Samuel Elliott Atkins, William Henry Overall

Some Account of the Worshipful Company of Clockmakers of the City of London

Samuel Elliott Atkins, William Henry Overall

Some Account of the Worshipful Company of Clockmakers of the City of London

ISBN/EAN: 9783337285180

Printed in Europe, USA, Canada, Australia, Japan

Cover: Foto ©ninafisch / pixelio.de

More available books at **www.hansebooks.com**

SOME ACCOUNT

OF THE WORSHIPFUL

COMPANY OF CLOCKMAKERS

OF THE

CITY OF LONDON.

COMPILED PRINCIPALLY FROM THEIR OWN RECORDS, BY

SAMUEL ELLIOTT ATKINS, FORMERLY CLERK OF THE COMPANY,

AND

WILLIAM HENRY OVERALL, F.S.A., LIBRARIAN TO THE CORPORATION
OF THE CITY OF LONDON.

1881.

PRIVATELY PRINTED.

THE COURT OF THE WORSHIPFUL
COMPANY OF CLOCKMAKERS.

MASTER.
CHARLES WELLBORNE, Esq.

WARDENS.
JAMES SCOVELL ADAMS, Esq.
SAMUEL ELLIOTT ATKINS, Esq.
SAUL ISAAC, Esq.

ASSISTANTS.
JOHN GRANT, Esq.
GEORGE WILLIAM ADAMS, Esq.
JOHN GARRETT CURTIS ADDISON, Esq.
WILLIAM LAWLEY, Esq.
GEORGE MOORE, Esq.
WILLIAM WING, Esq.
COL. ALEXANDER ANGUS CROLL.
WILLIAM PARKER, Esq.
EDWARD DANIEL JOHNSON, Esq.
EDWARD JOHN THOMPSON, Esq.
HERBERT JORDAN ADAMS, Esq.
JOHN NEATE DYMOND, Esq.

CLERK.
Mr. HENRY CHARLES OVERALL.

CONTENTS.

	PAGE
INTRODUCTION ...	i
THE COMPANY	
Charters and Bye-laws	1
Arms, Seals, Badges, Colours, &c. ...	72
Court of Assistants...	77
The Livery	96
Freemen	112
Apprentices	150
Biographical Notices of Members	161
Meeting Places ...	191
Feasts	196
Archives ...	199
Plate ...	206
Funds	212
Charities ...	217
Gifts to the Company ...	226
THE TRADE-	
Regulations of Workmen ...	231
Searches ...	235
Patents and Inventions	242
Importation and Exportation, False Marking and Engraving, Hall Marking, &c., &c.	255

ILLUSTRATIONS.

	PAGE
Initial Letter of Charter	7
Arms	72
Seal of Edward Walker, Garter King-at-Arms	74
Master's Badge	75
Wardens' Badge	75
Inscription on Tompion's Tomb	174
The Restoration of Harrison's Tomb	180
Plate of the Company	209
Adams's Cup (three plates)	210

INDEX.

*NOTE. The Figures in thick type (**161**) refer to Biographical Notices.*

Abbott, John, 234, 235
.... Sir Morris, Alderman, 52, 53
Adair, Mr. Serjeant, Opinion of, as to power of Company, 68, 69
Adams, Francis Bryant, 89, 90 — Banner presented by, 76
.... George William, 89, 90, 198, 209 — Three silver-gilt badges presented by, to be worn by the wardens, 75 — A silver cup and cover presented by, 210
.... James, 89
.... James Scovell, 90, 94
Adderley, Sir Charles, 342
Addis, George Curson, 108
.... William, 87 — Admitted to the livery, 104
Addison, John Garrett Curtis, 90, 179, 198
Airy, Sir G. B., K.C.B., Astronomer-Royal, 344
Aldermen, Court of, Steps taken by, to prevent the grant of letters patent to the French Clockmakers, 2, 3 — Petition of the Clockmakers' Company for incorporation referred to a committee, 5 — Report and certificate agreed to, 6 — Petition of the Blacksmiths' Company to, 52 — report upon, 53 — Petition of the Clockmakers' Company to, 53, 55 — report upon, 56 — Petition to, for a livery, 97, 98, 99, 100, 101 — Livery granted by, 102-4 —Petitions to, for increase to the livery, 106, 109, 110 granted, 108, 109, 110
Alcock, Thomas, 5, 51, 59, 85, 201
Aliens not to be employed by members of the Trade, 234 — Working in the City to be prosecuted, 232, 233
Allen, Elias, 85
.... George, 184
.... Mr., 235
Allenson, William, 60
Almond, Ralph, 73, 85 — A silver watch case presented by, 207
Alsop, Robert, Alderman, 104
Althorp, Lord, Chancellor of the Exchequer, Letter to, 294

Ambrose, Edward, 153
Ames, Richard, 73, 84, 85, 86, 237
Andrewes, Henry, Alderman, 56, 57
Antrobus, Richard, 65
Appleby, Joshua, 87, 98
Apprentices, to produce their masterpiece, iii, 150-1 — Authority exercised over, iii. — Petition of, to the Lord Mayor, 60, *et seq.* — Regulations with regard to the taking of, 70 — Bye-Laws relating to, 150 — Questions as to the number of, 151 — Thomas Loomes charged with keeping five, 151 — Ahasuerus Fromanteel and his Son charged with keeping too many, 151-2-3 — Females bound as, 155 — Fees upon binding reduced, 156 — Advice to, 156 — Gretton's gift to, 168, 218 — Roll of, 202 — Persons to be prosecuted for unduly taking, 233
Archer, Henry, 11, 20, 23, 49, 50, 51, 53, 78, 85, 172
Archives, 199, *et seq.* — Chest to preserve, 199, 200
Arms, grant of, 72, 73 — F. B. Adams presented the Company with a silk banner of the, 76 — in painted glass presented to Christ's Hospital and the Guildhall Library, 76
Arnold, John, **161**
.... John Roger, 88, 89, 282
Artisans, Emigration of, to America, France, &c., 277
Ash, Mr., 20
Aske, Henry, 166
Askell, Elizabeth, apprentice, 155
Assistants, The Court of — The first formal meeting of, 77 — Resolution passed to preserve their secrets, 77 — Regulation made to encourage good feeling, 78 — Fines for non-attendance, &c., 78, 79, 80, 81
Atcheson, Robert, gift to the poor, 221
Atkins, Francis, 87, 88 — Elected clerk, **92**
.... George, 88, 89, 134, 173, 185, 215

Atkins, George, elected clerk, **93** - Protest of, against removal of monumental stone from grave of Tompion and Graham, 174
...... Samuel Elliott, junior warden, 60—Elected clerk, **93**—Letter to Mr. J. Grant upon increasing the usefulness of the library, &c., 204
.... Thomas, 92
Atkinson, James, 114, 214
Atlantic and Pacific Ship Canal, 186
Aveline, Daniel, 87
.... Richard, admitted to the livery, 104
Avenell, Edward, chosen beadle, 95
.... John, chosen beadle, 95

Backquett, Davyd, 51
Bagge, Mr., Defective rules seized at shop of, 336
Bailey, Jeffery, 73, 85
Baker Henry, 184
.... John, 184
Barber, Elizabeth, 177
Barkham, Sir Edward, Alderman, 6
Barlow, Mr., 79
.... Edward, Application of, for patent for pulling or repeating watches, 170—Application successfully opposed, 244
Barometers, first made, 169 — Patent for making, granted to Daniel Quare, 170
Barraud, Frederick, 204
.... Henry, a silver gilt spoon presented by, 107
.... Paul Philip, 88, 232
Barrow, John, 65, 86
.... Nathaniel, 86, 116, 125, 154, 233
Bartram, Richard, 11, 20
.... Simon, 5, 23, 49, 50, 51, 59, 78, 81, 85
Basire, John, admitted to the livery, 105
Bate, Robert Brettel, 142, 145, 146
Battin, Thomas, fined for having a faulty contrate second wheel, 236
Baufre, Peter de, **163**
Bayes, John, 85
Bayley, Jeffery, 237
.... Thomas, 108
Beadles of the Company, list of, 95
Beardmore, Arthur, 127
Beck, Christopher, 108
Beckner, Abraham, 85 Silver beer bowl, presented by, 208
Bedford, Helkiah, 114, 236
Beeckman, Daniell, the Company's Arms engraved by, 74
Bell, Benjamin, 65, 73, 84, 85, 153, 230
...... John, 114
Bellas, George, 127
Benn, Anthony, 87, 101, 104
Bennett, Sir John, **181**

Bennett, Thomas, faulty watch movement belonging to, condemned and broken, 239
Beraud, James, admitted to work as the servant of Mr. Charlton, 232
Berry, John, 86
Bertram, William, 86
Bidlake, Thomas, 110
Billinghurst, Henry, admitted to the livery, 105
Birchmore, William, faulty rules seized in the shop of, at Newgate, 239
Bird, Samuel Joseph, 134, 135
Bishop, Samuel, 184
Bisse, Mr., prohibited from using the clockmakers' art, 232
Bittleston, John, 184
Black, William Henry, F.S.A., i. v
Blackborow, James, 87
Blackburn, William, 108
Blackett, Robert, 117, 124
Blacksmiths, the early makers of large clocks, 1—The art of the, described, 118
.... Company, petition of, against the formation of this Company, 2, 52—Extracts from the records of, 3, 52, 53, 54, 57 —Resolution of, for disenfranchising a member, 58 — Petition to the Common Council against the grant of an act for regulating the freedom of the Clockmakers' Company, 117, 124, 125 — Reasons against the bill, 118, 123—Agreement made with the Clockmakers, 119—To be heard against the granting of the bill, 124
.... Hall, 192
Blagrave, Daniel, 59, 60
Blew Bell, the sign of, in the Strand, 238
Blisse Ambrose, 62
Blundell, Richard, to be prosecuted for exercising the art of a clockmaker not being free, 233—Appeared and promised to take up his freedom, 234
Boddington, Colonel, James, 122, 123
Bombay Medical College, inscription on foundation stone of, 187
Booth, Richard, chosen beadle, 95
.... Samuel, chosen beadle, 95
Bosley, Charles, admitted to the livery, 105
.... Joseph, application of, for patent for an improvement in making watches, 255
Bouquet, David, 50
Bouquett, Solomon, 159
Bowen, Francis, 151
Bowly, Devereux, 87, 100, 105—Left £500 for the poor, 220
Bowyer, Mr., 20—A chamber clock, presented by, 207

INDEX.

Bradley, Dr., Astronomer, 167.
Brafeild, William, charged with making a bad gold watch-case, 240
Brewerton, Mr., 75
Bridger, Peter, Attorney, 239
Bridges, Mr., 246
.... Mr., Alderman, 285
Briggs, John, a soldier, admitted a freeman, 115
Briscoe or Bristoc, Mr., 120, 124
Broad Street, Mr. Cabriere's residence in, 162
Broderer's Company, see Imbroderers
Bromfield, Sir Edward, Alderman, 56, 57
Brooke, John. 51, 109
Brown, James, 87, 219, 220—Admitted to the livery, 105
Browne, Henton, 87, 97, 98—Admitted to the livery, 105
Browne. John, 66, 73, 85, 86, 114, 237
Browning, Dr., Report on the commerce and manufactures of Switzerland, 322
Bruhl, Count de, 169
Buck, William, 117, 124
Bucket, Mr., 21
Buckingham, Sir Owen. Alderman, 122, 127
Bucklee, David, 108
Bull, John, 51
...... Mr., 20
Bullby, John, 51
Bunhill Fields, Daniel Quare, buried in, 171
Burgis, John, 20, 51
Burnaby, Rev. S. B., M.A., Vicar of Hampstead, 179
Burnell, John, Alderman, 108
Burrill, Boys Err, 182
Bushman, John Baptist, 108
Butcher, William, 90
Butchers' Company, Charter, 69
Butlin, Mr., defective rules seized at the shop of, 238
Butter, Miss, a watch made by Henry Jones, presented by, 169
Bye-Laws for regulating the Company, 22-29—Ordered to be entered on record, 49 — For compelling freemen to take up their livery, 71—Cost of obtaining, 71.
Byfield, Mr., defective rule seized at the shop of, 236

Cabriere, Charles, 87, 162—Anderson prosecuted successfully for putting his name upon foreign-made watches, 259
Cabriere v. Anderson, the case of, 162
Cæsar, Mr., 246
Cambell, Sir James, Lord Mayor, 6
Campbell, Mr., opinion of, as to the grant of a livery, 100

Carpenter, Thomas, 108
.... William, 184
Carriage clocks smuggled into this country, 327
Carrington, Colonel, admitted to the livery, 104
.... George, 108
.... James, 87
.... Robert, admitted to the livery, 105
.... Thomas, admitted to the livery, 105
Carter, John, F.R.A.S., Alderman, 89, 90, 182, 198, 223—Lord Mayor, procession to Westminster, 76 —Arms of, 76—Banquet to, 198
Cartwright, John. Alderman, 104
Carver, Isaac, 114
Cateaton Street, meeting held at the Paul's Head Tavern in, 194
Cater, Widow, 237
Cathay, Daniel, chosen beadle, 95
Caveat, form of, agreed to, 131
Cavendish, Richard. 110
Cext, Catherine, Apprentice, 155
Chamberlain. Nath., 86
Chamberlain, fee paid to, 112, 113—Form of Caveat to be lodged with, 131—Petition of the Company to, 138
Change Alley. Cornhill, Mr. Frodsham's residence in, 166
Chaplin, Robert, 120
Charities, 217, et seq.
Charles I, charter granted by, 7, et seq.— Gold alarm watch made for, 165
Charles II, when Prince of Wales, 165— A watch with a pendulum spring made for, 174
Charlotte, Queen, a watch made for, 170
Charlstrom, William, 109, 110
Charlton, John, 5, 11, 20, 21, 23, 49, 50, 51, 78, 81, 85, 232
Charmes, David de, 163
.... Simon de, 163
Charter of Incorporation, 7-19—Description of, 19 — Enrolled in the city archives, 20—Cost of obtaining, and list of subscribers, 20, 21 — Copies of, written by Mr. Goodwin, 202—A MS. volume, containing copies of, purchased, 202
Chater, Eliezer, 87, 88—Admitted to the livery, 105
Cheney, Wither, 86
Chequers' Inn. Holborn, 236
Chest of the Company, keys belonging to, 83—Kept at Painter-Stainers' Hall, 191—Removed to St. Dunstan's Vestry, 199—To Mr. John Pennock's house in Lothbury, 199—Directions how to unlock, 200—New one ordered to be provided, 200— Deposited in the Guildhall Library, 201

Child, Henry, 83, 85
...... Mr., 21, 58
...... Mrs., widow of the late Master, the chest, books, and keys, delivered up by, 83
...... Richard, 51, 85
China Bowls presented to the Company, 210-11
Chisman, Timothy, 88, 108
Chitty, Mr., 125
Christ's Hospital, Arms of Company for painted window presented to, 76—Sir George Merttins, Alderman, elected Treasurer and President of, 183-4 — Dr. Thomas Simpson Evans, F.L.S., Mathematical Master of, admitted an Honorary Freeman, 187
Chronometers, improved by Thomas Earnshaw, 164—The perfection of, 276 — The first marine produced in England, 298—The importance of, 333—Prizes for the most accurate established, 344 — Regulations as to the competition, 344-6
Clark, Richard, Chamberlain, 138
Clarke, George, 51
.... Henry, 89, 173, 185, 186, 204, 215
—Portrait of, 186
.... Mr., defective rules seized at the shop of, 238
Claxton, Mr., 236
.... Thomas, 63, 85, 114
Clay, Charles, petition of, for patent for repeating watch or clock, 250-254
Clay, William, 62
Clayton, Sir Robert, Alderman, 246
.... Thomas, 73
Clement, William, 86
Clements, Mr., 123
Clerk, George, 108
Clerks of the Company, a list of, 90-95
Clewes, James, 159
Clitherowe, Mr. Alderman, 52, 53
Clocks, the Blacksmiths, makers of early, 1—Improvements in striking, 174—In large public, by Benj. Lewis Vulliamy, 176 — The manufacture of, in Switzerland, 322—Carriage, smuggled into England, 327
Clockmakers' Company, foundation of, 1, *et seq.*—Petition for incorporation referred to the Court of Aldermen, 5—Report and certificate upon, 6 — Charter granted, 7, *et seq.*—Bye laws, 22, 49—To be advertised, 67—Oaths of the Master, Wardens, Livery, Freemen, Clerk, Beadle, 45, 47—First Court held, 49—Second Court held, 50—Petition

Clockmakers' Company, *continued*, to the Court of Aldermen, 53, 55, 56—Charter submitted to a Committee of Parliament, 59—Referred to John Farwell to examine, 60—Returned to the Master and Wardens, 60 — Differences between the Freemen and Court of Assistants as to the charter, 60—Petition of Freemen and Apprentices to the Lord Mayor, 60, *et seq.*— Charter and Ordinances, digest of the, 67—Ordered to be annually read at the Christmas Court, 67—Compulsory powers of, 69—Reasons and petition against the Bill for regulating the, delivered in by the Blacksmiths' Company, 123-4—Bill brought in to the Common Council, 123—Bill rejected, 126—Petitions presented to the Common Council for an Act, 117, 126—Referred to a Committee, 127—Act passed, 128—Certificate to be given to Freemen, 136, 137—Petition to the Chamberlain and the Court of Aldermen against the Spectaclemakers' Company, 138, 143, *et seq.*—Jews admitted to the Freedom of, 149
Clocks and Watches as articles of dress, 2
Clock and Watchmakers to be required to take out a license, 281
Clock and Watchmakers' Asylum, 223-4
Closen, Mr., 20
Closon, Peter, 85
Clothworkers' Company, a silver cup given to, 112
Clows, John, 86
Cokayne, Francis, Alderman, 104
Coleman, John, 184
Collingridge, Edmund, 109, 110
Collingwood, Samuel, J., 109
Colours of the Company to be provided, 75, 76
.........A banner with the, presented, 76
Colts Dinner, the last held at Greenwich, 198
Comfort, William, 63
Common Council, Act of, regulating Freemen, 70—Petitions to, for an Act, 115, 126—Petition of the Blacksmiths' Company against, 117—Report to, upon Freemen, 121—Bill for regulating the Clockmakers' Company, brought into, 123—Petition of the Blacksmiths' Company against the Bill presented, 124—Bill rejected, 126—Act passed, 128—Act of, to provide loan of £50,000 to the King, passed, 207

Common Cryer, fees paid to, 112, 113
Coningsby, Lord, 246
Cook, Captain, chronometers made for, 161
Cooke, John, 62
.... Lewes, 5, 51
.... Robert, 114
Cooks' Hall, feast held at, 197
Copeland, Alex, 110
Copley, Sir Godfrey, 246
.... Thomas, 19, 50, 78.—Appointed Clerk, 90
Cordwell, Robert, 59
Corporations, Committee of Parliament upon, 59
Coulson, Robert, 109, 110
Coventry, Thomas Lord, Lord keeper of Great Seal, 22, 48
Coxeter, John, 85
.... Mr., 65, 79, 191
.... Nicholas, 73, 85, 199, 200, 237, 238
Cracraft, William, Alderman, 104
Cragg, Jno., 224
Crawford, R. W., M.P., 225
Crayle, Richard, 3, 5
Creek, Mr., 152
Creeke, Henry, submitted to the rules of the Company, 232
Croll, Colonel A. Angus, C.E., 90, **182**
Crosby, Brass, Alderman, 104, 108, 127
Cross, John Berryhill, gift of ten guineas to the poor, 226
Cross Keys, the sign of, within Newgate, 238
Crouch, Edward, 86
Cubitt, Messrs. W. & Co., 179
Cumming, Alexander, F.R.S., 167, 184, **186**
Cundee, Mr., 212
Cuper or Cwper, Josias, 3, 21, 51, 153
Customs, Commissioners of, Memorial to, upon the illicit importation of foreign watches and clocks, 267-268
Custom House Sale, foreign watches in metal cases, advertised as gold in the catalogue of, 331
Cutlers' Hall, 68—Meetings held at, 193—Leased to the Clockmakers' Company to hold their meetings in, 193, 194
Cutts, Lord, 246
Cylinder Escapement, invented by Tompion, 174

Daniel, Mr., 236
Daniell, Isaack, 62, 73, 85
.... Thomas, 63
.... William, 51
Danley, Charles, defective sun-dials seized at the shop of, 237
Danvers, J., 60
Darling, Sir Robert, Alderman, **183**—Gift of £100 to the poor, 219-20
Davis, Mr., 153

Davis, Samuel, chosen beadle, 95
.... Samuel, of Lothbury, fined for having faulty work, 236
Dawson, Thomas, 5, 21, 51, 113, 196
Day, Thomas, 117
Deane, George, engraver, copper plate of the Company's Arms, presented by, 74
Debaufree, Peter and Jacob, application of, for an enlargement of a patent for applying precious stones, &c., to watches and clocks, 245-7
Delafaye, Ch., letter upon Clay's application for a patent for repeating watches, 253
Delander or Delaunder, James, 159
.... John, 160
.... Nathaniel, 87, 97, 98, 159—Convened before the Goldsmiths' Company for making a false gold watch-case, 257
Dent, William, 160
Devereux Court, Fleet Street, 161
Deveris, Josyas, 120
Devil Tavern, 184
Devis, John, 184
Dewell, Mr., 20
Dhunjeebhoy, Sapooorjee, 189
Dial Plates, project for stamping, 254
Dickinson, Marshe, Alderman, 127
Dobree, Robert, 90
Dolley, Thomas, 88
Dorrell, William, 108
Downinge, Humfrey, 58
Drake, John, 54, 63, 151
...... Mr., 20
Drew, John, chosen beadle, 95
Dripping pan, the sign of, at Charing Cross, 236—At Smithfield, 236
Droeshout, John, 51
.... Martin, engraver, 201n
Drury, James, 86—Elected Clerk, 92
Ducie, Sir Robert, Alderman, 5, 6, 53
Dudds, Mr., admitted to the livery, 104
Dudley, Sir Matthew, 246
Duncombe, R., junr., 88
Dunlop, Conyers, 87—Admitted to the livery, 104—Left by will £50 to purchase a piece of plate, 226
Dunstan's, St., Vestry house, Fleet Street, 199
Durant, Oswald, 5, 21, 51, 85, 113, 196
Dutton, Matthew, 88
.... William, 169—Admitted to the livery—105
Dwerrihouse, John, 184

Earnshaw, Thomas, **164**—Portrait of, 164
East, Edward, 11, 20, 23, 49, 50, 51, 72, 73, 78, 80, 85, **164**, 168, 199, 213—Appointed Treasurer, 90, 208—£100 given to the poor of the Company by, 217, 218
...... Jeremie, 62
East India Company, chronometers made for, 161

Ebsworth, John, 86, 116, 125
Edlin, George, 109
Edwards, Hum., 60
Electric Telegraph Company, the United Kingdom, established by Col. Croll, 182
Elmes, William, 114, 237
Ellicott, Edward, 89
.... John, F.R.S., 87, **165**
Elwes, Sir Gervase, Alderman, 246
Emery, Josiah, 184
Epicycloid scape wheel, patented by Arnold, 162
Erbery, Henry, 62
Eryles, Mr., 21
Etherington, George, 86
Evans, Dr. Thomas Simpson, F.L.S., **187**
Ewart, Mr., return of the value of foreign watches imported, moved for in Parliament by, 316-17
Exchange Alley, 169
Exchequer, Chancellor of the, deputation received by, 337
.... Tallies, two ordered to be purchased, 212
Eyre, Sir James, Lord Chief Justice of the Common Pleas, 49

Facio or Faccio, Jacob, and Nicholas, 163 and Jacob Debaufree, application of, for letters patent for applying precious stones in clock and watches opposed successfully, 245-47
Fage, Edward, 114
Fairfax, Sir Thomas, letter of, to the Lord Mayor, on the approach of his corps to London, 217
Farwell, John, 60
Faulkingham, Mr., defective rules seized at the shop of, 238
Faulkner, Edward, 87
.... William, 109
Feasts of the Company, where kept, &c., 196-8
Febuce, Charles le, 160
Feilder, Thomas, 16
Fen, Sir Richard, Alderman, 52, 53, 57
Fenn, Daniel, 87, 88, 221—Admitted a liveryman, 104
...... Joseph, 89, 90, 114, 221
...... Samuel, 88—£200 left to the poor by, 221, 222
Ferdinand VI of Spain, watch made for, 170
Fines inflicted on Members for using abusive words, 78, 79, 80, 81—James Marwick, for speaking disrespectfully to the Master, 79—Imposed on Members neglecting their duties, 80—Alteration of, 81—To be paid by Members elected on the Court of Assistants, 81
Finch, Sir Heneage, Recorder, 5, 6, 56
...... John, 86, 125, 214

Fish, John, 130
...... Mary, 130
...... William, 130
Fisher, Rebeckah, apprentice, 155
Fishmongers' Hall, to be inspected, 192
Fladgate, John, 184
Fleet, the, money lent for the maintenance of, 213
Fleet Street, residences of Mr. East, Mr. Tompion, and Mr. Grant, in, 165-6-7—The Dial and One Crown in, 169—The Bolt and Tun in, 169
Fletcher, Thomas, prosecuted and fined for unduly taking apprentices, 233-4
Fole, Robert, 114
Foley, Mr., 246
Foreign Clocks and Watches, duty upon, 294, 295, 269, 299—Complaints as to the illicit importation of, 301—The marking of, 307—The right of search and seizure of, 307
Foreign Gold Watches, the number of, imported, 301, 302
Foreign Office, the, smuggling carried on through the messengers of, 317
Foreman, Francis, 4, 5, 11, 20, 23, 49, 50, 51, 78, 85
.... Michl., 110
.... Mr., fined for not attending Court of Assistants, 81
Founders' Hall, meetings of the Company, held at, 192, 193
France, money lent for carrying on the war with, 213—Trade opened with, in clocks and watches, 262, et seq.—Commercial treaty with, 294
Francis, William, 110
Freedom, the steps taken to obtain an Act of Common Council to regulate the, 115, et seq.—Draft of Bill read, 117—Petition of Blacksmiths' Company against, 117—Reasons of Blacksmiths' Company against, 118—Agreement between this Company and the Blacksmiths as to, 119—Report of the Common Council upon 121—A design for a Certificate of, agreed to, 136, 137—Fees upon taking, 149—Persons to be prosecuted for carrying on the trade, not having been admitted to the, 233
Freeman, Edward, 120
.... John, 73, £10, left to the poor of the Company by, 217
.... Sir Ralph, Alderman, 5, 6, 53
.... Samuel, 127, 128
Freemen, Sureties for their good behaviour, exacted, i—Authority exercised over, iii—Petition of, to the Lord Mayor, 60-63—Act of Common Council, regulating, 70

Freemen, *continued*.
— Decrease in the number of, 137 — Honorary, A list of, 184
French Clockmakers, Proposed grant of Letters Patent to, 2, 3
French Watchmakers, to be admitted to the Freedom, 115
Frewen, Mr., defective rules seized at the shop of, 237
Frodsham, Charles, 89, 90, 198
.... William, 184
.... William James, F.R.S. 89. **166** — £1000 left to the poor by, 222
Fromanteel, Ahasuerus, 3, 62, 63, 150. **166**, 236 — Charged with keeping too many apprentices, 151, 152 — Fined for steward, 196 — Fined for having a journeyman without orders, 232
Frying pan, the sign of at, Ludgate, 237
Funds of the Company, 212. *et seq.*
Funeral ceremonies, iii — Palls, the Companies who still preserve them, iii*n*
Furnivalls Inn, Holborn, 91

Gadlingstock, Samuel, defective rule seized at the shop of, 237
Ganion, Robert, deputy, 127, 128
Ganthony, Richard, 89
.... Richard Pinfold, 89
Gardiner, Thomas, Recorder, 57
Garle, Thomas, 87 — Admitted to the livery, 104
Gas Company, the Great Central Gas Consumers'. Colonel Croll appointed Engineer, 182
...... the Imperial founded, 186
Gatty, Mr., 68, 71
Gayre, Sir John, Alderman, 56, 57
George III, a watch presented to, 161
George, Daniel, chosen beadle, 95
George Inn, Ironmonger Lane, Feast held at, 197
Gibbons, Benjamin, £110 left to the poor by, 219
Gibbs, Thomas, 86
Gibson, Edward, 88, 108
.... James, 159
Gillpin or Gilpin, Edward, 5, 51, 73
Glenny, Joseph, 109, 110
Glover, Boyer, 87
.... Mr., one of the Wardens, Death of, 83
Glyn, Sir Richard, Bart., Alderman, 104
Godbud, William, 63
Gold, Christopher, chosen beadle, 95
Gold, The duty on wrought, 269 — The standard of, reduced, 271 — And Silver Manufacturers, Hall marking of, 342
Goldsmiths' Company, James Masters, transla ed to, 113 — Loans to the, 212. *et seq.* — Assaying of Goldsmiths' work by, 257*n*. —

Goldsmiths' Company, *continued*.
N. Delaunder summoned before them for making a false gold watch-case 257 — A silver tankard presented to, 192 — Two watches in gold cases with forged marks produced by their assay officer, 339 — Correspondence with, upon hall-marking, 340, 341
Goldsmiths' Hall The Company's meetings at, 192 — Feasts at, 79, 197 — Marks counterfeited on foreign watches, 287
Goods. Bill in Parliament to prevent the clandestine running of, 258
Goodwin, Thomas, chosen Clerk, 91
Gosling, Sir Francis, Alderman, 127
Goujon, Stephen, 87
Graham, George, F.R.S., 86, 98, **166**, 169, 178 — Executor of Thomas Tompion, 174 — £20 left to the poor of the Company by, 219
Grant, John, 88, 89, 184, **167** — Letter addressed to, concerning the Library, &c., 204
Gravell, William, 89
Graves, Benjamin, 86, 214 — Elected Clerk, 92
Gray, Timothy, 159 — Fined for leaving the Court, 81
Graye, Mr., 20
Gregory, Ann, 78
.... Jeremy, 62, 66, 72, 73, 78, 79, 83, 85, 153, 233 — A silver cup and dish, presented by, 208.
.... Mr., Warden, 199, 236
Green, James, 88 — Green, Macklin, 117.
Greene, John, Alderman, 65, 57
Gresham, Sir Thomas, 116
Gretton, Charles, 86, 116, **168** — £50 left by, to apprentice sons of deceased freemen, 218
Greville, Mr., 125
Griffith, James, 114
Griffiths, Edward, 109, 110
Griliat, Mr., project of, for stamping dial plates, 254
Grimes, Thomas, 159
Grinkin, Edmond, 62
.... Robert, 51, 58, 85, 199, 207
Grocers' Company, livery worn by, iv.
Grove, Richard, 108
Guildhall Library. Arms of the Company placed in window of, 76 — Company's Library and Museum deposited in, 206
Guilds of London, the origin of. i. — Divided into two kinds, ii — Foundation of Ecclesiastical, iii — Establishment of trading, iii — Adulterine Guilds fined, iii — Charter of the earliest, iii — Distinguishing dress worn by, iv

Haberdashers' Company, Ignatius Huggerford, a freeman of, 247
Hackett, Sir Cuthbert, Alderman, 6
.... Mr., 21, 199
.... Symon, 51, 59, 78, 85, 112, 113, 201—Nominated for treasurer, 90
Hales, Sir Charles, 246
Halley, Charles, 184
.... Dr. Edmund, 190
Hall Marking, gold watches with forged marks, produced by an Assay officer of the Goldsmiths' Company, 339 — Correspondence with the Board of Trade thereon, 340—Select Committee of the House of Commons appointed to enquire into, 342—Report of Select Committee, 342, 343
Halsted, Robert, 86, 116, 125 — Bad movements seized in the shop of, condemned and broken, 239, 240
Hamilton, George A., letter from, 338
.... Rev. Dr. Robert, 88, 204
Hamlin, Richard, a defective watch belonging to, seized, 239
Hammersley, Sir Hugh, Alderman, 6
Hammersmith, Grove Hall at, 163
Hampstead Churchyard, John Harrison's tomb in, restored, 177, 179—Inscription on the tomb, 179-80
Hampton Court Palace, Clock at, made by Daniel Quare, 170
Hancorne, Thomas, 66, 86n, 116
Hardy, Mr., admitted to the livery, 104
Hare, Alexander, 184
Harker, George, 89, 90
Harley, Right Hon. Thomas, Lord Mayor, 75, 105
Harmer, Jasper, 154
Harper, Henry, some defective watch or pocket clock chains seized at the shop of, 240
Harris, John, 11, 20, 23, 49, 50, 51, 59, 66, 78, 85, 86, 116, 209
.... Mr., 80 — Defective rules seized at the shop of, 238
.... William, 89
Harrison, Mrs. Elizabeth, 180
.... Henry, 177
.... John, the father of chronometry, 177 — Invented the Gridiron pendulum, 177—Made his first timekeeper, 177—Sent with it to Lisbon to test its performance, 178—£500 given to him by the Board of Longitude, 178—Obtained the gold medal of the Royal Society, 178—Produced a second instrument in 1739, 178—A fourth tried in a voyage to Jamaica, 179—Invented the metallic compensation and remontoir, 179—£20,000 awarded to him by the Board of Longitude, 179—His

Harrison, John, *continued*.
death and burial, 179—His tomb in Hampstead churchyard restored by the Company, 179, 180—The works of, in the Company's library and museum, 180, 181
Harrison, William, F.R.S., 179, 180
Hartington, Marquis of, 146
Hartley, Mr., sword cutler, 66
Harvey John, 122
.... Mr., 123, 125
Hassell, Joshua, 92
Hatton, Jos. York, 109
Hayes, Walter, 73, 85, 114, 237
Hearne, Mr., 20
Heath, Sir Robert, Knt., Lord Chief Justice of the Common Pleas, 22, 48
Heathcot, Sir Gilbert, Alderman, 246
Heerman, John, 160
Heldon or Holden, Onesipherus, 5, 20, 21, 51, 59, 85, 90, 201
Helena, St., Mr. Ellicott's clock at, 165
Helical or Cylindrical Spiral Spring patented, 161
Henshaw, Walter, 86, 114, 116
Herbert, Cornelius, 86, 97, 98
.... Estme, name of falsely put upon a watch, 256
.... Sir Thomas, gold alarm watch for, 165
Heriot, Master, 171
Hewes, Mr., 20
Hewitt, Francis, defective rule seized at the shop of, 238
Heywood, Mr., 20
Hicks's Hall, 235
Higgs, Peter, 83, 87
Hill, Benjamin, 85
...... John, 5, 20, 21
...... Mr., Warden, 191
...... Mr., 199, 236
...... Thomas, pocket dials taken from, not being perfect, 235
Hiorne, John, 87, 98
Hobler, Paul, 184
Hobson, John, petition against his project for stamping dial plates, 254
Hodges, Sir James, Knt., Town Clerk, 202
Hoe, Robert, 124
Holborn, High, Thomas Earnshaw's residence in, 161
Holborne Bridge, 236
Holden, Onesiphorus, *see* Heldon
Holker, Laurence, 127
Holland, George, 5
.... Mr. J., 21
.... Thomas, 20, 51, 85, 236—Appointed clerk & beadle, 91, 95—Suspended, 91—Discharged, 91
Hollidaie, Edward, 62
Holloway, Mr., 20
.... Robert, 51
Home, Henry, 98

Hopkins, Sir John, Alderman, 108
Horizontal escapement greatly improved by George Graham, 167
Hornblower, William, chosen beadle, 95
Horne, Henry, 87—Admitted to the livery, 105
Horne, Mr., 65
.... Samuel, 73, 85, 237—Master, 200
How, William, 214
Howes, John, 160
.... Wiliam, admitted to the livery, 104
Howse, Charles, 88
.... Thomas, 21, 51, 85
.... William, 87, 114
Hubert, Charlotte, apprentice, 155
.... David, 87, 98
.... Elizabeth, 155
.... James, 155
Hue, Pierry, 51
Huggerford, Ignatius, 159—Old watch with a stone fixed in the cock and balance made by, purchased, 247
Hughes, Thomas, 87, 260—Chosen clerk, 92—Admitted the first liveryman, 104
.... William, 184
Hulst, Jacob, a chaste oval sugar dish, presented by, 208
Hunt, John, 159
Hussey, William, 127
Hutchinson, John, pretended invention of, to keep dust out of watches, 248-50
.... Richard, a sum of money left to the poor by, 219
Hutton, Dr., 177

Imbroderers' Company, 113
.... Hall, the Company to meet at, 191
Inner Temple Gate, 169
Irland, Mr., 153
Ironmonger Lane, meetings held at the "George," 192, 197

Jackson, John, 88, 130, 143
.... John, jun., 88, 89, 204
.... Sir Henry, a Bill introduced into Parliament by, upon the subject of hall-marking, 342
.... Martin, 86
.... Richard, 51
Jacques, William, 86
James I, David Ramsay, clockmaker to, 171
James II, a watch made for, by Daniel Quare, 171
Jardin, John, 184
Jarratt, John William, 108
.... Richard, 66, 86, 197
Jeejeebhoy, Sir Cursetjee, 2nd Baronet, **188**
.... Sir Jamsetjee, 1st Baronet, **187**—£250 left by, for the poor, 222-3—3rd Baronet, **189**

Jeejeebhoy, The Hon. Rustomjee Jamsetjee **189**—£200 given to the poor by, 225
Jefferyes, Sir Jeffry, 246
Jekyll, Sir Jos., 246
Jesson, Mr., defective rules seized at the shop of, 238
Jews, first admitted to the freedom of the City, 148—Of the Company, 149
Johnson, Roger, 5
Jole, Robert, defective rules seized at the shop of, 237, 238
Jones, Evan, 62, 73
...... Henry, 65, 66, 74, 80, 86, 154, **168**, 169, 213, 223—£100 given to the poor of the Company by, 217, 218
...... John, 87
...... Mr., 236
...... Owen, 108
...... William, 108
Kellett, Thomas, fined for having a defective watch, 235
Kemp, William, 109
Kennedy, Richard Hartley, M.D., Alderman, 76, 89, 90, **183**, 222
Kenney, William, to be prosecuted for execising the art, not being free, 233
Kent, Henry, 73
Kenyon, Lord, Lord Chief Justice of the King's Bench, 49
Ker, J., letters from the Commissioners of Customs signed by, 305, 309, 316
Kilborne, Robert, 120
King, Mr., 68, 71
King's Head Tavern, Poultry, meetings held at, 194
Knottsford, William, 86, 233

Lack, Thomas, letter from, upon the complaint of the Liverpool watchcase makers, 304, 305—Reply of the Company, 305
Ladbroke, Sir Robert, Alderman, 127, 128
Ladies' feast to be discontinued, 198
Lafayette, General, 186
Laidlaw, Thomas, 184
Lambe, Thomas, 51
Land Tax, £500 lent upon the security of the, 213—Loan lent upon the credit of, 214
Lane, Mrs. Jane, 168
Langford, Thonias, 184
Latham, Mr., a clock given to, 112
.... Thomas, 151
Laundre Peter de, 159
Lawe, Mr., prohibited from working at the trade, not being free of the Company, 232
Lawley, William, 90, 198—Legacy of Mr. Warre, paid by, 226
Layher, Mr., Master of the Blacksmiths' Company, 3

Lea, Thomas, 88, 124, 171—Admitted to the livery, 105
Leach, Thomas, 235
Leather Lane, Holborn, 110
Leathersellers' Hall, 99—Meetings held at, 194—The Feasts held at, 196, 197, 198
Lecount, Peter, 109, 110
Leeming, Edward, 109
Lello, James, 151
Leman, Sir John, Alderman, 2
Lentall, Mr., 54
Leroux, John, 184
Levant Company, 173
.... Trade, 185
Lever escapement invented by Thomas Mudge, 170
Levett, Sir Richard, Alderman, 122, 123
Levy, Jonas, the first Jew admitted to the freedom, 149
Lewes, Sir Watkin, Alderman, 108
Lewis, Sir George Cornewall, letter from, 335, 337
Library, The, letter upon increasing the usefulness of, 104—The establishment of, 203, et seq.—Catalogue of, completed and issued, 204, 206—And museum to be deposited in the new library of the Corporation at Guildhall, 206
Licence, proposal made by the Company that dealers in foreign watches and clocks should take out an annual, 312
Lidiard, Richard, 117
Lindsay, Captain Sir James, 179
Liverpool, Lord, letter to, asking his assistance for the benefit of the watch trade, 276, et seq.
Livery, Distinguishing dress worn by the Companies, iv—Description of, iv—Mr. Sergt. Adair's opinion of, as to the power of the Company to compel freemen to take up their, 69, 70, 71—Bye-law, fixing a penalty for not taking the, 69, 71—Attendances of, in the pageants on Lord Mayor's day, 75, 76, 105—Bye-law referring to the, 96—Attempts made to obtain the, 96—Committee appointed to petition for a, 97—Petition to the Court of Aldermen for a, 97-101—Not granted, 100—Granted, 102-104— First liverymen admitted, 104, 105—Fine fixed, 104n—Petition to the Court of Aldermen for an increase to the 106-110—Complied with, and fine fixed, 107, 108-111—Members admitted to the, 108, 109—William Mansell and William Welborne fined for not taking up, 110—Invited to dine, 198—Admission book of the, 203

Lloyd, Sir Richard, opinion of, as to the livery, 100
Locker, John, elected clerk, 92
Loddington, Isaac, 155
London and Middlesex Archæological Society, 76
London Tavern, Meetings held at, 194
Longitude at sea, offer of £20 000, by the board of longitude for the best instrument for determining the, 162, 178
.... The Board of, £300 voted to Thomas Earnshaw by, for his improvements in chronometers, 164—£3,000 given to Thomas Mudge for the like, 170—£500 to John Harrison, by, to help him to proceed with his experiments, 178—£20,000 voted to him by, 179
Long Lane, meeting held at "The Cat" in, 192
Loomes, Thomas, 62, 159, 232—Charged with having five apprentices, 151
Lord Mayor's day, the livery walked for the first time in procession, 76
Lord, Richard, 51
Lothbury, the White Hart Tavern in, 66—The Mermaid in, 166—Mr. Pennock's house in, 199
Lowell, Paul, 21—a silver wine bowl presented by, 208
Lucas, Mr., portrait of George Atkins made by, 93
Lynaker or Linnaker, Samuel, 11, 20, 23, 49, 50, 51, 78
Lyons, Richard, 85, 86

Maberley, John, 87, 98
McCabe, James, 88, 109, 184
Magson, Henry, watch made by Huggerford purchased of, 247
Maisterson, Mr., 20
Major, Henry, 127, 128
Mansell, William, 110
Mansfield, Lord, the case of Cabriere, v. Anderson, tried before, 162—His judgment thereon, 259
Marchant, Samuel, 86, 214
Marke, John, 114
Markham, Mr., 123
.... Robert, defective rules seized at the shop of, 238
Markwick, James, 79, 86, 115, 116
Marriott, John, 88
Marsden, John, 86
Marsh, Anthony, chosen beadle, 95
.... Mr., City solicitor, 54
Marston, John, fined for having deceitful work on his premises, 236
Martin, John, fined for unduly taking apprentices, 233
Martin, Mr., 184
Maskelyne, Rev. Dr. Nevil, Astronomer Royal, 181, 189
Mason, Charles, 165
Massam, Sir Francis, 246

Master, Election of, 81, 82—None to be elected until he has been three years an assistant, 82—Steps to be taken on the death or resignation of, 82, 83
Masterpiece, to be produced by apprentices before being admitted as skilled workmen, iii, 150, 151
Masters, James, 110—Translated to the Goldsmiths' Company, 113
Masterson, Richard, 85, 112, 120, 159
Mathematical Instrument Makers admitted freemen of the Company, 114
.... Shops searched for defective work, 236-239 — Dispute between the Clockmakers' and Spectaclemakers' Companies, as to the admission of, 137-47
Mattchett, John. 63, 73, 80, 85
Matthew, Francis, 62
Matthews, William, 87—Admitted to the livery, 105
Mattocks, John, 108, 109
Maynard, George, 127
Maypole, the, the sign of, in the Stand, 238
Meeting places, 191-96
Melvill, John, 184
Meniall, James, a Frenchman, to be prosecuted for exercising the art, not being free, 233—Appeared, paid his charges, and took up his freedom, 234
Mercer, Mr., defective rule seized at the shop of, 237
Mercers' Hall, feast kept at, 197
Merchant, Samuel, 125
Merchant Taylors' Company, terms for meeting in the hall of, 193
Mercurial pendulum invented by George Graham, 167
Meredith, Launcellott, 63
Merigeot, John, admitted to the livery, 105
Merrill, Charles, 109, 110
Merry, Charles, 87—Admitted to the livery, 104
Merttins, Sir George, Alderman, 86, 183, 184
Metcalf, George Marmaduke, 108
Micabius, John, 20
Middleton, Sir Thomas, Alderman, 2, 5, 6
Middnall, John, see Mydnall
Miles, Septimus, 110
Miller, Mr., 153
Millington, Gilbert, 60
Million, William, 159
Mills, Sir Edward, 123
...... Thomas, sketch by, of the position of the graves of Tompion and Graham in Westminster Abbey, 175
Mina, General, 186
Mirehouse, J., Opinion of, as to enforcing the bye-laws, 111
Mitchell, Robert, admitted to the livery, 105
Mitford, Mr., admitted to the livery, 105

Mitre Tavern, Wood Street, feast held at, 197
Moliere, Mr., 76
Moodie, David, 62—A silver dish presented by, 207, 208
Moore, George, 90, 198
Mopes Alley, Southwark, 166
Morgan, Richard, 4, 5, 11, 20, 23, 78, 120 —A volume, containing copies of the charter, bye-laws, grant of arms, &c., presented by, 201
.... Thomas, chosen clerk and beadle, 91, 95
Morris, Edward, 116
.... Samuel, defective rules seized at the shop of, 236
Mosely, Elinor, 155
Moss, Mr., 54, 57
...... Thomas, 108
Motto, the Company's, 73
Moulinie, M., 323
Mowlson, Mr. Alderman, 5
Mudge, Thomas, admitted to the livery, 105, 169—Reward given to, by the Board of Longitude, for improvements in chronometers, 170—Lever escapement invented by, 170
.... Rev. Zachary, 169-170
Mulford, John, 87
Mullett, Edward, elected beadle, 95
Mydnall or Middnall, John, 11, 20, 23, 49, 50, 51, 78, 81, 85

Naked Boy, the sign of, in Cheapside, 237
Nash, John, 114, 237
Naval Architecture, society established for the improvement of, 173
Neale, Henry, 124
...... Samuel, 60
Needlemakers, the, proposal as to their incorporation with the Blacksmiths, 3
Negus, Willy, chosen assistant beadle, 95n
Nelson, George, Alderman, 127, 128
New, Mr., Warden of the Blacksmiths' Company, 3
Newcomb, Jos., 110
New Street, Shoe Lane, 60
Newell, William, 109
Newman, John, 110
.... Robert, 109
Newnham, Mr., Alderman, 107, 108
Nicaragua, The Lake of, 186
Nicasius, John, 59, 63, 72, 73, 85, 237— Suspended for using abusive words, 80
Noakes, James, defective rules seized at the shop of, 237
Non-freemen, carrying on the trade, powers of the Company over, 69, 70
Norris, Edward, 66, 86, 197
North, William, a silver drinking cup presented by, 208

Nourse, Thomas, admitted to the livery, 105

Oatlands, clock repaired at, by David Ramsey, 172
Okeham, Edward, 51
Orrery, Lord, the first planetarium made for, 167
Overall, Henry Charles, chosen clerk, 95
.... William Henry, F.S.A., 189—To prepare a new catalogue of the Company's library, MSS., and collection of watches and clocks, 206
Overzee, Gerard, 160

Painter-Stainers' Company, a chamber clock presented to, 191—Meeting of this Company held at their hall, 191
Pall Mall, residence of Edward East in, 165
Parker, John, 239
.... William, 90, 180—The master's badge made by, 75
Parkinson, William, 222
Parkwick, James, 125
Partridge, William, two apostle spoons, presented by, 208
Patents for Inventions, opposition of the Company to grants of, &c., 242-255
Paterson, John, Deputy, 127
Patmore, Peter, 135
Patrick, John, 244
Pattee, Thomas, 109
Paul, Nowell, an alien, to be prosecuted for working in the city, 233
Paul's Churchyard, St., meetings held at the Queen's Arms Tavern in, 194
Paul's Head Tavern, meetings at, 105, 107
Pawnbrokers, proposal of the Company to prohibit their receiving unfinished watches in pledge, 282
Payne, Nicholas, 73
.... Southern, 87—Admitted to the livery, 105
Peachy, Newman, admitted to the livery, 105
Pearce, William, 108
Peckham, Dr. Milner's school at, 173
Peel, Arthur W., letter signed by, 340
Peers, Richard, Alderman, 104
Pemberton, Mr., Serjeant, 65
Pembroke, the Earl of, 165
Pendulum, two seconds, first employed by Benjamin Lewis Vulliamy, 176
—The Gridiron invented by John Harrison, 177
Pennington, Sir Isaac, Alderman, 60
Pennock, John, 73, 85, 191, 199—A house clock presented by, 208
Pensioners of the Company, a list of the, 227
Pensions, Two new created, 215—The whole augmented, 215

Pepper, Thomas, 109
Pepys, John, 86, 87, 98, 214, 240
Perkins, Eysum, to be prosecuted for exercising the art, not being free, 233—Appeared, and promised to take up his freedom, 234
Perigal, Francis, 87, 89, 184—Admitted to the livery, 105
.... Francis, jun., 108
.... F. S., jun., 88
.... John, 184
Perry, J. A., 89
Petit, Guillaume, 5, 20, 51
.... William, Silver gilt cup and cover presented by, 207-209
Peto, Mr., forbidden to work at the trade, not being free, 232
Pheasant, Peter, Recorder, 56, 57
Phillips, Thomas, 124
Pickett, William, Alderman, 108
Pierce, William, 88
Piggott, Mr., defective rules seized at the shop of, 237
Pinchbeck, Christopher, 184
Pinson, John, apprentice, 239
Pitt, Thyar, 109
.... William, 109
.... The Right Hon. William, 267, 269, 270, 271, 294, 331
Pitts, Captain, 123
.... Thomas, 122
Planetarium, the first, made by George Graham, for Lord Orrery, 167
Plate belonging to the Company, description of, 206, *et seq.*
.... The duty upon gold, 266
.... William, 87
.... William, jun., 88
Poll Tax, loan upon the credit of the, 213, 214
Pond, John, F.R.S., Astronomer Royal, 189
Poole, Anthony, defective rules seized at the shop of, 238
.... Robert, 87, 88—Admitted to the livery, 104
Pope, Mr., to paint colours and streamers of the Company, 75
Porter, Harry, jun., 88
Potter, James, 110
.... John, beadle, 78, 95
.... Harry, senr., death of, 83, 88
Pound, Francis, 117
Prigg, John, admitted to the livery, 105
Procter, William, 110
Purefoy, William, 60
Pyrometer, an improved one made, 165

Quare, Daniel, 86, 170—Inventor of the repeater movement in watches, 170—A watch made by, for James II, 171—Buried in Bunhill Fields, 171—Patent granted to, for portable weather glasses, 244

INDEX.

Quarterage, Powers of the Company to enforce payment of, 68
Queen Street, Cheapside. The Rummer Tavern in, 168

Rainier, John, 108
Rainton, or Raynton Sir Nicholas, Alderman, 2, 52, 53
Ramsey, David, the first Master, 11, 23, 49, 50, 85, 171
Rawlings, Charles. £200 given to the poor by, 223
.... James, 108
Recusancy, John Mattchett, charged with, 80
Red Lion Square, John Harrison's residence in, 179
Reead, Thomas, 51
Reeve, Mr., 21
.... Thomas, 78
Reid, Thomas, 190
Renter Warden, duties of the, 84
Rice, Spring, letters on the illicit importation of foreign clocks and watches, 300, 306, 311
Richards. Hugh, 87
Richardson, James. 88
.... John, 110
...............Sir Thomas, Knt., Lord Chief Justice of the King's Bench, 22, 48
Richmond, the King's private observatory at, 179
Riddlesdon, Samuel, 130
Rigby, Joshua, 184
Rivers, David, 87—Admitted to the livery, 105
.... William, 88
Robins, William, 88, 143
Robinson, Christopher, 127, 128
.... Francis, 86
.... Robert. 62
Robson, William, 88, 89
Rogers, Isaac, 83, 88, 89. 143, 173, 185, 282—Plan matured by for the resuscitation of the Company, 173, 215—Thanks awarded to him, 173
.... Thomas, 109
.... William, 219n
Rogerson, William, 87—Admitted to the livery, 105
Rooke, John, 184
Rookes, Mr., 79
Rosoman Street, Clerkenwell, 110
Ross, Mr., Surveyor-General of Customs, 326
Rothwood, Robert, 51
Rowlands, Christopher, 224
.... William, 89, 90. 198—A silver salver, silver alms dish, a glass jug and two goblets, presented by, 209—His bequest for the benefit of the inmates of the clock and watchmakers' asylum. 223

Royal Observatory, Greenwich, deposit of chronometers at, for trial, 162, 344—Transit clock at, 164—Mr. Frodsham's chronometers tested at, 166—A mural arch and sector made for, by George Graham, 167
Russell, Concilius, 219
.... Lord Edward, 246
.... George, translated to the Salters' Company, 113
.... Mr., 240
.... Mrs., £10 given to the poor by, 218. 219
.... Captain Nicasius, 86, 116. 219, 233

Saddlers' Hall, report as to holding the meetings of the Company at, 192
Sadleir, Samuel, 86
Saldanha, General, 186
Salters' Company, George Russell, translated to, 113
Sanderson, James, Alderman. 108
Sargeant, Nathaniel, 88
Saunders, Daniell, 51
.... Mr., 20
Savory, Thomas Cox. 320. 321
Scafe, William, 87, 98
Scott, James, 130
...... John, 184
Scovell, C.A., Secretary of the Customs, letter from, 310
Scriven, Mr., 125
Seale, Mr. William, 247
Seals of the Company, 74
Search Courts, receipts and expenditure of, 241-42
Searches made for bad or defective work, 235-242
Seguier, Baron, Swiss consul, 338
Seignoir, Robert, 169
Sellars, John, 86, 114—Defective rules seized at the shop of, 237
Sewell, John, 142
Sharp, John, 89
Shaw, Anna Maria, apprentice, 155
...... John, 86
Shelton, John, admitted to the livery. 105
.... Sampson, 4, 11, 20. 23, 49, 50, 51, 59, 78, 85, 120—Bequest of £50 by, 217
.... Thomas, Elected clerk, 91
Shepherd, Mr., 20
Shepheard, Thomas, 51
Sherwood, William, 87
Shirley, John, Translated to the Vintners' Company. 113
Sidey, Benjamin, 87—Admitted to the livery, 104—Bequest of £300 to the poor, by, 221
Silver, Frederick, 110
Silvester, Joseph. several defective rules seized at the shop of, 237
Simpson, William Ellison, 184
Sinderby, Francis H., 109. 110

Skinner, Matthew, 87
Skinners' Company, Sir George Merttins, Alderman, translated to, 183
Skynner, John, Deputy, 127
Smellie, George, elected beadle, 95
Smith, James, 184
.... John, 11, 20, 21, 23, 49, 50, 51, 59, 78. 85—Fined for non-attendance, 81—Fined for putting Estme Herbert's name upon a watch, 256
.... Phillip, 114
.... Robert, 85, 207
.... Susanna, apprentice, 155
Smugglers bringing over watches, &c., 295, 298
Smuggling, proposal of the Company to put a stop to, 300, 301, 316
Snagg, Mr., 168
Snelling, James, 87, 97, 98
Soldiers, discharged, Act enabling them to trade, 115
Somersall, Richard, 108
South Sea Stock purchased, 214, 215
Sparkes, Nicholas, a piece of plate presented by, 208
Speakman, William, 86, 116, 154
Spectacle Makers' Company, dispute with as to admission of mathematical instrument makers to the freedom, 138, 146
Speidell, Francis, appointed clerk, 91—Charges brought against him, 92
Spelter Metal, a watch made of, 232
Spencer, Thomas, prosecuted for unduly taking apprentices, and fined, 233, 234
Ssmidt, Gersen, 4
Staff, to be provided for the beadle, 75, 76
Stafford, John, 87—Elected clerk, 92—Petition of, against a project for stamping dial plates, 254
Stamper, Mr. Francis, to be prosecuted for refusing to permit his workrooms to be searched, 240
Standards, three of brass received from the Court of Exchequer, 337
Stanley, Dean, his account of the restoration of the monumental stone over the graves of Tompion and Graham, 175
Stanton, Edward, 86, 116, 125
Starey, John, 109
Starr, Robert, 114
Stars, catalogue of, 1, 113
Stationers' Company, to be treated with for the use of their hall, 194
Stationers' Hall, feasts kept at, 197, 198
Steevens, Samuel, to be prosecuted for unduly taking apprentices, 233
Stephens, Daniel, chosen beadle, 95
.... Joseph, 87, 98—Admitted to the livery, 105
Stephenson, Thos. Samuel, 109, 110
Steveningham, William, 60

Stevenson, Adam, 108
Stewart, J., Letter from the Treasury and answers thereto, 313, 318, 319
Stocks, Confinement in the, iii
Stone, Mr., 52-54, 57
Stones, Thomas, 86
Stones, precious and common, applied to clocks and watches, 244-247
Storer, Robert, 184
Storr, William, 184
Strachan, Abraham, 155
.... Andrew, 154
Strange, Sir John, Attorney-General, 100
Street, Richard, 86
Strigil, George Philip, 184
Style, Nathaniel, 87, 98, 183—Admitted to the livery, 104—£10 given to the poor by, 220
.... Richard, 88 — Admitted to the livery, 104
Stubbs, Gabriell, 160
.... Mr., letter from, as to the gift of Conyers Dunlop, 226
Sun dials seized, being defective, 237
Sutton, Charles, 125
Swale, Jaques, an alien to be prosecuted for working in the city, 233
Sweeting's Alley, Cornhill, 165
Swindells, Jasper, 134
Swiss Consul, 293
.... Watches, increase in the number imported, 295—Those sold in France marked as to the quality of the gold, 307
Swithin's, St., London stone, 156
Switzerland, report on the commerce and manufacture of, 322
Swordhilts, bill in Parliament for permitting the exportation of, 257-8

Tailour, Edward, 3
.... John, 3
Tankards, Two Silver, purchased, 209
Taverns, A list of Old City, 195-196
Tayler, Edward, 109, 110
Taylor, George, 155
.... Jasper, 87, 97, 98—Elected clerk, 92—£10 given to the poor by, 220
.... Lucy, 155
.... Samuel, 88
.... Thomas, 62, 65, 66, 73, 85, 86
.... William, 124
Tebbatt, Benoni, a gold watch case made of unwarrantable gold seized at his shop in Little Old Bailey, 240
Theobalds, clocks at, repaired and a chime of bells made for, 172
Thorold, Sir John, 246
Thwaites, John, 88, 108, 143, 282
Tolley, Charles, chosen beadle, 95
Tomlinson, William, 86
Tompion, Elizabeth, 166
.... James, 166

Tompion, Thomas, 86, 116, 125, 166, **174**
— Buried in Westminster Abbey, 174
Tovie, Mr., 54
Town Clerk, 100 — Fees paid to, 112, 113
Townsend, John, forbidden to work at the Trade, 231
Trade, abuses in, referred to a committee, 65 — Regulations of Workmen, 231-35 — The distressed condition of the trade, petition to Parliament thereon. 283 84
Trade, Lords of the Committee of Council for, questions by and answers as to opening up trade with France, 262, *et seq.* — Representation to, as to the duty upon watches and clocks, 264 — Memorial to, for preventing false names being added to watches, 272
Trade, the Board of, Memorial to, upon the alteration of the Warehousing Act, 289-91 — Memorial to, upon the illicit importation of foreign clocks and watches, 320 — Their answer, 322
Translations to other Companies, 112, 113. 183
Treasurer, Edward East appointed, 90, 165
.... Simon Hackett, nominated, 90
Treasury, The Lords of the, Memorial to, for preventing the pirating of names on watches and clocks, 272 — Memorials to, upon the illicit importation of foreign watches and clocks, 293, *et seq.* — Letter to 307 — Letter from, upon the illegal importation of watches and clocks, 313 — Memorial to, 294. *et seq.*, 300, *et seq.*, 322, 330, 331, 336 — Replies to, 334 337, 338
Trecothick, Barlow, Alderman, 104
Tregent, James, 184
Trevithick, Richard, 185
Trubshaw, John, 86
Turner, Samuel, Alderman, 127
Tutet, Edward, 88 — Admitted to the livery, 105
Twyford, Robert. 184

Upjohn. Francis. 108

Valentine, Charles, D.F., 110
Vansittart, Hon. Nicholas, Memorandum sent to, upon the importation of foreign watches and clocks. 284-5
Vantrollier or Vautrollier James, 11, 20, 23, 49, 50, 51, 78, 81
Vernon, Samuel, 63. 73, 85
Vick, Richard, 86
Viet. Claude. 155

Viet, Mariane, apprentice, 155
Vigne, James, 184
Vincent, John, 235
Viner. Sir Robert, £100 lent to, 212
Vintners' Company. John Shirley, translated to, 113
Voland, or Volant, Elias, or Ely, 21, 51, 153
Vulliamy, Benjamin, 184, 204
.... Benjamin, Lewis, F.R.A.S., 88, 89. **176** — Presentation of plate to, 176
.... Justin, 204.
.... Justin Theodore, 88, 89

Waldron, John, 93
Wales, Henry Prince of, 3 watches made for, by David Ramsey, 171
Walker. Sir Edward. Garter King at Arms, 72, 73 — Seal of. 74
.... John, 51
.... Mr., 21 — Defective rules seized at the shop of 236
Wallace, the Right Hon., Lord President of the Board of Trade, 285, 324, 325, 326
Walter, Mr., 20
Warburton, —, chosen beadle. 95
Ward, John, 88
..... Mr., 21
..... Thomas, 51
Warden, Thomas, 155
Wardens, steps to be taken upon the death or resignation of, 82 — Election and removal of 83, 84
Warehousing Bill, petition of the Company against, 285-86 — Proposition of the Company inserted in the Bill, 286
.... Act, petition presented by the Company to Parliament for an alteration in, 288 — Clause inserted for the protection of the watch trade repealed, 288 — Memorials to the board of trade upon 289-92 — Amended, 292 — Notice of the clause in, advertised, 293
Warre, William Henry, £100 left to the Company by, 324
Watches, the smallest repeating made, 161 — Mudge's work on the improvement of, particularly those for use at sea, 169 — The repeating movement in, invented by Daniel Quare. 170 — One made by him for James II. 171 — One with a spiral balance or pendulum spring made for Charles II. 174 — The use of precious and other stones in, 245-47 — A patent for repeating, applied for by Mr. Barlow, 170 — Opposed successfully, 243 — Pretended invention to keep

Watches, *continued.*
the dust out of, 248-9—Application of Charles Clay for a patent for repeating watches or clocks, 251-254 — Application by J. Bosley for a patent for an improvement in making, 255— A tax imposed upon all wearers of, 269-70—Repealed, 271— Petition of the Company to Parliament against a Clause in the Customs Bill, relating to, 330—Memorial of the Company to the Treasury, upon, 330—Foreign, in metal cases, advertised in the Custom House sale as gold, 331—Memorial of the Company to the Lords of the Treasury and the House of Commons, upon, 332-337— Answer from the Lords of the Treasury, 334-337—The rate of duty upon, in France, 319 — Duty upon, Foreign, 294-296, 299, 303, 323—Endeavours of the Company to prevent the illegal importation or exportation of 255, 262, 263, 267-268, 278-281, 284-285, 293, *et seq.*, 305, 308, 316, 324—None to be exported without the name and residence of the maker engraved upon them, 280, 281, 304— Material for the manufacture of, exported from England, 297, 299, 304 — The number of foreign, imported, 301-302— Return to the House of Commons of the value of foreign, imported, 316 — Dealers in foreign, proposed to be compelled to take out a licence, 281, 312— Marking of, &c., at Goldsmiths' Hall, 255. *et seq.*—Forged marks of Goldsmiths' Hall, discovered upon, 288, 339—Proposal that they be marked when the duty has been paid, 325-26—Seizure of, with false names engraved upon, 239 — Proposal to increase the penalty for putting false names upon, 268 — Bill brought into Parliament for preventing other than freemen of London from putting " London " upon, 257-58—The Names of Tompion, Windmills, Quare, Cabrier, Lamb, and others falsely engraved upon, 258-59—Committee appointed to consider the best means of preventing the practice of putting false names upon, 272-6 — Foreign made, to have the name and residence of the maker en-

Watches, *continued.*
graved upon them, 280—The forging of names to be punished as a felony, 282—A case of foreign, with forged English names, imported and warehoused, steps taken by the Company, 287—Great quantities of, smuggled into this country, 279 —Representation to Lord Liverpool, as to the decay of the trade in, 276, *et seq.*—Memorial to the Lords of the Treasury upon the state of the trade, &c., 322—The manufacture of, in Switzerland, 322

Watch Cases, Reduction of the standard of gold in, 269—The difference in the cost of English and foreign made, compared, 269 — The number of gold and silver, marked in, 1796-97, 270, 271— The duty on gold and silver repealed, 271—The difference in quality of the gold made into watch-cases in England and abroad, 327—

Watch Makers, A public register of all proposed to be kept, 268

Watkins, Rev. H. G., M.A., his book entitled "Affectionate Advice to Apprentices," 156

Watson, Samuel, an invention by, to discover the hour of the day at sea, offered to the Company, 250

Weather Glasses, patent for making, granted to Daniel Quare, 170

Weavers' Company, charter granted to, iii
.... Hall, inquiries to be made as to the terms for holding meetings at, 194

Webb, Benjamin, 184

Webster, John, 117
.... Richard, 89, 110
.... Robert, 86, 214
.... Samuel, admitted to the livery, 104
.... William, 87—admitted to the livery, 105

Weekly Assessment ordered by Parliament, 206-7

Weeks, Thomas, charged with abusing Warden Coxeter and Ann Gregory, 78

Welborne, William, 110

Wellborne, Charles, 90

Wellke, Christianus de, 4

Wellowe or Willow, John, 11, 49, 50, 51, 59, 78, 85

Wells, Joseph, 114, 237

West, Mr., admitted to the livery, 104

Westminster, clocks at, repaired, 172
.... Abbey, Thomas Tompion and George Graham, burial of, in, 166, 174—Protest against the removal of the monumental

Westminster Abbey, *continued.*
    stone over their graves, 174, 175
    —Restoration of, 175
Whaplett, Thomas, a silver tankard presented by, 209
Wheeler, Thomas. 85, 86, 240
Whichcote, Samuel, 87, 98—Admitted to livery, 104
Whifflers, to attend the livery on Lord Mayor's day. 76
White Hart-court, Lombard-street, 173
Whitehead, John, 117
Whitlach, John, a silver cup, presented by, 208
Whitmore, Sir George. Alderman, 5, 6, 49, 50, 53. 172
Whittingham, William, 154—To be prosecuted for exercising the Art, not being free. 233, 234
Whitwell, Robert, three silver spoons and a silver wine bowl, presented by. 207-8.
Wickes, John, 108
.... J. Houghton. 110
Wightwick, John, 184
Wilbraham, Mr., 100
Williams, Mr., a china bowl, presented by, 210
Williamson, Jos., 86
.... Robert, 86. 116, 125
Willin, William, 110

Willow, John. *see* Wellowe
.... Mr., 20, 81
Wills, Edward, 122
Wilson, Alexander, 184
.... James, 155, 184
.... Hannah, 155
.... Richard, faulty rules seized in the shop of, at Newgate. 239
Windham, Sir William, 250
Windmills, Joseph, 86. 116. 159
Wing, William, 90
Winnie, Henry, 233
Wise, Peter, 86
Wontner, John, 110
Woodfielde, Mr., warden of the Blacksmiths' Company, 3
Woodmongers' Company, 52, 53
Wray, Hilton, 88
Wright, John. 184
Wrightson, Thomas, 87
Wyeth, John, a watch and box made of spelter metal, exhibited by, 232
Wynn Henry, 65, 66, 86, 116, 233
...... Mr. Warden of the Blacksmiths' Company, 3
Wythe, Lionel, 168—Chosen beadle, 95

Young, James. 108
.... John, 109
.... Richard, Sheriff of London, 181
.... William, 154

INTRODUCTION.

THE "Guilds" or "Mysteries" of London had their origin in the Old Saxon Law which exacted sureties from every Freeman above the age of 14 years for his good behaviour, and gave rise to associations called "Guilds" from the payment of money into one common fund for meeting any claims which might be made against their brethren of the craft.

Mr. W. H. Black, F.S.A., in his introduction to the history of the Leathersellers' Company, traces the origin of these Guilds back to a very early period of our history.

Gild is a true and pure British noun, signifying *contribution* or what is produced or contributed; and together with the British verb *gildiaw* (signifying to yield, produce, or contribute) and other derivations of the root *gil;* it may be found in any Welsh Dictionary. Both the idea, and the thing signified, are Roman; and the name is purely British, adopted by Saxon and Norman conquerors to express what they found existing among the natives. Hence came the *gild* or *geld* (whether as a verb or as a noun) of the Anglo-Saxon laws, and the *geldscipe*, the *geldum* and *geldare* of the Normans; the latter occurring perpetually in Domesday Book in the sense of *yielding* as revenue to the public Exchequer. The Anglo-Saxon legal word *gafol* (sometimes confounded with *geld* in sense) is but the British word *gafael*, meaning a tenure or holding; and is in like manner the origin of *gavelkind*, and of other terms occurring in our laws and records. These and many other words, hitherto referred to the Anglo-Saxon dialect for their etymology, and by consequence to a supposed Anglo-Saxon origin, can be more satisfactorily traced to the old British language, and be explained by existing usage among the Welsh people; in the same manner as the most ancient names of places, throughout Britain, Gaul, and Northern Italy, can be demonstrably explained by that language, and by it alone.—Page 3.

An important part of the functions attributed to the Roman *Urbi Præfectus* consisted in the supervision and regulation of trade, labour, markets, and prices; and in restraining or punishing "Illicit Colleges," that is, Companies or Societies which held nocturnal assemblies, or otherwise acted against the public good. So the Lord Mayor and Aldermen of London have from time beyond memory, regulated the tradesmen and artificers of London, both in their collective capacity as Crafts or Companies by framing "Ordinances" or rules and regulations, or by issuing Proclamations for the conduct of their affairs, and for allowing or disallowing, uniting, consolidating or severing Companies voluntarily associated; and also in their individual capacity upon complaints or accusations against fraudulent or disobedient craftsmen. The records of the City, so far back as they reach in regular series (into the thirteenth century) abound with such Ordinances and with instances of corrective and coercive jurisdiction, extending to forfeiture of wares, to fines and imprisonments, and to exposure on the pillory. The masters, or other chief officers of the several Societies or Companies, were commonly presented to the Mayor to be sworn as the Mayor himself was presented to the Imperial Court; and the Mayor and Aldermen received petitions, supplications, or "bills," as Senators in their "inner Chamber," where they held a Court of Record, and consulted on the laws and regulations which were proposed to them by Societies or their sworn Officers. This practice is so ancient, that there is no appearance of novelty in the earliest Ordinances now extant; on the contrary, some of the oldest refer to precedent regulations, and in some instances the largest terms of antiquity are applied to this part of the municipal jurisdiction, which was highly valued, and much frequented by the trades thereby regulated.—Page 7.

The Guilds were divided into two kinds, ecclesiastical and mercantile, the former devoted to religion and charity, the latter to the protection of trade. About the 14th century they became more blended, the mercantile being grafted on the ecclesiastical or devotional.

INTRODUCTION.

Mr. John Nicholls, F.S.A., in the history of the Ironmongers' Company,[1] sets out several Anglo-Saxon Charters of foundation of Ecclesiastical Guilds. By the reign of Henry II, many Guilds—some being exclusively Trading Guilds—had been established in the City. Eighteen of these, termed "Adulterine Guilds," for forming themselves into Fraternities without the King's licence, were fined.

The earliest existing Charter of a Trading Guild is that of the Weavers, granted by Henry II in 1184, in which he confirmed all the privileges granted to them by his grandfather, Henry I.

The system of apprenticeship became general in the early part of the 13th century, and the test of good workmanship before admission into a Fraternity was adopted about the 15th century, each Apprentice being compelled to produce his "Masterpiece" and to satisfy the Master and Wardens of his ability before being admitted to Membership as a skilled workman.

The authority exercised over the Apprentices and Freemen by some of the ancient Companies was of a very severe nature; not only had they power to inflict fines[2] and prohibit men from working at their trades, but in some cases confinement in the Stocks[3] was awarded to the refractory.

The whole body of each Company met upon certain days for the regulation and government of their trade, for convivial and social purposes, and also for making provision for the aged and helpless. Many of the crafts upon the decease of their members, and in some instances of their wives, took part in their funeral ceremonies, and the "Palls[4]" used upon these occasions are, in a few cases, still preserved.

---

[1] "Some Account of the Worshipful Company of Ironmongers." By John Nicholls, 1866, pp. 2—5.
[2] "History of the Carpenters' Company." By E. B. Jupp, p. 138 et seq.
[3] "History of the Vintners' Company," 1868, p. 18.
[4] The following Companies still preserve their Palls:—Fishmongers, Vintners, Saddlers, Merchant Tailors, Ironmongers, Watermen, and the Parish Clerks.

It does not appear until the reign of King Edward I that the Guilds had assumed a distinguishing dress or common habit to be worn by every Member alike. This distinguishing dress was known as the "Livery" or clothing of the Guild or Company. The word is probably derived from the French verb "*Livrer*" to deliver, since upon admission to full Membership the Badge, Cognizance or Clothing of the Fraternity was *livrée*, *i.e.*, delivered to the Member. It must not be understood, however, that the use of this word was confined to the common habit of these Guilds alone, since it was also applied to the retainers and adherents of the King, Noblemen, and others at an early period.

The term "Livery," as describing the clothing of a Fraternity, is thus used by Chaucer in his prologue to the "Knight's Tale:"—

> "An Haberdasher, and a Carpenter,
> A Webbe, a Deyer, and a Tapiser,
> Were alle yclothed in O livere,
> Of a solempne and grete fraternite."

The earliest Ordinances upon record, determining the dress to be worn by any of the existing City Guilds, are those of the Grocers' Company, in 1348. The Livery is particularized "An upper and under garment called a 'coat and surcote,'" being referred to as the common habit, whilst the cloak or gown, and the hood, which were reserved for ceremonials, completed what was termed "the full suit." Herbert[1] is of opinion that there also existed an undress, or part dress, called "the hooding," probably worn by Freemen only, who were not esteemed "full brothers," like the Livery, since in the Fishmongers' Ordinances, some years later, it is enacted that once in every year, every Member should have the livery, be it "hole clothing or elles hodying."

These Liveries varied in colour in the different crafts in early times, some of them being described in their ordinances.

---

[1] *See* his Introduction to the "History of the Twelve Great Livery Companies."—Page 59.

INTRODUCTION.

HE "Guilds" or "Mysteries" of London had their origin in the Old Saxon Law which exacted sureties from every Freeman above the age of 14 years for his good behaviour, and gave rise to associations called "Guilds" from the payment of money into one common fund for meeting any claims which might be made against their brethren of the craft.

Mr. W. H. Black, F.S.A., in his introduction to the history of the Leathersellers' Company, traces the origin of these Guilds back to a very early period of our history.

Gild is a true and pure British noun, signifying *contribution* or what is produced or contributed; and together with the British verb *gildiaw* (signifying to yield, produce, or contribute) and other derivations of the root *gil:* it may be found in any Welsh Dictionary. Both the idea, and the thing signified, are Roman; and the name is purely British, adopted by Saxon and Norman conquerors to express what they found existing among the natives. Hence came the *gild* or *geld* (whether as a verb or as a noun) of the Anglo-Saxon laws, and the *geldscipe*, the *geldum* and *geldare* of the Normans: the latter occurring

INTRODUCTION.

perpetually in Domesday Book in the sense of *yielding* as revenue to the public Exchequer. The Anglo-Saxon legal word *gafol* (sometimes confounded with *geld* in sense) is but the British word *gafael*, meaning a tenure or holding; and is in like manner the origin of *gavelkind*, and of other terms occurring in our laws and records. These and many other words, hitherto referred to the Anglo-Saxon dialect for their etymology, and by consequence to a supposed Anglo-Saxon origin, can be more satisfactorily traced to the old British language, and be explained by existing usage among the Welsh people; in the same manner as the most ancient names of places, throughout Britain, Gaul, and Northern Italy, can be demonstrably explained by that language, and by it alone.—Page 3.

An important part of the functions attributed to the Roman *Urbi Præfectus* consisted in the supervision and regulation of trade, labour, markets, and prices; and in restraining or punishing "Illicit Colleges," that is, Companies or Societies which held nocturnal assemblies, or otherwise acted against the public good. So the Lord Mayor and Aldermen of London have from time beyond memory, regulated the tradesmen and artificers of London, both in their collective capacity as Crafts or Companies by framing "Ordinances" or rules and regulations, or by issuing Proclamations for the conduct of their affairs, and for allowing or disallowing, uniting, consolidating or severing Companies voluntarily associated; and also in their individual capacity upon complaints or accusations against fraudulent or disobedient craftsmen. The records of the City, so far back as they reach in regular series (into the thirteenth century) abound with such Ordinances and with instances of corrective and coercive jurisdiction, extending to forfeiture of wares, to fines and imprisonments, and to exposure on the pillory. The masters, or other chief officers of the several Societies or Companies, were commonly presented to the Mayor to be sworn as the Mayor himself was presented to the Imperial Court; and the Mayor and Aldermen received petitions, supplications, or "bills," as Senators in their "inner Chamber," where they held a Court of Record, and consulted on the laws and regulations which were proposed to them by Societies or their sworn Officers. This practice is so ancient, that there is no appearance of novelty in the earliest Ordinances now extant; on the contrary, some of the oldest refer to precedent regulations, and in some instances the largest terms of antiquity are applied to this part of the municipal jurisdiction, which was highly valued, and much frequented by the trades thereby regulated.— Page 7.

The Guilds were divided into two kinds, ecclesiastical and mercantile, the former devoted to religion and charity, the latter to the protection of trade. About the 14th century they became more blended, the mercantile being grafted on the ecclesiastical or devotional.

INTRODUCTION.

Mr. John Nicholls, F.S.A., in the history of the Ironmongers' Company,[1] sets out several Anglo-Saxon Charters of foundation of Ecclesiastical Guilds. By the reign of Henry II, many Guilds—some being exclusively Trading Guilds—had been established in the City. Eighteen of these, termed "Adulterine Guilds," for forming themselves into Fraternities without the King's licence, were fined.

The earliest existing Charter of a Trading Guild is that of the Weavers, granted by Henry II in 1184, in which he confirmed all the privileges granted to them by his grandfather, Henry I.

The system of apprenticeship became general in the early part of the 13th century, and the test of good workmanship before admission into a Fraternity was adopted about the 15th century, each Apprentice being compelled to produce his "Masterpiece" and to satisfy the Master and Wardens of his ability before being admitted to Membership as a skilled workman.

The authority exercised over the Apprentices and Freemen by some of the ancient Companies was of a very severe nature; not only had they power to inflict fines[2] and prohibit men from working at their trades, but in some cases confinement in the Stocks[3] was awarded to the refractory.

The whole body of each Company met upon certain days for the regulation and government of their trade, for convivial and social purposes, and also for making provision for the aged and helpless. Many of the crafts upon the decease of their members, and in some instances of their wives, took part in their funeral ceremonies, and the "Palls[4]" used upon these occasions are, in a few cases, still preserved.

---

[1] "Some Account of the Worshipful Company of Ironmongers." By John Nicholls, 1866, pp. 2—5.
[2] "History of the Carpenters' Company." By E. B. Jupp, p. 138 *et seq.*
[3] "History of the Vintners' Company," 1868, p. 18.
[4] The following Companies still preserve their Palls :—Fishmongers, Vintners, Saddlers, Merchant Tailors, Ironmongers, Watermen, and the Parish Clerks.

It does not appear until the reign of King Edward I that the Guilds had assumed a distinguishing dress or common habit to be worn by every Member alike. This distinguishing dress was known as the "Livery" or clothing of the Guild or Company. The word is probably derived from the French verb "*Livrer*" to deliver, since upon admission to full Membership the Badge, Cognizance or Clothing of the Fraternity was *livrée*, i.e., delivered to the Member. It must not be understood, however, that the use of this word was confined to the common habit of these Guilds alone, since it was also applied to the retainers and adherents of the King, Noblemen, and others at an early period.

The term "Livery," as describing the clothing of a Fraternity, is thus used by Chaucer in his prologue to the "Knight's Tale:"—

> "An Haberdasher, and a Carpenter,
> A Webbe, a Deyer, and a Tapiser,
> Were alle yclothed in O livere,
> Of a solempne and grete fraternite."

The earliest Ordinances upon record, determining the dress to be worn by any of the existing City Guilds, are those of the Grocers' Company, in 1348. The Livery is particularized "An upper and under garment called a 'coat and surcote,'" being referred to as the common habit, whilst the cloak or gown, and the hood, which were reserved for ceremonials, completed what was termed "the full suit." Herbert[1] is of opinion that there also existed an undress, or part dress, called "the hooding," probably worn by Freemen only, who were not esteemed "full brothers," like the Livery, since in the Fishmongers' Ordinances, some years later, it is enacted that once in every year, every Member should have the livery, be it "hole clothing or elles hodying."

These Liveries varied in colour in the different crafts in early times, some of them being described in their ordinances.

---

[1] *See* his Introduction to the "History of the Twelve Great Livery Companies."—Page 59.

The favourable Certificate thus made on their behalf by the Court of Aldermen appears to have produced satisfactory results, and accordingly in the following year 1631, a Charter of Incorporation was granted by the King dated the 22nd of August, in the 7th year of His reign, constituting them a body corporate under the name of "The Master, Wardens and Fellowship of the Art or Mystery of Clockmaking of the City of London," the terms of which Charter are as follow :—

CHARLES, by the Grace of God, King of England, Scotland, France, and Ireland, Defender of the Faith, &c. To ALL MEN to whom these presents shall come, greeting.

"KNOW ye, that we, at the humble petition of the Clockmakers, as well freemen of our city of London, residing and inhabiting within the liberties and suburbs thereof, as also those that are foreigners, using the same trade, not of the freedom of the said city, and residing in or near the said city, liberties, and suburbs thereof, for the better order, rule, and government of them and every of them, and of others using the same Art or Mystery of Clockmaking, and also upon certificate made unto us from the Lord Mayor, Recorder, and Aldermen of the said city of London on their behalf, of our especial grace, certain knowledge and mere motion, HAVE willed, ordained, constituted, and granted, and by these presents, for us, our heirs, and successors, do will, ordain, constitute, declare, and grant :

Petition to the King by the Clockmakers, &c., praying to be incorporated. (7 Car. 1.)

THE CLOCKMAKERS' COMPANY.

Incorporation of all the Clockmakers both free and foreign; (i.e. persons not free of the city of London who practice the art of Clockmaking within the city of London and ten miles compass; with perpetual succession.

Title of the Company.

"THAT all and singular the *Clockmakers and other person and persons whatsoever, as well freemen of or in our city of London, as also all other our natural freeborn subjects, using the Art or Mystery of Clockmaking within the said city, liberties, or suburbs thereof, or within any place within ten miles of the said city, as well within liberties and places exempt, as in other places, be and shall be, by virtue of these presents, for ever hereafter, one body corporate and politic, in deed and name to have continuance for ever, by the name of* The Master, Wardens, and Fellowship of the Art or Mystery of Clockmaking, of the city of London, and them by the name of Master, Wardens, and Fellowship of the Art or Mystery of Clockmaking, of the city of London, we do for us, our heirs and successors, really and fully create, erect, make, ordain, and constitute, by these presents, one body corporate and politic, in deed and in name, to have continuance for ever.

"AND that by the same name they may and shall have perpetual succession.

"AND that they and their successors, by the name of Master, Wardens, and Fellowship of the Art and Mystery of Clockmaking, of the city of London, be, and shall be for ever hereafter, persons able and capable in law to purchase, have, **Power to purchase lands, tenements, &c.** receive, and enjoy any manors, messuages, lands, tenements, liberties, privileges, jurisdictions, franchises, and other hereditaments whatsoever, of whatsoever kind, nature, or quality they be, to them and their successors in fee and perpetuity, or for term of life or lives, year or years, or otherwise in what sort soever, not held of us, our heirs, or successors, in *capite* or by knight's **Power to sell and alienate lands,&c** service; AND ALSO all manner of goods, chattels, and things whatsoever, of what name, nature, or quality soever they be: AND ALSO to give, grant, alien, assign, and set over and dispose of any manors, messuages, lands, tenements, and hereditaments; AND ALSO to do and execute all and singular other acts and things whatsoever, by the name aforesaid.

"AND that by the name of Master, Wardens, and Fellowship of the Art or Mystery of Clockmaking, of the city of London, **Power to plead and defend any cause as any other subject.** they and their successors shall or may be able to plead and be impleaded, to answer and be answered unto, to defend and be defended, in any court or courts, place or places whatsoever, and before whatsoever judge or judges, justice or justices, or other persons or officers of us, our heirs and successors whatsoever, in all and singular actions, pleas, suits, plaints, matters, and demands of whatsoever kind, quality, or sort they shall be, in the same manner and form as any other of our liege people and subjects, of this our realm of England, being persons able and capable in law, or any other body corporate and politic, within this our realm of England, can or may have, purchase, receive, possess, enjoy, retain, give, grant, let, alien, dispose, and assign, implead or to be impleaded unto, answer or to be answered unto, defend and be defended, do permit or execute.

THE CLOCKMAKERS' COMPANY. 9

"AND that they the said Master, Wardens, and Fellowship of the Art or Mystery of Clockmaking, of the city of London, and their successors for ever hereafter, shall and may have and use a Common Seal, for the expediting of the causes and business of them and their successors. And that it shall and may be lawful to and for the said Master, Wardens, and Fellowship of the said Art or Mystery of Clockmaking, and their successors, to alter and make new the said seal from time to time, at their wills and pleasures, as they shall think fit. *To have a Common seal; with power to alter and make new from time to time*

"AND FURTHER, we will and ordain, and by these presents for us, our heirs and successors, do grant unto the said Master, Wardens, and Fellowship of the Art or Mystery of Clockmaking, of the city of London, that for ever hereafter there be and shall be *one of the said Art, Mystery, or Fellowship, in manner and form hereafter in these presents mentioned, to be chosen and named*, which shall be and shall be called *the Master of the said Fellowship* of the Art or Mystery of Clockmaking, of the city of London. *Power to elect one of the Fellowship to be Master;*

"AND that likewise there be and shall be *three of the said Fellowship, in manner and form hereafter mentioned to be nominated* and elected, which shall be and shall be called, *the Wardens of the Fellowship* of the Art or Mystery of Clockmaking, of the city of London. *and three of the Fellowship to be Wardens;*

"AND ALSO, that there be and shall be ten or more *Freemen of the said Fellowship, in manner and form hereafter in these presents expressed, to be named* and chosen, which shall be, and shall be called the *Assistants of the said Fellowship* of the Art or Mystery of Clockmaking, of the city of London. And from time to time shall be *assisting and aiding to the Master and Wardens* of the said Fellowship for the time being, in all causes, matters, and business, touching or concerning the said Fellowship. *also ten of the freemen to be called Assistants, to assist and aid the Master and Wardens for the time being.*

"AND that the said *Master, Wardens*, and *Assistants* of the said Fellowship for the time being, or the greater part of them (whereof the Master and one of the Wardens for the time being to be two), shall and may have *full power and authority* by these presents, to *make, constitute, ordain, and set down, from time to time, such reasonable* laws, statutes, decrees, ordinances, and constitutions, *in writing*, whatsoever, which to them, or the greater part of them, whereof the Master and one of the Wardens as aforesaid for the time being to be two, shall seem good, wholesome, profitable, honest, and necessary, *according to their discretions*, as well *for and concerning* such *oaths* as shall be fit to be administered *to the Master, Wardens, and Assistants, or any other of the said Fellowship*, free, foreign, or stranger. As also, *for, touching, or concerning the said Trade, Art, or Mystery, in the making of clocks, watches, 'larums, boxes, or cases for clocks, watches, or 'larums, or any other manner of work concerning their Art, Mystery, or Profession of Clockmaking*. As also for the punishment and reformation of such abuses, deceits, and other wrongful practices, as shall from *What persons must be present to constitute a court, having power to make laws and ordinances, (19 Hen. VII. 7.) for the government of its own members, free, foreign, and stranger: and also concerning the said Art or Trade in any respect. Deceitful practices punishable.*

time to time be practised, either in making, mending, or uttering any bad, deceitful or hurtful wares, whereby our loving subjects may be wronged, deceived, or abused, or any other wrong, cozenage, deceit, or abuse concerning the said art and mystery, offered or committed at any time within the said city, liberties, and suburbs thereof, or in any other place or places, privileged or not privileged, within ten miles compass of the said city. And also, for the good rule and government of the Master, Wardens, and Fellowship of the said Art or Mystery of Clockmaking aforesaid, and their successors, and of all and singular persons using, exercising, or trading in the said Art, Trade, or Mystery of Clockmaking, and every of them, both within the city of London and liberties thereof, and ten miles compass of the said city, in all matters and things touching or in any wise concerning the said Art, Trade, or Mystery of Clockmaking aforesaid. AND *for declaration after what manner, order, and form, the said* Master, Wardens, *and* Fellowship, *and their successors, and all and every other person and persons using and exercising the said Art, Trade, and Mystery of Clockmaking* within this our realm of England, shall behave, demean, carry, and use themselves in their said offices, mysteries, and work, for the public good and common profit of the said Master, Wardens, and Fellowship, and of the rest of our people, and for all other matters, things, and causes touching or concerning the said Art, Trade, or Mystery of Clockmaking, by any manner of means.

Power to make laws and ordinances for the government of all persons using the art, in all things appertaining thereto, within the city of London and ten miles compass of the same.

Power to regulate the manner in which all persons using the art throughout England shall carry on the same.

"AND WHENSOEVER *the said Master, Wardens, and Assistants* for the time being, or the greater part of them (whereof *the Master and one of the Wardens* for the time being *to be two*), do make, ordain, constitute, and establish such laws, ordinances, decrees, orders, and constitutions, to ordain, provide, and limit such pains, punishments, and penalties, either by fine or amercements, breaking the works deceitfully made, or by any other lawful ways or means whatsoever, upon all offenders or breakers of such laws, ordinances, decrees, orders, and constitutions, or any of them, as to them or any of them, or the greater part of them (whereof *the Master and one of the Wardens* for the time being *to be two*), shall seem necessary, fit, and convenient to be made, set, imposed, limited, and provided for the keeping of the same laws, orders, and constitutions.

Power to fine and punish offenders against their laws.

"THAT then, and at any time after, the said Master, Wardens, and Fellowship of the Art or Mystery of Clockmaking, of the city of London, and their successors, shall and may by virtue hereof, have and levy the same fines and amercements to their own use, and put in execution the said other penalties, without the let or hindrance of us, our heirs and successors, or without giving or rendering any thing therefore to us, our heirs or successors, or any other persons whatsoever.

To recover fines and penalties to their own use.

"ALL which laws, ordinances, statutes, decrees, and constitutions so as aforesaid to be made, we will to be observed and kept upon the pains therein contained.

All laws and ordinances to be obeyed.

THE CLOCKMAKERS' COMPANY.

The favourable Certificate thus made on their behalf by the Court of Aldermen appears to have produced satisfactory results, and accordingly in the following year 1631, a Charter of Incorporation was granted by the King dated the 22nd of August, in the 7th year of His reign, constituting them a body corporate under the name of " The Master, Wardens and Fellowship of the Art or Mystery of Clockmaking of the City of London," the terms of which Charter are as follow :—

𝕳𝕬𝕹𝕴𝕰𝕾, by the Grace of God, King of England, Scotland, France, and Ireland, Defender of the Faith, &c. To ALL MEN to whom these presents shall come, greeting.

" KNOW ye, that we, at the humble petition of the Clockmakers, as well freemen of our city of London, residing and inhabiting within the liberties and suburbs thereof, as also those that are foreigners, using the same trade, not of the freedom of the said city, and residing in or near the said city, liberties, and suburbs thereof, for the better order, rule, and government of them and every of them, and of others using the same Art or Mystery of Clockmaking, and also upon certificate made unto us from the Lord Mayor, Recorder, and Aldermen of the said city of London on their behalf, of our especial grace, certain knowledge and mere motion, HAVE willed, ordained, constituted, and granted, and by these presents, for us, our heirs, and successors, do will, ordain, constitute, declare, and grant :

Petition to the King by the Clockmakers, &c., praying to be incorporated. (7 Car. 1.)

THE CLOCKMAKERS' COMPANY.

Incorporation of all the Clockmakers both free and foreign; (i.e. persons not free of the city of London) who practice the art of Clockmaking within the city of London and ten miles compass; with perpetual succession.

Title of the Company.

"THAT *all and singular the Clockmakers and other person and persons whatsoever, as well freemen of or in our city of London, as also all other our natural freeborn subjects, using the Art or Mystery of Clockmaking within the said city, liberties, or suburbs thereof, or within any place within ten miles of the said city, as well within liberties and places exempt, as in other places, be and shall be, by virtue of these presents, for ever hereafter, one body corporate and politic, in deed and name to have continuance for ever, by the name of* The Master, Wardens, and Fellowship of the Art or Mystery of Clockmaking, of the city of London, and them by the name of Master, Wardens, and Fellowship of the Art or Mystery of Clockmaking, of the city of London, we do for us, our heirs and successors, really and fully create, erect, make, ordain, and constitute, by these presents, one body corporate and politic, in deed and in name, to have continuance for ever.

"AND that by the same name they may and shall have perpetual succession.

"AND that they and their successors, by the name of Master, Wardens, and Fellowship of the Art and Mystery of Clockmaking, of the city of London, be, and shall be for ever hereafter, persons able and capable in law to purchase, have, *Power to purchase lands, tenements, &c.* receive, and enjoy any manors, messuages, lands, tenements, liberties, privileges, jurisdictions, franchises, and other hereditaments whatsoever, of whatsoever kind, nature, or quality they be, to them and their successors in fee and perpetuity, or for term of life or lives, year or years, or otherwise in what sort soever, not held of us, our heirs, or successors, in *capite* or by knight's *Power to sell and alienate lands,&c* service; AND ALSO all manner of goods, chattels, and things whatsoever, of what name, nature, or quality soever they be: AND ALSO to give, grant, alien, assign, and set over and dispose of any manors, messuages, lands, tenements, and hereditaments; AND ALSO to do and execute all and singular other acts and things whatsoever, by the name aforesaid.

"AND that by the name of Master, Wardens, and Fellowship of the Art or Mystery of Clockmaking, of the city of London, *Power to plead and defend any cause as any other subject.* they and their successors shall or may be able to plead and be impleaded, to answer and be answered unto, to defend and be defended, in any court or courts, place or places whatsoever, and before whatsoever judge or judges, justice or justices, or other persons or officers of us, our heirs and successors whatsoever, in all and singular actions, pleas, suits, plaints, matters, and demands of whatsoever kind, quality, or sort they shall be, in the same manner and form as any other of our liege people and subjects, of this our realm of England, being persons able and capable in law, or any other body corporate and politic, within this our realm of England, can or may have, purchase, receive, possess, enjoy, retain, give, grant, let, alien, dispose, and assign, implead or to be impleaded unto, answer or to be answered unto, defend and be defended, do permit or execute.

"AND that they the said *Master, Wardens,* and *Fellowship* of the Art or Mystery of Clockmaking, of the city of London, and their successors for ever hereafter, shall and may have and use a Common Seal, for the expediting of the causes and business of them and their successors. And that it shall and may be lawful to and for the said *Master, Wardens,* and *Fellowship* of the said Art or Mystery of Clockmaking, and their successors, to alter and make new the said seal from time to time, at their wills and pleasures, as they shall think fit.

To have a Common seal; with power to alter and make new from time to time.

"AND FURTHER, we will and ordain, and by these presents for us, our heirs and successors, do grant unto the said *Master, Wardens,* and *Fellowship* of the Art or Mystery of Clockmaking, of the city of London, and their successors, that for ever hereafter there be and shall be *one of the said Art, Mystery, or Fellowship, in manner and form hereafter in these presents mentioned, to be chosen and named,* which shall be and shall be called *the Master of the said Fellowship* of the Art or Mystery of Clockmaking, of the city of London.

Power to elect one of the Fellowship to be Master;

"AND that likewise there be and shall be *three of the said Fellowship, in manner and form hereafter mentioned to be nominated and* elected, which shall be and shall be called, *the Wardens of the Fellowship* of the Art or Mystery of Clockmaking, of the city of London.

and three of the Fellowship to be Wardens;

"AND ALSO, that there be and shall be ten or more *Freemen of the said Fellowship, in manner and form hereafter in these presents expressed, to be named* and chosen, which shall be, and shall be called the *Assistants of the said Fellowship* of the Art or Mystery of Clockmaking, of the city of London. And from time to time shall be *assisting and aiding to the Master and Wardens* of the said Fellowship for the time being, in all causes, matters, and business, touching or concerning the said Fellowship.

also ten of the freemen to be called Assistants, to assist and aid the Master and Wardens for the time being.

"AND that the said *Master, Wardens,* and *Assistants* of the said Fellowship for the time being, or the greater part of them (whereof the Master and one of the Wardens for the time being to be two), *shall and may have full power and authority* by these presents, to *make, constitute, ordain, and set down, from time to time, such reasonable* laws, statutes, decrees, ordinances, and constitutions, *in writing,* whatsoever, which to them, or the greater part of them, whereof the Master and one of the Wardens as aforesaid for the time being to be two, shall seem good, wholesome, profitable, honest, and necessary, *according to their discretions,* as well *for and concerning* such *oaths* as shall be fit to be administered *to the Master, Wardens,* and *Assistants, or any other of the said Fellowship,* free, foreign, or stranger. As also, *for, touching, or concerning the said Trade, Art, or Mystery, in the making of clocks, watches, 'larums, boxes, or cases for clocks, watches, or 'larums, or any other manner of work concerning their Art, Mystery, or Profession of Clockmaking.* As also for the punishment and reformation of such abuses, deceits, and other wrongful practices, as shall from

What persons must be present to constitute a court, having power to make laws and ordinances, (19 Hen. VII. 7.) for the government of its own members, free, foreign, and stranger: and also concerning the said Art or Trade in any respect.

Deceitful practices punishable.

time to time be practised, either in making, mending, or uttering any bad, deceitful or hurtful wares, whereby our loving subjects may be wronged, deceived, or abused, or any other wrong, cozenage, deceit, or abuse concerning the said art and mystery, offered or committed at any time within the said city, liberties, and suburbs thereof, or in any other place or places, privileged or not privileged, within ten miles compass of the said city. And also, for the good rule and government of the Master, Wardens, and Fellowship of the said Art or Mystery of Clockmaking aforesaid, and their successors, and of all and singular persons using, exercising, or trading in the said Art, Trade, or Mystery of Clockmaking, and every of them, both within the city of London and liberties thereof, and ten miles compass of the said city, in all matters and things touching or in any wise concerning the said Art, Trade, or Mystery of Clockmaking aforesaid. AND *for declaration after what manner, order, and form, the said* Master, Wardens, *and* Fellowship, *and their successors, and all and every other person and persons using and exercising the said Art, Trade, and Mystery of Clockmaking* within this our realm of England, shall behave, demean, carry, and use themselves in their said offices, mysteries, and work, for the public good and common profit of the said Master, Wardens, and Fellowship, and of the rest of our people, and for all other matters, things, and causes touching or concerning the said Art, Trade, or Mystery of Clockmaking, by any manner of means.

"AND WHENSOEVER *the said Master, Wardens, and Assistants* for the time being, or the greater part of them (whereof *the Master and one of the Wardens* for the time being *to be two*), do make, ordain, constitute, and establish such laws, ordinances, decrees, orders, and constitutions, to ordain, provide, and limit such pains, punishments, and penalties, either by fine or amercements, breaking the works deceitfully made, or by any other lawful ways or means whatsoever, upon all offenders or breakers of such laws, ordinances, decrees, orders, and constitutions, or any of them, as to them or any of them, or the greater part of them (whereof *the Master and one of the Wardens* for the time being *to be two*), shall seem necessary, fit, and convenient to be made, set, imposed, limited, and provided for the keeping of the same laws, orders, and constitutions.

"THAT then, and at any time after, the said Master, Wardens, and Fellowship of the Art or Mystery of Clockmaking, of the city of London, and their successors, shall and may by virtue hereof, have and levy the same fines and amercements to their own use, and put in execution the said other penalties, without the let or hindrance of us, our heirs and successors, or without giving or rendering any thing therefore to us, our heirs or successors, or any other persons whatsoever.

"ALL which laws, ordinances, statutes, decrees, and constitutions so as aforesaid to be made, we will to be observed and kept upon the pains therein contained.

"So ALWAYS, *as such laws, ordinances, constitutions, fines,* Provided that no *amercements, or other ways or means be reasonable, and not* contrary to law *repugnant or contrary to the laws of this our realm of England, nor* or custom *to the customs or usage of this our city of London.*

"AND FURTHER, our royal will and pleasure is, for the better All apprentices strengthening of the said government, that if any person or persons to persons using the art to be hereafter professing the trade of Clockmaking, and being free of bound to a free that Company, or of any other company whatsoever, within the Clockmaker only. city of London, liberties, and suburbs thereof, or the limits hereby proposed, and shall take unto him or them an apprentice for the term of seven years or otherwise, according to the custom of the said city, that the said apprentice or apprentices shall for ever hereafter be bound to some free brother of the said Company of Clockmakers, *to the end the said Brotherhood in time may become an able body of itself, without the disturbance of any other society or government.*

"AND for the better executing of this our grant in that behalf, Creation of the we have assigned, named, constituted and made, and by these first Master by name; presents, for us, our heirs, and successors, do assign, name, constitute, and make our well-beloved servant David Ramsey, Esquire, to be the first and present Master *of the said Fellowship, he being or having been a professed Clockmaker,* and *to continue in* who is to con-*the same office until the feast-day of Saint Michael the Archangel, next* tinue his office until the ensuing *ensuing* the date of these presents, if he shall so long live; and Michaelmas-day from thence until one other of the said Fellowship shall be and until the election of a chosen and named unto the office of Master of the said Fellow-successor. ship in due manner, according to the ordinances and provisions hereafter in these presents mentioned and expressed.

"AND also, we have assigned, named, and constituted, and by Creation of the first Wardens by these presents, for us, our heirs and successors, do assign, name, name; constitute, and make our well-beloved Henry Archer, John Wellowe, and Sampson Shelton, to be the first and present Wardens *of the said Fellowship, they being also, or having been, professed Clockmakers,* and they and either of them respectively *to continue in their said office until the said feast-day of Saint* to continue their office until the *Michael the Archangel next ensuing* the date of these presents, if ensuing Michael-they or either of them shall so long live. And from thence until mas-day, and until the election three other of the said Fellowship, according to the ordinances of successors. and provisions in these presents expressed and declared, shall be newly chosen.

"AND we have assigned, named, constituted, appointed and Creation of the first Assistants made, and by these presents for us, our heirs and successors, do by name; assign, name, constitute, and make our well-beloved James Vautrollier, John Smith, Francis Forman, John Harris, Richard Morgan, Samuel Lynaker, John Charlton, John Midnall, Simon Bartram, and Edward East, to be the first and present Assistants to continue dur-of the said Fellowship, to continue in the said office of Assistants ing life, unless they shall be during their natural lives, unless they or any of them respec-removed for some reasonable tively shall fortune to be removed for the misbehaving him or cause.

themselves in their said office, or for some other reasonable cause, whom for such reasonable cause we will shall be removable from time to time, at the pleasure of the *Master, Wardens,* and *Assistants* of the said Fellowship or the greater part of them, whereof the Master and one of the Wardens to be two.

Assistants removable, and by what authority.

"NEVERTHELESS, our will and pleasure is, that the said David Ramsey, before mentioned, to be *Master of the said Fellowship, before he enter into the execution of the said place and office, take his corporal oath upon the Holy Evangelists,* for the faithful and due execution of the said office before the Lord Mayor of our city of London, unto which Lord Mayor we do hereby give power and authority *to administer an* oath *unto the said first and present Master, and the three first Wardens,* by virtue of this our present grant hereby mentioned accordingly, without any further commission or warrant from us, our heirs or successors, to be procured in that behalf.

First Master sworn before the Lord Mayor, as also the three first Wardens.

"AND afterwards we will, and by these presents for us, our heirs, and successors, do for ever hereafter grant and give unto the said Master, Wardens, and Fellowship of the Art and Mystery of Clockmaking, of the city of London, and their successors also That the *Master, Wardens, and Assistants* of the said Fellowship for the time being, or the greater part of them *(whereof* we will *the Master and one of the Wardens* for the time being *to be two),* from time to time, for ever hereafter, shall have full power and authority, yearly and every year, upon the said feast-day of Saint Michael the archangel, if it fall not out to be on the Sabbath-day, or in such case the next day following, and so from day to day until election and acceptation of officers as after followeth shall be made, to elect *and nominate* one *of* the *Freemen* of the said Fellowship, *he being or having been a professed Clockmaker at the time of his election,* to be the Master *of the said Fellowship,* for one year then next ensuing, and from thence until one other of the said Fellowship be chosen into the said office of Master of the said Fellowship, according to the ordinances and provisions in these presents expressed and declared, unless in the mean-time he shall die, or be removed as aforesaid.

Power to elect officers annually on Michaelmas-day.

One of the FREEMEN *to be elected Master, who must be or have been a professed Clockmaker:*

"AND that he which shall be so chosen and named into the office of Master of the said Fellowship, *before he* be admitted or *execute his said office, shall take his corporal oath before the last Master* of the said Fellowship *then living, and the Wardens* of the said Fellowship *for the time being, or two of them,* well and truly to execute the said office of Master of the said Fellowship, unto whom, and their successors, we do hereby give full power and authority to administer an oath or oaths accordingly. And that after the said oath or oaths so as aforesaid taken, he shall have and exercise the office of Master, until one other be chosen and sworn into the said office, in manner and form aforesaid.

and he shall take the oath before the last Master and two Wardens before he be admitted into his office.

Power for the old officers to administer the oaths to the new ones.

"AND that then likewise *they may* elect, nominate, and choose, three *other of the Freemen* of the said Fellowship to be Wardens of the said Fellowship, *which shall be, or have been, professed Clockmakers as aforesaid,* to continue in the same office one year then next ensuing, and from thence until three others of the said Fellowship be chosen in the said office of Wardens of the said Fellowship, according to the ordinances and provisions in these presents expressed and declared, unless, in the mean-time, any of them shall die or be removed as aforesaid.

Three of the FREEMEN to be elected Wardens, who must be or have been professed Clockmakers.

"AND that they which shall be so chosen and named into the office of Wardens of the said Fellowship, before they be admitted to execute the said office, *shall take their corporal oath before the Master and last Wardens* of the said Fellowship *then living, or two of them,* well and truly to execute the said office of Wardens in all things touching and concerning the said offices, unto whom and their successors we do hereby give power to administer an oath accordingly. And that after such oaths so as aforesaid taken, they shall and may execute their office from thence, until three other be chosen and sworn in form aforesaid into the said office of Wardens of the Fellowship, in manner and form afore in these presents expressed and declared.

New Wardens to take the oaths before the last Master and two Wardens, before they be admitted into their offices.

"AND FURTHER, by these presents for us, our heirs and successors, we will and do grant unto the said Master, Wardens, and Fellowship of the Art or Mystery of Clockmaking, of the city of London, and their successors, That *if it happen the* Master *of the said Fellowship* for the time being, at any time within one year after that he be chosen into his office, do die, *or be removed* from the same *(whom we will shall be removable upon reasonable and just cause, at the pleasure of the Wardens and Assistants* of the said Fellowship for the time being, or the greater part of them, *whereof one of the Wardens to be one),* That then, and so often, it shall and may be lawful to and for the *Wardens and Assistants of the said Fellowship* for the time being, or the greater part of them *(whereof one of the Wardens to be one), within one month* next after such decease or removal, *to choose,* elect, and swear one other *of the* Wardens *or* Assistants of the said Fellowship for the time being, to be Master *of the said Fellowship,* to execute and exercise the said office of Master of the said Fellowship *until the feast of St. Michael the Archangel then next following,* and from thence until one other be chosen in the said place in manner aforesaid, *he* or *they first taking his or their corporal oath* or oaths, in manner and form aforesaid. And so as often as the cause shall so require.

Power to elect a Master on death or removal of the old one.

Master removable for reasonable cause.

Election to take place within one month after death or removal, and must be either a Warden or Assistant; and to continue only until Michaelmas-day following;

but not to act until sworn.

"AND if it shall happen *the* Wardens of the Fellowship, *or one of them,* at any time within one year after they or any of them be chosen into his or their office or offices *to die, or be removed* from his or their office or offices, *whom we will upon reasonable and just cause shall be removable at the pleasure of the Master, Wardens, and the Assistants* of the said Company, or the greater part of them for the time being, that then and so often it shall and may

Power to elect Wardens on death or removal.

Wardens removable for reasonable cause;

and other of the Fellowship may be chosen instead.

New Wardens not to act until sworn,

and to continue until ensuing Michaelmas-day.

be lawful to and for the said *Master, Wardens, and Assistants,* and their successors, *which shall be then living* or remaining, or the greater part of them, at their pleasure, to elect, choose, and give oath unto one, two, or three other of the said Fellowship to be Warden or Wardens according to the orders and provisions before in and by these presents expressed and declared, to execute and exercise the said office of Warden or Wardens of the said Fellowship *until the said feast of Saint Michael the Archangel then next following,* in form as aforesaid, and so as often as the cause shall happen or require.

Power to elect Assistants on vacancies occasioned by death or removal,

"AND FURTHER, we will, and by these presents, for us, our heirs and successors, we do grant unto the said Master, Wardens, and Fellowship of the Art or Mystery of Clockmaking, of the city of London, and their successors, that *whensoever it happeneth any* the Assistants of the said Fellowship for the time being *to die, or to be removed* by the greater part of the said *Master, Wardens,* and *Assistants,* for the time being *(whereof the Master and one of the Wardens* for the time being *to be two),* for evil government or misbehaviour, or for any other reasonable cause, that then and so often, it shall and may be lawful to and for the

which elections may be made at the pleasure of the Court as often as the case may require.

said *Master, Wardens, and so many of the said Assistants* for the time being, *which shall then survive and remain,* or the greater part of them *(whereof the Master and one of the Wardens* as aforesaid, for the time being *to be two),* at their will and pleasure, from time to time, *to choose or name* one other. or more of the Fellowship *aforesaid to be* Assistant or Assistants *of the said Fellowship,* in his or their place or stead, *which shall so happen to*

New Assistants not to act till sworn.

die or to be removed as is aforesaid. And that he or they after they be so chosen and named to be Assistant or Assistants of the said Fellowship as aforesaid, before that he or they, or any of them, be admitted to the execution of the office or offices of Assistant or Assistants of the said Fellowship, shall take his or their corporal oath or oaths, before the Master and Wardens of the said Fellowship, well and truly to execute the said office and offices, and so, as often as the cause shall so require. Unto which Master and Wardens, and their successors, we do by these presents give power and authority to administer an oath or oaths accordingly, for the general good of the said Society or Fellowship of Clockmakers.

Power to administer oath to any person admitted under the government of the Company, for the due performance of all things appertaining to the art.

"AND FURTHER, that it shall and may be lawful to and for the said *Master, Wardens,* and *Assistants* of the said Fellowship for the time being, or the greater part of them *(whereof the Master and one of the Wardens to be two),* to give and administer an oath *or oaths,* from to time, to every particular freeman, foreigner, denizen, or stranger, or any others that shall be admitted by the *Master, Wardens,* and *Court of Assistants,* or the major part of them (whereof the Master and one of the Wardens to be two), under the government of the said Fellowship, for performance of such things as shall be requisite and necessary by them to be done and performed in their several Arts and Mysteries of Clockmaking.

"And we will, and by these presents, for us, our heirs and successors, for the better order, rule, and government of all and singular person and persons which shall be admitted by the *Master*, *Wardens*, and *Court of Assistants*, a member of that Fellowship, of the Art or Mystery of Clockmaking, or which now do use, or hereafter shall use, either making, mending, buying selling, ingrossing, or retailing, or do any manner of work generally or particularly belonging to the Trade, Art, or Mystery of Clockmaking, or the making, buying, selling, transporting, and importing any bad, deceitful, and unsufficient *Clocks*, *Watches*, *'larums*, *Sun-dials*, *Boxes or Cases*, *for the said Trade*, *Art*, *or Mystery of Clockmaking*, be they of what metal or of what nature, condition, or fashion soever; or any other work peculiarly belonging to the said Trade of Clockmaking, coming either from foreign parts or provinces forth of our dominions, or within our dominions, and made, sold, or brought to be sold within the said city of London, liberties, and suburbs thereof, or ten miles of the said city, or within our realm of England or dominion of Wales. We do will, and for us, our heirs and successors, do grant to the said *Master*, and *Wardens* and *Assistants*, or any two of them (whereof the said Master or one of the said Wardens for the time being, *to be one*), or their lawful sufficient deputy or deputies in that behalf lawfully deputed and assigned, together with a constable or other officer or officers of us, our heirs or successors, from time to time, when they shall think necessary or expedient to enter into any ship bottom, vessel, or lighters, or any other warehouse or warehouses, houses, shops, or any other place or places whatsoever, where they or any of them shall suspect any such watches, 'larums, sun-dials, or any the premises before mentioned, to be so brought in, made, or wrought as aforesaid, to be and remain, and then and there to make search for all the said clocks, watches, 'larums, sun-dials, or cases made for any clocks, watches, or 'larums, or any other works as aforesaid peculiarly belonging to the said trade of Clockmaking, made within this realm, or brought into the same to be put to sale and them to view and survey, and such of them as shall be faulty and deceitfully wrought, to seize on them and to break them, or cause them, if they shall think fit it may be well done, to be amended, and to take such order and security, that none of them that shall not be substantially and truly wrought be put to sale, or not made of good and lawful metals, or by such men who have not served out the full term of seven years, according to the statute in that case made and provided, and the parties themselves suppressed, or such of them, and all such works as shall be deceitfully wrought, and cannot be by art well and sufficiently amended, that then it shall be lawful for the said Master and Wardens, or one of them, or their sufficient deputy so assigned from time to time, upon due search, as often as they shall think fit, to seize the same faulty and deceitful work or works, and every part and parcel thereof, into their hands, in the names of us, our heirs and successors ; and in presence of the Mayor, Sheriff, Bailiff, Constable, Headborough, or other chief officer or officers of the place or county where such seizure shall be made, shewing the deceitfulness or insufficiency

Mayor, &c. the same to be broken.	of the work to him or them, and he or they approving thereof, to break the same.
In case the Mayor, &c. cannot judge of such insufficiency,	"BUT if in such case the Mayor, Sheriff, Bailiff, or other chief officer of that place or county cannot sufficiently judge of the reasons, that the said Master, Warden or Wardens, or some of the Assistants of the said Fellowship of Clockmaking, of our city of London, or their sufficient and lawful deputy or deputies, shall give and shew them that the work or works is deceitful and fit to be broken, then our will and pleasure is, that the said work or wares, by virtue of these presents, shall be brought to the common hall or place of meeting of the Fellowship of Clockmaking, in our city of London, there to be viewed by the *Master, Wardens*, and the *whole Court of Assistants*, and there to be adjudged by them or the greater part of the assembly (whereof the Master and one of the Wardens to be two.) And then if they shall think fit to break or deface it, they then to do it so that it may not hereafter be put to sale, except the owner thereof do appeal to the Lord Mayor of our city of London, to be further judged there.
then the seized work to be brought to the Company's hall to be adjudged	
and if condemned, to be broken, except the owner appeal to the Lord Mayor for further judgment	
Power to break open any place if refused entrance to search it.	"AND in case the said *Master, Wardens*, or *Assistants*, or their sufficient deputy or deputies and officers aforesaid, shall be denied entrance into any the places aforesaid, or shall be denied to have the sight of any such wares as aforesaid, that then it shall and may be lawful for them, or any of them with such assistants as aforesaid, to break open any locks, doors, bolts, latches, chests, trunks, boxes, or other thing or things whatsoever, where they shall suspect any such work, wares, or tools to be, and the same to take and seize as aforesaid.
and to seize work and tools therein concealed.	
Power to sue in the Exchequer all such as act contrary to this Charter.	"AND if the said *Master, Wardens*, and *Assistants*, or the greater part of them, shall so think fit to make presentment or information of the workers or putters to sale, either by wholesale or retail, or by piece-meal or otherwise, of all such deceitful work, works, or wares, or other the offenders, aforesaid, in our Exchequer as aforesaid, of us, our heirs and successors, to the end that the said workers or putters to sale thereof, and other the said offenders, may receive such condign punishment, as by the laws or our prerogative royal can, or may be, required for the same.
No Alien or Stranger shall work within the limits of this grant, but with an allowed and professed Clockmaker.	"AND our pleasure is that no alien or stranger whatsoever, born out of our dominions, not naturalized or denized, (saving such as are already allowed of by us), shall attempt to work in any place whatsoever, either chamber, house or any other place or places whatsoever, within the limits and circuits of this our royal grant, either privileged or not privileged, saving only to or with an allowed and professed Clockmaker.
To prevent frauds and abuses on the public,	"AND for the further preventing of abuses and frauds in uttering and selling such deceitful wares, made or imported to the abuse of our subjects; It is our will and pleasure, and we do

hereby for us, our heirs and successors, straightly charge and command that no person or persons, whatsoever, Englishmen, or denizens strangers, which shall import or bring into this our realm of England, or the dominions of Wales or any part of them, or either of them, any clocks, watches, 'larums, boxes, sun-dials, or cases for watches, clocks, or 'larums, or any other wares properly belonging to the Art or Mystery of Clockmaking, by way of merchandize, do presume, attempt or go about at any time or times, to utter, vent, or make sale of the same, or any of them, to any person or persons within the said realm or dominion, before the same be brought to the hall or meeting-place of the said Clockmakers, in our said city of London or elsewhere, to be viewed and approved of, and receive a mark by them to be ordained, testifying the allowance of the *Master*, *Wardens*, and *Assistants* of the said Company, upon pain of forfeiture of such clocks, watches, 'larums, boxes, cases, or sun-dials, or cases for watches, clocks, or 'larums, or any other wares or works so uttered or sold, or attempted or offered to be sold, (which do properly belong to the Art of Clockmaking) contrary to this our pleasure, and upon such further pains and penalties as by the laws or statutes of this realm may be inflicted upon the offenders for contempt of this our royal command.

no persons whatsoever import any clocks, watches, &c.

or offer the same for sale,

before such work be brought to the Company's Hall to be viewed, and marked, upon pain of forfeiture of such work,

and further penalties.

"NEVERTHELESS, if the maker, merchant, or owner of such clock, watch, alarum or other such work, shall not rest satisfied with the judgment of the said *Master*, *Wardens*, *and Assistants*, of and in the goodness or deceitfulness of the same, that then and in every such case our will and command is, that the said *Master*, *Wardens*, and *Assistants*, do forbear to break or deface the said work, until such further trial thereof be had as the Lord Mayor of the city of London, and the Court of Aldermen of the said city (if the same shall be in London) shall allow of and direct. And in the meantime the same to be safely kept by the Master or Wardens, until such further trial thereof shall be had as aforesaid.

Should the judgment pronounced by the Company be disputed, the work shall not be defaced but an appeal made to the Lord Mayor, &c. the work in the mean time to be safely kept by the Master and Wardens.

"AND THEREFORE, we do by these presents, for us, our heirs and successors, give power and authority unto the *Master*, *Wardens*, and *Assistants* of the said Fellowship, for the time being or any of them, with the assistance of a constable, or some other officer or officers of us, our heirs and successors in due and lawful manner, to make search in all and every place and places convenient, as well privileged as not privileged, within our said realm and dominion, or either of them, as well within liberties as without, for such clocks, watches, or 'larums, sun-dials or cases, for either of them, great or small, or any other work or wares peculiarly belonging to the Art of Clockmaking, as shall be so imported, made, uttered, or sold, or offered to be sold, contrary to the true meaning hereof. And having found any such, to seize and take the same as forfeited to the use of us, our heirs and successors. And if the said *Master*, *Wardens*, and *Assistants*, or the greater part of them as aforesaid, shall so think fit, further to prosecute the offenders, according to the laws of this realm.

Power to the Master, Wardens, and Assistants, or any of them, with the assistance of a constable, to search through-out England and Wales for such foreign clocks, &c. and for the several productions enumerated, and such as are not lawfully imported and marked to seize,

and prosecute the offenders.

One half of all forfeitures to be to the use of the king and the other half to be taken by the Company.	"AND for the care pain and expence of the said *Master, Wardens, and Assistants,* in the execution thereof, and toward the supportation of the public charge of the said Fellowship or Company: We do hereby, for us, our heirs and successors, so far as in us lieth, give and grant unto the said *Master, Wardens, and Fellowship,* and their successors, the moiety or one half of all and singular the said forfeitures, without any account or any thing therefore to us, our heirs and successors, to be rendered, paid, made, or given.
All officers of Justice are to assist the Company in the execution of the powers herein granted and contained.	"And FURTHER, we will, and by these presents for us, our heirs and successors, we do straightly charge and command, all and singular Mayors, Justices of Peace, Sheriffs, Bailiffs, Constables, Headboroughs, and all other officers, ministers, and subjects of us, our heirs and successors whatsoever, that they and every of them, from time to time, and at all times, as often as cause shall require, with their best power and ability, to be aiding, helping, assisting, and comforting to the said *Master, Wardens, and Fellowship of Clockmakers of London,* for the time being, and every of them and their successors, in the doing, enjoying, having, and executing all and singular thing and things whatsoever, by us before by these presents granted unto the said *Master, Wardens, and Fellowship* as aforesaid, and every or any part or parts thereof, according to the tenor and true meaning of these presents.
To have a clerk of the said fellowship	"AND FURTHER, we will, and by these presents for us, our heirs and successors, do grant unto the said *Master, Wardens,* and *Fellowship* of the Art or Mystery of Clockmaking of the city of London aforesaid, and their successors, that they and their successors shall and may have one honest and discreet person, in manner and form hereafter, in these presents expressed, to be chosen and named, which shall be, and shall be called the Clerk of the said Fellowship of that Art or Mystery of Clockmakers of the city of London.
The first clerk named, and to continue for life unless removed for misconduct.	"AND we have assigned, constituted, and made, and by these presents for us, our heirs and successors, do assign, constitute, make, name, and ordain, our well-beloved subject Thomas Copley, to be the first and present Clerk of the said Fellowship, to continue in the said office during the term of his natural life, (unless upon some misdemeanor there shall be just occasion to remove him.)
On death or removal, one other to be chosen.	"AND that from time to time, and at all times, after the death of the said Thomas Copley, the *Master, Wardens, and Assistants* of the said Fellowship for the time being, or the greater part of them as aforesaid, shall and may choose, name, and make one other discreet person, to be Clerk of the said Fellowship.
who shall continue during the pleasure of the Master, Wardens &c.	"AND that he which shall be chosen and made Clerk of the said Fellowship, after the death of the said Thomas Copley as is aforesaid, shall and may exercise and enjoy the said office of Clerk of the said Fellowship during the good-will and pleasure of the said

Master, Wardens and *Assistants,* of the said Fellowship for the time being, or the greater part of them as aforesaid.

"THE *said Clerk* so to be named and appointed after the death of the said Thomas Copley as aforesaid, first *taking his corporal oath* before the *Master, Wardens,* and *Assistants,* for the time being, or the greater part of them, *well and truly to execute the said office of Clerk of the said Fellowship, in and by all things appertaining to the said office, according to his best skill and knowledge, and according to the tenor and true meaning of these presents.* {to be sworn truly to execute his office before he be allowed to act}

"UNTO which *Master, Wardens,* and *Assistants,* and their successors, now and for the time being, or the greater part of them, we do by these presents for us, our heirs and successors, give and grant full power and authority, to administer such oath and oaths as aforesaid, as well to the said present Clerk, as to all other future Clerk or Clerks, or to any other Officer, Beadle or Beadles, whom they shall choose or think fit to entertain in and *for the service* of the said Fellowship, without any further warrant or commission from us, our heirs or successors, to be in that behalf had, procured, or obtained. ALTHOUGH express of the true yearly value or certainty of the premises, or any of them, or of any other gift or grant, by us or by any of our progenitors or predecessors, to the said *Master, Wardens,* and *Fellowship* of the Art or Mystery of Clockmaking, of the city of London, heretofore made in these presents, is not made, or any statute, act, ordinance, provision, proclamation, or restraint, to the contrary thereof, heretofore made, ordained, or provided, or any other matter, cause, or thing whatsoever, in any wise notwithstanding. {Power granted to the Master, Wardens, and Assistants, to administer oaths to all clerks, beadles, and other officers.} {To have and to hold their several places, privileges, immunities, &c. any law to the contrary notwithstanding.}

"IN WITNESS whereof, we have caused these our letters to be made patent. Witness ourself at Canbury, the two-and-twentieth day of August, in the seventh year of our reign. {Anno Domini 1631.}

"*Per Breve de privato Sigillo.*

"WOLSELEY."

The foregoing Charter is engrossed on two large skins of parchment richly emblazoned, having in the right-hand corner a full-length Portrait of King Charles the First in his Coronation Robes, holding the Sword of Justice in his right-hand, and in his left the Orb. At the top are the Arms of England, in the right-hand margin the Arms of Scotland and Ireland, and in the left-hand margin the Arms of France. The border consists of flowers, fruits, birds and insects, beautifully entwined.[1]

---

[1] Att a Court holden the 3rd day of November 1634 was paid unto Mr. John Chappell £4 for the flourishing and finishing of the Companys Charter. Company's Journal I.

A copy of this Charter is enrolled in the Archives of the Corporation. (Journal No. 36, fol. 54-58ᴮ.)

The costs of obtaining the Charter were defrayed by the subscriptions of individual Members. In addition to those already referred to in the Memorandum of Agreement of the 31st March, 1630, the following List of Contributors, preserved among their Records, affords evidence of the number of persons engaged in the trade in London at the date of the application, and includes names of men whose works have since rendered them celebrated, and to whom reference will be hereafter made :—

"The particular names of such persons as the Company have concluded the Collectors shall demand money of for the accomplishment of their Incorporation viz. :—

		1630.	£	s.	d.
"Lent £5.	Imprimis of	Mr. Archer ...	10	0	0
		Mr. Peteet ...	10	0	0
		Mr. Bull ...	3	0	0
		Mr. fforeman ...	3	0	0
		Mr. Smith ...	3	0	0
		Mr. Harris ...	1	0	0
hath Lent £5.		Mr. Vaultroleir ...	3	0	0
hath Lent £5.		Mr. Shelton ...	3	0	0
hath Lent £5.		Mr. Willow ...	3	0	0
		Mr. Morgan ...			
hath Lent £5.		Mr. Charlton ...	1	15	0
hath Lent £5.		Mr. Lynnaker ...	1	0	0
hath Lent £5.		Mr. East ...	1	15	0
hath Lent £5.		Mr. Bowyer ...	5	0	0
hath Lent £5.		Mr. Closen ...	5	0	0
		Mr. Holden ...	1	15	0
		Mr. Burgis ...	1	16	0
hath Lent £5.		Mr. Bartram ...	3	0	0
		Mr. Tho. Holland ...	1	10	0
hath Lent £5.		Mr. Maisterson ...	2	0	0
		Mr. Ash ...	2	0	0
		Mr. Graye ...	2	10	0
		Mr. Shepherd			
		Mr. Saunders ...	1	0	0
		Mr. Walter			
hath Lent £5.		Mr. Midnall			
		Mr. Drake ...	1	10	0
		Mr. Heywood ...	4	0	0
		Mr. Holloway ...	2	0	0
		Mr. Hill ...	2	0	0
		Mr. Dewell ...	2	0	0
		Mr. Hearne			

		1630.	£	s.	d.
hath Lent £5.	Mr. Hewes	...	1	15	0
	Mr. Jo. Holland				
	Mr. Volant				
	Mr. Josias Cuper		2	0	0
Lent £5.	Mr. Dawson	...	2	0	0
	Mr. Eryles	...	2	0	0
	Mr. Bucket				
	Mr. Walker	...	2	0	0
	Mr. Smith	...	3	0	0
	Mr. P. Lowell	...	5	0	0
	Mr. Howse	...	5	0	0
	Mr. Hackett	...	5	0	0
	Mr. Reeve	...	2	0	0
	Mr. Charlton		3	0	0
	Mr. Helden	...	3	0	0
	Mr. Josias Cuper		2	10	0
	Mr. Oswell Durant		2	10	0
	Mr Thomas Dawson		5	0	0
	Mr. John Hill	...	5	0	0 "

Some of them did not immediately fulfil their promises, and as soon as the Company was regularly constituted, measures were taken to enforce the payment of their share of the expenses, as the following extracts shew :—

1632. October 23rd. "This daye the Court have Ordered that John Micabius shalbe taken Course withall by Law for not paying his contribution towards the Companie's Charter Ordinaunces and other charges according to his promiss." [1]

1632. November 19th. "This daye Mr. Child paid in Court the some of £3 3s 6d in part of five pounds formerly promissed towards the Corporation the remainder he faithfully promissed to pay at Christmastide." [2]

1633. April 1st. "This day Mr. Ward did pay twenty shillings in part of three pounds that he promissed to the Company towards the procuring of the Charter and Ordinances." [3]

1633. September 2nd. "This day Onesepherus Holden did faithfully promiss to pay the 3ˡⁱ which he subscribed unto by the 1st of November following which was towards the procuring of the Charter and Ordinances." [4]

Mr. Paul Lovell promissed to pay £5 for the same purpose, and the names of others follow who had made promises to the same effect.

In conformity with an Act of Parliament of the 19 Henry VII 1503-4, Cap. 7, which enacts—

" . . . That no Maisters, Wardens & felishippes of Craftes or mysters, nor eny of them, nor eny rulers of guyldes or fratnities, take uppon them to

[1, 2, 3, 4] Company's Journal I.

make eny actes or ordinaunces, ne to execute eny actes or ordinaunces be them hereafore made, in disheritaunce or diminuc͠on of the p̃rogatyſſe of the King, nor of other, nor ageynste the comen p̃fite of the people, but yf the same actes or ordinaunces be examyned & approved by the Chaunceller Tresorer of Englonde & cheſſe Justices of ether Benche, or thre of them; or before bothe the Justices of Assises in ther cyrcuyte or p̃gresse in that Shyre wher suche actes or ordinaunces be made, uppon the peyne of forfeytoure of xl. li for ev͠ry tyme that they doo the contᵃrie."

Bye-Laws for the good government of the craft were duly submitted for approval, and were granted and confirmed on the 11th of August, 1632, in these words :—

"To ALL XTIAN PEOPLE to whom this present writing shall come, Thomas, Lord Coventrye, *lord keeper of the great seal of England*, Sir Thomas Richardson, knight, *lord chief-justice of his Highness' Court of King's-Bench;* and Sir Robert Heath, Knight *lord chief-justice of his Highness' Court of Common Pleas;* send greeting in our Lord God Everlasting.

<small>19th Hen. 7th. Concerning</small>

"WHEREAS, *in a certain Act, of Parliament*, holden at Westminster, the five-and twentieth day of January, *in the nineteenth year* of the reign of the late king, of famous memory, Henry, after the conquest the Seventh, *made and ordained for the weal*

<small>the enacting of bye-laws by guilds or fraternities,</small>

and profit of his subjects: it was amongst other things *ordained, established, and enacted, that* no Master, Wardens, or Fellowship of Crafts or Mysteries, *or any of them, nor any rulers of guilds or fraternities, should take upon them* to execute any acts *or ordinances by them thentofore made* in disinheritance or diminution of the prerogative of the king, nor of any other, *nor against* the com-

<small>by whom the same are to be examined and approved, under forfeiture of £40.</small>

mon profit of the people. But *if the same Acts and Ordinances be examined and approved by the chancellor treasurer of England; or chief-justices of either bench, or three of them ; or before both the justices of assize, in their circuit or progress in the shire where such Acts and Ordinances should be made*, upon pain of forfeiture of forty pounds *for every time they did thereunto contrary*, as by the said Act of Parliament more plainly doth and may appear.

<small>Acts and ordinances presented 2d Jan. 1632.</small>

"KNOW YE, that the *Master, Wardens*, and *Fellowship* of the Art or Mystery of Clockmaking, of the city of London, the second day of January, in the seventh year of the reign of our sovereign lord Charles, by the Grace of God, King of England, Scotland, France, and Ireland, Defender of the Faith, &c. Have *exhibited and presented unto us a book, wherein are contained divers* Acts,

<small>Ratification by the Judges applied for,</small>

Ordinances, and Constitutions, *heretofore devised, ordained, and* made by the *Master, Wardens, and Assistants of the same Fellowship, being thereunto enabled by* letters patent *of our said sovereign lord the* King, *bearing date the two and twentieth day of August, in the seventh year of the reign of our said sovereign lord* Charles ; and *thereupon have instantly desired us, that we,* all and every *the said Acts*, Ordinances, and Constitutions, set down and by them unto us exhibited, *would examine;* and *if there should be cause, to allow and approve, and those and every of them to correct and amend* in due and convenient manner and form, if need should so require, as the said recited Act of Parliament requireth.

"WE, well perceiving and considering their supplications to be good and acceptable, according to their said petition, and desires, by the authority of the said Act of Parliament, to us in that behalf given, all and every the said *Acts and Ordinances have seen, read, and well understood;* and considered of, and them *and all and every of them examined, corrected, reformed, and so examined, corrected, and reformed, have approved:* all which Acts, Ordinances, and Constitutions, so examined, corrected, reformed by us, following in these words: and obtained.

"ACTS, *Ordinances, and Constitutions, made and ordained by* David Ramsey, Master of the Fellowship of the Art or Mystery of Clockmaking of the city of London; Henry Archer, John Willowe, and Sampson Shelton, Wardens of the said Art or Mystery of Clockmaking; and James Vautrollier, John Smith, Francis Foreman, John Harris, Richard Morgan, Samuel Linnaker, John Charlton, John Midnall, Symon Bartrum, and Edward East, Assistants of the said Fellowship, of the said Art or Mystery *being assembled at a public meeting, the last day of November, in the seventh year of the reign of our Sovereign lord, Charles,* by the grace of God, King of England, Scotland, France, and Ireland, defender of the faith, &c. *for that purpose:* by virtue of letters patents of our said sovereign lord the King, bearing date the two and twentieth day of August, which Acts, Ordinances, and Constitutions, were made and ordained in the presence, and with the advice of divers others of the said Fellowship, to whom the same were then publicly read, and were by them approved, viz.:

Acts, Ordinances, and Constitutions by whom made; in what manner ordained; dated Nov. 30, 1631; By what authority; being first publicly read to, and approved by, the Freemen at a general meeting duly assembled.

I.

"IMPRIMIS, where there hath been a long time (as time out of mind), *a great multitude of Clockmakers* in number, which have wrought *within the* City of London, *liberties and suburbs thereof, although never incorporated, until* it hath of late pleased his Majesty, of his especial grace, by *his highness's letters patents,* bearing date at Westminster, the two and twentieth day of August, *in the said seventh year of his Majesty's reign,* to make them a body corporate and politic, and *thereby ordained* that of the same *Fellowship there should be* a Master, three Wardens, *and* ten Assistants or more, *wherein is expressed in what manner the said* Master, Wardens, and Assistants, *should be chosen,* as by the said letters patents doth appear *for the better order and rule to be held amongst the said Company here incorporated.*

The first incorporation of Clockmakers in England, 22d Aug. 1631. To have a Master, three Wardens, and ten Assistants, to be chosen conformably to the directions of the Charter.

II.

"IT is hereby ordained, that of the said Master, Wardens, and Fellowship, *and of the Fellowship and of the Fellows thereof,* there shall be a Livery of Company, as is used in other companies

To have a livery of company.

THE CLOCKMAKERS' COMPANY.

who shall be of the livery, and by whom they shall be chosen;

within the city of London, for the better service of his Majesty and of the said city. And that the *Master, Wardens,* and *Assistants* of the said Fellowship; and so many others *of the Fellows* of the said Fellowship, as the said *Master, Wardens,* and *Assistants,* being assembled, or the more part of them *(whereof the Master and one of the Wardens shall be two)* shall elect from time to time, shall be of the said Livery. AND that every person of the said Fellowship chosen into the said Livery, shall accept and take upon him to be of the said Livery, and shall within fourteen days after notice of such election, take such oath as by these ordinances shall be appointed for him.

every person then shall take the clothing and the oaths within fourteen days.

III.

Courts to be holden the first Monday in every month, and that day fortnight,

" ITEM, it is ordained, that upon the first Monday of every month, and that day fortnight, shall be *the usual and ordinary days of assemblies for the* Master, Wardens, and Assistants of this Fellowship, and upon every of these days a court to be held at the hall *or other meeting-place of the said* Company, *for view and correction of such things as to the same Art or Mystery pertaineth,* and other the affairs and business of the said Master, Wardens, and Fellowship. And *if occasion do require,* then such court or assembly *to be oftener,* and at such times as by the *Master and Wardens* of the said Company shall be thought fit and caused to be summoned.

at the hall or other Meeting place of the company.

Master and Wardens may summon other courts as occasion may require.

In case the said courts should fall on certain holidays, the court to be held on the next day.

" PROVIDED always, that if any such Monday shall happen to be the feast of All Saints, the feast of the Birth of Christ, the feast of the Circumcision, the feast of the Epiphany, or the feast of the Purification of the Blessed Virgin Mary: then such assembly shall be the day next following.

IV.

A general assembly of the whole company to be held four times in every year;

" ITEM, there shall also be a general assembly or court of the said Master, Wardens, Assistants and Fellowship of the said Company, four times in every year, which shall be called quarter-day courts, which shall be in every year, one of them upon *the first Monday* sevennight after the Annunciation of the blessed lady St. Mary the Virgin; *the second quarter-day* upon the first Monday sevennight next, and immediately after the feast of St. John Baptist; *the third-quarter-day* upon the first Monday sevennight next, and immediately ensuing the feast of St. Michael the Archangel, *and the fourth quarter-day* upon the Monday next and immediately ensuing after the feast of the Epiphany, between *the hours of nine in the forenoon and three in the afternoon* of the same days: All their said courts to be kept at their common hall, or other convenient meeting place of the said company *within the city of London.*

on what days

to be kept within the city of London; between the hours of nine in the forenoon, and three in the afternoon.

V.

Quarterage to be paid by every member, and other persons using any branch of the incorporated arts, other than servants.

" ITEM, that *in every of the said quarter-days,* or quarter courts, every person of the said Fellowship or Incorporation, and every person of the said Fellowship or otherwise, using, selling, buying, importing, exporting, or any way trading in clocks, watches, 'larums, sun-dials, casemaking, graving, mathematical-instruments-making, in any nature, condition, or material whatsoever, by *by whom to be received.* piecemeal, wholesale, or retail, or by way of merchandizing, under the government of this Company, *(other than servants,)* shall then and there satisfy and *pay for* quarteridge, *twelve-pence* in money *in every quarter*, to the hands of the Master of the said Company for the time being, for the common use of the Master, Wardens, and Fellowship, as by every fellow of the said Company ought to be done.

VI.

" ITEM, that *every person* of the said Fellowship *making default of* Fines for default *appearance*, after reasonable summons and warning to him or them of appearance when summoned given, to be at the said *court or meetings, or any of them*, at any time, to attend courts. shall so often forfeit as ensueth : *(viz.)* The Master, *or any of the* The Master not appearing at the Wardens, not appearing there by the hour appointed, having no hour appointed, reasonable excuse, the Master *to forfeit and pay one shilling and six-* to forfeit 1s. 6d. *pence*, and the Wardens *and* Assistants *each of them twelve-pence*. the Wardens and Assistants 1s. And *not coming at all* to the said court, *(having no lawful excuse)*, the Master not *or departing without licence before the court be ended*, the Master *to* coming at all, *pay six shillings eight-pence*, and the Wardens and Assistants *each of* or departing without licence, *them five shillings*, every other member of the said Company or to forfeit 6s. 8d. the Wardens and Fellowship, or person under their government as aforesaid, sum- Assistants 5s. moned or warned according to the nature of the court or meeting, and *not appearing* there by the hour appointed (except he can shew some lawful impediment, such as the *Master, Wardens*, and every other mem-*Assistants*, or the most part of them shall allow of), *shall forfeit* ber not appearing *six-pence*, and *not coming at all* to the said court, *or departing* in time, to forfeit 6d. and not *thence* without licence *before the court be ended*, shall forfeit three appearing at all, *shillings four-pence*. And if the *Master*, or any of the *Wardens*, to forfeit 3s. 4d. or any of the *Assistants*, or any of the *Livery* of the said Company shall repair to any of the said courts or meetings *without his livery gown*, or being otherwise undecently attired, he *shall forfeit* No officer or any *for every such time, and so often as he shall offend, twelve-pence*. shall appear in And *every person* under the government of this incorporation, gown, denying, *refusing or neglecting to pay his* quarterage, or any other right or duties to be as aforesaid paid and answered *at any the* under penalty of *said quarter days* or quarter courts ; for every such default *shall* every person not *forfeit thirteen shillings four-pence*. Except *the same be* moderated then paying is quarterage shall and *dispensed with, by the Master, Wardens, and Assistants* of the forfeit 13s. 4d. said Company, in the same or the next assembly.

VII.

" ITEM, *if* for attendance upon the King's Majesty, his heirs or successors, at his or their repair, to or towards the city of London, or for other reasonable or just occasion or consideration, *any of* Members of the *the Assistants or Livery* of the said Company, *or other of the said* Fellowship summoned upon any *Company* or Fellowship, *shall be* by the Master and Wardens public occasion, by horse or foot, *appointed to any reasonable or convenient service* or attendance, in to attend under livery or otherwise, by horse or foot ; *and* upon warning thereof, penalty of 20s. shall *not attend*, and in good sort provide attire and furnish himself, *and perform* and do *accordingly* what he shall be so appointed, he shall for every such default and neglect, *forfeit the sum of twenty shillings :* except he shall make and have allowed unto him in like sort as aforesaid, some reasonable matter of excuse.

VIII.

Members of the Livery (if request) to attend the dead body of a Liveryman, or his wife, to the grave, within three miles of London, under penalty of 10s.

"ITEM, *that if request* at any time shall be made, by the Master and Wardens of the said Company, *to have those of the livery* of the said Company *to accompany to the grave* within the circuit of London, liberties, and suburbs thereof, or within three miles compass of the same, *the dead corpse of any one of the livery* of the said Fellowship or Company *deceased*, or of his wife, at the time of the funeral of such man or woman, then the said Master and Wardens (if they shall think it fit) shall cause a warning of all those of the said livery accordingly; and *every one of the said livery shall*, upon reasonable warning, *attend* with his livery at the time and place appointed, *upon pain of ten shillings* by every particular person of the said livery, who shall make default *upon such warning*, so often as he shall make *default* to attend (except he shall make and have admitted some reasonable excuse for his absence).

IX.

Three of the Assistants to be chosen, to take bond of the new Master and Wardens, previous to their election;

"ITEM, that *at* such Yearly assemblies as shall be held *for the choice of Master and Wardens* for the year next ensuing, *there shall be chosen* at that court, *before the election of the new Master and Wardens*, three other fit persons of the said Assistants *to take obligation of the Master and Wardens that be newly chosen*. And

who shall not be admitted or sworn, until they have severally given bond in two securities,

that none nominated and agreed upon to be the *new Master*, or any of the *new Wardens*, for the year following, shall be admitted or sworn until each of them *shall* have *become bound* by a several obligation in the sum of fifty pounds (or more or less according to the discretion of the *Master*, *Wardens*, and *Assistants*, or the greater part of them, as cause shall require) *unto the said three*

who shall then be none of the Assistants.

Assistants, with two sufficient sureties, who shall then be none of the Assistants of the said Company, that he shall so use, employ, and dispose all, every, and any such sum and sums of money, rents, plate, and other things of the said Master, Wardens, and Fellowship, which he shall receive and be possessed of, or shall any way come to his hands or custody, in the time of his being Master or Warden, as shall be orderly directed or appointed by

Accounts to be rendered within one month after expiration of their office, to the auditors appointed,

the said *Master*, *Wardens*, and *Assistants* of the same Fellowship from time to time, and not otherwise; and *that* within one month after the determination of his Mastership or Wardenship, by time, death, removal, or otherwise, *he shall make and deliver* to the use of the said Master, Wardens, and Fellowship, *a perfect*, true, and full *account of the said money, plate, and other things, to and before such persons,* and at and by such time, *as* by the said *Master, Wardens*, and *Assistants, shall be* for that purpose nominated and

and the balance, &c., to be delivered up to such persons who shall be appointed.

appointed; and after such account so made, *whatsoever remain* shall be found in his hands or custody belonging to the said Master, Wardens, and Fellowship, *he shall without diminution,* covin, or delay, *deliver* over the same at such time and place, and to such person and persons *to the use of the said* Master, Wardens,

on true account rendered and balance, &c., paid, the bonds to be given up to be cancelled.

and Fellowship, as by the *Master, Wardens*, and *Assistants* of the said Fellowship shall be appointed; and after such account and delivery made, the said bond shall be re-delivered to them that shall be so bound respectively to be cancelled.

X.

"ITEM, it is further ordained, that *if any Person*, Freeman of the said Company, which shall be chosen Master or Warden *of the said Company*, shall upon notice thereof deny, *refuse*, or neglect to take *the same office* upon him; or to *become bound* as aforesaid; or *to take such corporal oath* as by these ordinances or by any other hereafter, shall be lawful and lawfully appointed, approved, or allowed, then for every time so offending, he shall *forfeit the sum of ten pounds*, to the use of the said Master, Wardens, and Fellowship; and then after *there shall be* proceeding to *a new* nomination or *choice* of any other *in his place*, in like sort, as shall be done when any Master or Warden shall decease in the time of his said office, or as if such person had never been so elected and chosen, and that like *forfeiture and proceeding* shall run and be upon every such person of the said Fellowship *being chosen of the said* Assistants, after he is so chosen to take such oath as by these ordinances, or any other hereafter shall be lawfully appointed, approved, and allowed; and *every person hereafter chosen to be of the Assistants* since his Majesty's Charter of Incorporation, *shall pay* the sum of *six pounds, thirteen shillings, four-pence*, to the Company, *or more or less* according to the quality, and true propriety and worth of the party, and to the clerk, six shillings, eight-pence, and to the beadle two shillings, six-pence.

[margin: Any freeman refusing to take the offices of Master and Warden, or to give bond, or to take the oaths, shall forfeit 10l. and proceed to a new election. every person chosen an Assistant shall pay to the Company 6l. 13s. 4d.; clerk 6s. 8d.; beadle 2s. 6d.]

XI.

"ITEM, *that if* for service of the King's Majesty, his heirs or successors, or of the city of London, or of the proper affairs of the Master, Wardens, and Fellowship, or for other reasonable and just consideration, *any taxation or assessment* shall be *by the Master and Wardens* for the time being, or two of them, whereof the Master to be one, *and the Assistants of the Company*, or the greater part of them, be assessed or imposed, and to be rated *upon particular* person and persons, *members* of the said Fellowship; then and so often the same shall be in all things obeyed and performed, according to such orders as shall be by them set down for the collection of the same; and that *every person denying, refusing, or omitting to satisfy and pay such*, and so much of the said *assessment or taxation*, as shall so at any time be rated and assessed upon him or them, *shall forfeit* to the use of the said Master, Wardens, and Fellowship, the sum of *ten shillings, or more or less according to the quality of the said assessment*, for such denial or refusal.

[margin: Every member refusing or neglecting to pay any assessment made for the service of the King, the city of London, or this Company, shall forfeit 10l.]

XII.

"ITEM, *that no person*, member of this Fellowship, or any other under the government of the said Fellowship, *shall* at any time *revile, give any blows, or opprobrious or scornful speeches or words*, or other acts, to, of, or towards the Master, or any of the Wardens, or other person, member of the said Fellowship, *whereby the King's peace or brotherly love may be broken* or impaired amongst them; and *if any shall offend* in this behalf, *then* if upon complaint of such mis-behaviour, any such person shall at an assembly of the said *Master, Wardens, and Assistants*, be thereunto called, and

[margin: Any member giving blows, or using opprobrious words, on complaint thereof, being made within three months,]

shall be found to have so offended, he shall obey, undergo, and perform such reasonable order and sentence, as by the said *Master, Wardens, and Assistants,* shall be set down concerning the same; *so as Complaint* shall be made *within* the space of *three months;* and if he shall refuse and neglect so to do, then he *shall forfeit* the sum of *forty shillings,* or more or less, according to the quantity or quality of their offence or offences, to the use of the said Master, Wardens, and Fellowship.

shall forfeit 4.

XIII.

"ITEM, for that *many persons of ill behaviour,* and so known in places where they have dwelt *in the country, and* from other parts and provinces *beyond the seas,* and elsewhere, *do* much *resort to the city of London,* and places near thereabouts; for better discovery of such persons, as for other good purposes, it is ordained *that none* using, or which shall use or occupy within the said city, liberties, and suburbs, or within ten miles thereof, the Art, Mystery, or Trade of Clockmaking, in any kind whatsoever, *shall* receive, *entertain,* employ, *or use* in the Art, Trade, or Mystery of Clockmaking, any *person or persons* whatsoever, except *he shall present every such person* personally by true certificate, both of the certainty of his name, and place of his or their birth or abode, *unto the said Master, Wardens,* and *Assistants,* being assembled, *the next court* day after his or their entertainment; expressing also the time and purpose of his retainer, *to the end the same court may examine,* take view, and notice of *him,* and, *if they shall find him fit to be allowed,* then to enter his or their names, with other certainties, *upon pain of* every fault found to the contrary in *the master* so offending in not certifying, *to pay* the sum of *twenty shillings* to the Master, Wardens, and Fellowship, *to the use of the poor,* and *the party so entertained two shillings six-pence;* but, if he be certified, then there shall be paid to the clerk for such entrance, one shilling six-pence, and to the beadle six-pence.

To prevent persons of ill behaviour resorting to London, no Clockmaker, within ten miles thereof, shall employ any workman without personally presenting him, together with a certificate of his name, birth, &c., &c., for the Company's approval.

under penalty of 20s. to the poor, and the person employed 2s. 6d. but, if approved, to clerk 1s. 6d.; beadle 6d.

XIV.

"ITEM, it is ordained, that *no person,* or persons, using the Art, Trade, or Mystery of Clockmaking, within the said city, liberties, suburbs, or limits aforesaid, *shall hire, receive, take, or entertain,* to his apprentice, or into his service, *any person* whatsoever, *formerly* apprentice unto or *serving and using the trade* of Clockmaking, *within* any *the limits* aforesaid, *without the consent of his former master,* (if any such be), or by order of the *Master, Wardens,* and *Court of Assistants,* or the more part of them, and *notice given* with all like certainties *as aforesaid*; to the end the entertainment, passage, honest departure, and setting over of such an apprentice, servant or servants, may be truly known; with like payment *only to the clerk,* for entrance thereof, and *upon pain* that every person offending contrary *to* the true meaning of this article in any thing, shall *pay* for such offence the sum of *forty shillings for every month* for his so entertaining any servant contrary to this act, to the use of the said Master, Wardens, and Fellowship; *and so monthly,* until he make his presentment of the said servant before the *Master, Wardens, and Court of Assistants.*

No person shall take as apprentice, or into his service, any one without the consent of his former master, or by order of the Master, Warden, &c., and the same registered.

under penalty of 40s. per month until presented.

XV.

"ITEM, *for the avoiding of confusion* and disorder in the said Fellowship, which may grow and arise *by taking of apprentices* as many in number as they please; and *to the end that journeymen freemen*, having truly served all their time of apprenticeship, *may be* the better *employed* and provided for, it is hereby ordained, that *no person* or persons whatsoever of the said Fellowship hereafter, but such as shall be allowed a master workman, as in these presents is hereafter mentioned, *shall take to* himself *any apprentice or apprentices, but first to have leave* and licence of the *Master, Wardens*, and *Assistants, (the which without just cause shall not be denied)* and *then to have but one, until he shall be called to bear office of Master, Warden, or Assistant*, in the said Company; and *after* he shall be so called as aforesaid, *not to exceed* the number of *two apprentices at any time* whatsoever. *To the end that journeymen freemen who have duly served their apprenticeship may be better employed, no person of the Fellowship, except a master workman, shall take any apprentice without leave of the Master, Wardens, &c. and only one until he be chosen Master, Warden, or Assistant, and then not to exceed two at the same time;*

"NEVERTHELESS, it is thought fit, that any one of the said Fellowship before the said first apprentice shall have so served forth his full term of years for which he became bound an apprentice, that, by virtue hereof, *it shall* and may *be lawful* for every particular master *to bind one other apprentice* at his pleasure *the full term of five years*, and no sooner, *before his* said *former apprentice his time be expired*, by reason that for the present time he shall not be left destitute of an apprentice; *upon forfeiture*, for every time so offending, the sum *of ten pounds*, or more or less, at the discretions of the *Master, Wardens*, and *Court of Assistants*, to the use of the said Master, Wardens, and Fellowship. *but when the first apprentice has served five years complete, he may take another, but not sooner, under penalty of 10l.*

XVI.

"ITEM, that *for the better ordering of dissolute and ill-disposed persons*, such as will hardly be brought under the rule of any good government, it is hereby ordained and established, that *what person* or persons soever *free of the said Fellowship, or under their government*, now or hereafter using the said trade or mystery of Clockmaking, *shall depart this city and liberties as aforesaid, into any* other remote *place within the realm of England, shall,* notwithstanding, observe the rules and orders, and *be subject to* live under *the government of the* said Master, Wardens, and Fellowship, according to the Charter in that behalf granted; and *if default be made* by any such person or persons whatsoever hereafter, that *then* it shall and may be lawful to and for *the* said *Master and Wardens*, according to the tenor of his Majesty's Grant of Incorporation, *to proceed against them* for misdemeanor, *for not doing and performing such duties*, as shall be appointed by the *Master, Wardens*, and *Court of Assistants*, (whereof the Master and one of the Wardens for the time being to be two) *either in themselves*, *or in* the deceitfulness and *false workmanship* of or *in their trade;* upon their due search and oversight, *by way of fine or otherwise*, *as if they* yet lived and did *reside within the said city* and liberties aforesaid; which *fine* is likewise *to be imposed* by and at the discretion of the *Master, Wardens*, and *Assistants, according to the quality of his* or their *offence* or offences, to the use of the said Master, Wardens, and Fellowship. *Freemen following the trade, though removed from London to any part of England, shall still be subject to the laws of this Company. and may be proceeded against for default of duties, deceitful workmanship, &c., as if they yet resided in the said city, and fined, at the discretion of the Court.*

XVII.

Apprentices who have duly served, and been admitted Freemen, shall serve two years as journeymen.

"ITEM, it is ordained, that *every apprentice having truly served* his apprenticeship, *and being admitted a Freeman* of the said society, *shall*, according to the custom of other Companies, *serve his Master, or some other of the same Fellowship*, by the space of *two years as journeyman;* and, *at the end of* the same *two years*, it *shall be*, by virtue hereof, *lawful for the* Master, *or* Warden, *or* Wardens, of the said Fellowship, *with the consent of the* greater part of the Assistants of the said Fellowship, *to call any person* or persons *whatsoever, being a member or professor of the same trade,* before he or they be admitted, or allowed of, to be a lawful master,

and also produce his masterpiece before he be admitted a workmaster.

to bring in his or their masterpiece or masterpieces, *which he* or they *shall be appointed to make* by the *Master, Wardens,* and *Assistants,* or the major part of them, (whereof the Master and one of the Wardens to be two), what piece, or what manner of a whole or intire piece, he shall make, and where he shall make it, which, *being* by the *Master, Wardens,* and *Assistants,* of the said Company or Fellowship, or the more part of them, allowed and *approved of he shall,* from thenceforth, *be admitted* to be *a work-*

Fines payable on such admission 20s.; clerk 3s 4d.; beadle 1s.

master, of the said Society, and not before; *for which* said *admittance,* he shall *pay* to the use of the said Master, Wardens, and Fellowship, the sum of *twenty shillings,* and to the clerk three shillings four-pence, and to the beadle twelve-pence.

Any journeyman, who has served one year, may petition to produce his masterpiece, and if approved, be admitted a workmaster, on payment of a fine at the discretion of the Court.

"YET, *if* at any time, *after the* time and *expiration of the first year, any* journeyman whatsoever *shall make suit unto the Master, Wardens,* and *Court of Assistants, to have* the privilege and *leave to* make and *bring in* his masterpiece, to be allowed of by them at a General Court of Assistants to be by them holden, that *then,* upon such suit made, if *upon his sufficiency* it shall please the said *Master, Wardens,* and *Court of Assistants,* or the major part of them, upon view of his workmanship, to admit of the same, then *it shall be,* by virtue of these presents, *lawful to admit him* or them accordingly, *upon* such *reasonable fine* or fines as, in the discretions of the *Master, Wardens,* and *Court of Assistants,* or the major part, shall be thought fit.

XVIII.

"ITEM, it is ordained, that *no person* or persons whatsoever using, or *that* shall use, the Trade, Art, or Mystery of Clockmaking; and *hath* or shall have *any apprentice* or more *once bound,* and presented to the Master or Wardens of the said Company, by him

No apprentice to be assigned or turned over to a new master without consent of the Court,

or them allowed, *shall,* at any time after, *assign, set, or turn over any such apprentice* to any person or persons whatsoever, *without* first *presenting* him *to the Master and Wardens* of the said Company for the time being, to the end their consents may be thereunto required, upon pain to *forfeit* to the said Master, Wardens, and

under penalty of 40s.; clerk 3s. 4d.; beadle 1s.

Fellowship, for every act done to the contrary, the sum of *forty shillings,* and to the clerk three shillings four-pence, and to the beadle twelve-pence.

XIX.

"ITEM, it is ordained, that *no person* or persons whatsoever, *which* hereafter *shall not have served seven years* at the least as an *apprentice* to the said Trade, Art, or Mystery of a Clockmaker, Mathematical Instrument-maker, Sundial-maker, Graver, Case maker, or any thing otherwise peculiarly belonging to the same trade, *(unless such as be the Clockmakers' widows of the city of London, and of the said several arts and professions as aforesaid : and for so long time only as they shall so continue widows,)* shall use the said Trade, Art, or Mystery of a Clockmaker, *or any thing thereunto appertaining*, as his Trade, Art, or Mystery; nor *shall*, within the city of London, or liberties thereof, *teach or instruct any person* or persons *other than his apprentice* or apprentices, *in the same Trade* or Mystery, *upon* pain to *forfeit* to the said Master and Wardens and Fellowship, *for every month* he or they shall so use the said Trade as a Trade, or teach or instruct any person or persons other than his or their apprentice or apprentices, in the said Trade, the sum of *forty shillings*, and to the clerk three shillings four-pence, and to the beadle twelve-pence.

No person to use the trade, or any part thereof, (as enumerated) but who shall have served seven years as an apprentice, (Clockmakers' widows, so long only as they shall remain widows excepted)

nor teach any other than his own apprentice,

under penalty of 40s. per month; clerk 3s. 4d.; beadle 1s.

XX.

"ITEM, it is ordained, that *no Freeman* of the said Company *using the said Trade*, Art, or Mystery, *do keep in his service*, to work in and about the said Trade or Mystery, *any foreigners*, alien or English, *not being free of the said Company* of Clockmakers, *or bound* as an *apprentice thereunto*, unless he be (at the next court after *he shall be* first received into the said service,) *presented* unto the said *Master, Wardens*, and *Court of Assistants, and* be by them *allowed*, upon pain to *forfeit* to the said Master, Wardens, and Fellowship, for every time so doing, the sum of *forty shillings*, and to the clerk three shillings four-pence, and to the beadle twelve-pence.

No foreigner shall be employed by any Freeman unless presented to and approved by the Court

under penalty 40s.; clerk 3s. 4d.; beadle 1s.

XXI.

"ITEM, it is ordained, that *no Freeman* of the said Company of Clockmakers, *or any person* or Persons *using the Trade*, Art, or Mystery of a Clockmaker, shall *set at work, keep, or maintain, any foreigner or journeyman*, not being admitted into the freedom of the said Company, *or not* being or *having been retained, brought up, or bound seven years to the same Trade*, Art, or Mystery, *to work* as a journeyman or servant in any shop, shops, chamber, or any other place or places, either public or private, *within the said city, or liberties thereof*, upon pain to *forfeit* to the said Master, Wardens, and Fellowship, *for every day* so doing, *ten shillings*, and to the clerk one shilling six-pence, and to the beadle four-pence.

No person shall be employed as a journeyman who has not been brought up or served seven years to the trade,

under penalty 10s. per day; clerk 1s. 6d.; beadle 4d.

XXII.

"ITEM, it is also ordained, that *every person*, Freeman of the said Company of Clockmakers, using, or *which shall use the Trade*, Art, or Mystery of Clockmaking *within the said city, or within ten miles compass* of the same, *shall, within one month after he* or they *take any apprentice* to serve him in the said Trade, Art, or

Apprentices to be presented to and approved by the Court within one month.

Mystery, *present the same apprentice* or apprentices *unto the said Master, Wardens*, and *Court of Assistants*, of the said Company, *to the end that they may admit and allow such apprentice* to serve such freeman or foreigner, *upon* pain to *forfeit* to the said Master, Wardens, and Fellowship, to the use of the said Company, *for* *every month* so offending, *three shillings four-pence;* and to the clerk for entering the said presentment, twelve-pence.

under penalty
4 / per month;
clerk 12.

"AND that *no denison or foreigner* using the said Trade, Art, or Mystery of Clockmaking within the said city, liberties, and suburbs thereof, or within ten miles compass of the same, *shall take any apprentice* or apprentices, *servant or servants, not born within his Majesty's dominions, to work in or about the same Trade,* Art, or Mystery, and, *if any, alien or others, shall do contrary* to this ordinance, or anything therein contained, he shall *forfeit* and pay to the said Master, Wardens, and Fellowship, for the use of the Company, the sum of *five pounds* lawful money of England, and to the clerk six shillings eight-pence, and to the beadle one shilling six-pence.

No alien shall take as an apprentice or journeyman any one born out of his Majesty's dominions.

under penalty 5*l*; clerk 6*s*. 8*d*.; beadle 1*s*. 6*d*.

XXIII.

"ITEM, it is ordained, that *no journeyman* that is or shall be hired to work to or with any brother of the Company, *shall depart from the Master with whom he* or they *shall be hired*, except he or they give his or their said Master *three months' warning* at the least, of his or their intention to depart from his or their said Master. And that *no Master* or Brother of the said Company shall hereafter *turn* or put *away any such journeyman*, except *he* or they *give his* or their said *journeyman three months' warning* at the least; and that *no Master* or Brother of the Company *having* knowledge or *notice of any journeyman departing without consent* as aforesaid, *shall* hereafter *entertain* into his or their work or service *any such journeyman* that shall so depart, *without such warning* to be given to him as aforesaid, *upon* pain to *forfeit* and pay for his and their offence therein *five pounds* to the said Master, Wardens, and Fellowship, to the use of the said Company.

No journeyman shall depart from his master's service without giving three months warning;
nor shall any Master turn away any journeyman without the like warning.
No Master shall employ any journeyman who has left his former service without such warning.

under penalty 5*l*.

"AND that *no Brother* of the said Company *using the said Trade,* Art, or Mystery of Clockmaking, *shall* hereafter *set at work*, or employ *any journeyman that is not admitted a Brother* of the Company, *upon* pain to *forfeit* to the said *Master, Wardens,* and *Fellowship, for every week* he or they do the contrary, the sum of *six shillings eight-pence*, to the clerk for entry of such departure twelve-pence, and to the beadle four-pence.

No Brother shall employ any journeyman who has not been admitted a Brother.

under penalty 6*s*. 8*d*. per week; clerk 1*s*.; beadle 4*d*.

XXIV.

"ITEM, it is ordained, that no person *shall* hereafter *be admitted* a *journeyman*, or otherwise, to use the Trade, Art, or Mystery of Clockmaking, *unless he shall bring true testimony of his* true service of *apprenticeship*, and *every* such *journeyman shall be hired for one whole year*, or for a longer or shorter time, and *make trial of his workmanship* by the space of fourteen days, and such trial being

No journeyman shall be admitted unless he has duly served an apprenticeship, then shall be hired for a fixed time, and after trial of 14 days made, *then* the said journeyman *shall be presented before the Master and Wardens* of the same Company, and *shall not depart* from his Master *without especial licence* obtained, *upon such penalty as shall be thought fitting* by a Court of Assistants, or *else upon three months' warning* to be orderly given as aforesaid; and that *every such journeyman* received into the said Company *shall work only with* such as are *free Brothers* admitted of the said Company, and with no other person or persons whatsoever; and whosoever shall do *contrary* to this ordinance, shall forfeit to the said Master, Wardens, and Fellowship, for every offence, to the use of the said Company, the sum of *twenty shillings* a week, and for such entry to the clerk, by every particular party, twelve-pence.

XXV.

"ITEM, it is ordained, that no person, *shall teach* or instruct *in the Art* of Clockmaking *any other person* or persons whatsoever, *not being presented or admitted into the said Company*, upon pain to *forfeit* and pay to the said Master, Wardens, and Fellowship, to the use of the said Company, the sum of *five pounds* of lawful money of England, *for every month* so offending, and to the clerk for every such month twelve-pence, and to the beadle four-pence.

XXVI.

"ITEM, it is ordained, that *no person using the said trade* of Clockmaking *shall take* as his *apprentice the son of any which is free of the said Company*, or shall *teach* or instruct *any such freeman's son* in the said Art, except *the said son be his own*, upon pain to *forfeit* to the said Master, Wardens, and Fellowship, to the use of the same Company, *forty shillings for taking* such apprentice, *and forty shillings for every month he shall keep and instruct him* (except the said freeman's son shall be *first presented to the said Company* before he shall be taught and instructed), and to the clerk such fine as the Company shall think fit.

XXVII.

"ITEM, it is ordained, *that no Brother* of the Company *shall receive into work any* manner of journeyman Clockmaker *without a certificate* of his departure *from his former master*, upon pain to *forfeit* to the said Master, Wardens, and Fellowship, to the use of the said Company, *thirteen shillings four-pence* for every such offence, to the clerk two shillings six-pence, and to the beadle four-pence.

XXVIII.

"ITEM, it is ordained, *that* what person of this Company that taketh any apprentice or *apprentices* into his service, after the custom of London, and causeth not him or them, *within one month* after the beginning of the term of such an apprentice, to *be* inrolled *before the* Chamberlain of the said city, shall *forfeit* and pay to the said Master, Wardens, and Fellowship, to the use of the said Company, *six shillings eight-pence*, without remission or pardon, to the clerk *twelve-pence*, and to the beadle *four-pence*.

XXIX.

Persons making search for frauds &c.

shall also enquire respecting disorders and abuses and report such to the next Court, who shall fine the party 40s. And to the clerk at discretion.

"ITEM, it is ordained, that those *persons that shall view and make* search for frauds and deceits *in the said trade* as aforesaid, *shall make diligent search and inquiry of all disorders and inconveniences* used in the said art of Clockmaking. And *all such disorders and abuses* as they shall find, they *shall* justly and truly *present to the Master, Wardens, and Court of Assistants* of the said Company, at the next court of Assistants after the discovery or finding thereof; and *such person* or persons *as shall commit any such disorder*, shall *forfeit* and pay to the said Master, Wardens, and Fellowship, the sum of *forty shillings*, or such lesser sum as shall be imposed by the discretions of the *Master, Wardens, and Assistants* of the said Company: and such fee to the clerk as they shall think fit.

XXX.

Every freeman within the city and liberties, shall be warned to attend at the quarter-day Courts,

"ITEM, it is ordained, that every person or persons, being free of the said Company, *or using the Trade,* Art, or Mystery of a Clockmaker, *within the city of London, or the liberties thereof,* shall by the beadle, or some other known officer of the said Company, *be* warned to appear *once every quarter of a year,* (that is to say) upon the first Monday sevennight after every of the quarter days, (as they are formerly ordained and appointed) *before the Master, Wardens, and Assistants* of the said Company of Clockmakers, *or the greater number of them,* there *to hear read such good fitting and wholesome orders as are or shall be made for the bettering of the said trade, and suppressing of enormities and abuses therein;* and that *if any* such *person being summoned as aforesaid, or notice thereof left at* his or their *dwelling-houses,* or other places of abode, *he being at*

and being absent therefrom without reasonable cause,

home, do *make default and be absent from any the Quarterly Meetings* aforesaid and cannot nor will not shew, (or otherwise prove) to the Master and Wardens for the time being, some lawful impediment or lett, which was the cause of his absence; or

as also every person using the Art not appearing whenever summoned, shall forfeit 2s. 6d.; clerk 6d.

if *any freeman* of the said Company, *or any person* or persons *using the said Trade,* Art, or Mystery, of Clockmaking, *or anything thereto pertaining,* and *being warned before the said Master, Wardens,* and *Court of Assistants, either against a Monthly Court* (as aforesaid,) *or upon any other occasion,* shall *not,* at the place and time appointed, *appear* there to remain and abide, unless he be by the Master and Wardens, or some of them discharged, not having such lawful excuse as aforesaid; that *then* every person and persons so offending shall *forfeit* and pay to the said Master, Wardens, and Fellowship, for every such offence, *two shillings, six-pence,* and to the clerk for entering such default, *six-pence.*

XXXI.

Every Freeman or person using the Art within ten miles of the city, and obstinately refusing to attend and perform reasonable service,

"ITEM, it is ordained, that if any person or persons, *free of the said Company of* Clockmakers, *or using the said Trade,* Art, or Mystery, within the said city or liberties, or within ten miles compass of the same, *being specially required* thereunto, *shall* obstinately and wilfully *refuse to appear or meet at any place appointed by the* Master *and* Wardens for the time being, or *to pay* or bear *any sum* or sums of *money, or any other common charges* whatsoever, for or to the King's Majesty, Lord Mayor, or city of London, or for the Commonwealth or worship of the said Company, or *to do* or perform *any public service*, meet or decent to be performed or done as aforesaid, *within the same Company*, or by any members of the same: that *then every person* and persons, *being free of the said* Company of Clockmakers, so refusing to do or perform all or any those things, *shall forfeit* to the said Master, Wardens, and Fellowship, for such refusal, the sum of *forty shillings*, and to the clerk three shillings, four-pence.

<small>shall forfeit 40s., clerk 3s. 4d.</small>

XXXII.

" ITEM, it is ordained, that *no person* of the said Company *shall discover or disclose* any of *the lawful secrets concerning the said Trade*, Art, or Mystery of Clockmaking, in their own occupation, or *any secret counsel of the* said *Company*, which ought in reason and conscience secretely to be kept, without any utterance thereof, to any other person, of another Mystery, and out of the same Company, to the hurt and prejudice of this Company, *upon the* penalty and *forfeiture of forty shillings*, to be paid to the said Master, Wardens, and Fellowship, and to the clerk three shillings four-pence, and to the beadle twelve-pence, for every time so offending.

<small>Any person of the Company, who shall disclose to any person of another mystery, any secret counsel</small>

<small>shall forfeit 40s.; clerk 3s. 4d.; beadle 1s.</small>

XXXIII.

" ALSO, it is ordained, that *every man of the said Company using the said Trade*, Art, or Mystery of Clockmaking, from this time forthwards, *after his degree and power, shall be contributary and bear charge of, and in, all manner of Sessings, Prests, Costs, Contributions, Impositions, and all other charges appertaining to the worship, benefit, and credit, of the said Company:* upon the pain of *forfeiture* of *forty shillings*, to be paid to the said Master, Wardens, and Fellowship, for every such offence, and to the clerk three shillings four-pence.

<small>Every man of the Company shall be contributary to all just charges, or forfeit 40s.; clerk 3s. 4d.</small>

" AND that all and *every person* and persons, *as well strangers, denizens, foreigners, and others* whatsoever, *free of the said Company, or using the said Trade*, Art, or Mystery of Clockmaking, or any thing thereunto appertaining or belonging *within the said city and liberties* thereof, *shall obey*, observe, and keep *all the lawful orders, rules, and ordinances, made and written in this present Book;* and *if any person* or persons *shall offend or transgress any of the same orders, rules, and ordinances, or refuse to pay such penalties and forfeitures* as are here set down for the breach thereof; that then it shall and may be lawful to and for the same Master, Wardens, and Fellowship, *by their officer or lawful |attorney* to distrain, and the distress and distresses so from time to time taken, to lead, drive, carry, or bear away, and the same to keep and detain to the use of the Master, Wardens, and Fellowship, of the said Company, *until the said penalties, forfeitures, fines, or sums of money for which the said distress so be taken shall be fully satisfied and paid*, with *caution and provision*, notwithstanding, that *if the* party, *owner of these goods* and chattels so taken and *distrained* as aforesaid, *shall* within fourteen days next after such taking and

<small>All persons whatsoever using the Art, shall obey all rules and ordinances;</small>

<small>and if any transgress or refuse to pay the penalties, the Company may distrain, and detain the same</small>

<small>until the fines or forfeitures shall be paid;</small>

<small>if paid within fourteen days,</small>

distress, *satisfy or pay* to the Master or one of the Wardens, to the use of the said Fellowship, *such duties, rights, and sums of money for which the said distress was so taken*, then *he* or they *shall have* to him or *them restored* all the goods and chattels so taken and distrained for all and every the pains, penalties, forfeitures, sum and sums of money so forfeited, or to bring an action of debt for recovery thereof.

XXXIV.

"ITEM, it is also ordained, that all Clocks, Watches, Larums, *and all Cases for Clocks, Watches, and Larums, plain or graven, made of metals or of any other nature, condition, or fashion whatsoever, or any other* work or works, *as Sun-Dials, Mathematical-Instruments, or any other work peculiarly* belonging to the Art of Clockmaking, be it for great or small, brought *into* this realm of *England, or* dominion of *Wales, or from the parts beyond the seas, to be put to sale*, shall be first customed, and *then brought to the* hall *of the said* Clockmakers in London, or their meeting place, and *there presented to the Master, Wardens, and Assistants, to be viewed and approved* of according to the said Letters-patents of Incorporation; and *upon* the *approbation of the Master, Wardens, and Assistants*, or the greater part of them, *shall*, according to the usual custom of the said Company in such cases, *receive* the mark and allowance of the said Company, *before the same be offered or put to sale, upon* pain of *such* reasonable *penalties as by the* said *Master, Wardens, and Court of Assistants*, or the more part of them (whereof the Master and one of the Wardens for the time being to be two) *shall* in such cases *appoint* and ordain.

XXXV.

"ITEM, it is also hereby ordained, that the Master, Wardens, and Fellowship of Clockmakers of London, for the time being, and their successors, *in respect of their* said extraordinary *care and pains*, which shall from time to time be taken, *in the viewing, search, and oversight of all such Clocks, Watches, Larums, Sun-Dials, and Mathematical-Instruments coming from beyond the seas, or otherwise. either by themselves, or* such other person or persons, *their lawful deputy* or deputies, as shall be *appointed for the same*, to receive of every such person and persons, *according to the worth and value of all such* as shall be so found as aforesaid, or in any other work or wares by the way of merchandizing, *peculiarly belonging to the same trade*, how many or few, and of what nature, kind, or property, soever they be, either for quantity or number *in every pound sterling, the sum of four-pence, for* the correcting and *viewing* the insufficiency of the said work, and for *marking and allowing the same* to be good, sufficient, and merchantable.

XXXVI.

"AND it is ordained, *that the Master, Wardens*, and *Assistants* of the said Company of Clockmakers, or the major part of them (whereof the Master and one of the Wardens for the time being to be two) if they shall think fit to call *together with* them for their better strength, *a constable*, headborough, *or some other*, his

Majesty's chief officer or officers, who, together with the said *Master, Wardens*, and *Assistants*, or some of them, *shall shut up the shops of all such person and persons* whatsoever, *either free or foreign, that shall or will attempt to take any apprentice, or to work* in any shop, chamber, or other place or places whatsoever, privileged or not privileged, exempt or not exempt, *he himself having not served*, with a professed Clockmaker, the full term and time of seven years within his Majesty's dominions, according to the several statutes and laws in that case made and provided, *and* having likewise *not* formerly *made his allowed master-piece*. {tice, or who shall work in any place whatsoever, he himself not having served seven years, who shall not within the King's dominions, or have made his master-piece.}

XXXVII.

" ITEM, it is ordained, that *if any person* or persons, hereafter *professing the Trade*, Art, or Mystery of Clockmaking, *and being free of that Company, or of any other Company* whatsoever, within the city of London, liberties, and suburbs thereof, or the limits hereby proposed, and *shall take* unto him or them *an apprentice* for the term of seven years, or otherwise, according to the custom of the said city; and *shall not bind him or* them to *some free brother of* this Company, according to the letters-patent of incorporation granted to this Society, *to the end the same brotherhood in time may become an able body of itself, without the disturbance of any other society or government*, he shall *forfeit* the sum of *ten pounds* to the said Master, Wardens, and Fellowship, to the said Company's use. {Every person whatever using the trade, and taking any apprentice, shall bind him to some free brother of this Company, under penalty of ten pounds.}

XXXVIII.

" ITEM, it is ordained, that if any person or persons, alien or stranger whatsoever, *coming from beyond the seas or otherwise*, shall work in a shop, chamber, cellar, warehouse, or any other place or places whatsoever, either exempt or not exempt within the city of London, liberties, or suburbs thereof, or within ten miles *compass, and being not conformable*, and yielding obedience, in all due respects, to *the government of this society*, and his Majesty's aforesaid letters of incorporation; that then it shall be lawful for the *Master, Wardens*, and *Assistants*, or their lawful deputy or deputies in that behalf, in such case *to seize, and take into their hands*, on his Majesty's behalf, *all such working-tools, or other materials* whatsoever, as often as cause shall require, *and them detain*, and keep, *until* he or they, or any of them, *shall be conformable* herein, and likewise pay such fine or fines as shall from time to time be imposed upon him or them by a court of Assistants, in that behalf. {Any alien who shall work in any place whatsoever within ten miles of the city, and not yielding obedience to this Company, may have his tools and materials seized and detained by the Master, Wardens, &c., until compliance and payment of fines imposed.}

XXXIX.

" ITEM, it is ordained, *where many* journeymen and others are from time to time set at work by several workmen, admitted into this Society, which upon their first entertainments, and afterwards in their several services, in respect of their wants and necessities, and other pretended employments, they *have obtained* several sum or *sums of money of* those *several masters* they do or have so wrought unto, before any part of the same be by his workmanship {Any journeymen hired and receiving money before hand, or quitting their employers service without completing their work;}

earned, *and before the same be wrought out, go from their several workmasters to others of the same trade,* supplying only their wants and necessities, and *very dishonestly :*

and the same being known by the second master he shall immediately dismiss such workman, under penalty of paying the debt due to the former master, and such other fine as shall be imposed by the Master, Wardens, &c.

"BE it therefore ordained, that *if any master* workman of this Society shall at any time hereafter, *(after notice given by the said former workmaster,) set any such workman or journeyman a work,* in any manner of work whatsoever, peculiarly belonging to the same trade, *either at home or abroad,* in any place or places whatsoever, but *presently disemploy the same man,* and take away such work from him, if any such delivery were, *to the intent the said former master, which so trusted him* and was so deceitfully dealt withal, *may be fully satisfied,* he shall forfeit, besides the full debt of arrearage due to the former workmaster, such other fine and penalty to the said Master, Wardens, and Fellowship, to the use of the said Company *as shall be adjudged by the Master, Wardens, and full Court of Assistants.*

XL.

Master and Wardens, &c., to arbitrate any disputes which may arise amongst the freemen,

"ITEM, it is ordained, that *if any suit, controversy,* disagreement, discord, *or falling out, by or between any brothers or freemen,* of the said Company, *happen* to arise, grow, or be between or amongst any of them, *other than debt or in point of interest or property* that then each suit, disagreement, controversy, *and falling out, shall be made known to the* Master *and* Wardens of the said Company, or the *Master, Wardens, and Assistants* of the said Company, for the time being, *before* such time as *suit in law be commenced* and begun by and *between them,* upon pain to *forfeit*

who wilfully contemning the award made, shall forfeit 40s.

for every one wilfully refusing, or contemning this order, the sum of *forty shillings, to the end that the Master and Wardens may endeavour to make peace and love between them, and thereby prevent suits in law, if it so may be.*

XLI.

The Master, one Warden, and six Assistants, at the least, must be present to form a court;

"ITEM, it is also ordered, that *if* it happen the Assistants of the said Company *be sent for by the* Master *and* Wardens, *for matters and causes, and other things concerning* the common profit *of the same,* then it is ordained, they shall have and take *six Assistants,* besides the *Master and one of the Wardens at the least,* for the

No act, &c., under seal, to pass but in open court, under penalty of 10l. for every particular person so offending, and the acts or deeds declared null and void.

redressing and ordering of such matters, causes, and doubts, as before them shall be alleged and shewed; and also it is ordained, *that* no grant or gift pass under their common seal, for term of years or term of life, *to any person* or persons, nor judgment, nor sentence, pass *under the same seal,* without it be done in open court, where the said Master, Wardens, and Assistants, *according to the number aforesaid,* shall be present, *or the more part of them,* and consenting to the same, upon pain of every particular man so offending to *forfeit ten pounds* to the said Master, Wardens, and Fellowship, as often and when as such case shall happen, *besides the disannulling of the said act or deed,* and the same pain to be levied of the Master, Wardens, and Assistants doing the contrary, to the use of the said Company.

XLII.

"ITEM, *to the intent enormities and abuses in the trade* aforesaid *may be* the better *found out and reformed*, it is further ordered, that it shall and may be lawful to and for *the Master and Wardens* of the same Company, for the time being, *or two of them*, as also to and for such other person and persons whom they shall bring with them, or in that behalf any wise authorize or appoint, and will answer for, *at all convenient time* and times hereafter, *to enter and come into the house, shop, warehouse, or working-house*, sellers, sollars, or other place or places, *of any person* or persons whatsoever, *using or exercising, or which shall use or exercise the Trade*, Art, or Mystery of Clockmaking, within the city of London, liberties and suburbs thereof, or within ten miles compass of the same, to *search, survey, and view the making and working of any* wares or merchandizes, or other *works belonging to the Trade*, Art, or Mystery of Clockmaking, *without the hindrance* or interruption *of such person* or persons to whom the said shops, warehouses, workhouses, or rooms aforesaid, do appertain, *and all things found* by them *deceitfully and insufficiently wrought, to take*, carry away, and after sufficient trial to deface, and that *every one refusing and hindering such view and search* to be made as aforesaid, shall *forfeit* and pay to the said Master, Wardens, and Fellowship, to the use of the said Company, the sum of *five pounds*.

For the better finding out and reforming abuses in the trade, the Master and Wardens or their Deputy may enter any house, &c. within ten miles of the city, and search for and survey the working and making, and seize, carry away, and deface all wares deceitfully wrought, every one hindering such search to forfeit 5l.

XLIII.

"ITEM, it is ordained, that *no person* whatsoever, being once made free of the said Art or Mystery, *shall without licence* of the *Master, Wardens*, and *Assistants* of the said Company for the time being, or the greater part of them *change or leave his Company to be free of another* Fellowship or Company, upon pain of *forfeiture* of *twenty pounds*, except he change his copy by reason of his election into any head or chief office in London.

No freeman shall quit this Company to enter another under penalty of 20l. unless he be elected to some chief office in the city.

XLIV.

"ITEM, that *if any apprentice shall misbehave himself towards his master* or mistress, or that he shall be of a rude behaviour, that the persuasion or reasonable correction of his master or mistress will not cause him to reform his misbehaviour, or if he shall be any drunkard, haunter of taverns, ale-houses, bowling-alleys, or other lewd suspected places, or evil company, or houses where unlawful games shall be used, or gamester, dicer, or runnereway, or shall be out of his master or mistress's house without his or her privity, or shall be an enticer of other men's servants to the like; he shall be brought to the hall of the said Company by his said master or mistress, and there these or such like notorious faults justly proved against him, at or before the said *Master, Wardens, and Assistants*, the *party so offending shall receive such condign punishment as shall be reasonable and suitable to his offence*, by corporal penance, or otherwise, in presence of the Master or some of the Wardens, and six of the Assistants of the Company, at the least,

Disorderly and incorrigible apprentices to be brought before the Master, Wardens, &c. and on proof to receive condign punishment;

and for any his *second offence*, or oftener offending, being proved, as aforesaid, he shall be punished in like sort as aforesaid, and it shall be and rest in the power of the *Master, Wardens, and Assistants*, to order and publish him disabled, and he shall from thenceforth stand, and for ever be disabled and barred to demand, enjoy, or have his freedom of this Society; or *if any serving* Journeyman, or hired servant, *shall offend in any the like kinds* and degrees aforesaid, and the same being proved against him at a Court of Assistants, in like sort aforesaid, *he shall satisfy* and undergo *such reasonable pecuniary penalties* as by the said *Master, Wardens, and Assistants* shall be imposed on him; and *if he shall refuse* or omit to satisfy the same, he shall be and stand, (if by the said *Master, Wardens, and Assistants*, he shall be so ordered,) for ever after *dismissed* and debarred *from* using and working at *the trade* of Clockmaking.

XLV.

"ITEM, it is ordained, if upon search hereafter made by the *Master, Wardens, and Assistants*, or any of them at any time, by virtue of his Majesty's charter, *any insufficient or deceitful* Clocks, Watches, Larums, or other *works to the said Trade*, Art, or Mystery, *belonging*, be made or put to sale shall be *found;* then it shall be lawful for *the Master, Wardens, and Assistants to seize upon them, and* after sufficient trial of the said insufficiencies or deceits, *to break such* Clocks, Watches, or Larums, or other *work* thereto appertaining, if *the party* so offending *shall not* desire to be admitted to *pay a reasonable fine* by the said *Master, Wardens, and Assistants*, to be made and rateably assessed, which they shall admit of *on that behalf;* so in such case, *that no such Clock, Watch, Larum, or other work* thereto pertaining, *shall be offered* to be put *to sale until it shall be* mended and *made sufficient* in all things; and that therefore the party so offending *shall put in security that it shall not be sold before it be mended, in* all points, according to the order, direction, and appointment of the *Master, Wardens, and Court of Assistants;* and *that the same so amended shall not be sold* or offered to be put to sale, *before it be viewed again*, and allowed of by the said *Master, Wardens, and Court of Assistants*, or the major part of them, or else to be broken without any further view or order.

"And it is also ordained, that in regard of the extraordinary care and pains to be taken in viewing and searching as aforesaid, *every particular person, members of the said Fellowship*, shall *pay to the said Master, Wardens*, and *Assistants*, the sum of *four-pence quarterly* to the use of the said Fellowship.

XLVI.

"ITEM, whereas *there hath formerly been divers and great abuses offered to divers expert and sufficient workmen in the said Art or Trade of Clockmaking, as well by importing from beyond the seas, as by making within the realm, faulty and deceitful work, upon which have been set the names or marks of some other workmen who made it not, to the discredit and disgrace of them the said wronged workmen, whereby the others dishonesty and deceit is not discovered.*

"It is therefore ordained, *that whosoever* hereafter *shall be found* by the *Master, Wardens,* and *Assistants,* of the Fellowship of Clockmakers, or by any of them, or their lawful deputy or deputies, *to have imported such work* from beyond the seas, *falsely marked,* to sell or exchange by way of merchandizing, or *to have set any man's name or mark upon any work* made within this kingdom or dominion of Wales, *other than the name or mark of the true maker or finisher thereof,* shall *forfeit the said work or works* to the King's Majesty, his heirs and successors, *and* also be fined to the use of the said Master, Wardens, and Fellowship of Clockmakers, *for every time so offending, and for every piece of work* which he or they shall be found to offend in, the sum of *forty shillings, or other greater or lesser sum, according to the nature* and quality *of the said offence,* to be taxed by the *Master, Wardens,* and *Court of Assistants* of the said Company. whoever shall import work falsely marked, or put any name thereon other than that of the true maker, shall forfeit the same to the king, and be fined by the Company 40s. or more or less according to the nature of the offence.

XLVII.

"ITEM, it is ordained, *that if any person* or persons whatsoever, other than a free licensed and admitted Clockmaker, either a freeman, foreigner, denizen or stranger, or any other for them, or by their means, *go about the streets,* hawking or proffering *their wares* to sell *from shop to shop,* or in any inn, or any other place or places, within the liberties and franchises of this city, or within ten miles compass thereof, (being made and wrought within his Majesty's dominions, or coming from beyond the seas) *other than to a free Clockmaker, admitted by the said Company,* and being not allowed of according to his Majesty's aforesaid letters-patents, that *thereby his Majesty's subjects may not be deceived,* shall hereby *forfeit the same* to his said Majesty, his heirs and successors, according as is hereby set down and proposed : *and the parties themselves,* for their several contempts from time to time fined, as *in the discretion of the Master, Wardens,* and *Court of Assistants,* or the major part of them, from time to time, shall be thought fit, *according to* the quantity and quality of *their offences.* None but admitted Clockmakers shall hawk their wares within the city of London or within ten miles thereof, other than to admitted Clockmakers, under penalty of forfeiting the same, and paying such fine as the Court shall determine.

XLVIII.

"ITEM, it is ordained, *that all person and persons* dwelling within the city of London and the liberties thereof, or within ten miles compass, as well within places privileged and exempt as not privileged and exempt, free of the said Company, that *doth, or shall use or exercise the said Art, Trade, or Mystery,* or any thing appertaining thereunto, *shall be contributary* and bear, and pay *unto the said* Master, Wardens, and Fellowship *of Clockmakers,* to the use aforesaid, all *such reasonable sums of money* as shall be thought good and reasonable, *to be assessed* by the *Master, Wardens,* and *Assistants* of the said Fellowship, or the more part of them for the time being, as well *for the affairs of his Majesty, this honourable city,* as also *for any other thing belonging to this Society,* in such manner *as other Freemen of the said Fellowship, and of other companies* of the said city, from time to time *are and shall be charged,* according to their abilities, upon pain of *forfeiture* of *ten* All persons whatsoever exercising the Art within the city of London or within ten miles thereof, shall be contributary to the Company, under the penalty of 10l.

pounds to the said *Master, Wardens*, and *Assistants*, to the use of the said Fellowship.

XLIX.

A chest shall be provided with four several locks, in which shall be kept such effects as are valuable, the keys to be kept by the Master, and three Wardens, who shall all four of them in person together open the same, and not one, two, or three of them alone.

"ITEM, It is ordered, that *the said* Company *or Fellowship shall have one substantial* chest, *with* four several locks *thereupon, with* four *different several* keys *to the same:* which chest shall stand in some convenient place appointed for the same; wherein *shall be put all such monies, plate, jewels, books, and such like treasure,* as shall belong to the said Company or Fellowship; which keys shall be *in the custody of the* Master *and* three Wardens, every one of them to have a key; so that *they shall all four of them in person together, go to the said chest,* and open the same when and so often as there shall be occasion to put any thing therein, or to take any thing forth of the same; and *not one, two, or three of them to have all the keys;* neither *to go alone to the said chest* about the occasions aforesaid, but *all four, Master and Wardens, to go together;* and *if* it happen any *the said Master or Wardens to be sick, or out of town, or to have any other lawful business,* that *the same Master or Warden shall appoint* one of the ancientest that hath been Master or Warden before, *to take his key,* and in his absence *for that time, to go and help to the opening of the chest* to the occasions aforesaid.

remedy in case of sickness, &c.

L.

Recital of abuses by evil-disposed persons.

"ITEM, where *divers* of the *nobility* themselves attending his royal majesty at court, and elsewhere, *as also divers others* in the like kind, *and not only they, but divers other persons of quality,* both of the city and country, many times, by the bad condition of ill-disposed persons, by way of purloining, or plain felonious stealing, taking, or other indirect embezzling from such noble and right honourable personages, and the rest as aforesaid, have and may, from time to time, *lose all sorts of Watches, Clocks, Larums, Cases, Dials, Mathematical-Instruments, and such other commodities, being wrought and sold by the* Master, Wardens, and Assistants, *and the whole body of the said Company,* or by some of them detained, or by any other:

Stolen work frequently sold to goldsmiths, brokers, &c. who by altering the names and marks conceal the offenders.

"AND whereas by common experience it hath been heretofore found by those, that it hath pleased his Majesty to make, in his gracious letters-patents, Master, Wardens, and Assistants, that divers watches that have, from time to time, in such purloining and felonious manner been bought *from and by such several persons who,* after their purloining and false taking as aforesaid, *have delivered the same to some Workmen coming from foreign parts,* and others *who have sold the same* to some goldsmith, broker, or others, and *have, by altering the names, and other particular parts or marks* of the said work, *defaced and obscured the same,* whereby the same might not be known, either from what party the same was so stolen or purloined, or who made it, that the parties themselves might not be apprehended:

Master and Wardens may search in any place

"BE it therefore ordained hereby, for prevention of the like abuses hereafter, that it shall and may be lawful to and for the

Master and Wardens of the said Company of Clockmakers, *or any two of them,* their or any two sufficient deputies allowed by the said Master and Wardens, by and with a full Court of Assistants, or the major part of them, *to make* and take diligent View, *Search,* Inquiry, and Oversight, *in all places suspicious,* and in all and every the houses, shops, warehouses, working-houses, cellars, sollars, place or places, of any person or persons whatsoever, *either of Clockmakers,* goldsmiths, brokers, *or any other whatsoever,* whereby, by their true search, care, and oversight, as aforesaid, *the same wicked and evil actors and offenders may be rooted out* and reformed, and his Majesty's true and lawful subjects, in such case and cases, righted and relieved.

<small>whatsoever, for articles which may have been so stolen, so that the offenders may be discovered, and the aggrieved party obtain redress.</small>

LI.

"ITEM, where, in the fifteenth ordinance made it is ordained, *that none hereafter admitted to be a brother of this society, shall take to himself any apprentice or apprentices, but first to have leave and licence of the Master, Wardens* and *Court of Assistants, or the more part of them, and then to have but one until he shall bear office of Warden or Assistant of or in the said Company; and after he shall be so called to be Warden or Assistant of the said Company, not to exceed the number of two at any time whatsoever;* now forasmuch as *the benefit* of being admitted to be Warden, or one of the Assistants, in *not paying* the several *fines of admittance into the* clothing *and to* the place of stewardship, will be of great advantage to the party or parties, so to be admitted Warden or Assistant:

<small>Fifteenth bye-law recapitulated. A Brother to have but one apprentice, a Warden or Assistant may take two apprentices and no more.</small>

"BE it therefore ordained, that *every* such *party* that shall be so *admitted, before he be called to the clothing, or being Steward, shall pay* to the Master and Wardens of the said Company, to the use of the said Fellowship or Society, the sum of *twenty pounds,* and to the clerk thirteen shillings four-pence, and to the beadle three shillings four-pence.

<small>Persons admitted Warden or Assistant, before they have been admitted to the clothing, or been steward, to pay 20*l*., clerk 13*s.* 4*d.*, beadle 3*s.* 4*d.*</small>

LII.

"ITEM, it is also ordained, that *no servant or apprentice* that is, or *hath unlawfully,* without just and reasonable cause, *departed from his master, mistress, or dame,* not having served the full time of his or their Apprenticeship, or Term of Covenant, *shall be admitted to work for himself, or with any Master, before such time that the said servant or Apprentice hath fully accomplished his Time* or Term of his or their Apprenticeship as aforesaid, *and given content to his said Master, Mistress, or dame,* their or any of their Executors, Administrators, or Assigns; *And* their Departure shall be registered in the Common Hall of the said Company, upon a Court-Day, before the MASTER, WARDENS, and COURT of ASSISTANTS, or the major part of them, whereby Notice may be taken of such unlawful Departure as aforesaid; that they thereby, may give no permission to any such Apprentice or Apprentices, unlawfully departed, to work; *and those that shall set any such to work,* having been forewarned thereof, *shall pay* to the said *Master, Wardens, and Fellowship,* to the Company's Use, the sum

<small>No apprentice shall be admitted to work for himself, or for hire, who shall not have duly served his full time.

Unlawful departure to be registered.

Whoever shall employ such unlawfully shall forfeit £5.</small>

E

THE CLOCKMAKERS' COMPANY.

Clerk 6s. 8d.
Beadle 2s. 6d

of *five pounds*, to the Clerk six shillings, eight pence, and to the Beadle two shillings sixpence: *And* for his or their *further Offence*

And for further offence to be further punished

in that degree, from time to time, *to be further punished*, according to the discretion of the MASTER, WARDENS, and COURT of ASSISTANTS, or the major Part of them, until he or they leave off

Servants unlawfully leaving their employers, shall not the admitted to the Freedom, until the former employers shall acknowledge satisfaction in open Court, then to pay 2s. 6d. Clerk 1s Beadle 4d

setting any such unlawful Servant to work. *And that Servant* so unlawfully departed, *never to have* the Benefit, *Freedom*, or Liberty to work for himself, or for or with any other, *until* such time as *the said Master, Mistress, or Dame*, their or any of their Executors, Administrators, or Assigns, come in open Court as aforesaid, and there publicly *acknowledge satisfaction for such Wrong* received, as formerly: and for the Entry, to pay the Company two shillings, to the Clerk twelve pence, and to the Beadle four pence.

LIII.

To prevent abuses in the trade through insufficient workmen, and that every apprentice that shall be bound, may become a true Artist.

"ITEM, whereas, of late, *many Abuses have crept up by bad and insufficient Workmen*, that have no true knowledge in the finishing any Work they take in hand, whereby it may prove saleable, and no deceit used to the Subject, and especially those that should have been instructed by them, *Now therefore to the end that all and every Apprentice and Apprentices hereafter, that shall become bound to any Person or Persons whatsoever using the Art, Trade, or Mystery, of a professed Clockmaker, may in time become a true Artist in the said Trade and Profession of a Clockmaker, after the full expiration of their term.*

Every person using the Art within the limits of this Charter shall duly teach his Apprentice (who shall be resident in his house) the whole Art, to the end that he may make up his masterpiece with credit.

"BE *it hereby ordained, that every Person* or Persons whatsoever *using, or that* hereafter *shall use the Trade*, Art, and Mystery of Clockmaking, within the City of London, Liberties, and Suburbs thereof, or within Ten Miles compass, according to the Letters Patent of Incorporation, shall hereafter *teach and instruct his said Apprentice* and Apprentices in such manner and form *as their Predecessors formerly have done, which is to keep daily and duly him and them in his House, and there, by himself or his sufficient Journeyman, teach or instruct them in the making of Cases or Boxes of Silver or Brass, and likewise the several Springs belonging to a Watch, Clock, or Larum, and likewise all other particular and peculiar things belonging to such Watches, Clocks, Larums, Mathematical Instruments, and Sun-Dials, his or their said Master shall teach and instruct them in;* to the end they may, in time, make up their Masterpiece with sufficiency of credit, and truly understand both the beginning and ending of their Work, from time to time,

None to buy the several Articles but of a professed Clockmaker or sufficient Workman under penalty of £5.

which they shall take in hand. *And none to buy any Boxes, Cases, Springs, or otherwise, but of such a professed* and allowed *Clockmaker*, or such other sufficient Workman, as by the said MASTER, WARDENS, and COURT of ASSISTANTS, or the major Part of them, shall be thought fit and allowed of, and as is hereby set down, whereby the sufficiency and true goodness thereof may be known, *upon Penalty for the first Offence*, to pay the Master and Wardens, to the use of the Company, *five pounds*, or such other reasonable penalty, as by the MASTER, WARDENS, and COURT of ASSISTANTS, of the said Company, or the greater Part of them (whereof the Master and one of the Wardens for the time being, to be two) shall be thought meet, according to the nature and quality of the Offence; *And for the second Offence, such Fine or other Punishment, according to* the quantity and quality of *their Offence or Offences, as* in the discretions of the MASTER, WARDENS, and COURT of ASSISTANTS, or the major Part of them (whereof the Master and one of the Wardens for the time being, to be two), *shall be thought fit.* and for the second offence, such other fine as the Court may determine.

LIV.

"ITEM, *to the end* it shall appear *what* Oath and Oaths, *every* Person and Persons which shall become *Master or Wardens*, or of the *Assistants or Livery*, or a *Freeman* of this Company, Fellowship, or Fraternity, or the *Clerk, Beadle, or Beadles,* of this Fellowship, *and every Person* at any time to be *allowed to work as Servants* to any of this Fellowship, or *within their Government, shall take,* or enter into; Every person admitted Master, Warden, Assistant, Livery, Freeman, Clerk, or Beadle, shall take the Oaths required.

"*It is ordered and ordained, that* they and every of them, shall severally take such several Oaths as are here respectively set down, and the Oath of loyalty and supremacy to the King's Majesty, his Heirs and Successors, according to the Laws of this Realm, as they now be, or hereafter shall be, provided. and also the Oath of Loyalty and Supremacy.

LV.

"ITEM, *every Master or Warden* agreed upon, in sort as aforesaid, to be Master and Warden for the succeeding Year, *to take Oath before the ancient Master, and both or one of the Wardens and Court of Assistants,* in this sort ensuing, viz.

"You shall be true to our Sovereign Lord the King and to his Heirs and Successors, you shall endeavour yourselves the best you can, whilst you continue in the Office whereunto you are now chosen, justly and indifferently to execute, and cause to be executed, your Offices in every respect, and to put in due execution all the good and lawful Laws and Ordinances in the Book of Ordinances expressed and contained, without assessing or punishing any Person for envy, hatred, or malice, or sparing any Person for reward, meed, dread, favor, or affection: And of all and every such Goods, Plate, Jewels, Sums of Money, or any other thing or things, that, by reason of your said Office, shall come to your hands, charge, and custody, you shall, according to the Ordinances made touching the same, yield and make a good, true, and plain Account within convenient time, after you shall be thereunto required by the Master and Wardens of the Company and Fellowship for the time being; or else you shall pay your Fines according to the same Ordinances. So HELP YOU GOD. The Oath to be taken by every person admitted Master or Warden and before whom.

LVI.

"ITEM, *the Oath of every one chosen from time to time of the Assistants, to be taken before the Master, and all or one of the Wardens and Court of Assistants,* to the effect ensuing, viz.

"You shall swear to be true to our Sovereign Lord the King, his Heirs and Successors; you shall assist the Master and Wardens of this Fellowship of Clockmakers for the time being, in their Rule The Oath to be taken by every person chosen an Assistant, and before whom.

and Government of the said Fellowship, so long as you shall continue one of the Assistants, with your best and soundest advice: and shall endeavour yourselves, to the utmost of your skill and knowledge, justly and indifferently to execute your said Place and Office in every respect; and to put in due execution all the good and lawful Ordinances of this Society, contained, and which shall be expressed and contained, in the Book of Ordinances, without punishing or assessing any Person for envy, hatred, or malice, or sparing of any Person for love, fear, dread, favor, or affection, or for reward, or for hope or promise of reward. So HELP YOU GOD.

LVII.

"ITEM, *the Oath of every one of the Livery to be taken in sort aforesaid*, and to the effect ensuing, viz.

The Oath to be taken on admission to the Livery.

"YOU shall swear to be true to our Sovereign Lord the King, his Heirs and Successors; and that you shall perform and obey all that to you appertaineth to be done, by the true meaning of this Book of Ordinances of this Society, and be honest for you to perform, and approved or warranted by the Laws of this Realm. So HELP YOU GOD.

LVIII.

"ITEM, *when any of the said Livery of this Society shall be at any time chosen and appointed, according to the said Book of Ordinances, to be Auditor for any accounts or reckonings touching this Fellowship*, to be passed or taken by or from any Master, Wardens, or others, he *shall take Oath in sort aforesaid*, to the effect ensuing, viz.

The Oath to be taken by every person chosen Auditor.

"You shall faithfully, and to the best of your skill and knowledge, hear and examine all such Accounts and reckonings, which by any Person or Persons shall be made and offered, in any wise touching or concerning the Affairs of this Fellowship or Company; and the same accounts and reckonings so by you heard and examined, shall deliver up in writing under your hand, to the Master, Wardens, and Assistants, of this Fellowship or Society for the time being, upon reasonable request to you made, and at such time as the Master and Wardens for the time being shall appoint, with your allowance and disallowance of the said account: you shall not allow any thing for love or favor, nor disallow any thing for hatred, or malice: but shall justly and indifferently hear and examine the same account, so near as God will give you Grace. So HELP YOU GOD.

LIX.

"ITEM, *that the Clerk of the Fellowship shall take his Oath in manner and to the effect here ensuing*, viz.

The Oath to be taken by the Clerk.

"YOU shall be true to our Sovereign Lord the King's Majesty, and his Heirs and Successors, and to the *Master, Wardens*, and *Fellowship* of this Society; and all the commandments of the Master and Wardens of the same Fellowship, being lawful and honest, and touching and concerning the affairs and business of this Fellowship, belonging to your Office, willingly you shall do and execute. True entries of all things belonging to your Office, you shall make, without any partiality for favour or affection, lucre or gain, hatred, envy, or malice whatsoever. You shall not wittingly or willingly do or commit any thing that may be hurtful and prejudicial to the said *Master, Wardens,* and *Fellowship;* but shall honestly, justly, and truly execute your Office of Clerkship in all things appertaining to the same, as the Clerk of the said *Master, Wardens,* and *Fellowship* of this Society ought to do, so long as you shall continue and be in the same Office, according to your best skill, power, and ability, without any partiality. SO HELP YOU GOD.

LX.

" ITEM, *that every one that shall be, at a Court of Assistants, chosen and allowed to be a Beadle of this Company, Fellowship, or Society, shall take his Oath to the effect here ensuing,* viz.

" You shall be true to our Sovereign Lord the King's Majesty, his Heirs and Successors; and obedient shall be to the Master and Wardens of this Fellowship for the time being; their commandments lawful and honest touching the affairs and business of this Fellowship, to the utmost of your power, willingly you shall do; And generally you shall justly and truly do and execute all and every thing and things appertaining to the said Office, as the Beadle of the said *Master, Wardens,* and *Fellowship,* ought to do, to the utmost of your skill, power, and ability, as long as you shall continue in the said Office, without any partiality whatsoever. SO HELP YOU GOD.

The Oath to be taken by the Beadle.

LXI.

" ITEM, *every one that shall hereafter be received to be a Freeman or Brother of this Fellowship, shall take the Oath of Supremacy, and likewise another Oath to the effect here ensuing,* viz.

" You shall swear to be true to our Sovereign Lord the King's Majesty, his Heirs and Successors, and at all times obedient to the Master and Wardens of this Fellowship and Society, and their Successors after them, in all honest and lawful things touching the affairs of this Fellowship. You shall be ready at all manner of Summons, and bear scot and lot in all manner of reasonable Contributions of, and to, this Fellowship; and the Fellowship of the COMPANY of CLOCKMAKERS of the CITY OF LONDON, you shall, to the best of your skill, power, and ability, uphold and maintain. You shall not know nor suspect any manner of Meetings, Conspiracies, Plots, and Devices against the King's Majesty, his Heirs or Successors, or the Government of this Fellowship, but you shall the same, to the utmost of your power, let and hinder, and speedily disclose to the Master or one of the Wardens of this Society. *And* this City of London, and Fellowship of Clockmakers, you shall keep harmless, as much as in you lieth: *also* you shall be ready at all times to be at the Quarter Days, and every other Assembly, Matter, or Cause, that you shall be warned or called unto for the affairs of this Fellowship; unless you shall

The Oath to be taken on admission to the fellowship.

have lawful and reasonable excuse in that behalf. *And* all other Ordinances of this Fellowship or Society, ratified according to the Laws of this Realm, or otherwise lawful for this Fellowship or Society to make and ordain, you shall, to the utmost of your power, well and truly submit yourself unto and keep. So HELP YOU GOD.

LXII.

"ITEM, *that forasmuch as it may often happen, by reason of sickness or other necessities, that the Master or Wardens of this Fellowship or Society may be absent,*

<small>The Master and Wardens may appoint a Deputy by approbation of the Court, but not to act until sworn.</small>

"IT *is ordained,* That *the Master or Wardens* of this Company, *by order of a Court of Assistants, shall have power to make a Deputy* in any of their Places, for such time as shall be allowed at the said Court; *And that all things* touching the Affairs or Ordinances of this Company, *which shall be done, by, to, or before, such Deputy, of any* Master or Warden, *(so as such Deputy shall have taken such Oath as is there before in this Book of Ordinances, appointed for the Master, or Wardens to take,* the same Oath, being taken before the Master and Wardens, or any two of them and before the whole Court of Assistants, or the greater part of them) *shall be held in state and case, as if the same were in the presence of, or done, or executed by, to or before, the Master or Warden himself,* who shall have made or assigned such deputy without any quarrel, question, or exception to be made or moved, of, to, or upon the same.

"ALL *which Acts, Ordinances, and Oaths, in form aforespecified, at the request of the said Master and Wardens of the Company or Society of Clockmakers of the City of London, by authority of the said Act of Parliament,* We the said Chancellor, *and Justices of either Bench aforesaid, for good, laudable, and lawful Acts, Ordinances, and Oaths, do accept and admit, and as much as in us*

<small>All the Bye Laws ratified 11th August 1632, 8th Car: 1st.</small>

is, ratify, laud and approve by these presents; In Witness whereof to this present Book, we have subscribed our Names and set to our Seals, the eleventh day of August, in the year of the Reign of our Sovereign Lord Charles, by the Grace of God, King of England, Scotland, France, and Ireland, the eighth; Anno Domini, 1632.

" THO. COVENTRYE.
" THO. RYCHARDSON.
" RO. HEATH.

" Examinat per me Johem Page in Cur^a Cancellar' Magrm."

Additional Bye-Law passed 4th April, 1796 :—

LXIII.

<small>Any Freeman refusing (without good and sufficient cause)</small>

"ITEM, *it is further ordained, that if any Person* of the said Fellowship, *being* so, as aforesaid, *chosen to be of the* said *Livery, shall* (without any reasonable and sufficient cause, to be allowed and admitted by the said MASTER, WARDENS, *and* ASSISTANTS) *refuse to accept and take upon him* to be of *the said Livery; And* for 14 days to take the Livery *shall refuse to take*, within fourteen days next after Notice to him after being given of such his Election as aforesaid, *such Oath*, as by the chosen, to forfeit Ordinance in that behalf made, is *appointed* to be taken ; *That* £15. then, and in every such Case, *every such Person* so refusing, *shall forfeit* and pay to, and for the use of, the said *Master, Wardens,* and *Fellowship*, the sum of *fifteen pounds*, to be recovered by action of debt, or levied by distress.

"WE *have perused and do approve of, and allow this Order, Rule, and Ordinance, to be one of the Orders, Rules, and Ordinances of the Company of* CLOCK-MAKERS *of the City of* LONDON.

"LOUGHBOROUGH. C.

"KENYON.

"JA. EYRE."

The Bye-Laws were in accordance with custom submitted to the Court of Aldermen, and by them ordered to be entered on Record, as is shewn by the following entry on their Minutes :—

"1632. October 11th. Whitmore Mayor. ITEM: this day upon a moĉon made unto this Court for and in the behalfe of the Company of Clockmakers lately incorporated it is ordered by this Court that their ordinances be entered upon Record."[1]

The necessary preliminaries having thus been gone through, the several persons designated in the Charter as the first Master and Wardens of the Company, attended before the Lord Mayor and took the Oath of Office thereby prescribed. On the same day, the 12th October, 1632, the Assistants being summoned to attend, the first duly constituted Court of the Company was held, and as the proceedings at this and the subsequent Court Meetings are of considerable interest, they are given at length, as follows :—

"Whittmoore Maior.

[2] "At a Court holden the 12th daye of October 1632. present

Davyd Ramsey Esquier Master.	Frauncis Foreman }	
Henry Archer }	John Harris }	
John Willow } Wardens.	Samuell Lynnaker }	
Sampson Shelton }	John Charlton }	Assistants.
James Vaultrollier	John Mydnall }	
John Smith	Symon Bartram }	
	Edward East }	

[1] Repertory 46, fol. 426b. [2] Company's Journal I.

Master and Wardens sworn before ye Lord Mayor.

"ITEM: this daye the Master and Wardens above named having taken their Corporall Oathes before the R^t Ho^{ble} George Whittmore now Lord Maior of the Citty of London, according to his Maties most gratious graunt of Incorporation did afterwards assemble themselves togeather, callinge before them the whole Assistants of which such as are above named did appeare, And by vertue of their said Charter, and the Judges Ordinaunces of the Lawe, made by the R^t ho^{ble} the Lord Keeper and the two Lord Chief Justices on either bench the said Master and Wardens did their in Open Court give Thomas Copley their Clarke by Corporation his Oath according to the said ordinaunces, and after he was soe sworne he did likewise give Oath to the severall Assistants above named, who were also sworne accordingly.

Lo: Coventry Lo: Richardson Lo: Heath

Clerk sworn.

Comon Prayer on Court dayes.

"This daye the Court hath ordered, That at all Courts heereafter to be holden by the Master Wardens and Assistants of this Fellowshipp of Clockmakers, before the said Court begin their shalbe Common Prayers redd by the Clarke or some other free Brother of this Societie in his absence, to th'end such proceedings as the Court shall (from tyme to tyme) take in hand, and what discourse either in privacy or publiquely the companie may mutually have in love and Brotherhood may be all donn in the feare of God and sincerity of hert.

Mr. Archer Deputy Master.

"This daye the Court hath elected Mr. Henry Archer as Deputy Master untill Mr. Davyd Ramsey returned forth of the Country or untill his opportune occasions fitt him to take the same place upon him againe."

[1] "At a Court holden the 16th of October 1632. present

Henry Archer Deputy Master.		John Harris	
John Willow	} Wardens.	Richard Morgan	
Sampson Shelton		Samuell Lynaker	
James Vaultrollier		John Charlton	} Assistants.
John Smith		John Middnall	
Frauncis Foreman		Symon Bartram	
		Edward East	

A n^d of submission to ye ordinaunces and charter

"M^d Wee whose names are hereunder written have publiquely here read in open Court His Maties Charter of Incorporation graunted to the Clockmakers of London and elswhere within His Maties Dominions, As also the Judges Ordinaunces of the Lawe, by which said Charter wee being all of us Incorporated into a Brotherhood as well Free as Forreyne, And by vertue therof enjoyned to submit ourselves to be under that gouvernment, have with a willing and free consent submitted ourselves to the same accordingly the daye and yeare first above written.

[1] Company's Journal I.

"The particular names of those that did this day subscribe, viz. :—

Henry Archer Deputy Master.
John Willow } Wardens.
Sampson Shelton }
James Vaultrollier
Frauncis Foreman
John Smith

John Harris
Richard Morgan
Samuell Lynaker
John Charlton   } Assistants.
John Middnall
Symon Bartram
Edward East

Robert Rothwood
Thomas Holland
Thomas Dawson
John Brooke
Onisipherus Heldon
Symon Hackett
Pierry Hue
Oswold Durant
Richard Child
Thomas Shepheard
Josias Cuper
Thomas Alcock
Davyd Backquett
Ely Volant
Robt Grinkin
Thomas Howse
William Petit
John Burgis

William Daniell
John Droeshout
Edmund Gillpin
Lewes Cooke
John Walker his mark ×
Thomas Reead
Edward Okeham
Thomas Ward
Thomas Lambe
George Clarke
Robt Holloway
John Bullby
John × Bull his mark
William Daniell
Richard Jackson
Richard × Lord his mark
Daniell Saunders.

"ITM : forasmuch as it hath pleased his Matie out of his prerogative Royall to graunt to this fellowshipp power by his Charter of Incorporation to admitt such Bretheren as by vertue of the same ought to be subject to the orders, rule and govournment of the said Companie. Now this daye the Master Wardens and Assistants according to the marginall directions of the now Lord Keeper signified by his hand in the booke of ordinaunces of the Lawe have hereby ordered that what person or persons shalbe hereafter thought fitt to be allowed of and admitted into this Society shall pay such Fees as hereafter enseweth viz$^{t.}$ *An order for admittaunces.*

"Imprimis to pay noe Fees to the Companie but to be admitted gratis.

"ITM: to the Clarke for entring of every Freeman 2s and to the Beadle 8d and for every Forreigner 3s and to the Beadle 12d.

"At a Court holden on the 23 of October 1632 the Deputy Master together with his Wardens and Assistants tooke their Oathes of Brotherhood as the rest of the body of the Companie have donne formerly."

The newly incorporated body, notwithstanding the favour shewn them by the King and the Court of Aldermen, seem soon to have incurred the displeasure of the Blacksmiths, some of whose Members and Office-bearers were found taking prominent positions in the new Company, accordingly they determined to petition the Court of Aldermen against them, as the undermentioned order shows :—

"At a Court of Assistants of the Blacksmiths' Company held on the 1st November 1632.

"This daie it is Ordered that ye Clarke shall draw a Peticõn to ye Lord Mayor & Courte (of Aldermen) to shew the Clockmakers that are made free into ye Woodmongers to bee disfranchised and ye Clockmakers to p'duce their Charters and ye Clark to be paid¹ for what he shall do therein."²

Their Petition was accordingly presented to the Court of Aldermen in the following January, and by them referred to a Committee for consideration in these terms :—

"1632-3. 8 Charles I. January 22. Raynton Maior. ITEM: this day upon reading of a peticõn exhibited in the name of the Wardens and Assistantes of the Company of Blacksmithes London whereby they shewe that the Clockmakers have lately obteyned a Chrē of incorporation to the great p'iudice of the peticoners who humbly desire that they may sue the recognizances of such as being Clockmakers by trade are made free of other Companys, It is thought fitt and soe ordered by this Court that Mr. Recorder, Mr. Aldrān Clitherowe, Mr. Aldrān Fen and Sr Morrice Abbott Knight and Aldrān and Mr. Stone or any three or more of them shall peruse the said Chrē and ordinances confirmed to the said Clockmakers, and examine how and in what manner the same were procured and take consideracon thereof as alsoe what is fitt to be done for releife of the peticoners in what they have desired as aforesaid, And certifie unto this Court in writing under their hands how they finde the same and their opinions."³

Before the Committee had made a Report, a second Petition from the Blacksmiths was presented, and permission was given them to put in suit the recognizances of such Clockmakers as had become free in other Companies. At a subsequent Court of Aldermen, held two days afterwards, a counter-petition was submitted by the Clockmakers, in which reference is made to the fact, that some of the trade (probably after the negociations of 1628 with the Blacksmiths

---

¹ Entry among receipts and payments.

27 Nov. 1632. Spente at Guildhall about ye Clockmakers 2 2 0
15 Jan. 1632-3. Spent at Guildhall about ye Clockmakers 1 0 0

² Extract from Minute Book of Blacksmiths' Company. Vol. V.

³ Repertory 47, fol. 98^b.

had fallen through) had become Members of the Woodmongers' Company, and the Court of Aldermen thereupon withdrew their sanction to the Blacksmiths to commence hostile proceedings pending the report of the Committee.

"1632-3. 8th Charles I. February 26. Raynton Mayor. ITEM: this day upon the humble peticõn of the Wardens and Assistants of the Company of Blacksmithes London It is thought fitt and soe ordered by this Court that Mr. Recorder, Sir Robert Ducie Knight and Baronett Sir George Whitmore Knight and Aldrañ Mr. Aldrañ Freeman Mr. Aldrañ Clitherowe Mr. Aldrañ Fen Sir Morris Abbott Knight and Aldrañ and Mr. Stone or any five or more of them shall puse and consider of the Chrẽ of late obteyned by the Clockmakers and of their ordinances, as also of the first draught of the said Chrẽ allowed by some of the said Comittes who formerly certified their opinions unto this Court touching the same, And examine whether any alteracõn or addicõn hath binc made thereunto since it was pused and allowed of by the said former Comittees and what prejudice is thereby likely to happen unto the said peticõners, And consider what is fitt to be done for their reliefe, And the said Comittees to certifie unto this Court in writing under their hands how they finde the same and their doings and opinions. And this Court doth give libty unto the said peticõners to put in suite the Recognizances of such Clockmakers by trade as are not free of the Blacksmithes but have obteyned their freedome of this City by redempcõn of other Companys."[1]

"1632-3. 8th Charles I. February 28. Raynton Mayor. ITEM: this day upon the humble Peticõn of the Company of Clockmakers London it is ordered by this Court that the Company of Blacksmithes shall forbeare to put in suite the Recognizances of such Clockmakers by trade as are free of the Company of Woodmongers untill the Comittees lately appoynted by this Court to heare the differences betweene the said Company of Blacksmithes and Company of Clockmakers have made Certificate unto this Court of their p̃ceedings and opinions touching the same. And soe as the said Clockmakers doe p̃nte unto the said Coñittees the first draught of their Chrẽ wch is now in question betweene them and the Blacksmithes."[2]

The Records of the Court of Aldermen do not contain any evidence that the subject was further pursued before them by the Blacksmiths, but from the following entries taken from their Records, it will be seen that they took proceedings in the Exchequer Court against several Members of the Clockmakers' Company—Drake, Archer and others.

"At a Court of Assistants of the Blacksmiths' Company held on the 10th October, 1633.

[1] Repertory 47, fol. 138b. [2] Repertory 47, fol. 142b.

"This daie it is ordered that ye Clockmakers shalbe forthwith pceeded against in the Exchequer and that the Clerk shall take care in the followinge and psecucon thereof.[1]

"Book of receipts and payments of the Blacksmiths' Company, 1631 to 1633:—

"Paid to Mr. Mosse for his advise to goe unto the
    Court of Aldermen about our petition to disin-
    franchise 3 Clockmakers . . . . .   x^s
"Paid Mr. Mosse and Mr. Clarke for going unto ye
    Court about ye same . . . . .   vj^s viij^d
"Paid Mr. Clarke in ye suite against ye Clockmakers
    Archer, and Drake . . . . . .   xlvj^s vj^d
"Paid Mr. Tovie his fee in ye Chequer .   iij^s iiij^d
"Paid Mr. Stone his fee . . .   xx^s
"Paid Mr. Stone more . . .   xx^s
"Paid Mr. Mosse for his paines thereon .   xx^s
"Paid to Mr. Clarke for his paines .   iij^s iiij^d
"Paid to Mr. Lentall his fee .   x^s

"1633—1635
"Received of the Clockmakers for a composition in
    Drake's business . . . . .   vj^li
"Paid to Mr. Recorder his fee against ye Clockmakers
    touching Drake's suite . . . . .   xl^s
"To Mr. Marsh the Cities Solicitor for his paines in
    going to Mr. Attorney General and Mr. Recorder   x^s
"To Mr. Attorney General for his fee in that suite .   xl^s
"Paid the Clarke for his paines in John Drake's suite
    and against the Clockmakers upon ye Committee   xlvij^s ij^d
"Spent in attending Mr. Attorney General and Mr.
    Recorder about Drake's business . . .   vj^s viij^d

"1633. November 5. This daie att a full Court itt was agreed that if the Clockmakers would give £6 and a supper they spendinge xx$^s.$ more att the supper than our Company, that then a peace shall be concluded for John Drake suite.

"That the 14 of November the Clockmakers did agree to give us a supper, touchinge Drake business and Drake paid £vj which is afterwards accounted in the Wardens accompt as by the next accompt daie appeareth."[2]

---

[1] 1633. October 17.
   Spente att severall daies (upon the Clockmakers' business) &c. £2 16 10
   Paid to Mr. Attorney his fee about the Clockmakers . .   2   0   0
[2] Extracts from Minute Book of Blacksmiths' Company. Vol. V.
   1633-4. January 23. Account brought in by Mr. Warden Murron.
   Spent att a supper with the Clockmakers at the ending of
       Jo. Drake business £2   3   5

In the year 1635 the Clockmakers again addressed themselves to the Court of Aldermen, and after reciting their Charter, they set out the difficulties under which they laboured, being freemen of other Companies, and they sought permission to bind their Apprentices to themselves, not through the intervention of the Companies of which they were free, but through the new Company of Clockmakers of which they were members.

The Court thereupon referred the application to a Committee for consideration.

"1635. 11th Charles I. October 22. Parkhurst Maior. ITEM: This day the Maister Wardens and Society of the Clockmakers in and about this City p̃ferred unto this Court their humble peticon thereby intymating that it hath pleased his Ma'y to incorporate the said peticõners thereby to inhable them the better to search and governe the workemen and workemanshipp belonging to the Arte of Clockmakers within this Citty and places adioyning and to p̃vent and reforme the abuses therein comitted the which they are not hable to doe in regard that (they) are not free of the corporacõn of Clockmakers and therefore humbly desired being free of this City of diverse Companyes who have noe relacõn to their said trade that they may have liberty to binde their Apprentices to themselves as Citizens and Clockmakers of London and at th' end of their termes they may bee made free of this Citty the peticõners being willing to remayne unto the severall Companyes whereof they are now free and to pay their quarteridge during their lives upon consideracõn whereof it is thought fitt and soe ordered by this Court that Sir Thomas Mowlson Knight & Aldrān Mr. Aldrān Bromfeild Mr. Aldrān Garoway Sir William Acton Knight and Baronett Mr. Aldrān Andrewes Mr. Aldrān Gurney Mr. Shereife Gayre or any three or more of them and Mr. Greene and Mr. Pheasaunt shall take due consideracõn of the peticõners said peticõn and certifie unto this Court in writing under their hands how they finde the same and their doings and opinions." [1]

The subject was some time under the consideration of the Committee, who in December of the following year, 1636, presented a Report in which they recapitulated the several proceedings taken to establish the Clockmakers in accordance with the custom of the City; and recommended that their petition should be complied with, and that such of them as were willing to be translated from other Companies of which they were free, might, with the consent of such bodies, be admitted to Citizenship as Clockmakers, and that such as could not get the assent of their Companies to their translation, should nevertheless cause their Apprentices, using the

---

[1] Repertory 49, fol. 345.

trade of Clockmaking, to be bound to a Freeman of that Craft, and at the end of their Apprenticeship to be admitted Citizens and Clockmakers.

[1] " 1636. 11th Charles I. December 1. Bromfeild Maior. ITEM : This day was openly read heere in Court a report in writing under the hands of Mr. Recorder, Edward Bromfeild now Lord Maior, Richard ffen, Henry Andrewes, and John Gayre Aldren and Mr. Greene; and Mr. Pheasant the tenor whereof is as followeth vizt. :—

" To the right hono^{ble} the Lord Maior of the City of London and to the right Worshipfull the Aldren of the same.

" According to an order of this hono^{ble} Court of the nynteenth day of November last. Wee whose names are subscribed have taken consideracōn of the matters thereby referred unto us concerning the Watchmakers and Clockmakers in and about London beeing Freemen of the said Citty, who doe desire that by the favour of this hono^{ble} Court, they may bee intituled and called by the name of Cittizens and Clockmakers of London and that they may bind theire Appntices unto them and make them free by that name. And haveing called the Company of Blacksmiths before us who opposed them in their said desire and haveing heard them and their Councell sev^{r}all tymes wee find that his Mai$^{ty:}$ in his tender care and respect to the Citty and the Goverment thereof was graciouslye pleased before he would incorporate the said Clockmakers to require a Certificate from this Court concerning the same. And wee alsoe find that after consideracōn had and taken thereof by Sir Henneage ffinch kt. then Recorder and diverse Aldermen Committees appointed for that purpose, who found the same fitt to be granted, and Certificate thereof by them made unto this Court a report was made unto his Ma^{te} by this hono^{ble} Court that they had taken consideracōn of the petition and reasons of the Clockmakers and of the draught of a Charter desired by them which had bin perused by the said Recorder and did conceave that the incorporating of them would not bee pjudiciall to any other Corporacōn or gov'ment then established. But they did think it a likely meanes to incourage them in their trade and increase their number of good and sufficient workemen, and reforme abuses wch did and might happen for want of gov'ment. And wee alsoe find that the said Sir Henneage ffinch beeing required by the right hono^{ble} the Lord Keeper did certify that the clause for the binding of Apprentices to some free brother of the Company was very fitt to bee inserted into the Charter and noe inconvenience to other Companies of the Citty. And thereupon his Matie was pleased to incorporate the said Clockmakers by the name of Mr. Wardens and ffellowship of the Art or Mistery of Clockmaking of the Citty of London, and that they should have succession for the continuance of their said Corporacōn for ev^{r}. And for that purpose they are thereby authorized to bind Apprentices to themselves, whereby in tyme they may beecome an able body without the disturbance of any other Society or Gov'ment and alsoe to make lawes and ordinances for the better rule and Gov'ment of the said Clockmakers. And after mature and deliberate consideracōn there upon had and taken in regard it appeares that the Corporacōn was obtayned upon the Certificate of this Court, and upon such consideracōn had as aforesaid. Wee doe therefore think fitt that such psons as use the Art

---

[1] Repertory 51, fol. 18^{b}.

of making Watches and Chamber Clocks beeing freemen of this Citty who are willing to bee translated and can proove the consent of the Company whereof they are free to give way thereunto shall forthwith be translated from the sev'all Companies whereof they are free unto the said Society of Clockmakers in such manner as in translations is used within this Citty. And further wee think fitt that such persons as shall use the Art of making Watches and Chamber Clocks and will not bee translated to the said Society of Clockmakers or cannot p̄cure the Company whereof they are free to give their consent thereunto shall not withstanding bee enjoyned to bind their Apprentices to some freemen of the said Society of Clockmakers of London by the names of Cittizens and Clockmakers. And soe having served their Tearmes according to the custome to be made free of the said Society of Clockmakers. And wee think fitt that the Chamberlaine of this Citty shall soe receave and inrolle them and admitt them into the freedome of this Citty by that name and title when they are to be made free. And that he bee directed and ordered by this Court to take notice thereof and doe accordingly. All which notwithstanding wee humbly submitt to the grave judgement of this hono^{ble} Court. This 16 day of June 1636.

       "Thomas Gardiner, Recorder.

    "John Gayre.   "Edw Bromfeild.

    "John Greene.   "Rich Fenn.

    "Peter Pheasant.   "Hen Andrews.

"The which report was allowed of by this Court and ordered to be entered into the Repertory and to bee accordingly pformed."

The Blacksmiths' Company lost no opportunity of opposing the Company of Clockmakers as well as the individual Members. The accompanying Extracts abundantly show the steps taken Counsel being retained to urge their claims before the Committee and to prosecute offending Members.

"1635—1637.
[1] " Paid Mr. Mosse to move the Court of Aldermen about the Clockmakers . . . . . v^s
" Paid Mr. Stone his fee twice when the Committees sate about the Clockmakers . . . . xx^s
" Paid Mr. Mosse his fee about the Clockmakers . v^s
" Spent when we went to the Comityes about the Clockmakers . . . . ij^s vj^d
" Spent when we went to Mr. Mosse about ye Clockmakers . . . . iiij^s vj^d
" Spent when we went to the Court of Aldermen . viij^s j^d
" Spent when the Comityes sate about ye Clockmakers vij^s iiij^d "

---

[1] The Receipts and Payments Account Book of the Blacksmiths' Company, 1625 to 1646.

At a meeting of the Court of Assistants of the Blacksmiths' Company on February 8, 1637, the following resolution was passed :—

' " It is ordered that some course shall be taken to disfranchise Humfrey Downinge a Clockmaker being inrolled and bound to Mr. Grinkin yet havinge obtayned his freedome by patrimony of the Barbar Surgeons."

" 1638. 9th May. Court of Company. AUDIT :

"Spente the 6th of March in goinge to the Courte of Aldren about disfranchinge Downinge the Clockmaker . . . .   3' 0^d

" Spente the 13 March upon the same occasion.   3 3

" 1638. 19th of July.

" Spente att a Meetinge the 24 May aboute the Clockmakers att my Lord Maiors . . .   3 7

" Spente the 13th of June in goinge to my Lord Maiors about the Clockmakers 1 8

" 1638. July 19.

" This daie it is ordered that our Master and Wardens shall take advice to sue Child the Clockmaker in the spiritual court for breach of his oath and shall do therein accordinge as they shalbe advised.

" Spent the third of July in goinge to my Lord Maiors with Child when wee served warrant on him 2 5

" Spent att Guildhall the 10th of July in going to the Court of Aldren about Child 2 1

" Paid my Lord Maior's officer for carryinge Child to the Compter 2 6

" Spent on Thursday the 11th day of July in goinge to Guildhall about the Clockmakers . . .   5 5

" Spent this 19th of July 1638, in goinge to Guildhall about Childe 5 0

" 1638.

" Accounts from the 9th of May to the 19th of July 1638.

" For copy of the Clockmakers' reporte of the Aldren 3 4

" For the order and fee to Mr. Clarke touching Child the Clockmaker before my Lord Maior .   5 0

" For a Warrant for him 1 0

" For my attendance [The Clerk] about Child many tymes att my Lord Maiors and Court of Aldren and Meetinge att the hall speciall about the Companies business . . . . . .   15 0 "

' Journal V of the Blacksmiths' Company.

The powers conferred by the Charter and Bye-Laws were soon found in practice to be insufficient to prevent the abuses practised by unskilful workmen and unscrupulous masters, and the Court of Assistants long debated the propriety of applying to the Legislature for an Act of Parliament confirming the Charter and conferring increased powers on the Company, but the expenses attendant upon such a proceeding appear to have deterred them. In 1646 an attempt was made to get over the difficulty by raising a subscription among the Members for that purpose, but it failed.

"1646. October 12. This day Mr. Wansey said in open Court that when the Charter was confirmed by Parliament, he would give the Company £10 there being present in Court Simon Hackett, Mr. Thomas Alcock and Onesipherus Holden, Wardens, Sampson Shelton, John Willow, John Harris, John Smith, Symon Bartram, David Bouquet, Robert Cordwell and John Nicasius."[1]

On the 14th September, 1652, the House of Commons passed the following order, viz. :—

"'Ordered that it be referred to the Committee for Corporations to take into consideration how Corporations may be settled as may be suitable to and agreeable with the Government of a Commonwealth and how their respective Charters may be altered and renewed to be held from and under the authority of this Commonwealth.'"[2]

The Company subsequently received a letter directing them to submit their Charter for inspection. The letter, together with the proceedings which thereupon ensued, are detailed in the following documents :—

[3] "Gentlemen,—The Committee for Corporations having taken into their consideration an Order of Parliament of the fourteenth of September 1652, touching the alteration and renewing of the several and respective Charters of this Nation, and upon serious debate had thereon (judging it most agreable with, and suitable to, the Government of a Commonwealth, that they be held from and under the authority of the same) commanded me to signify unto you their pleasure therein (vizt) that in pursuance of the said order of Parliament, you fail not to bring or cause to be brought unto the said Committee upon the fourth day of January next at two of the clock in the afternoon (sitting in the Queen's Court in Westminster) the Charter or Charters by which you are incorporated, this being all I have in command
"I remain, Gentlemen,
"Your friend and Servant,
"DANIEL BLAGRAVE.
"Queen's Court, Westminster,
"December 21st, 1652."

---

[1] Company's Journal 1.   [2] Journals of the House of Commons.
[3] Original Letters, No. 2.

"By the Coṁitee for Corporations, January 4th, 1652. Ordered that ye Charter of the Company of Clockmakers this day brought unto this Coṁittee bee referred to John Farwell Esq. Councell to this Coṁittee in behalfe of the Coṁonwealth, who is desired to peruse the same, and give this Coṁittee an accompt of the heads thereof.'

"A true coppy examined by
    Saml. Neales Clerk to ye s^d Coṁittee

" Da. Blagrave
" Hum. Edwards
" Gilbt. Millington
" J. Danvers
" Is. Penington "

"By the Coṁittee for Corporations, January 27th 1652. Upon Report made by John Farwell Esq. Councell unto this Coṁittee in behalfe of the Coṁonwealth that he hath in his hands a true coppy of the originall Charter by which the Company of Clockmakers are incorporated, it is ordered that the said Mr. Farwell do deliver unto the Master and Wardens of the said Company their originall Charter back againe, they giveing him a receipt for the same.[3]

"A true coppy examined by
    Saml. Neale Clerk to ye said Coṁittee

" Da. Blagrave
" Willm. Allenson
" Wm. Purefoy
" Wm. Steveningham
" Hum. Edwards."

In 1656 a serious difference of opinion arose between the Freemen of the Company and the Court of Assistants as to the manner in which the latter carried out the powers granted by the Charter and Bye-Laws which led to great dissatisfaction among the Apprentices and Workmen, and at last found its expression in a petition to the Lord Mayor, of which the following is a copy :—

"To the Right Honourable the Lord Mayor of the Citty of London.

"The humble petiĉon of several Freemen of the Company of Clockmakers.

"Sheweth,—That having obteyned a Charter of the late King about 25 yeares since for the better improving and regulating of the same trade and that the nation might not be abused with unserviceable worke, and the members of it live honestly by their calling, which reformaĉon we have for many years patiently expected, but notwithstandinge many complaints both public and private wee finde ourselves now in a worse condiĉon then ever we were before the Charter was granted, for then such as were agrieved sought their remedy by the law of the land and ye customs of this Citty, but since the power hath bin in the Courte of Assistants all manner of evils have flowed in upon

---

[1] Original Documents No. 3.
[2] He was a Member of the Fishmongers' Company, and was elected Alderman of Bridge Ward Without 29th January, 1638. Served the office of Sheriff in 1638, and the office of Lord Mayor in 1641-42. He was one of the Commissioners who sat upon the trial of King Charles the first, for which he was condemned to death at the Restoration, but was not executed. He was imprisoned in the Tower, where he died 17th December, 1661.
[3] Original Documents No. 4.

THE CLOCKMAKERS' COMPANY. 61

us, as may appear by theis particulars. First, whereas, considering the exacting of xii^d. per quarter besides money from each member and many donations at admissions some place might have bin purchased, where we might have mett in an orderly and decent manner, we have bin constantly sumoned to Taverns and Ale houses and such disorderly places to ye great desparagement of ye Company.

"Whereas the Charter was in especiall manner procured for ye restraint of strangers and foreigners, they have not only countenanced and abetted them but entertayned for many years in their own houses although never soe often complained of to the great trouble and hindrance of the Freemen, and not only so but have frequently bound Apprentices to Freemen for foreigners and strangers and with them they have served their whole time, and then the Court of Assistants by their Warden presents them to the Chamberlaine and soe they become Freemen, as if they had served their whole time with Freemen, by which the Citty is abused and the Company prejudiced nor can wee reasonably expect reliefe while Frenchmen who are foreigners are admitted to rule the Freemen, yea they have lately endeavoured to bring in another Frenchman to their Assistants who was no wayes capable to judge of our Art and to effect this, they privately in an evening sumoned a Taverne Court or a Court at a Taverne, such Government being suitable to such place.

"Whereas there is an Order, which hath bin often renewed, for restraining the multiplicity of Apprentices, they have yet contrary to the said Order permitted Apprentices to be multiplied whereby the Trade is almost ruined.

"And that these abuses might be without remedy, when from time to time complaints have bin made by severall of ye Company, as if they were conscious of their guilt, instead of reforming they have presently taken into ye Assistants the most active of such complayners and soe ye complainte ceased. Now the unreasonableness of such practises hath bin so evident that several of our Apprentices having observed it, and fearing that the end of their services would be the beginning of beggary, they made their address to the late Lord Mayor for reliefe, and being sensible of the reasonablenes of their demands have since taken it into our own hands and did then acquaint his honour how the case stood, whereupon the Master and Wardens being warned to appear before his honour they chose to invite us to meet them at ye Rose Tavern that if possible there might be an accomodacon, where being mett they tould us, as they had done many yeares before, that they were resolved to reforme the abuses wee complained of, but wee being wearied out with such promises and no performance we had no ground to believe them. Several expedients were propounded and at last it was agreed that for our better security two of our number should attend every Court to see the execucon of these Orders, and as it was then also agreed, there should bee delivered to the said two subjoined officers a Register of all the Masters and Apprentices, all which was after confirmed at a full Quarter Court, and accordingly the same subjoined Officers did meet and act with them several Courte Dayes in the execucon of the said Orders, though with their great regret as appeared by their reproaching them that the Company needed noe Supervisors and asking them what they came for, and when they saw all this would not beate them from their duty, and that we would noe longer accept of dead orders without execucon, they then at a Court held at the Rose Tavern declared the said Orders null, and that ye sub-officers should noe more bee sumoned to attend at their Courts.

F 2

THE CLOCKMAKERS' COMPANY.

"And whereas it was agreed by them lately that if we would bring in a list of those foreigners and strangers by whom we were agrieved they would joine with us in the prosecuting of them, when at a Court we since presented them with a list, they asked us if wee would have them tear out the bowells of ye Companie, soe deare are those strangers and foreigners to them, and bad us seek our remedy ourselves.

"All which promises considered and your petic̃oners observing a more then ordinary readiness in your Lordship to reform abuses wee are encoraged to beseech and implore your honour's assistance and power for our relief.

"Signed by Thomas Loomes

"Ahasuerus Fromantell and 31 other Members."

A counter petition was also presented to the Lord Mayor from some other Freemen of the Company denying the foregoing allegations and stating that several who had signed that Petition were not even Members of the Company, and further praying his Lordship not to allow this false clamour to injure the best interests of the Company.

"To the Right Honourable the Lord Maior of the Cittie of London.

"The humble petic̃on of the Freemen and Clockmakers of the Citty of London.

"Humbly Sheweth,—That whereas your Petitioners are given to understand that severall petic̃ons have been lately presented to your Honour by divers persons who style themselves by the name and title of the Company of Clockmakers of London, whereas indeed some of them are not members of the said Company and many of them most guilty of the grievances complained of by them in the said petic̃ons.

"And Whereas there was a meeting the 8th of this instant September by the Maister and Wardens of the said Company divers of the said grevances were presented, and your former petitioners found all readiness and willingness in the said Maister, Wardens and Assistants to the utmost of their power to redresse the same. But notwithstanding all their endeavours in order to a reconciliation nothing would content or satisfy them, but pressed to have the elecc̃on of Maister, Wardens and Assistants amongst themselves, or soe many of them to be joyned to the Assistants as might equalize them in number, which is contrary to the true intent and meaning of the Charter and thereby would make a final distrucc̃on of the whole Company.

"Your Petitioners therefore humbly beseech your Honour that the Corporac̃on and Government of the said Company may continue as now it doth, and that no obstrucc̃ons or disadvantages may happen to the said Company by any such false clamours and pretences, and that your petic̃oners may find all lawfull favour for the suppression of the said disorders.

"And your Petitioners shall pray &c.

"Thomas Taylor   "Jerimie Gregory
"Edmond Grinkin   "Edward Hollidaie
"Jeremie East   "Francis Mathew
"Evan Jones   "William Clay
"David Moodie   "Robert Robinson
"Henry Erbery   "John Cooke
"Ambrose Blisse   "Isaack Daniell."

The Company appear to have submitted an answer to the Lord Mayor in which they gave a general denial to the complaints alleged, especially as to strangers ruling the Company, except one who was a principal man in procuring the Charter in which his name was inserted.

The intervention of the Lord Mayor does not appear to have brought matters to a peaceable solution, as is shewn by the following supplementary Petition of some of the Freemen :—

[1] "To the Right Honourable the Lord Maior of the Citty of London.

"The humble petition of [the several Freemen of] the Company of Clockmakers.

"SHEWETH,—That your Petitioners having formerly made their addresse to your Lordship for redresse of their greevances wee thought it our duty to give your Lordship this further accompt that your Lordship may understand our moderation and readines to compose our differences in an orderly way, wee desire your Lordship to take notice that according to an agreement between us since our being with your Lordship wee gave a meeting to the Court of Assistants and wee did then deliver to them in writing some of our principall greivances, which they having examined and also abundantly acknowledged to be true, they desired us to propose a remedy, which we then also gave them in writing, which according to our understanding they might justly grant as an effectual remedy to our grevances.

"The Copies of both which writings are hereunto annexed, and when upon their refusall wee saw no hopes of a right understanding or composure of our differences, wee then propounded that the matters in debate might be referred to the determination of your Lordship and the honourable Court of Aldermen, to whose wisdome and censure we still desire to refer ourselves, but all our tenders were with much scorne rejected so that we are againe necessitated to cast ourselves againe upon your Lordship for direction and assistance herein. My Lord we doe humbly beseech your Lordship to compassionate the grievances of a poor expiring Society. If our demands were the sence of a factious parte wee should not dare to approach to your Honour, but both the greevances and the remedy wee have proposed being the joint sence of the whole Company being a greate number of Artists made poore by these grievances wee thought our desires to your Honour might be the more considerable.

	"SAMUEL VERNON
"WILLIAM GODBUD	"THOMAS CLAXTON
"LAUNCELLOTT MEREDITH	"AHASUERUS FROMANTEEL
"JOHN MATTCHETT	"JOHN DRAKE
"THOMAS DANIELL	"WILLIAM COMFORT.

[1] Original Documents, No. 12.

"8 September 1656.

[1] "Wee the Company of Clockmakers doe present our Agrievances in generall

"1. Imprimis for allowing fforiners to worke & trade wthin ye citty and ye Liberties thereof.

"2. For ye number of Prentices sufferd to be bound by your orders contrary to ye Charter.

"3. For making free prentices wthout their proofe pfecte.

"4. For making men free turnd-over to fforiners and strangers.

"5. For presenting men to be made free of ye City wthout satisfying ye Company.

"6. For not being diligent in their searches.

"8th September, 1656.

[2] "To the end that we may for the time to come enjoy the benefit of our Charter we make these proposals (viz.)

"Imprimis, that an order be made that for time to come such as are admitted to be members of the Company, should have their voyce in chusing of Master, Wardens and Assistants, and to the end that it might be done orderly wee desire to make choice of so many and no more as are in the Court of Assistants and they jointly to have their vote with the Court of Assistants in the choice of their Officers from time to time as often as there shall be need of chusing of Officers for the Company, for as wee are all the freedome we have is to make our Complaints to the Court of Assistants and wee find them so generally disaffected to the publick good and so troubled at our proceedings that wee have rather cause to feare that some order or other will be made to crosse us, and so wee lesse able to relieve ourselves in time to come.

"2. And therefore our next proposition is that the Master and Wardens and Assistants doe governe the Company according to the orders in being, and that no alteration be made by making new orders without the consent of such who shall have power to chuse the Officers of the Company.

"3. And if you are free to these propositions wee shall not desire to lay open our greevances unto the magistrate any farther, but shall endeavour to the best of our abillities both in purse and person to assist you to recover the Company out of that confusion wherein wee are brought."

What steps, if any, were taken by the Court to satisfy the Complainants, whose chief object appears to have been to obtain a voice and authority in the government of the Company, which belonged to the former, and the concession whereof would have been in contravention of the Charter, does not appear, and for several years afterwards no further reference to such matters is contained amongst the Records.

[1] Original Documents, No. 6.   [2] Original Documents, No. 7.

In the year 1677 the abuses in the trade became so great and patent that the attention of the Court of Assistants was again directed to the question how best to deal with them. Several plans were proposed and examined, and after considerable debate a Committee was on the 23rd of August in that year appointed to advise the Court thereon, and the terms of the reference as entered in the Minute Book are as follow:—

"Whereas there hath been and is some doubt made of the sufficiency of the authority and power which the Company hath and a suspect that there needeth some further and better power in some especiall cases for the better government of the Members thereof, and for their proficiency in the Art and performance of workes and matters relating thereto, and especially that such deceipts or abuses as might otherwise be put upon his Majesties subjects may be prevented for the future, This Court for these ends did desire and appoint that the Master and Wardens and these five Assistants, namely, Mr. Horne, Mr. Bell, Mr. Barrow, Mr. Wynn, and Mr. Jones, or any four, should be a Committee to peruse the Charter and Ordinances of the Company and consult and consider all things conducing or relating to those ends, and if need shall be to cause a breviate to be drawne by the Clarke fitt to be perused by such Councell as they shall thinke fitt to apply themselves to and receive their opinion and advice in the case and to report." [1]

On the 4th of September, 1677, Mr. Coxeter, Mr. Nicasius and Mr. Taylor, of Holborn, were added to the Committee.

On the 17th September, 1677, the Charter and Ordinances having been abbreviated, and a Case prepared for Counsel's opinion, it was ordered that Mr. Serjeant Pemberton be waited upon and his[2] opinion obtained.

In 1680 the subject was again brought under the notice of the Court of Assistants, and their Minutes bear evidence of their anxiety to obtain some satisfactory settlement of the difficulty.

[3] At a Court held on the 21st February, 1677-8, a consultation was had as to the desirability of obtaining an Act of Parliament for strengthening the Company's Charter and Ordinances, and for additional or enlargement of power where wanting. It was resolved that Mr. Richard Antrobus should be consulted as to the matter, and that the Court should meet

---

[1] Company's Journal I.   [2] Fee to be paid Two Guineas.
[3] Company's Journal I.

at the White Hart Tavern, Lothbury, on the 4th of March, then following, for that purpose.

[*No entry is to be found of the results of this action*].

[1] "1680. May 3. Upon consideration that there are many refractory and unconformable Members of this Company and divers who exercise the Art or some branch of it and do not come into the Company or conform to the search, rule, and government thereof, and many irregularities inconveniences and abuses are grown in and put upon the Company and the Art. It was thought fit, resolved and ordered That

" The Master and Wardens   " Mr. Thomas Taylor (Holborne)
" Mr. Jeremie Gregory   " Mr. John Harris
" Mr. John Browne   " Mr. Nathaniel Barrow
" Mr. Richard Jarratt   ." Mr. Henry Wynn
" Mr. Edward Norris   and
" Mr. Thomas Hancorne   " Mr. Henry Jones

or any five of these before named ten Assistants with the Master and Wardens, or the Master and one Warden, or in the absence of the Master two of the Wardens, shall be and are a Committee to continue for three months to be accounted from this day, to meet from time to time, at such time and place as the Master shall think fit and appoint and to consider consult and resolve upon the wayes and meanes of bringing those refractory Members of the Company and others exerciseing the Art to conformity, and for reformation and future prevention of those or the like irregularities inconveniences and abuses, which are grown and put, or may grow and be put upon the Company, and the Art and for punishment of the Offenders. And that the said Committee shall from time to time acquaint the Court with their proceedings therein."

The Committee thus appointed met from time to time, and from their proceedings entered in the Court Minute books the following Extracts have been taken:—

"1680. May 21. The said Committee Resolved to acquaint the next Monthly Court That they conceive it fit and needful

"1. That the Company's Charter shall be publicly read to the Master Wardens and Assistants at the next Quarter Court.

"2. That the Ordinances of the Company shall be perused and those put in due execution that are for the good of the Company.

"3. That the Members of the Committee shall at the next Court give in their opinions what are the reasons of the decay of the trade.

"4. And that Mr. Hartley, Sword Cutler, living in New Street near Shoe Lane, who maketh pin cases and tradeth in Watches and Clocks, not having served seven years to the Trade, and such others as at the next Monthly Court shall be thought fit and appointed, shall be summoned by a particular Summons to appear at the next Quarter Court.

---

[1] Company's Journal I.

"1680. May 24. The Committee Resolved to acquaint the next Monthly Court that they conceived it fit and needful

"1. That the Clerk write a copy of the Ordinance of the Company of Blacksmiths, which is ingrossed in the Book of Ordinances of this Company giving allowance, That those free of the Blacksmiths and professing Clockmaking (not being great Church Clockmakers of Iron) may bind their Apprentices to some free Clockmaker to the intent that some of the Committee may (as they are intended) discourse the Master of that Company and endeavour to have the full consent of that Company for the performance thereof for the future."

On the 7th June, 1680, the Reports of the Committee were submitted to the Court, who selected a certain number of persons, carrying on the trade in Watches, Clocks, &c., to be summoned to attend at the next Quarter Court, some of whose names appear at the next Meeting as having been admitted to the Freedom.

For more convenient reference, and to facilitate the business of the Company by affording its Members a better knowledge of its powers, rights, and privileges, a Committee was appointed in the year 1722 to digest the Charter and Ordinances, and suitably arrange the several provisions thereof under proper heads :—

"1722. February 4. Whereas the severall points contained in the Companies Charter and book of Ordinances have not as yett been putt into any regular method, and the severall orders and constitutions since made from time to time by the said Company are only entered in the books of the Company in order of time as they were made, whereby the search for any one single point is rendered difficult and troublesome. To remedy which it is this day ordered that the Master and Wardens or any three of them, whereof the Master to be one, be appointed a Committee to examine Charter and Ordinances, and all the severall orders since made, and digest them under proper heads for the more ready turning to the same, and report their proceedings to the next Quarter Court with what they shall think further needfull to compleat the end proposed, and the said Committee are hereby empowered to defray the necessary expences of their proceedings out of the Companies stock." [1]

In order that the Charter might be better understood by all, it was on the 4th November, 1765, determined that the Clerk should in future read it, immediately after dinner at the Christmas Quarter Court.

On the 2nd of December following the Bye-Laws were ordered to be advertised in the *Gazette* on the Saturday before Christmas Day, and in the *Daily Advertizer and*

[1] Company's Journal III.

Gazetteer on the Tuesday before Christmas Day, and in the *Public Ledger* on the 5th or 6th of January following.[1]

By their Charter the Company was authorised to consist of Members using the Art or Mystery of Clockmaking, whether freemen of London or otherwise, within ten miles of the City, and to make laws and ordinances for the good rule and government of all persons using the trade within those limits, or within the realm of England or dominion of Wales, but doubts appear to have arisen as to their authority to enforce some of their powers, notably those for compelling the trade outside the City to become Freemen of the Company or to pay Quarterage, and accordingly the Court on the 2nd November, 1795, determined to obtain legal advice thereon, and appointed a Committee to consult a Solicitor, Mr. King, of Cutlers' Hall, being selected for that purpose. The Committee, whose proceedings are duly recorded in the Minutes, determined to obtain the opinion of Mr. Serjeant Adair (afterwards Recorder of London), and on the 1st February, 1796, they duly presented their Report, which was taken into consideration by the Court on the 11th of the same month, and the Report, together with the proceedings of the Court thereon, are contained in the following Extract :—

"1796. February 11. The Master declared the purpose of the Meeting, agreable to the order of the last Monthly Court, when a motion was made

"That the report of the Committee be now read, which being seconded and carried the report was accordingly read, and is as follows, viz.

"The report of the Committee appointed by the Court of Assistants of the Worshipful Company of Clockmakers of the City of London, pursuant to a resolution made by the said Court on the 2nd day of November 1795, whereby it was

"Resolved that application should be made to some professional Gentleman of the Law to examine the Charter and Bye Laws of the Company, and that Mr. King, of Cutlers Hall, should be applied to for that purpose.

"That in pursuance of the said resolution the Committee applied to the said Mr. King, and that he with Mr. Gatty his partner have examined the said Charter and Bye Laws, and that several doubts existing thereon, they have prepared a case and submitted the same with several Queries thereon to the opinion of Mr. Sergeant Adair,

"That the first Query stated for the said Counsel's opinion, was whether the Court could by any and what means, under the Charter and Bye Laws, compel Freemen of the Company to take upon them the Livery.

[1] Company's Journal IV.

"That the said Counsel is of opinion that the Bye Law is certainly deficient, in not having annexed a specific penalty and though he is inclined to think (upon the authority of the case, in the 2 Leo: 200 & 5 Mod: 319) that upon complaint to the Mayor, and Aldermen of London, the Court might commit the party elected to the Livery, for refusing to take upon him such Livery, yet as such proceeding has not been very usual, and he knows of no instance later than that reported in 5 Mod., he would rather advise the Company to make a new Bye Law annexing a reasonable penalty.

"That the Committee have considered of the 1st Query and the opinion of Counsel thereon, and are of opinion that it will be beneficial to the said Company, that a Bye Law should be immediately made annexing a penalty of Fifteen Pounds on any person refusing to take up the Livery of the said Company.

"That the 2nd Query stated for the said Counsel's opinion was—Are Freemen of the Company and Freemen of other Companies, but carrying on the business of Clock and Watchmakers, and Non-Freemen who reside out of the City of London, but within ten miles thereof and carry on the business of Clock and Watchmakers, liable to pay Quarterage or any and which of them.

"That the said Counsel in his opinion says, he has entertained great doubts respecting the validity of the Charters of those Companies of the City of London which extended their jurisdiction beyond that City and the liberties thereof and also of the efficacy of such their Bye Laws, as professed to bind persons without those limits, and not free of the Company, but in a late Case of the Butchers Company, whose Charter incorporated all those of the City of London or within two miles thereof, upon a Case reserved for the Opinion of the Court of Common Pleas, upon the validity of a Bye Law, both these objections were taken, and were overruled by the unanimous opinion of that Court. He is therefore of opinion that all the persons who are the subject of this Query are liable to the payment of Quarterage, under the Bye Laws on that subject.

"The Committee are therefore of opinion and recommend, that all persons who are the subject of the above Query should be immediately applied to for payment thereof, and in case of refusal, proper steps should be taken to enforce it.

"That the 3rd Query stated for the said Counsel's opinion was—Can the Clockmakers Company compel Clockmakers, who are free of another Company, to become Members of the Clockmakers' Company, and can they also compel Non-Freemen who follow the business of Clock and Watchmakers and reside within the City, or ten miles thereof, to become Members of the same Company, by any and what means.

"That the said Counsel in his opinion says that he does not think the Clockmakers' Company have any means of compelling persons exercising that Trade to become free of their Company, otherwise than by the aid of the Act of Common Council above stated [1] which cannot operate beyond the City and liberties of London, and therefore they cannot compel persons exercising the trade within ten miles of London, but beyond the liberties thereof, to take up their Freedom, but such persons may continue to exercise the Trade under

---

[1] This Act is dated 15 October, 1765, and is given at length under the Chapter on Freemen.

the direction and government, and subject to the reasonable Bye Laws of the Company, without being free thereof, the Act however of the Common Council appears to him to be valid in itself and binding upon all persons, within the City and liberties of London, this and similar Acts being supported by the customs of the City of London, confirmed by divers Acts of Parliament; he is therefore of opinion that Freemen of other Companies, who were not so in December, 1765, and Non-Freemen, resident within the City and liberties of London, using the Trade in question, may be compelled to become free of the Clockmakers' Company, or desist from their business, by enforcing the Act of Common Council of the City of London which affixes a penalty of £5 for every such offence.

"The Committee are therefore of opinion and recommend that Freemen of other Companies who were not so in December 1765, and Non-Freemen resident within the City and liberties of London using the Trade in question be immediately called upon to take upon them the freedom of the Clockmakers' Company, and in case of refusal, that proper steps be taken to enforce the due observance thereof.

"The 4th Query stated, for the said Counsel's opinion was—Are Members of the Clockmakers' Company who are of other Companies and Clock and Watchmakers, who are free of other Companies, but not of the Clockmakers', and those who follow the Trade, but are Non-Freemen, liable to any, and what penalty in case they take an Apprentice who is bound to any other person than a free brother of the Clockmakers' Company and properly entered as such in the Company's Books.

"'That the said Counsel is of opinion: that Members of the Clockmakers' Company, and Freemen of other Companies, are liable to the penalty of Ten Pounds if they take an Apprentice who is bound to any other person than a free Brother pursuant to the Clause of the Charter above stated; but neither the words of the Charter relative to this, nor the Bye Law imposing the penalty extend to Non-Freemen, and therefore he does not think the penalty could be levied against them, but as no person can exercise that, or any other Trade, within the City and liberties of London without being free, the provision of the Charter and Bye Laws taken together with the Act of Common Council, which oblige all persons exercising that Trade to be free of the Clockmakers' Company, seemed to be sufficient within the limits of that City and Liberties, but as to persons residing out of those limits, though within ten miles, he saw no remedy provided for this Case of Apprentices, but by a prosecution under the Statute of the 5th of Eliz., Chap. 4th., Sec. 31st.

"The Committee are therefore of opinion that it will be proper and right to proceed against any one who shall bind an Apprentice contrary to the Charter and Bye Law.

"'The 5th Query stated for the said Counsel's opinion was—That if he should be of opinion that the Charter, Bye Laws and Act of Common Council were not sufficient to enforce the above objects or either of them, in what manner would he advise the Company to act, so as to obtain power to carry the several matters into effect.

"That the said Counsel in his opinion says, the Cases in which it appears to him that the powers of the Company were insufficient to effectuate the objects referred to in the Case, were

THE CLOCKMAKERS' COMPANY.

" 1. In the means of compelling Freemen of the Company to take upon them the Livery—where he had already suggested the remedy for that to be, by making a new Bye Law, affixing an adequate penalty, payable to the Company, to be recovered by action of debt or levied by distress. To which the Committee has already submitted its opinion.

" 2. The means of compelling persons exercising the Trade to become free of the Clockmakers' Company either as to those residing within or without the City and Liberties of London ; as to those resident within the said City and liberties, the Act of Common Council is sufficient for that purpose ; as to those resident without the City and Liberties, but within ten miles, he thought nothing short of an Act of Parliament could enable the Company to compel them, and he did not incline to think that such an Act of Parliament could be obtained.

" 3. In the means of preventing persons taking Apprentices in the Art or Mistery of Clockmaking who are not free of the Clockmakers' Company, and reside out of the City and liberties of London, this also he thought could only be done by Act of Parliament."

The Court having debated on the report by putting each Article separate, it was moved, that this Court do agree with the Committee in their report, which was accordingly carried.

" 1796. April 4. Resolved, That the following be an additional Bye Law of the Company, viz.

" It is further ordained that if any person of the said fellowship being so as aforesaid chosen to be of the said Livery shall, without any reasonable and sufficient cause, to be allowed and admitted by the said Master, Wardens and Assistants, refuse to accept and take upon him to be of the said Livery, and shall refuse to take, within fourteen days next after notice to him given of such his election as aforesaid, such Oath as by the Ordinance in that behalf made is appointed to be taken ; That then and in every such case, every such person so refusing, shall forfeit and pay to, and for the use of the said Master, Wardens and fellowship, the sum of Fifteen Pounds to be recovered by action of debt or levied by distress."

On the 14th of April, 1796, Messrs. King and Gatty were ordered to apply to obtain a confirmation of the proposed Bye-Law. They submitted the same to the Lord Chancellor, and the Chief Justice, of the King's Bench and Common Pleas, who approved and allowed it in the terms above stated.[1]

The costs incurred, amounting to £52 10s. 0d., were on the 10th of October, 1796, ordered to be paid by the Renter Warden.

---

[1] *Vide* page 49.

ARMS, SEALS, BADGES, COLOURS, &c.

It was not until the year 1671 that the Company obtained the right to bear Arms. On the 15th of January of that year the Court of Assistants determined to apply for a grant, their Resolution being in the following terms :—

> "'It was agreed voated and ordered That the Company shall take upon them a Coat of Armes fitt and proper for them to beare and that for the procureing thereof all fees whatsoever for perfecting the same and the pattent as shall be needfull in the case, so that it may be brought and shall be brought free of all further charge to the Master or Wardens of the Company, the Renter Warden shall expend and pay ffive and twenty pounds, And the Master and Wardens Mr. East Mr. Nicasius and Mr. Jeremie Gregorie are desired and ordered to treat and agree with Sir Edward Walker King at Armes and to act in this business according to this order.'"[1]

The following is the text of the Grant of Arms eventually obtained :—

To all and singular UNTO whom these presents shall come S^R· EDWARD WALKER KNIGHT GARTER PRINCIPALL KING OF ARMES OF ENGLISHMEN sendeth greeting

Whereas the generous Actions and Virtuous Endeavours of Worthy Men, as also of Bodyes Politique and Incorporate have beene from time to time remembred to Posterity by certaine Honourable signes and markes commonly called ARMES, as proper testimonyes of the worth and meritt of those to whom such have been assigned. **And Whereas** his late Maiestie KING CHARLES the first of ever glorious and blessed memory, for divers Causes and Considerations him thereunto moveing Did of his especiall grace certaine knowledg and meere motion by his Letters

---

[1] Company's Journal I.

Patents under the Great Seale of England, bearing Date the Two and Twentyth day of August in the seaventh yeare of his Reigne, Incorporate, Create, Make, Erect, Ordeyne, and Constitute The CLOCKMAKERS resideing in the City of London, Suburbs thereof or within Tenn Miles of the said City, To be one Body, Corporate and Politique by the name of THE MASTER WARDENS AND FELLOWSHIP OF THE ART OR MISTERY OF CLOCKMAKING OF THE CITY OF LONDON, To have perpetuall Succession and Continuance for ever With divers other Grants, Libertyes, Priviledges and Franchises, as in the said Letters Patents the same are more amply expressed. Amongst which his said late Maiestie Did authorise the said Master Wardens and Fellowship of the Art and Mistery of Clockmaking To use a Common Seale for the Expediting of the Causes and Businesses of them and their successors In which regard And also for the greater Honour and Splendor of the said Company and Fellowship it is and will be necessary that proper and peculiar Armes and Ensignes be assigned them to be used in their Comon Seal and all other fitt occasions.

Know yee therefore that I the said S^R EDWARD WALKER KNIGHT GARTER PRINCIPALL KING OF ARMES by the power and authority annexed unto my Office and confirmed unto me by Letters Patents under the Great Seale of England Do by these presents give grant and assigne, unto the said Incorporate Company and Society useing the Art and Mistery of Clockmakeing in the City of London the Suburbs and within Tenn Miles thereof, whereof at present Nicholas Coxeter is Master, Samuell Horne and Jeffery Baily are Wardens as also Edward East the only person now living of those mentioned in the said Letters Patents of Incorporation, John Nicasius, John Pennock, Edmond Gilpin, Jeremie Gregory, Thomas Taylor, Thomas Clayton, John Freeman, Evan Jones, Isaac Daniell, John Matchett, Ralph Almond, Samuell Vernon, Henry Kent, Walter Hayes, John Browne, Nicholas Payne, Richard Ames and Benjamin Bell are Assistants and to the rest of the Fellowship and Company thereof, and to their successors for ever The Armes, Crest, Supporters and Motto hereafter mentioned, vizt. SABLE, A CLOCK Y^e 4 PILLARS THEREOF ERECTED ON FOUR LYONS, AND ON EACH CAPITALL A GLOBE WITH A CROSSE, AND IN THE MIDDEST AN IMPERIALL CROWNE ALL OR, AND FOR THEIR CREST UPON AN HELMET PROPER MANTLED GULES DOUBLED ARGENT AND WREATH OF THEIR COLOURS A SPHEARE OR, THE ARMES SUPPORTED BY THE FIGURES OF A NAKED OLD MAN HOLDING A SCITHE AND AN HOUR GLASSE REPRESENTING TIME, AND OF AN EMPEROUR IN ROABES CROWNED HOLDING A SCEPTER: THEIR MOTTO

TEMPVS RERVM IMPERATOR

As in the Margent they are all more lively Depicted. The which ARMES, CREST, SUPPORTERS and MOTTO, the said Master Wardens, Fellowshipp and Company useing the Art and Mistery of Clockmakeing commonly called Clockmakers and their successors for ever, may and shall lawfully use in their Common Seale and beare and sett forth in Shield, Coat Armour, Standard, Pennon, or otherwise, upon all occasions without the lett or interruption of any person whomsoever.

In Witness whereof I have hereunto subscribed my Name and affixed the seale of my Office, this One and Thirtyth day of January in the Four and Twentyth yeare of the Reigne of our Soveraigne Lord CHARLES the Second.

by the grace of God, King of England, Scotland, France, and Ireland. Defender of the Faith, etc. Annoq Domini 167⅜

EDW WALKER

GARTER

The Grant which bears the Signature of Sir Edward Walker,[1] and the Seal of his Office, cost the Company £25.

The Arms thus obtained have since been in constant use by the Company, and the following references to their employment on plates, seals, badges, etc., have been gathered from their Records.

"1677. September 24. Mr. George Deane, Engraver, a Member of this Company, having by the hands of Mr. Henry Jones presented to this Court the Company's Coat of Arms engraved on a copper plate fit to be used for tickets and divers other occasions of the Company which was very well liked, This Court did kindly accept it and returned him thanks.[2]

"1695. June 3. It was Ordered that Daniell Beeckman be paid by the Renter Warden forty shillings for engraving the Company's Coat of Arms on a new Copper Plate to be used on Quarter Court days Bills or Summonses.

SEALS.

"1692. March 6. It was resolved and ordered that for the Company's occasions and convenience the Master shall with what speed he conveniently can cause a Common Seal of Silver about the breadth or circomference of a milled Half Crown piece, or Oval to be made as the Company are impowred to do by their Charter of Incorporation. Which seal is to be so and according to the Company's Coat of Armes, Supporters, Mantling, Crest and Motto.[3]

"1819. October 11. It was resolved to provide an Official Seal engraved with the Company's Arms in lieu of that now in custody of the Clerk. This was carried into effect at a cost of £7.17.6.

---

[1] Appointed by King Charles I in 1645, but upon the death of the King he was deprived of his Office, restored by Charles II, October 1662, died February 19, 1677.
[2] Company's Journal I.   [3] Company's Journal II.

MASTER'S BADGE.

WARDEN'S BADGE.

BADGES.

"1873. January 13. The desirability of providing a Badge to be worn by the Master on all official occasions having been suggested by several Members and Mr. Parker Member of the Court having been requested to furnish a design for the same, that Gentleman laid before them a sketch of one which he had specially prepared for that purpose when it was Resolved unanimously That a Badge composed of the Company's Arms, Crest and Motto be furnished for the use of the Master for the time being, to be worn by him on all official occasions, and that the same be made in 18 Carat Gold and Enamel at an expence not exceeding sixty pounds.[1]

"1873. April 7. Mr. Parker laid before the Court the Gold Badge to be worn by the Master on all official occasions. The same having been inspected was pronounced to be a highly artistic specimen of Goldsmith's work and received the unqualified approval of the whole Court. The Master was then formally invested with his insignia of office.

"1874. July 6. George William Adams Esq. presented to the Court a set of three Silver Gilt official Badges containing the Arms of the Company in accordance with the design submitted at the last Court to be worn by the Wardens during their tenure of office. The Master having accepted the same on behalf of the Court and having invested each of the Wardens with his distinctive Badge, it was Resolved unanimously That the best thanks of this Court be and are hereby presented to G. W. Adams Esq. for the very handsome gift so kindly presented for the use of the Wardens and that the Clerk be instructed to convey to that Gentleman the Court's high appreciation of his kind and liberal consideration."[2]

In 1767, the year following the grant of a Livery by the Court of Aldermen, the Company provided the necessary paraphernalia to enable them to take their place in processions on State and other occasions, and from the following Extracts having reference thereto, it would seem that they first appeared as a Livery Company in the pageant of the Right Hon. Thomas Harley, Lord Mayor in the above-mentioned year:—

"1767. April 6. Ordered that Colours and Beadle's Staff be provided by the Company against Lord Mayor's Day and that application be made to the City Surveyor to know where the Stand for the Company should be. Ordered that there be a Committee of the whole Court for the above business and that five of them be a Quorum to do business, of which the Master and one of the Wardens to be two.

"1767. May 4. Ordered that the Crest on the Beadle's Staff be of Silver, and that Mr. Pope be employed to provide and paint the Colours and Streamers proper for the Company.

"1767. September 29. Ordered that Mr. Brewerton do attend the next Quarter Court with a dress proper for the porters.

---

[1] [2] Company's Journal X.

"Ordered the Whifflers and the lads to hold up the Train: the Beadle's Staff and a Wainscot Box for Colours, and the Ribbons and the Music, and all the other things necessary for the Lord Mayor's Day be left to the Master and Wardens to provide.'

"1767. October 28. Paid Mr. Moliere for chasing the Beadle's Staff, and for Silver and for making it £36 9 5.

"1767. November 9. The Master attended by the Livery, walked in procession, agreable to the precept sent by the Lord Mayor and Court of Aldermen."[1]

The costs incurred by the Company on the above occasion were not inconsiderable, as will be seen from the following items from their accounts:—

	£	s.	d.
"1768. March 14.			
"Expence of the Dinner on Lord Mayors Day	21	12	9
" do for ordering the last mentioned	1	3	11
" do for 8 Staves	0	6	0
" do for Music	4	4	0
" Paid for Robes for Lord Mayors Day	5	8	0
" do Mr. Pope for painting the Colours	49	2	0
" do for a Chest for the Colours	2	12	6"

On the 9th of November, 1859, Mr. Alderman Carter, the Master of the Company, being Lord Mayor, the Company occupied the post of honor in the Civic procession to Westminster Hall, to present him in accordance with ancient custom to the Barons of the Exchequer, for which occasion a handsome silk banner of the Arms of the Company was presented by Francis Bryant Adams, Esq., a Member of the Court.

The Company also possesses the following Colours:—
The City Arms and Supporters.
The Arms of Mr. Alderman Carter.
The Arms of Mr. Alderman Kennedy.

In connexion with the subject of the Arms of the Company, it may be mentioned that upon applications made to them they have aided in the embellishment of public buildings in the City, by presenting their Armorial bearings in painted glass; thus in the year 1841, at the request of the Governors of Christ's Hospital, they gave part of a window for the Great Hall of that establishment; and again in 1872, at the instance of the Council of the London and Middlesex Archæological Society, they joined with other Companies in similarly contributing to the decoration of the New Library and Museum of the Corporation at Guildhall.

---

[1] Company's Journal IV.

COURT OF ASSISTANTS.

BY the terms of the Company's Charter, the governing body is to consist of the Master, three Wardens, and ten or more Assistants, the first holders of those Offices being named in the Charter.

Their first formal Meeting was held on the 12th October, 1632. At their second, on the 23rd of the same month, they determined by Resolution their usual hour of Assembling.

"1632. October 23rd. This daye the Court have thought and soe ordered that the howerly meetinges at the severall Courts hereafter for the Master Wardens and Assistants shalbe at the hower of Nyne, and their departure from the said Courts by Twelve at the furthest the same day upon the penalty conteyned in the ordinaunces of the Lawe."[1]

They next passed a Resolution intended to ensure the preservation of their secrets, and bound themselves by a penalty to observe the same.

[2] "1632. October 23rd. Forasmuch as many Inconveniences may happen in not keeping the secrettes of the Companie that from tyme to tyme may be spoaken of and done at a Court of Assistants, It is thereupon hereby ordered that if Master, Wardens, Assistant or Servaunt shalbe at any tyme found to be guilty of such a fault committed in that kind in falsefying his oath of trust in not keeping the Companies secrettes which may tend to the prejudice of the Companie in generall or of any particular Member, he or they soe offending shall forfeit the some of ffive pounds. In wittnes whereof and for confirmation

[1] [2] Company's Journal I.

of the same wee hereundernamed did setto our hands to the same order of Court viz.

Henry Archer Deputy Master
John Willow
Sampson Shelton } Wardens
James Vaultrollier
John Smith
Frauncis Foreman
John Harris
Richard Morgan

Samuel Lynnaker
John Charlton
John Middnall } Assistants
Symon Bartram
Edward East
and
Thomas Copley, Clarke."

A regulation was also made to encourage good feeling and brotherhood, and for prohibiting the use of profane and uncivil language.

"1632. October 23rd. This daye the Court have ordered That if any person or persons admitted of this Societie shall hereafter be found to be profane or lavish in uncivil manner to blaspheame in takinge the Name of the Lord in vaine to the dishonor of his name and discredditt both of the Companie and himself he shall for ever hereafter be subject to what censure the Companie in their judgment shall thinke fitt either by fine or other punishment."[1]

Numerous instances of Fines being imposed are contained in the Court Minute Books, but a few will suffice to show the custom :—

"1638. October 8. At this Court Mr. Thomas Reeve did justifye ye abusive words spoken by John Potter, Beadle against Mr. Symon Hackett Warden, which were not to passe without punishment or fine according to the judgement of this Court and the words were further to be considered on at the next Quarter Court and likewise all other matters as shall be then objected against him.

"1657. April 20. The same day upon complaint of Mr. Jeremy Gregory against Thomas Weeks, the said Weeks having abused Warden Coxeter Ann Gregory and others that were in the search, He was fined a Marke in English Money for his offence, and in not coming to this court day.[2]

"1668. September 29. Forasmuch as Mr. John Nicasius one of the Assistants of this Company did at an Assembly of the Master Wardens and Assistants of this Company upon the 30th day of July last utter divers undecent words and opprobrious speeches revileing and villifying Mr. Jeremy Gregory the Master of the Company and to the breach of brotherly love, of which the Master made his complaint at the last Court, and thereupon and by order of the same Court the said Mr. Nicasius hath bin duly sumoned to appeare at this Court that he might make his defence and that such proceedings might be therein as by the ordinances of the Company is in such case appointed and he hath nevertheless made default in appearance :—therefore this Court have thought fit and doe judge determine and order that he shalbe

---

[1,2] Company's Journal 1.

againe somoned to appeare, att the next Court being Monday the 5th day of October next, and in case he doe not appeare then and give fitting satisfaction he shall pay for such his misdemeanor, the sume of fforty shillings (being the ffine sett by the Ordinances in this Case) to the Master and Wardens of the Company for the use of the Company.[1]

"1668. December 7. The difference betweene Mr. Nicasius and Mr. Gregory arisen upon occasion of some passionate words by each to the other at a meeting the 30th of July last was by this Court, composed, and the ffine sett upon Mr. Nicasius by the Court on the 29th of September last was remitted and the said parties were fully reconciled.[2]

"1673. April 7. Whereas at this Court, It was proved That Mr. John Nicasius hath spoken divers opprobrious and reproachfull words of the Master, one of the Wardens and one of the Assistants of the Company, tending much to their damage and disreputation and also as to the lessening the validity of the Charter, he for that his offence and misdemeanour is ffined and ordered to pay Forty Shillings to the use of the Master Wardens and ffellowship.[3]

"1673-4. February 2. Mr. Nicasius appeared and laid downe his ffine of fforty shillings which at the Court of the 7th of April last he was ordered to pay, and did acknowledge himselfe to be sorry for the injury he had by his passionate words done to the Master Warden and Assistant agrieved, and in regard of that his acknowledgment this Court did return him 35s. and ordered him to put the other ffive shillings into the poores Box which he accordingly did.[4]

"1677. August 23. Whereas at the time of solempnity of the ffeast at Goldsmiths' Hall upon the 26 day of July last, the then Stewards especially Mr. Barlow, Mr. Rookes and Mr. James Markwick did utter words which tended to the diminution of the worth of the Master Mr. Jeremie Gregory and did soe demeane themselves as that the peace of the Company was then disturbed and Brotherly love impaired, the said Mr. Rookes and Mr. Markwick haveing been summoned to appeare this day, that they might be discoursed and soe proceeded with as the Court should according as the case, and the Ordinances of the Company in such behalfe doe require and direct, they did appeare, and those their words and demeanoure were debated.[5]

Mr. Rookes and Mr. Markwick were fined 5s. each but they did not pay at that time desiring time to consider.

1677. September 4. Mr. Rookes paid his fine.

1677. September 24. Mr. Markwick not having paid his fine of 5s. was fined 20s.

1677. December 3. Mr. Markwick not having paid his fine proceedings against him before the Lord Mayor were ordered to be taken to compel him to pay.

1677-8. February 1. The difference between Mr. Markwick and the Company was settled by the good offices of Mr. Coxeter the Master. Mr. Markwick acknowledged his misdemeanor and paid 10s. of which 5s. were returned to him and the other put in the poor's Box.

[1,2,3,4,5] Company's Journal I.

"1679. May 5. Whereas Mr. Henry Jones one of the Assistants did att this Court make complaint against Mr. John Nicasius one other of the Assistants for that att the Meeting after the search made the 9th of Aprill last he had uttered many abusive words and comitted some abusive acts against him the said Mr. Jones and other Members there, all which the Master and divers Assistants then present were eye and eare witnesses of, and the Company was thereby much disturbed. It was therefore at this Court ordered that the said Mr. Nicasius before he shalbe admitted to sitt att any Court for this Company shall pay to the use of the poor of the Company 20s. which this Court hath fined him for that his misdemeanor against the Company, and if he shall hereafter offend he is from thenceforth to stand suspended from being an Assistant.

"1679. June 2. The Order of the last Court which relateth to Mr. Nicasius being read in his hearing he refused to pay the fine of 20s. then sett upon him and so departed the Court: It was resolved that he be summoned before the Lord Maior.

"1679. July 7. After considerable debate it was resolved until Mr. Nicasius paid the fine and cost of proceeding he should stand suspended from all priviledges of an Assistant."[1]

In the year 1678 one of the Court of Assistants charged with recusancy was suspended from his attendance at the Meetings of the Court.

"1678. November 4. Forasmuch as Mr. John Matchett an Assistant of this Company is well knowne to be a popish recusant, this Court did by vote (noe man gainsaying) suspend him from being warned to appear att and sitting in any Court or Meeting with the Master Wardens and Assistants of this Company or any of them upon the Company's occasions or concerns untill it shalbe otherwise thought fitt and ordered.[2]

By the Ordinances of the Company, fines were imposed upon the Members of the Court who neglected their duties.

If late the penalty was :—

	s.	d.
For the Master - - -	1	6
For Wardens and Assistants - -	1	0

If absent, or leaving without permission before the Court ended :—

	s.	d.
For the Master - - -	6	8
For Wardens and Assistants - -	5	0

"1632. October 23rd. This day Mr. Harris paid his fine of xii^d according to the Ordinaunces of the Lawe for not appearing in dew tyme after the Court was sett, and likewise prayers and the booke of orders being read.

"This daye Mr. East for the like occasion in comeing late to the Court paid his fine accordingly.

[1] Company's Journal I.

"This daye Mr. Foreman was fined for not appearing at all two Court dayes formerly, and Mr. John Smith for one, according to the Ordinaunces of the Lawe.

"1632. November 29. This daye Mr. Vaultrollier, Mr. Bartram, Mr. Charlton, Mr. Middnall, Mr. Smith, Mr. Willow and Mr. Foreman all paid their fines for coming too late to the Court.

"1633. August 5. This Court day Timothy Gray appeared and was fined for his contempt in going away the last quarterday without leave iii[s.] iiij[d.] which he laid down and the Court took but one shilling."

In 1676 and 1704 the Fines were varied, the alterations being shewn in the following Resolutions:—

"1676. February 5. It was ordered on account of the neglect of divers of the Members of the Court of Assistants to attend the Court at the appointed time, that there should be paid to the use of the Company by the person making default the undermentioned fine, viz.: If the Master or Warden 12 pence If an Assistant 6 pence; and in case of not appearing at all If the Master or Warden 5s. If an Assistant 3s. 4d.

"1704. November 6. Ordered that each Member of the Court of Assistants not appearing by the first hour after summons shall pay 6d. the second hour 1s. and not appearing the 3rd hour be deemed as not coming at all, The Master in each case to pay for the 1st hour 1s. 6d. 2nd hour 3s. and the 3rd hour as not coming at all and to pay 6s. 8d., The Wardens in each case of default to pay 1s. for the first hour 2s. for the 2nd and not appearing the 3rd hour to be deemed as not coming at all.

"All defaults to be decided as Members come to Court."

The fee paid by Assistants upon their election to the Court in 1761 was £7 2s. 6d.; in 1827 it was increased to £30, with 20s. to the Clerk and 10s. to the Beadle; and in 1864 it was again increased to Fifty Guineas, the Clerk being allowed thereout 40s. and the Beadle 10s.

On the 8th of October, 1759, it was agreed that a Member chosen an Assistant might be excused for the usual fine of Ten Pounds, though he had not served the office of Steward.

MASTER.

In the Company's early days it was not an unusual thing for the Master to be re-elected and to serve for two years in succession, or to be elected a second time after a lapse of a short interval. This practice, however, which prevented junior members of the Court from attaining the Chair, was successfully opposed, and on the 29th September, 1683, the following entry appears in the Minutes of the Court :—

"1683. September 29th. Memorandum That upon debate and by vote it was determined and accordingly ordered That neither the now present Master nor for the future either the then present Master nor any old or former Master shall either upon the Annual or other Election of a Master be put in nomination for Master of the Company, but that only those three persons who are next in course in point of seniority, and as they are in seniority shall be put in nomination, that one of them may be chosen Master of the Company for the year ensuing.'

A few years later the practice was again amended, and the past Masters made eligible for re-election, one of them being required to be put up with the Upper and Renter Wardens for election, as appears by the following Extract :—

"1701. July 7. At this Court the consideration was resumed of putting again in nomination those of the Court of Assistants that have been Master of the Company to be chosen again Master :—and it was upon the question put agreed unto, that one that had been Master shall be again put in nomination by putting all that have been or are Masters so that he of the past Masters that has the majority of votes shall be one of the three to be put up for Master at the election with the Upper and Renter Wardens yearly."

On the 5th of July, 1813, it was Resolved : That no person should be elected to the office of Master or Warden until he had been five years an Assistant, the regulation not to affect either of the then Members of the Court ; but on the 6th of April, 1824, in consequence of the great inconvenience experienced by the operation of this rule, the term was reduced to three years.

DEATH OR RESIGNATION OF MASTER OR WARDENS.

It is provided by the Charter that in the event of the Master or Wardens dying or resigning during his or their year of office, the Court shall meet within one month and elect one of the Wardens or a Member of the Court of Assistants to exercise the office so vacant for the remainder of the term, and swear him in accordingly.

' Company's Journal II.

The following Extracts upon this subject shew instances of the course of proceeding adopted on these occasions :—

"1665-6. February 9. Mrs. Child the Widow of Mr. Henry Child' our late deceased Master appeared upon the summons given her, And it was determined and ordered that to-morrow being Saturday the 10th instant Mr. Warden Gregory shall receive from her the Company's chest and bag of bookes and keys in her custody and upon receipt of them in good and true state shall deliver to her the bond which he and his surety gave to the Company for the true execution of his Office the said bond being delivered to Mr. Warden Gregory for that end." [2]

"1768. February 1. At this Court a letter was read from Mr. Higgs wherein he desired to resign the office of Master and that the Court would accept his resignation on account of his ill state of health; and the question being put, the majority of the Court agreed to accept thereof.

"Ordered that a special Court be called for Wednesday the 10th instant on the occasion at five o'clock in the afternoon.

"1768. February 10. At this Court Mr. Higgs' letter was read and the Court were unanimously of opinion to accept his resignation on account of his ill state of health, and appointed the next Monthly Court for the Election of a Master in his room, and ordered the Clerk to send him a letter of the resolution of the Court thereon, and the Company ordered thanks to him for his past services.

"The Master then declared the office of Warden vacant by the death of Mr. Glover, and the Court ordered that the vacancies occasioned by the resignation of Mr. Higgs and the death of Mr. Glover be filled up the next Monthly Court, and that in the notices it be mentioned a special Monthly Court, reciting the extra business.

"1813. September 6. The Wardens and Court of Assistants met for the election of a Master in the room of Mr. Harry Potter deceased. A letter was read from his executors stating that on the 30th of August he died very suddenly.

"The Clerk having read so much of the Charter and Bye Laws as related to the election and swearing of a New Master in the event of a death, the Court proceeded to the election by ballot, when the ballot fell upon Mr. Isaac Rogers, who was sworn in and the various Books and the Key of the Chest given to him." [3]

WARDENS.

According to the power given in the Charter of Incorporation three Wardens are to be elected on Michaelmas-day and upon death or removal from their office a fresh election is to be held.

---

[1] The last Court he attended was held on the 3rd of July, 1665.
[2] Company's Journal I.
[3] Company's Journal IV.

In the troublous times at the latter part of the reign of King Charles I, it appears that only two Wardens were appointed, for what reason is not explained. The practice was continued throughout the Commonwealth and the reign of King Charles II until the year 1677, when the following Resolution for returning to the original course, which has since been uninterruptedly followed, is found in the Records:—

"1677. September 29. This Court for divers reasons did think fit and vote, That there shall (be) according as the Charter directs and impowers that there should be and as heretofore was, but for some years past hath been discontinued a third Warden of the Company, And thereupon Mr. Richard Ames and Mr. Benjamin Bell were put in nomination and Mr. Ames was chosen the third and youngest Warden for the year ensuing."

RENTER WARDEN.

It is the duty of the Renter Warden to receive and pay all moneys, to keep an account of the same; and he is required to deliver in his Statement of Receipts and Expenditure at the close of his year of office.

The following Resolution was passed July 6th, 1640, whereby his duties were specifically defined:—

"1640. July 6. It was ordered, whereas divers inconveniences are found to growe in this fellowshipp by the confusion of severall notes of paper and loose accounts, and the never orderly enteringe the same in the booke prepared for that purpose. It was therefore ordered by this Court, that the Renter Warden then beinge or hereafter to be chosen shall betweene the severall quarter dayes of the yeare fitt his accompt exactly drawne upp of his payments and receipts and present the same to the Clarke of the Company, to be fayrely entred and publicly read on every quarter daye before the whole Court upon payne of every default, to pay the somme of Twenty Shillings to the use of the Company, and in case there shall be any Court of Assistants betweene the said quarter dayes, then the said Renter Warden is ordered to deliver up the same to the Court without farther delay upon payne of 10s. for every neglect:—This Court also considering whereas there hath not formerly bin bond given for the true accompt of the Renter Warden to the said Company to re-deliver the Charter, Ordinances and other things trusted with him whereby the Company may receive much prejudice; It was therefore ordered, that every Renter Warden hereafter to be chosen shall immediately upon his election enter into bond of £200 penalty to the Company to deliver up his accompts, and all that trust reposed in him exactly without confusion, and every such Warden soe refusing shall forfeit and pay to the use of the Company Five Pounds."[1]

[1] Company's Journal I.

THE CLOCKMAKERS' COMPANY.

A LIST of the MASTERS and WARDENS, from the formation of the Company to the present time.

Year.	Month.	Master.	Senior Warden.	Renter Warden.	Junior Warden.
1632	Oct. 12	David Ramsey	Henry Archer	John Willow	Sampson Shelton
1634	,, 13	Sampson Shelton	John Willow	John Harris	Francis Forman
1635	Jan. 18	John Willow	John Charleton	Elias Allen	John Midnall
1636	,, 19	Elias Allen	Peter Closon	Richard Masterson	Simon Hackett
1638	July 29	John Smith	Peter Closon	Richard Masterson	Simon Bartram
1639	,, 13	Sampson Shelton	Peter Closon	Edward East	Simon Bartram
1640	Sep. 29	John Charleton	Simon Bartram	Edward East	Robert Grinkin
1641	,, 29	John Harris	Simon Hackett	Robert Grinkin	Richard Child
1642	,, 29	Richd. Masterson*	Simon Bartram	Robert Grinkin	Thomas House
1643		John Harris	Simon Hackett	Robert Grinkin	Richard Child
1644	‡				
1645	Sep. 29	Edward East	Robert Grinkin	Oswell Durant	Thomas Alcock
1646	,, 29	Simon Hackett	Thomas Alcock	Onesipherus Helden	
1647	Oct. 11	do.	do.	do.	
1648	Sep. 29	Robert Grinkin	Onesipherus Helden	John Nicasius	
1649	Oct. 8	do.	do.	do.	
1650	,, 14	Simon Bartram	John Nicasius	Robert Smith†	
1651	,, 20	do.	do.	do.	
1652	,, 4	Edward East	Thomas Holland	Benjamin Hill	
1653	Sep. 29	John Nicasius	do.	do.	
1654	,, 29	Robert Grinkin	Benjamin Hill	John Pennock	
1655	Oct. 1	John Nicasius	do.	do.	
1656	Sep. 29	Thomas Holland	John Pennock	Nicholas Coxeter	
1657	Oct. 1	Benjamin Hill	do.	do.	
1658	‡	...	...	Nicholas Coxeter	John Bayes
1659	Oct. 3	Simon Hackett	do.	do.	
1660	,, 1	John Pennock	Henry Child	Jeremy Gregory	
1661	,, 7	John Coxeter	John Bayes	do.	
1662	,, 6	do.		Thomas Taylor	
1663	,, 5	John Pennock	Jeremy Gregory	do.	
1664	,, 3	Henry Child §	do.	Abraham Beckner	
1665	Feb. 27	Jeremy Gregory	Thomas Taylor	Abrhm. Beckner‖	
1666	Jan. 14	Do. to Michaelmas	do.	Thomas Claxton	
1667	,, 20	do.	do.	do.	
1668	Sep. 29	Thomas Taylor	Thomas Claxton	Samuel Horne	
1669	,, 29	do.	do.	do.	
1670	,, 29	Thomas Claxton	Samuel Horne	Jeffery Bailey	
1671	,, 29	Nicholas Coxeter	do.	do.	
1672	,, 30	Samuel Horne	Jeffery Bailey	Isaac Daniel	
1673	,, 29	do.	do.	do.	
1674	,, 29	Jeffery Bailey	Isaac Daniel	John Matchett	
1675	,, 29	do.	John Matchett	Ralph Almond	
1676	,, 29	Jeremy Gregory	do.	do.	
1677	,, 29	Nicholas Coxeter	Ralph Almond	John Browne	Richard Ames ¶
1678	,, 30	Ralph Almond	Samuel Vernon	Richard Ames	Benjamin Bell
1679	,, 29	Samuel Vernon	Walter Hayes	Benjamin Bell	Richard Lyons
1680	,, 29	Walter Hayes	John Browne	Richard Lyons	Thomas Wheeler

* Died in 1653. Journal 1, p 64.   ‡ No entry of Election.
† Died 1654. Journal 1, p. 71.   § Died in office.
‖ Died in office.
¶ The re-appointment of a third Warden agreed upon at this date.

THE CLOCKMAKERS' COMPANY.

Year.	Month.	Master.	Senior Warden.	Renter Warden.	Junior Warden.
1681	Sep. 29	John Browne	Richard Ames	Thomas Wheeler	Richard Jarratt
1682	,, 29	{ Richard Ames * { Benjamin Bell }	Thomas Wheeler	Richard Jarratt	Edward Norris
1683	,, 29	Richard Lyons	Richard Jarratt	Edward Norris	Thomas Taylor †
1684	,, 29	Thomas Wheeler	Edward Norris	Thomas Taylor	John Harris
1685	,, 29	Richard Jarratt	Thomas Taylor	John Harris	Nathaniel Barrow
1686	,, 29	Edward Norris	John Harris	Nathaniel Barrow	Henry Wynn
1687	,, 29	Thomas Taylor	Nathaniel Barrow	Henry Wynn	Henry Jones
1688	,, 29	John Harris	Henry Wynne	Henry Jones	Nicasius Russell
1689	,, 30	Nathaniel Barrow	Henry Jones	Nicasius Russell	William Knotsford
1690	,, 29	Henry Wynne	Nicasius Russell	William Knotsford	William Clement
1691	,, 29	Henry Jones	William Knotsford	William Clement	Wither Cheney
1692	,, 29	Nicasius Russell	William Clement	Wither Cheney	John Sellars
1693	,, 29	William Knotsford	Wither Cheney	Walter Henshaw	Edward Stanton
1694	,, 29	William Clements	Walter Henshaw	Edward Stanton	John Ebsworth
1695	,, 30	Walter Henshaw ‡	Edward Stanton	John Ebsworth	Robt. Williamson
1696	,, 29	Edward Stanton §	John Ebsworth	Robert Williamson	Robert Halsted
1697	,, 29	John Ebsworth	Robert Williamson	Robert Halsted	Charles Gretton
1698	,, 29	Robert Williamson	Robert Halsted	Charles Gretton	Wm. Speakman
1699	,, 29	Robert Halsted	Charles Gretton	William Speakman	Josh. Windmills, Jr.
1700	,, 30	Charles Gretton	William Speakman	Joseph Windmills	Thomas Tompion
1701	,, 29	William Speakman	Joseph Windmills	Thomas Tompion	Robert Webster
1702	,, 29	Joseph Windmills	Thomas Tompion	Robert Webster	Benjamin Graves
1703	,, 29	Thomas Tompion	Robert Webster	Benjamin Graves	John Finch
1704	,, 29	Robert Webster	Benjamin Graves	John Finch	Samuel Marchant
1705	,, 29	Benjamin Graves	John Finch	John Pepys	Daniel Quare
1706	,, 30	John Finch	John Pepys	Daniel Quare	Geo. Etherington
1707	,, 29	John Pepys	Daniel Quare	Geo. Etherington	Thomas Taylor
1708	,, 29	Daniel Quare	Geo. Etherington	Thomas Taylor	Thomas Gibbs
1709	,, 29	Geo. Etherington	Thomas Taylor	Thomas Gibbs	John Shaw
1710	,, 29	Thomas Taylor	Thomas Gibbs	John Shaw	John Barrow
1711	,, 29	Thomas Gibbs	John Shaw	John Barrow	George Merttins
1712	,, 29	John Shaw	John Barrow	George Merttins ‖	Thomas Feilder
1713	,, 29	Sir Geo. Merttins	Thomas Feilder	William Jaques	John Clows ¶
1713	Oct. 30 **	do.	John Barrow	Thomas Feilder	William Jaques
1714	Sep. 29	John Barrow	Thomas Feilder	William Jaques	John Trubshaw
1715	,, 29	Thomas Feilder	William Jaques	Nath. Chamberlain	Richard Street
1716	,, 29	William Jaques	Nath. Chamberlain	Thomas Windmills	Edward Crouch
1717	,, 30	Nath. Chamberlain	Thomas Windmills	Edward Crouch	James Markwick
1718	,, 29	Thomas Windmills	Edward Crouch	James Markwick	Martin Jackson
1719	,, 29	Edward Crouch	James Markwick	Martin Jackson	George Graham
1720	,, 29	James Markwick	Martin Jackson	George Graham	John Berry
1721	,, 29	Martin Jackson	George Graham	John Berry,	Jos. Williamson
1722	,, 29	George Graham	John Berry	Jos. Williamson	Francis Robinson
1723	,, 30	John Berry	Jos. Williamson	Francis Robinson	Samuel Sadleir
1724	,, 29	Jos. Williamson ††	Francis Robinson	Peter Wise	Langley Bradley
1725	June —	Francis Robinson	Peter Wise	Langley Bradley	Cornelius Herbert
1725	Sep. 29	Peter Wise	Langley Bradley	Cornelius Herbert	James Drury
1726	,, 29	Langley Bradley	Cornelius Herbert	James Drury	Richard Vick
1727	,, 29	Cornelius Herbert	James Drury	Richard Vick	Thomas Stones
1728	,, 30	James Drury	Richard Vick	Thomas Stones	John Marsden
1729	,, 29	Richard Vick	Thomas Stones	John Marsden	William Bertram
1730	,, 29	Thomas Stones	John Marsden	William Bertram	Wm. Tomlinson

* Died the 12th of October following, before he was sworn in.
† Thomas Hancorne elected, but excused upon a fine both for this and all the other offices.
‡ Wither Cheney elected Master for this year, but was excused at his own request upon making a suitable acknowledgment to the Poor Box.
§ John Sellar chosen Master, but excused on account of bad health.
‖ Alderman of Bridge Ward.
¶ Unable to serve the office on account of ill health.
** A re-election took place.
†† Died in office June, 1725.

THE CLOCKMAKERS' COMPANY.

Year.	Month.	Master.	Senior Warden.	Renter Warden.	Junior Warden.
1731	Sep. 29	John Marsden	William Bertram	Wm. Tomlinson	John Ellicott
1732	,, 29	William Bertram *	Wm. Tomlinson	John Ellicott †	Edward Faulkner
1733	,, 29	Wm. Tomlinson	Edward Faulkner	Hugh Richards	James Snelling
1734	,, 30	Edward Faulkner	Hugh Richards	James Snelling	William Webster ‡
1735	,, 29	Hugh Richards	James Snelling	Thos. Wrightson	John Maberly
1736	,, 29	James Snelling	Thos. Wrightson	John Maberly	John Pepys
1737	,, 29	Thos. Wrightson	John Maberly	John Pepys	Wm. Sherwood
1738	,, 29	John Maberly	John Pepys	William Sherwood	John Stafford
1739	,, 29	John Pepys	William Sherwood	John Stafford	Thomas Hughes
1740	,, 29	William Sherwood	John Stafford	Thomas Hughes	David Hubert
1741	,, 29	John Stafford	Thomas Hughes	David Hubert	John Hiorne
1742	,, 29	Thomas Hughes	David Hubert	John Hiorne	Joshua Appleby
1743	,, 29	David Hubert	John Hiorne	Joshua Appleby	Jas. Blackborow
1744	,, 29	John Hiorne	Joshua Appleby	James Blackborow	Matthew Skinner
1745	,, 30	Joshua Appleby	Jas. Blackborow §	Matthew Skinner	Nathanl. Delander
1746	,, 29	Matthew Skinner	Nathaniel Delander	Samuel Whichcote	William Scafe
1747	,, 29	Nathaniel Delander	Samuel Whichcote	William Scafe	John Mulford ‖
1748	,, 29	Samuel Whichcote	William Scafe	Henry Horne	Nathaniel Style
1749	,, 2 ¶	William Scafe	Henry Horne	Nathaniel Style	Joseph Stephens
1750	,, 29	Henry Horne	Nathaniel Style	Joseph Stephens	Henton Browne
1751	,, 30	Nathaniel Style	Joseph Stephens	Henton Browne	Jasper Taylor
1752	,, 29	Joseph Stephens	Henton Browne	Jasper Taylor	William Webster
1753	,, 29	Henton Browne	Jasper Taylor	William Webster	Francis Perigal
1754	,, 30	Jasper Taylor	William Webster	Francis Perigal	Charles Cabrier
1755	,, 29	William Webster	Francis Perigal	Charles Cabrier	Conyers Dunlop
1756	,, 29	Francis Perigal	Charles Cabrier	Conyers Dunlop	Devereux Bowly
1757	,, 29	Charles Cabrier	Conyers Dunlop	Devereux Bowly	Stephen Goujon
1758	,, 29	Conyers Dunlop	Devereux Bowly	Stephen Goujon	Benjamin Sidey
1759	,, 29	Devereux Bowly	Stephen Goujon	Benjamin Sidey	John Jones
1760	,, 29	Stephen Goujon	Benjamin Sidey	John Jones	Anthony Benn
1761	,, 29	Benjamin Sidey	John Jones	Anthony Benn	William Addis
1762	,, 29	John Jones	Anthony Benn	William Addis	Thomas Hughes
1763	,, 29	Anthony Benn ¶	William Addis	Thomas Hughes	Daniel Fenn
1764	,, 5	Sam. Whichcote			
1764	,, 29	William Addis	Thomas Hughes	Daniel Fenn	Peter Higgs
1765	,, 30	Thomas Hughes	Daniel Fenn	Peter Higgs	Boyer Glover
1766	,, 29	Daniel Fenn	Peter Higgs	Boyer Glover	William Matthews
1767	,, 29	Peter Higgs **	Boyer Glover **	James Carrington	Charles Merry
1768	Mar. 7	S. Charrington ††	Charles Merry	Thomas Garle	James Brown
1768	Sep. 29	Charles Merry	Thomas Garle	James Brown	Daniel Aveline
1769	,, 29	Thomas Garle	James Brown	Daniel Aveline	Eliezer Chater
1770	,, 29	James Brown	Daniel Aveline	Eliezer Chater	David Rivers
1771	,, 30	Daniel Aveline ‡‡	Eliezer Chater	David Rivers	William Rogerson
1772	,, 29	Eliezer Chater	David Rivers	William Rogerson	Francis Perigal
1773	,, 29	David Rivers	William Rogerson	Francis Perigal	Joseph Stephens
1774	,, 29	William Rogerson	Francis Perigal	Joseph Stephens	William Howse
1775	,, 29	Francis Perigal	Joseph Stephens	William Howes	Southern Payne
1776	,, 30	Joseph Stephens	William Howes	Southern Payne	William Plumley
1777	,, 29	William Howes	Southern Payne	William Plumley	Francis Atkins
1778	,, 29	Southern Payne	William Plumley	Francis Atkins	Robert Poole

* Died during his year of office (August).
† Succeeded upon his decease, June, 1733, by Edward Faulkner. Hugh Richards chosen Junior Warden in the room of Faulkner.
‡ Thomas Wrightson chosen in the room of William Webster, deceased, September 1st, 1735.
§ Died in July, 1746; Skinner was chosen Upper Warden, Delander Middle Warden, and Samuel Whichcote was chosen Junior Warden.
‖ Died April, 1748; Henry Horne chosen in his room.
¶ Died in office.
** In conequence of the illness of the Master, Mr. Higgs, and the death of Boyer Glover, a new Election was held on March 7th, 1768 [see New Election].
†† September 13th, Henry Horne elected Master for the remainder of the year, in the room of Samuel Charrington, deceased.
‡‡ Died in his year of office [August].

THE CLOCKMAKERS' COMPANY.

Year.	Month.		Master.	Senior Warden.	Renter Warden.	Junior Warden.
1779	Sep.	29	William Plumley	Francis Atkins	Robert Poole	Thomas Lea
1780	,,	29	Francis Atkins	Robert Poole	Thomas Lea	Nath. Sargeant
1781	,,	29	Robert Poole	Thomas Lea	Nath. Sergeant	James Green
1782	,,	30	Thomas Lea	Nath. Sergeant	James Green	Hilton Wray
1783	,,	29	Nath. Sergeant	James Green	Hilton Wray	Edward Tutet
1784	,,	29	James Green	Hilton Wray	Edward Tutet	Charles Howse
1785	,,	29	Hilton Wray	Edward Tutet	Charles Howse	James Richardson
1786	,,	29	Edward Tutet	Charles Howse	James Richardson	Eliezer Chater
1787	,,	29	Charles Howse	James Richardson	Nath. Sergeant	Richard Style
1788	,,	29	James Richardson	Benjamin Sidey	Richard Style	Daniel Fenn
1789	,,	29	Benjamin Sidey	Richard Style	Daniel Fenn	Rev. Dr. Robert Hamilton
1790	,,	29	Richard Style	Daniel Fenn	Rev. Dr. Robert Hamilton	Samuel Fenn
1791	,,	29	Daniel Fenn	Rev. Dr. Robert Hamilton	Samuel Fenn	William Rivers
1792	,,	29	Rev. Dr. Robert Hamilton	Samuel Fenn	William Rivers	Harry Potter, Jun.
1793	,,	30	Samuel Fenn	William Rivers	Harry Potter	John Jackson
1794	,,	29	William Rivers	Harry Potter, Sen.	John Jackson	John Ward
1795	,,	29	Harry Potter	John Jackson	John Ward	R. Duncombe, Jr.
1796	,,	29	John Jackson	John Ward	Richd. Duncombe	John Marriott
1797	,,	29	John Ward	Richd. Duncombe	John Marriott	Matthew Dutton
1798	,,	29	Richd. Duncombe	John Marriott	Matthew Dutton	W. Plumley, Jun.
1799	,,	30	John Marriott	Matthew Dutton	William Plumley	Edward Gibson
1800	,,	29	Matthew Dutton	William Plumley	Edward Gibson	Timothy Chisman
1801	,,	29	William Plumley	Edward Gibson	Timothy Chisman	William Pierce
1802	,,	29	Edward Gibson	Timothy Chisman	William Pearce	William Robins
1803	,,	29	Timothy Chisman	William Pearce	William Robins	F. S. Perigal, Jun.
1804	,,	29	William Pearce	William Robins	F. S. Perigal, Jun.	Samuel Taylor
1805	,,	30	William Robins	F. S Perigal, Jun.	Samuel Taylor	Thomas Dolley
1806	,,	29	F. S. Perigal, Jun.	Samuel Taylor	Thomas Dolley	W. Robson
1807	,,	29	Samuel Taylor	Thomas Dolley	William Robson	Paul P. Barraud
1808	,,	29	Thomas Dolley	William Robson	Paul P. Barraud	James McCabe
1809	,,	29	William Robson	Paul P. Barraud	James McCabe	George Atkins *
1810	,,	29	Paul P. Barraud	James McCabe †	Isaac Rogers	John Thwaites
1811	,,	30	do.	Harry Potter	do.	do.
1812	,,	29	Harry Potter ‡	Isaac Rogers }	John Thwaites	John R. Arnold
1813	,,	6	Isaac Rogers	William Robins }		
1813	,,	29	William Robins	John Jackson	John Thwaites	John R. Arnold
1814	,,	29	do.	do.	do.	do.
1815	,,	29	John Thwaites	William Robson	John Roger Arnold	Benjamin Lewis Vulliamy
1816	,,	30	William Robson	John RogerArnold	Benjamin Lewis Vulliamy	Matthew Dutton
1817	,,	29	John RogerArnold	John Thwaites	do.	William Plumley, Jun.
1818	,,	29	William Robson §	William Plumley, Jun.	do.	JohnJackson, Jun.
1819	,,	29	John Thwaites	Benjamin Lewis Vulliamy	PaulPhilipBarraud	do.
1820	,,	29	do.	do.	John Jackson, Jun	Justin Theodore Vulliamy
1821	,,	29	Benjamin Lewis Vulliamy	John Jackson, Jun.	Justin Theodore Vulliamy	William Robson

* Resigned upon his election as Clerk the 22nd December, 1809; John Grant elected Junior Warden, January 8th, 1810; Mr. Grant's death announced May 7th, and Isaac Rogers elected Junior Warden, June 4th, 1810.
† Deceased; Harry Potter elected in his room, October 7th, 1811.
‡ Deceased 30th August, 1813; Isaac Rogers elected September 6th, 1813.
§ Third time elected Master. At the close of his year of office the thanks of the Company were voted to him.

THE CLOCKMAKERS' COMPANY.

Year.	Month.	Master.	Senior Warden.	Renter Warden.	Junior Warden.
1822	Sep. 30	John Jackson, Jun.	Justin Theodore Vulliamy	William Robson	Henry Clarke
1823	,, 29	Benjamin Lewis Vulliamy	do.	Isaac Rogers	do.
1824	,, 29	Isaac Rogers	Francis Perigal	Henry Clarke	Richard Webster
1825	,, 29	Benjamin Lewis Vulliamy	Henry Clarke	Richard Webster	Richard Ganthony
1826	,, 29	John Jackson	do.	Richard Ganthony	William Harris
1827	,, 29	Benjamin Lewis Vulliamy	Richard Ganthony	William Harris	John Sharp
1828	,, 29	Richard Ganthony	William Harris	John Sharp	Edward Ellicott
1829	,, 29	do.	do.	do.	do.
1830	,, 29	William Harris	John Sharp	Edward Ellicott	William James Frodsham
1831	,, 29	do.	do.	do.	do.
1832	,, 29	do.	do.	do.	do.
1833	,, 30	John Sharp	Edward Ellicott	William James Frodsham	John Grant
1834	,, 29	Edward Ellicott	William James Frodsham	John Grant	William Gravell
1835	,, 29	do. *	do.	do.	do.
1835	July —	John Sharp			
1836	Sep. 29	William James Frodsham	John Grant	William Gravell	Joseph Fenn
1837	,, 29	do.	do.	do.	do.
1838	,, 29	John Grant	William Gravell	Joseph Fenn	Richard Pinfold Ganthony
1839	,, 30	do.	do.	do.	do.
1840	,, 29	William Gravell	Joseph Fenn	Richard Pinfold Ganthony	John Roger Arnold
1841	,, 29	do.	do.	do.	do.
1842	,, 29	Joseph Fenn	Richard Pinfold Ganthony	John Roger Arnold†	George Atkins
1843	,, 29	do.	do.	George Atkins	B. L. Vulliamy
1844	,, 30	Richard Pinfold Ganthony ‡	George Atkins	Benjamin Lewis Vulliamy	Francis Bryant Adams
1845	Jan. 24	George Atkins			
1845	Sep. 29	George Atkins	John Grant	B. L. Vulliamy	F. B. Adams
1846	,, 29	John Grant	B. L. Vulliamy	F. B. Adams	J. A. Perry
1847	,, 29	B. L. Vulliamy §	F. B. Adams	J. A. Perry	G. Harker
1848	,, 29	F. B. Adams	J. A. Perry	G. Harker	J. Adams
1849	,, 29	do.	do.	do.	do.
1850	,, 30	J. A. Perry	George Harker	James Adams	Charles Frodsham
1851	,, 29	do.	do.	do.	do.
1852	,, 29	George Harker	J. Adams	C. Frodsham	John Carter, Ald. and Sheriff
1853	,, 29	do.	do.	do.	John Carter, Ald.
1854	,, 29	James Adams	C. Frodsham	John Carter, Ald.	R. H. Kennedy, Ald.
1855	,, 29	Charles Frodsham	John Carter, Ald.	R. H. Kennedy, Ald. and Sheriff	John Grant
1856	,, 29	Ald. Carter	Ald. Kennedy	John Grant	Wm. Rowlands
1857	,, 29	James Adams	John Grant	William Rowlands	G. W. Adams.
1858	,, 29	John Grant	Wm. Rowlands	George W. Adams	Charles Frodsham
1859	,, 29	Ald. Carter Lord Mayor elect	do.	do.	do.

* Died in July.
† Died in February, 1843, and George Atkins elected in his room, and B. L. Vulliamy elected Junior Warden.
‡ Died in January, 1845.
§ Five times Master. The Court presented him with a piece of Plate, July, 1849.

THE CLOCKMAKERS' COMPANY.

Year.	Month.	Master.	Senior Warden.	Renter Warden.	Junior Warden.
1860	Sep. 29	W. Rowlands	G. W. Adams	C. Frodsham	J. Fenn
1861	,, 30	George W. Adams	Charles Frodsham	Joseph Fenn	George Harker
1862	,, 29	Charles Frodsham	Joseph Fenn	George Harker	Ald. Carter
1863	,, 29	Joseph Fenn	Ald. Carter	F. B. Adams	J. G. C. Addison
1864	,, 29	Ald. Carter	F. B. Adams	J. Addison	R. H. Kennedy
1865	,, 29	F. B. Adams	John Addison	William Rowlands	G. W. Adams
1866	,, 29	J. G. C. Addison	Wm. Rowlands	G W. Adams	William Lawley
1867	,, 30	W. Rowlands *⎱	G. W. Adams	W. Lawley	George Moore
1868	,, 29	John Grant † ⎰			
1868	,, 29	G. W. Adams	Wm. Lawley	George Moore	Charles Frodsham
1869	,, 29	William Lawley	George Moore	Chas. Frodsham	F. B. Adams, Jr.‡
1870	,, 29	George Moore	Chas. Frodsham §	Wm. Wing	Chas. Wellborne
1871	,, 29	J. G. C. Addison	Wm. Wing	C. Wellborne	Wm. Lawley
1872	,, 30	Wm. Wing	Charles Wellborne	Wm. Lawley	George Moore
1873	,, 29	Charles Wellborne	W. Lawley	George Moore	J. S. Adams
1874	,, 29	William Lawley	George Moore	J. S. Adams	Alex. Angus Croll
1875	,, 29	George Moore	J. S. Adams	Col. A. A. Croll	Wm. Parker
1876	,, 29	J. S. Adams	Col. A. A. Croll	Wm. Parker	Wm. Butcher ‖
1877	,, 29	Col. A. A. Croll	Wm. Parker	Robert Dobree ¶	Wm. Wing
1878	,, 29	William Parker	William Wing	Charles Wellborne	J. S. Adams
1879	,, 29	William Wing	Charles Wellborne	J. S. Adams	S. Elliott Atkins, Deputy

TREASURER.

In the year 1647 a Treasurer was appointed for the reasons given in the following Resolution :—

"1647. October 11. The day above said it was likewise ordered, That whereas Mr. Helden being Renter Warden and refusing to give security for the stock of the Company, the Company thought it fit that it should be put to voices that Mr. East and Mr. Hackett should be putt in nomination for Treasurer and then Mr. East was chosen and it was ordered that the money should be paid unto him, and he to give bond to the Company for it." [1]

The office ceased with the death of Mr. East.

CLERK.

The following is a list of the Clerks of the Company since its formation ; with extracts, where obtainable, from the minutes of proceedings of their admission, etc., to office :—

1631. August 22. Thomas Copley appointed by the Charter to hold office for life.

---

* Deceased during his year of office, 22nd September, 1868.
† Five times Master. See distinguished Members.
‡ Deceased 11th March, 1870, W. Wing elected April 4th, 1870.
§ Died during his year of office, J. G. C. Addison elected July 3rd, 1871.
‖ Died on the 4th of January, 1877. R. Dobree elected January 8th, 1877.
¶ Died during his year of office, W. Wing elected April 8th, 1878. Charles Wellborne being elected Junior Warden.
[1] Company's Journal I.

Sworn into office at the first Court held 12th October, 1632. Power was given to the Master, Wardens and Court of Assistants by the Charter from time to time and at all times after his death to choose, name, and make, one other discreet person, to be Clerk of the fellowship to hold office during the good will and pleasure of the Court.

1636. August 1. Thomas Shelton was elected.

"This day was freely elected and chosen and sworn Clerk of the Company of Clockmakers Thomas Shelton of Furnivalls Inn in Holborne, Gent, and it is ordered that the said Clerke shall not at any tyme receive any writings or copies from henceforth in anywise touching the Company but shall from time to time bring in and redeliver the same from one court day to another as occasion shall require for the confirmation of him in the said place." [1]

1651-2. January 5. Thomas Morgan was chosen.

1659. January 16. Thomas Holland was admitted.

"This day Thomas Holland according to his petition was admitted for Clerk and Beadle to the Company and to officiate in the said places that so his abilities may be seen for them by Ladyday next being the next quarter day.

"1662. August 20. This Court day Mr. Thomas Holland was suspended from acting any more as Clerk or Beadle to this Company *(nemine contradicente)*.

"1662. September 1. This Court day Mr. Holland the former Clerk to this Company delivered up the Bookes and all other things belonging to the Company and was paid what the Company did owe him and discharged of his service for the time to come."

1662. September 1. Thomas Goodwin chosen.

"This Court day Mr. Thomas Goodwin (upon his petition) was chosen to execute the place of Clerk to this Company.

"1683. April 2. Ordered that annually on the 29th of September when the Master and Wardens are put in nomination and chosen so shall the Clerk and Beadle likewise be then nominated and chosen."

17—. Francis Speidell. The date of his election is not recorded, but in 1704 appear the following entries with reference to him :—

---
[1] Company's Journal I.

"1704. September 29. This Court was petitioned by the present Clerk Franc Speidell acknowledging his faults and misapplication of some of the Company's money come to his hands, promiseing amendment and reparation and praying to be continued Clerk. It was upon debate and consideration had thereon, Ordered That the said Speidell shall have time till the Monthly Court in November to make out his accounts of what money is in his hands unanswered of the Orphan duty received by him, and also shall make up the account of the Law Charges and the Moneys paid to the Attorney in the suit against Bird, and produce the receipts for the same, and what the whole of that charge amounts unto, and also that he perfect his entries and other business of the Company by that time and deliver the books belonging to the Company to the Master, and then the Company will come to a resolution whether they continue him the said Speidell as their Clerk or suspend or discharge him from that Office.

"1704. October 4. the Master reported that there had been received at several times of the Clerk towards the Money paid at Guildhall and for Stamps £18 . 16 . 9.

"1704. November 6. It was Ordered that the settlement of the Clerk be adjourned to the next Quarter Court."

The matter was finally allowed to pass over, and he continued in office until 1719.

1719. April 6. Benjamin Graves was elected Clerk in the room of Francis Speidell, deceased.

1731. December 6. James Drury elected in the room of Benjamin Graves, deceased, was sworn accordingly, and thereupon surrendered his place as an assistant.

1740. May 5. John Stafford was elected Clerk in the room of William Drury, deceased.

1740. June 2. John Locker was elected in the room of John Stafford, deceased.

1760. July 15. Jasper Taylor was elected in the room of John Locker, deceased.

1770. March 14. Thomas Hughes chosen Clerk.

1785. December 5. Francis Atkins was elected.

The son of Thomas Atkins Citizen and Barber Surgeon. Born in 1730. Apprenticed to Joshua Hassell December 1 1746; admitted to the Freedom of the Company April 2 1759; to the Livery December 4 1769; chosen on the

Court of Assistants April 5, 1773; served the office of Warden 1777-79; chosen Master September 29, 1780; elected Clerk of the Company December 5, 1785; died 1809.

1809. December 22. George Atkins elected.

The Son of the above Francis Atkins; born March 25 1767; apprenticed to John Waldron, admitted to the Freedom September 1, 1788 and to the Livery October 13, 1788. Chosen on the Court Assistants April 4, 1808; resigned upon succeeding his Father as Clerk to the Company December 22, 1809. He held this office for Thirty-one years. He was again elected on the Court of Assistants upon his resigning the office of Clerk, October 11th 1841. He served the office of Warden 1842-44 and upon the decease of Mr. R. P. Ganthony, January 24, 1845, he was elected Master, which office he held again the following year. At the termination of his year of office the following resolution was passed unanimously and ordered to be presented to him by the Master of the Company in Open Court. 1847. January 4th. "That the Thanks of this Court be presented to George Atkins Esq., the late Master, for the very able and zealous manner in which he had for two successive years filled that office; for the undeviating punctuality of his attendance, his obliging demeanour at all times towards the whole of its members, and for his sincere desire to promote the best interests of the Trade in general and this Corporation in particular. But the services of the late Master have been so multifarious and have extended over so long a period that the Court feels specially called upon to enumerate them on the present occasion. In the year 1788 he was admitted to the Livery, and elected a Member of the Court of Assistants in 1808, which situation he relinquished after having served the office of Warden to accept the much more useful but arduous duty of Clerk to the Company, which he filled to the great advantage of the Corporation and with infinite credit to himself for the long period of Thirty-One Years, when he resigned and was again elected a Member of the Court. And this Court on his retiring from the Chair feels that it cannot too strongly express the high sense it entertains of his past services in the various situations he has filled, and earnestly prays that they may long continue to enjoy the advantage of his society and the benefit of his assistance. By order of the Court (Signed) S. Elliott Atkins, Clerk to the Company." In 1852 he was requested by the members of the Court of Assistants to sit for his portrait to Mr. Lucas. This is now preserved with the other portraits belonging to the Company in the Guildhall Library. He died in 1855 in his 88th year having been connected with the Company for the long period of 67 years.

1842. January 10. Samuel Elliott Atkins was elected to succeed his Father.

He was born April 13, 1807; apprenticed to his Father May 7th 1821; admitted to the Freedom March 7th 1831, and to the Livery December 2, 1839; succeeded his Father as Clerk January 10, 1842. In 1865 he was chosen to represent the Ward of Cornhill in the Court of Common Council and was appointed Deputy to the Alderman of that Ward. In 1874 upon his completing his thirty-second year of office as Clerk to the Company he received the unanimous thanks of the Court of Assistants with a presentation of Plate.

1874. July 6. On the conclusion of the business of the Court Mr. Adams laid before the Members for their inspection the Plate he had manufactured at their request, and for which they had individually subscribed, to be presented to Mr. S. E. Atkins, the Clerk of the Company, consisting of a large Silver oval Salver and a Claret Jug engraved with the Arms of the Company, as well as those of Mr. Atkins, each piece bearing the following inscription.

"Presented to Samuel Elliott Atkins Esq., by the Master, Wardens and Court of Assistants of the Worshipful Company of Clockmakers of the City of London, in acknowledgement of the great and valuable services rendered by him as Clerk of the Company during the long period of Thirty two years, and as a tribute of their personal regard and esteem A.D. 1874."

On the 13th of January, 1879, he was chosen on the Court of Assistants, having previously resigned the office he had held for 37 years, but at the request of the Court continued to act as Clerk, *pro. tem.*, until the appointment of his successor, when on his giving up the office, the following Resolution was unanimously passed, and ordered to be ornamentally written and presented to him in open Court:—

"That the best thanks of this Court be presented to Samuel Elliott Atkins Esq. Deputy, on his retirement from the office of Clerk to this Company, after filling that position for the long period of thirty seven years, during the whole of which time this Court and the Livery have received more attention and devotion than is ordinarily found in the discharge of mere official duties; and this Court cannot omit from their notice the fact that the zeal evinced by Mr. Atkins in promoting the display of their collection of articles pertaining to the Art and Mystery of Clockmaking in the Guildhall of this City, as well as the collation of the past Records of the Company again entitle him to more than ordinary thanks. It is right that reference should be made to the circumstance that the Father and Grandfather of the retiring Clerk have conjointly with him contributed to the advantage of this Company by the faithful and honourable discharge of the duties of the office during Ninety-six years. By order of the Court (Signed) H. C. Overall, Clerk to the Company."

Upon his resignation becoming known to the Livery, a subscription was set on foot among themselves, which resulted in a silver tea and coffee service being presented to him by that body, bearing the following inscription :—

"Presented to SAMUEL ELLIOTT ATKINS, Esq., Deputy for the Ward of Cornhill, by the Livery of the Clockmakers' Company, in testimony of their

THE CLOCKMAKERS' COMPANY.   95

high esteem and regard for his long and valuable services as Clerk to the Company, 1879."

On the 29th of September, 1879, he was elected to the office of Junior Warden, the Resolutions of the Court of the 6th of April, 1824, which directs that Members of the Court shall be required to be three years thereon before they are eligible to take the office of Warden, being specially suspended to enable him to take that office.

1879. April 7. Henry Charles Overall chosen Clerk.

BEADLE.

1633.	October 3.	John Potter was admitted and sworn.
1641.	September 29.	— Morgan admitted and sworn.
1659.	January 16.	Thomas Holland. [1]
1662.	August 20.	William Rogers.
1665.	February 9.	Lionel Wyth.
1674.	January 18.	Samuel Davis. [2]
1680.	September 29.	Daniel Stephens.
1697.	January 17.	Richard George.
1712.	April 7.	John Drew.
1713.	September 29.	Christopher Gold.
1718.	January 16.	— Warburton.
17—.		Charles Tolley.
1730.	September 29.	Edward Avenell. [3]
1749.	January 22.	John Avenell. [4]
1756.	July 4.	Anthony Marsh.
1775.	April 3.	Daniel Cathay.
1779.	April 12.	William Hornblower. [5]
1798.	April 2.	Richard Booth. [6]
1830.	January 11.	Samuel Booth. [7]
1851.	October 13.	George Smellie elected. [8]
1864.	September 29.	Edward Mullett elected.

---

[1] Elected Clerk and Beadle; suspended from his Office, August 20, 1662; discharged September 1, 1662.
[2] Discharged for neglect of duty September 29, 1680.
[3] Chosen in the room of Charles Tolly, deceased.
[4] Chosen in the room of his father, deceased.
[5] On account of the great age of William Hornblower, Willy Negus was chosen Assistant Beadle, September 7, 1795; resigned October 12, 1795; and was succeeded by Richard Booth.
[6] Died November 2, 1829; he had filled the office for 30 years.
[7] July 7, 1851. The death of Samuel Booth reported.
[8] Deceased 1864.

THE LIVERY.

HE Bye-Laws made by the Company on the 11th of August, 8th Charles I, 1632, and confirmed by the Lord Keeper and the Lord Chief Justices of the King's Bench and Common Pleas, contain in Bye-law 2 an Ordinance to the following effect :—

"It is hereby ordained, that of the said Master, Wardens, and Fellowship, and of the Fellowship and of the Fellows thereof, there shall be a livery of Company, as is used in other Companies within the City of London, for the better service of his Majesty, and of the said City. And that the Master, Wardens, and Assistants of the said Fellowship; and as many others of the Fellows of the said Fellowship, as the said Master, Wardens, and Assistants, being assembled, or the more part of them (whereof the Master and one of the Wardens shall be two) shall elect from time to time, shall be of the said Livery. And that every person of the said Fellowship chosen into the said Livery shall accept and take upon him to be of the said Livery, and shall within fourteen days after notice of such election, take such oaths as by these ordinances shall be appointed for him."

This, however, it was not within the power of the Company to create. It is difficult to understand at this distance of time how such a provision was confirmed by the Judges ; a Livery being, according to the custom of the City of London, granted to a Company by the Court of Aldermen only, and that upon a proper application made to them for that purpose. The Clockmakers made several fruitless attempts to obtain such a grant, but it was not until the year 1766 that their efforts were crowned with success, and then the number of the Livery was limited to Sixty. Their first application was made in the year 1748, and the circumstances which gave rise to it and the results which ensued may be best gathered from the following Extracts from the Minutes of the Court of Assistants, and the Repertories of the Court of Aldermen respectively.

On the 16th of January, 1748, the Court of Assistants met, and after a long and serious debate upon the decline of the Company, they passed the following Resolution :—

"It being observed that the whole number of the Members of this Company is considerably decreased, fewer persons coming now to be bound or made free than formerly, an evil among others which seems to be owing to the want of the Livery of the City:—it was therefore resolved, that a petition be drawn up and presented to the Lord Mayor and Court of Aldermen and all proper means used for the obtaining of a Livery, and that there be a Committee of the whole Court which the Master may call together from time to time, as he shall think fit: that seven of them (of which the Master and one of the Wardens to be two) are empowered to draw and present such a Petition, and the Company will defray the attending charges.[1]

"1748. January 23. The Charter was read, and the Bye Laws with the Oath intended for the Liverymen of the Company.

"The Committee agreed to attend the Lord Mayor in relation to the Company's design of applying for the Livery of this City.

"The Master and Wardens, Mr. Herbert, Mr. Snelling, Mr. Delander, Mr. Browne and Mr. Taylor or any four of them were desired to prepare heads for a Petition.

"1748. January 28. The Committee met, and agreed to a Petition to be presented on Tuesday next to the Lord Mayor and Court of Aldermen."

The Petition was presented to the Court of Aldermen and was by them referred to a Committee for consideration, as appears from the following Extract from their Repertory:—

[2] "1748. January 31. This day the humble Petition of the Master Wardens and Assistants of the Company of Clockmakers was presented unto this Court (of Aldermen) and read in these words

"To the Right Honourable the Lord Mayor
 and Court of Aldermen of this City of London.

"The Petition of the Master Wardens and Assistants of the Company of Clockmakers

"Sheweth,—That a Charter was granted to the said Company in the Seventh year of the Reign of King Charles the First by which they became an incorporated Body with power to make Ordinances for the well governing their Corporation.

"That in pursuance of this authority in the succeeding year of the said Reign it was ordained that there should be a Livery of the said Company and directs among other things the Oath to be taken by those admitted thereon.

"That it having been found by experience that the not being of the Livery hath been in many instances of great disadvantage:—that the number coming to be bound Apprentices and others to be made free either by servitude or purchase is considerably decreased which your Petitioners cannot ascribe to any other cause than that before mentioned.

"Your Petitioners therefore pray your Lordship and this Honourable Court to grant them the honour and priviledge of the Livery of this City in order to remove those inconveniences and put them in a respectable condition with the rest of their fellow Citizens in such manner as to your Lordship and this Court shall seem meet.

---

[1] Company's Journal IV. [2] Repertory 153, fol. 125 *et seq.*

"Signed by the Master Wardens and Assistants of the said Company 28th January 1748.

Saml. Whichcote, Master.

Wm. Scafe
Henry Home } Wardens.
Nat^{l.} Style

Geo^{e.} Graham
John Pepys
Langl. Bradley
John Maberly } Assistants.
David Hubert
John Hione
Josh^{a.} Appleby

Corn^{s.} Herbert
Henton Brown
Nathl. Delander
James Snelling
Jos. Stephens
Jasper Taylor.

"Whereupon it is referred to a Comittee of the whole Court or any three of them who are desired to examine the allegations and report their opinions thereon to this Court."

Whilst the matter was still under the consideration of the Court of Aldermen, some differences of opinion arose amongst the Members of the Company as to the propriety of the course adopted, although their action was ultimately confirmed by the unanimous vote of the Company and a new Petition agreed to be presented to the Court of Aldermen.

[1] "1749. April 3. Resolved that the Committee of the whole Court be continued to proceed in the business of the Petition before the Court of Aldermen.

[2] "1749. June 19. The Petition of the Master, Wardens and Assistants to the Lord Mayor and Court of Aldermen to be made a Livery Company was read.

"And an additional Petition of the other members in favour of it was also read.

"Then the question was put, whether this Court doth approve of the said Petitions?

"Resolved unanimously in the affirmative.

"Resolved unanimously, that it appears to this Court that no undue influence hath been used to induce the freemen to sign the additional Petition, but that the same was obtained fairly and with their free and ready consent.

"Resolved unanimously, that there is not the least shadow of pretence that the application for the Livery is founded on any consideration of Party, and that whoever are the authors of such an insinuation, can in no wise be looked on as friends to the Company.

"Resolved, that the several steps that have been taken by the Master, Wardens and Assistants for the obtaining a Livery are entirely agreeable to this Court and they are desired to continue their care therein, and to take all other measures which they shall judge proper to accomplish it, it appearing to this Court that a Livery is absolutely necessary to raise the Company from the low estate in which they are at present, which can be ascribed to no other cause than the want of a Livery.

---

[1] [2] Company's Journal IV.

"Resolved unanimously that the Master, Wardens and Assistants be empowered to draw up and present a fresh Petition to the Right Hon. the Lord Mayor and Court of Aldermen, in the name of themselves and the rest of the Members of this Company, for the purposes aforesaid if they shall see occasion.

"Ordered, that the resolutions of this Court be printed in the public papers.

"After these proceedings several persons subscribed the Petition, who had not done it before.

"1749. June 27. A Petition to the Lord Mayor and Court of Aldermen of the Master, Wardens and Assistants in the name of themselves and the rest of the freemen of the Company, was signed by the Members present, sealed with the Company's seal and afterwards presented to the Court of Aldermen."

The entries in the Repertory of the Court of Aldermen in relation thereto are as follow :—

"1749. June 27. This day a new Petition of the Master Wardens and Assistants of the Company of Clockmakers in behalf of themselves and the rest of the Freemen of the said Company, pursuant to the power unanimously given to them at a General Court held at Leathersellers Hall the Nineteenth instant, under their Comon Seal was presented unto this Court and read. Whereupon this Court doth appoint Tuesday the Eleventh day of July next to take into consideration the matter of the said Petition And it is Ordered that the said Master Wardens and Assistants do then attend this Court."[1]

"1749. July 11. This Court proceeded (according to the Order of the 27th June last) to take into consideration the Petition of the Master Wardens and Assistants of the Company of Clockmakers in behalf of themselves and the rest of the Freemen of the said Company, pursuant to the power given unanimously to them at a General Court held at Leather-sellers Hall, the Nineteenth of June last, which was then presented unto this Court; and the said Master Wardens and Assistants attending they were called in and the said Petition was read setting forth that a Petition of the said Master Wardens and Assistants was presented to this Court the thirty first day of January last, for the reasons therein contained, praying to be admitted on the Livery, which Petition was referred to a Comittee of the Whole Court:—That the Petitioners laid before the Comittee the proofs necessary to support the allegations of that Petition but some objections arising thereto, as not being done by consent of a General Court, in order to remove those, and every other objection a General Court was called by six days publick notice, and held the nineteenth day of June last at Leather-sellers Hall, when the Court came to several Resolutions which they were ready to produce:—That the Petitioners conceived there cannot now remain one possible objection against them :—They therefore prayed this Court to admit the said Company to the priviledge of the Livery of this City, in comon with the other Companies, in order to raise them from the low estate to which they were reduced, and which can only be ascribed to the want of a Livery:—And after hearing what the said Petitioners had further to offer in support of the said Petition they were ordered to withdraw :—And,

[1] Repertory 153, fol. 332.

after this Court had fully debated the matter, at length a Motion was made and Question put, That this Court do grant the said Company a Livery according to the prayer of their said Petition? The same was Resolved in the Negative."[1]

The entries in the Company's Minute Books of their proceedings and the course they determined to adopt, are thus recorded :—

"1749. July 11. The Committee met and attended the Lord Mayor and Court of Aldermen. And, being called in, the Petition drawn and presented according to the direction of a general Court on the 19th of June was read by the Town Clerk, the resolutions of the general Court were also read, and several questions relating to the Company being asked and answered, the Committee withdrew. After waiting a considerable time a message was brought by the Common Crier, that it was not the pleasure of the Court to admit the Company to the Livery.

"Resolved that the Master and Wardens with the Clerk, draw up a Case for the opinions of the Attorney General and Sir John Strange with respect to the proceeding on Mandamus or otherwise to obtain the Livery of the City.

"1749. August 7. Resolved that a Committee of the whole Court (of which the Master and one of the Wardens to be two) be empowered to take such measures as they think fit for obtaining the Livery either by Mandamus or otherwise.

"1749. October 9. Resolved that the Committee concerning the Livery be revived and the opinion of Council taken in the Case as the Master and Wardens shall think fit.

"1750. November 5. On reading the Opinions of Mr. Wilbraham, Sir Richard Lloyd and Mr. Campbell on the Company's Case with respect to the Livery, Resolved that it be considered at another summoned Court.

"1751. March 28. On a question, whether the Minute made to empower the Committee to take all proper measures for obtaining the Livery, be a standing Minute? It passed in the affirmative.

"1751. April 1. The Master reported from the Committee of 28th March their resolution that the Minute made to empower the Committee to take all proper measures for obtaining a Livery be a standing Minute. And it was ordered accordingly."

The Members of the Company were still dissatisfied, and on the 1st of July following—

"Mr. Devereux Bowly, and several other Members of the Company attended the Meeting and being called in desired to know what had been done in consequence of the orders of the General Court 19 June 1749. The said Orders being read, after some debate the question was put, whether the Court would proceed in consequence of the said Orders respecting the Livery?—and it was agreed in the affirmative. Being called in the Members were made acquainted with the said Resolution."

---

[1] Repertory 153, fol. 352 *et seq.*

The subject appears to have been quiescent during the ensuing three or four years, the next entry relating to it being as follows:—

"1755. April 7. The affair of the Livery being again under consideration and it appearing to the Court that the Company have a right to the Livery by the Ordinances confirmed according to the directions of the Act of Henry VII, It was solemnly first put to every Assistant present whether the Company should on the foundation of the Ordinance take up the Livery?—And a motion being made for balloting on that question, it was carried in the affirmative ten against five, Wherefore the Court doth order, that the Livery be taken up according to the Ordinance of this Company, as they are directed and empowered by the Ordinance to do."

The Company, however, in 1766, again determined to apply to the Court of Aldermen, and the following proceedings were thereupon agreed to :—

"1766. April 7. Ordered that the Livery be applied for, it being voted almost *nem. con.* advantageous for the Company. Ordered that the Committee be of the whole Court and that five of them be a quorum.

"1766. April 22. Ordered that the Clerk do prepare a Petition on account of obtaining the Livery for the Recorder, Common Serjeant, and Town Clerk to settle, and that he be allowed the assistance of an Attorney, and Mr. Benn being named was accepted. Ordered that Mr. Benn be invited to the next Monthly Court. Ordered that the Livery Fine be not less than Ten pounds.

"1766. April 30. At this Court the question was put, whether there should be an application to the Lord Mayor and Court of Aldermen for the obtaining the Livery of the City of London?

"It passed in the affirmative. And the next question was put whether the Livery Fine should be fixed for Ten pounds? It passed in the affirmative. And that the Court will use their utmost endeavours not to exceed that sum."

The Company's Minutes record that on the 10th June, 1766, the Petition was presented to the Court of Aldermen, and by them read and referred to a Committee. The terms of the Petition are as follow :—

"To the Right Honourable the Lord Mayor
and Court of Aldermen of the City of London.

"The Humble Petition of the Master, Wardens and Assistants and Fellowship of the Art or Mystery of Clockmaking of the City of London,

"Sheweth,—That his late Majesty King Charles the First (with the consent of this Honorable Court) by his Charter dated the 22nd of August in the 7th year of his reign 1631, did constitute and grant that all the Clockmakers and other persons as well Freemen of London as also all other natural born subjects using the Art or Mystery of Clockmaking within the said City or Ten Miles thereof should be for ever thereafter One Body Corporate by the name of the Master, Wardens and Fellowship of the Art or Mystery of Clockmaking of the City of London, And thereby gave and granted to them divers Immunities and Privileges and particularly a power to make Bye Laws and Ordinances for the better Rule and Government of the said Corporate Body.

"That in pursuance of such authority the said Company made several Bye Laws and Ordinances which were approved of and signed on the 11th of August 1632 by the then Lord Keeper and the two Chief Justices of the King's Bench and Common Pleas, agreable to the Act of Parliament amongst which Ordinances there is one to the following effect—That of the Master, Wardens and Fellowship there should be a Livery Company as was used in other Companies for the better service of his Majesty and of the City, and that the Master, Wardens and Assistants should elect such as should be of the Livery, and that such person so chosen should take the Oath therein mentioned.—That divers of the Members of the said Company are of considerable substance and are able and willing to bear the expence of a Livery and to contribute and assist on all public occasions for the honour and service of this City.

"That by an Act of Common Council made on the 15th day of October 1765 all persons following the trade of Clockmaking are obliged to be free of the said Company whereby the said Company will in a short time be greatly increased—the number of Shopkeepers at this time following the said trade within the City and not free of the said Company exceeding that of the present Members thereof.

"That your Petitioners humbly apprehend that if a Livery was granted to the said Company it would be a great benefit and advantage thereto and an encouragement to an ingenious, valuable and extensive branch of trade, as by means thereof the persons using the Art or Mystery of Watch and Clockmaking would be upon a respectable footing, equal with the rest of their fellow Citizens who are entitled to the benefit and privileges which by the customs of this City can be enjoyed by Liverymen only.

> "Your Petitioners therefore most humbly pray this Honorable Court to grant them the Livery of this City under such restrictions and regulations as to this Honorable Court shall seem meet.
>
> "And your Petitioners shall ever pray &c."

On the 24th of June, 1766, the Committee of the Aldermen met, and in the Company's Minutes it is stated that they—

"Examined the validity of the allegations mentioned in the Petition and declared that the Court had fully answered them and ordered a Report accordingly, which they would report to the Court of Aldermen the next Court day, which would be next Tuesday and that we should attend accordingly."

On the 1st of July, 1766, it is recorded that—

"The Court of Aldermen received the Report of the Committee, and after some time, the Petitioners being called in, the Lord Mayor was pleased to declare that they were constituted a Livery Company, and that the Fine should be Ten Pounds, and the number allowed to be Sixty—after which his Lordship wished us joy thereof, with peace and unanimity."

The Extract from the proceedings of the Court of Aldermen is as follows:—

"1766. 6 George III. 1 July. This day the Committee appointed the tenth day of June last to examine the allegations of the Petition of the Master, Wardens, Assistants and Fellowship of the Art or Mystery of Clockmaking of the City of London relating to their being made a Livery Company of this City, did deliver into this Court a Report in writing under their hands which was read in these Words,

"To the Right Honorable the Lord Mayor and Court of Aldermen,

"In obedience to an Order of this Honorable Court of the tenth day of June last, We whose Names are hereunto subscribed being appointed (amongst others) to examine the allegations of the Petition of the Master, Wardens, Assistants and Fellowship of the Art or Mystery of Clockmaking of the City of London relating to their being made a Livery Company of this City, and to report out opinions thereon to this Court. Do humbly certify that We have accordingly met and examined into the allegations of their said Petition, and do find that His late Majesty King Charles the First by his Charter dated the twenty-second of August in the seventh year of his Reign, 1631, did constitute and grant that all the Clockmakers and other persons as well Freemen of London as also all other natural born subjects using the Art or Mystery of Clockmaking within the said City or Ten Miles thereof should be for ever thereafter One Body Corporate by the Name of the Master, Wardens and Fellowship of the Art or Mystery of Clockmaking of the City of London, And thereby gave and granted to them divers immunities and privileges and particularly a power to make Bye Laws and Ordinances for the better Rule and Government of the said Corporate Body—That in pursuance of such authority the said Company made several Bye Laws and Ordinances which were approved of and signed on the eleventh of August 1632 by the then Lord Keeper and the two Chief Justices of the King's Bench and Common Pleas agreable to the Act of Parliament, amongst which Ordinances there is one to the following effect, That of the Master, Wardens and Fellowship, there should be a Livery Company as was used in other Companies for the better service of His Majesty and of the City, And that the Master, Wardens and Assistants should elect such as should be of the Livery, And that such person so chosen should take the Oath therein mentioned—That divers of the Members of the said Company are of considerable substance and are able and willing to bear the expense of a Livery and to contribute and assist on all public occasions for the honour and service of this City. That by an Act of Common Council made on the fifteenth day of October 1765, all persons following the trade of Clockmaking are obliged to be free of the said Company, whereby the said Company will in a short time be greatly increased, the number of shopkeepers at this time following the said trade within the City not free of the said Company exceeding that of the present Members—And after duly considering thereof it does appear to us that the complying with the prayer of their Petition will be beneficial to the said Company by encouraging and promoting the increase of their Members and contribute to the dignity and service of this City by enabling them to attend and assist on all public occasions; We are therefore of opinion that they should be created and made a Livery Company of this City and that the said Livery be granted unto them under the qualifications and conditions following (that is to say) That their

Livery fine be set at the sum of Ten Pounds Sterling—That the number on their Livery shall not at any time exceed Sixty—That they shall be subject to the several Orders of this Court respecting Livery Companies—That no Member of their Company who is of the Clothing of any other Company of this City shall be called on the Livery of their Company before he be translated from such other Company openly in this Court according to the ancient custom of this City—That they be enjoined to a constant attendance upon the Lord Mayor for the time being upon all public solemnities—And that their Charter and Bye Laws shall be enrolled among the Records of this Court. All which nevertheless We humbly submit to the judgement of this Honorable Court. Dated this first day of July 1766.

" F. Cokayne.
" Robert Alsop.
" Richard Peers.
" Richard Glyn.
" John Cartwright.
" William Cracraft.
" Barlow Trecothick.
" Brass Crosby.

"Which was well liked, approved of and confirmed by this Court, and ordered to be entered in the Repertory, and in all things performed—And it is further ordered that the Attorneys of the Outer Court do take care that Precepts be for the future sent to the said Company of Clockmakers upon all occasions as to the other Livery Companies of this City."

The Court of Assistants was summoned to meet on the 7th of July, 1766, when the Master was admitted the *First Liveryman*.

[1] " Mr. Thomas Hughes the Master was admitted on the Livery, put on the Clothing, and was sworn accordingly, as were afterwards the following gentlemen:—[2]

Mr. Fenn and Mr. Higgs, Wardens.

Mr. Whichcote		Mr. Sidey
Col. Carrington		Mr. Style
Mr. Dunlop	Assistants.	Mr. Merry
Mr. Webster		Mr. Addis
Mr. Garle		

Mr. Dudds	Mr. Aveline
Mr. Rd. Style	Mr. West
Mr. Benn	Mr. Rt. Poole
Mr. Howes	Mr. Hardy

All which put on the Clothing and were sworn accordingly."

---

[1] Company's Journal IV.
[2] Each Liveryman was required to pay to the Clerk 6s. 8d. and to the Beadle 3s. 4d. for their fees.

[1] "1766. July 16. At a Summoned Court held at the Paul's Head near Guildhall, the fifteen following were admitted on the Livery—

> Mr. Stephens } Assistants.
> Mr. Matthews
> Mr. Mitford } Past Stewards and fined
> Mr. Mudge   for Assistant.
> Mr. John Shelton
> Mr. Robt. Carrington } Past Stewards.
> Mr. Robt. Mitchell
> Mr. Chas. Bosley
> Mr. Wm. Rogerson
> Mr. Wm. Dutton
> Mr. Davd. Rivers
> Mr. Eliezer Chater
> Mr. Jno. Basire
> Mr. Hen. Billinghurst
> Mr. Newman Peachy

"1766. July 29.

> Mr. Henry Horne
> Mr. Henton Browne } Assistants.
> Mr. Devereux Bowly

Were admitted on the Livery.

"1766. August 6. The five following were admitted to the Livery—

> Mr. Edward Tutet
> Mr. John Merigeot
> Mr. John Prigg
> Mr. Tho. Nourse
> Mr. Tho. Lea.

"1766. September 3. The five following were admitted on the Livery—

> Mr. Francis Perigal } Assistants.
> Mr. James Browne
> Mr. Tho. Carrington
> Mr. Saml. Webster
> Mr. Southern Payne."

On the 9th of November, 1767, at the Inauguration of the Right Hon. Thomas Harley, brother to the Earl of Oxford, as Lord Mayor, the Master, attended by the Court and Livery, walked in procession for the first time; Robes, Flags and Music being provided for the occasion.[2]

The grant of the Livery gave new life to the Company, and in a few years the number limited to sixty was found to be insufficient for the full requirements of the Trade, which had then made great strides; and at a Meeting of the Master,

---

[1] Company's Journal IV.
[2] *Vide* pages 75, 76.

Wardens, and Court of Assistants on the 3rd of July, 1786, it was determined to apply to the Court of Aldermen for an increase in the number of the Livery, when it was—

"Moved and resolved that the Clerk do give notice in the summonses for the next Court, that the Company intend to take into their consideration the expediency of enlarging the number of the Livery and the fines."[1]

And on October the 9th it was—

"Resolved unanimously that it be referred to the Master and Wardens to make application to the Court of Lord Mayor and Aldermen to increase the number of the Livery to one hundred, and to endeavour that the fine be not less than Ten Pounds or more than Fifteen."[2]

Accordingly on October 23rd, a Draught of a Petition to the Court of Aldermen being produced, was read in the following words, viz.:—

"To the Right Honorable the Lord Mayor and Court of Aldermen.

"The humble petition of the Master Wardens and Assistants of the Fellowship of the Art or Mystery of Clockmakers of the City of London,

"Sheweth,—That on the tenth day of June One Thousand, seven hundred and sixty six a Petition of the said Fellowship of Clockmakers was presented to this Honorable Court which after reciting several parts of the Charter of the said Fellowship of the Art or Mystery of Clockmakers prayed that they might be allowed and constituted a Livery Company of this City; that this Honorable Court did on the same day refer the said Petition to a Committee of Aldermen who were desired to examine the allegations thereof and report their opinion thereon.

"That on the first day of June following the said Committee did report their opinion that the prayer of the said petition should be complied with, and this Honorable Court was pleased to approve and confirm the said report, and the said Fellowship of the Art or Mystery of Clockmakers was constituted one of the Livery Companies of this City accordingly.

"That your Petitioners beg leave to represent that when a vacancy happens by the death of any one of the Livery they are under great embarrassments from the various applications of a considerable number of respectable Freemen of the said Fellowship of Clockmakers who have been for a long time and now are desirous to take upon them the Clothing of the same, which number is greatly increased by persons becoming free of this City and following the profession of Clock or Watchmaking, being prohibited by Act of Common Council from being admitted into any other Company.

"Your Petitioners therefore humbly pray that this Honorable Court will be pleased to take the premises into consideration and grant an increase to the number of the Livery of the said Fellowship of the Art or Mystery of Clock-

---

[1,2] Company's Journal V.

makers under such regulations and orders for the honour and dignity of this City as this Honorable Court shall think fit.

"And a question being put That the said Petition be approved by this Court? the same was unanimously resolved in the affirmative.

"Ordered that the said Petition be fairly copied, sealed with the Company's Seal and presented to the Court of Aldermen forthwith.'

"1786. October 31. The Master with the Wardens and Messrs. Rivers, Stephens, Sergeant and Wray met at the Paul's Head Tavern, and affixed the Company's Seal to the Petition agreed to on the 23rd instant, in order to present it to the Court of Aldermen, and being clothed in their Livery Gowns, attended by the Clerk and Beadle proceeded to Guildhall. The Petition being given by the Master to Mr. Alderman Newnham who had passed the chair and was one of the City Representatives, he having previously undertaken to present it to the Court, in a short time the Master, Wardens &c. were called in and heard it read, and being asked by the Lord Mayor whether they had anything farther to say the Master answered no, and withdrew, and was presently informed by one of the Aldermen that their Petition was referred to a Committee.

"1786. November 28. The Master and Wardens with the Clerk attended a Committee of Aldermen, and being called in were examined concerning that part of the Petition (presented the 31 October) which sets forth that the Company were embarrassed by the number of applications on a vacancy in the Livery, and being satisfied with regard to the number and respectability of the applicants, they were desired to withdraw, and being called in again were informed that the Committee had agreed to report to the Court of Aldermen that the Livery should be extended to 120 and the fine be raised to £15, and made no doubt but the same would be confirmed by the Court.

The following are the proceedings of the Court of Aldermen thereon :—

"1786. December 5. This day the Committee appointed the thirty first day of October last to examine the allegations of the Petition of the Master, Wardens and Assistants of the Fellowship of the Art or Mystery of Clockmakers of this City, praying an increase to the number of their Livery, did this day deliver into the Court, a Report in writing under their hands which was read in these words

"To the Right Honorable the Lord Mayor and Court of Aldermen.

"In obedience to an order of this Honorable Court of the thirty-first day of October 1786, We whose names are hereunto subscribed being appointed amongst others to examine the allegations of the Petition of the Master, Wardens and Assistants of the Fellowship of the Art or Mystery of Clockmakers of this City, praying an increase to the number of their Livery, and to report our opinions thereon to this Court, Do certify that we have accordingly met and examined into the allegations of their said Petition.

"After duly considering thereof it does appear to your Committee that the complying with the prayer of their Petition, will be beneficial to the said Fellowship by encouraging and promoting the increase of their members.

---

¹ Company's Journal V.

" We are therefore of opinion that the number of their Livery should be increased to One Hundred and Twenty, and shall not at any time exceed the same; and that their Livery Fine be set at the Sum of Fifteen Pounds Sterling instead of Ten Pounds as heretofore directed by this Honorable Court. Dated this twenty eight day of November 1786.

"WM. PICKETT.
"JOHN HOPKINS.
"JAS. SANDERSON.

"BRASS CROSBY.
"WATKIN LEWES.
"NATHL. NEWNHAM.
"JOHN BURNELL.

"And a Motion being made and Question put, That this Court doth agree with the Committee in their said Report? the same was resolved in the Affirmative and ordered accordingly."

A Special Meeting of the Court of Assistants was convened on the 11th of December following, when—

"The Master informed the Court that their application had been successful and that this Court was called for the particular purpose of considering who were proper to be called on the Livery.

"Ordered that the following Twenty-seven Gentlemen be summoned to take up their Livery at the next Quarterly Court to be holden on the 8th day of January 1787 viz.

Mr. Francis Perigal, Junr.
,, Christopher Beck
,, Richard Grove
,, Thomas Carpenter
,, William Blackburn
,, Richard Somersall
,, Adam Stevenson
,, John Baptist Bushman
,, James Rawlins
,, Edward Gibson
,, William Jones
,, Timothy Chisman
,, Owen Jones
,, George Marmd. Metcalf

Mr. George Clerk
,, John Thwaites
,, George Carrington
,, John Willm. Jarratt
,, John Wickes
,, William Dorrell
,, John Mattocks
,, David Bucklee
,, Thomas Bayley
,, William Pearce
,, Thomas Moss
,, James Young
,, John Rainier."

On the 8th of January, 1787, the following seventeen Gentlemen were admitted on the Livery, paid their fines, were clothed and sworn:—

"Mr. Francis Perigal Junr.
,, Chris'r. Beck
,, Thos. Carpenter
,, Richd. Somersall
,, Edwd. Gibson
,, Willm. Jones
,, Timy. Chisman
,, Geo. Curson Addis
,, Fran. Upjohn

Mr. Geo. Marmd. Metcalf
,, Geo. Clarke
,, Jno. Wm. Jarratt
,, Wm. Dorrell
,, David Bucklee
,, Wm. Pearce
,, Thos. Bayley
,, John Rainier."

On the 2nd of April—

"Mr. Willm· Faulkner
,, Thos· Pepper
,, Edwd· Leeming
,, Jas. Mc Cabe

Mr. Willm· Kemp
,, Thyar Pitt
,, Jno. Mattocks
,, Bern^d· Jarrett."

On the 7th of May—

"Mr. Saml· Jno· Collingwood
,, John Brooks

Mr. Jno· Starey
,, John Young."

And on the 24th of May—

"Mr. William Pitt was admitted."

The Company still continued to make steady progress, and the numerous applications that were made by Freemen to take up their Livery, rendered it in the opinion of the Court of Assistants desirable to make a further application to the Court of Aldermen to increase the number, and accordingly on the 2nd of April, 1810, they again referred the matter to a Committee for consideration, who after consulting precedents submitted a form of Petition to the Court of Aldermen, which was adopted in similar terms to the last recited. It was presented to the latter body on the 15th May, 1810; the usual course of referring it to a Committee for consideration was followed by them, and the report of their Committee, recommending that the number should be increased to 200, was sanctioned and approved.

On the 26th July the Court of Assistants met to give effect to the permission thus obtained, and

"The following Gentlemen, Citizens and Clockmakers, were (on their respective solicitations) elected upon the Livery by shew of hands :—

Mr. Willm· Newell
,, Chas. Merrill
,, Robt· Coulson
,, Joseph Glenny
,, Peter Lecount
,, Thos· Pattee
,, Jos^h· York Hatton
,, Sep^ts· Miles
,, Willm· Procter
,, Jas. Hatton

Mr. Thos. Saml· Stephenson
,, Frans. Hay^d· Sinderby
,, Edwd· Tayler
,, Edm^d· Collingridge
,, Robt· Newman
,, Thos. Rogers
,, Robt· Newman
,, Geo. Edlin
,, Willm· Charlstrom
,, Edwd. Griffiths

Mr. Mich{}^{l.} Foreman
" J{}n^{o.} Haughton Wickes
" John Wontner
" Jos^{h.} Newcomb
" Richd. Webster
" J{}n^{o.} Richardson
" Willm. Francis
" Richd. Cavendish

Mr. Chas. D^{rs.} F^{k.} Valentine
" Jas. Potter
" Alex. Copeland
" Thos. Bidlake
" Jas. Masters
" John Newman
" Fred^{k.} Silver
" Willm. Willin

and they were directed to be summoned to take upon them the Clothing at the next Monthly Court which was held on the 3rd of September when the following Gentlemen attended and were sworn :—

Mr. Chas. Merrill, jun^{r.}
" Robert Coulson
" Joseph Glenny
" Peter Lecount
" Thos. Saml. Stephenson
" Frans. Hay^{d.} Sinderby
" Edmund Collingridge
" Edward Tayler
" William Charlstrom
" Edwd. Griffiths
" John Haughton Wickes
" John Richardson
" Richard Webster

Mr. Thomas Pattee
" Septimus Miles
" William Procter
" James Hatton
" Richard Cavendish
" James Potter
" Alexander Copeland
" Thomas Bidlake
" James Masters
" Robert Newman
" Frederick Silver
" William Willin.

"1813. November 2. William Mansell of Rosoman Street Clerkenwell Watch Case Maker who was summoned to take the Livery on the 19 August 1812, again on 7 September 1812 and repeated on the 11th October last was peremptorily summoned to be at this Court and being now in attendance for the first time refused to take the Clothing and the penalty of Fifteen Pounds being awarded against him for such refusal he paid the same in Court and his Election to the Livery was thereupon discharged.

"William Welborne of Leather Lane Holborn having been summoned to take the Livery in November 1811 and also in January, February and July 1812, but having failed so to do was again summoned for that purpose to the last Quarter Court when he attended and requested until this day promising either to take the Clothing or pay the penalty for refusal, he being now present and declining to take the same, the penalty of £15 was ordered to be enforced, which being paid in Court his Election to the Livery was likewise thereupon discharged."[1]

In the year 1826, the Livery, upon the application of the Company, was again increased by the Court of Aldermen, the usual proceedings having previously been adopted as on former occasions. Their order, dated the 11th April, 1826, authorises the number of Liverymen to be 250, and directs the Livery Fine to be set at £21, including the fees payable to the Clerk and Beadle, at which it still remains.

[1] Company's Journal.

The Court having had some doubts as to the ability of the Company to enforce their Bye-Laws for compelling Members to take upon them the Livery when elected thereto, the Master was requested to have a Case drawn and to obtain the opinion of Counsel thereon, which he accordingly did, and submitted the same to Mr. Mirehouse, one of the Common Pleaders of this City, and subsequently Common Serjeant, who was requested to advise the Company whether they could compel Freemen to take up their Livery, and by what means, and in case of refusal, whether the Company could safely adopt the course prescribed by the 63rd Bye-Law to recover the penalty thereby inflicted on individuals refusing to take up the Livery.

The opinion thereon is as follows :—

"1830. July 5th. I am of opinion that the Company may compel Freemen to take up their Livery, and that if they refuse to do so, the Company may recover the penalty under the Bye Law by an Action of Debt.

"(Signed) J. MIREHOUSE.

"12, Paper Buildings, Temple,
June 30, 1830."

FREEMEN.

Upon the Incorporation of the Company, the original Members were Freemen of the Blacksmiths' and other Guilds, and, as has been shewn in the Chapter on the Charter and Bye-Laws, such of them as could obtain the consent of their Companies were translated and recorded as Citizens and Clockmakers ; those, however, who could not obtain such consent, bound their Apprentices to other Freemen of this Company, whereby in time they acquired the right of admission to the Freedom thereto by servitude.

The ranks of the Freemen were also constantly being augmented by the admission of persons using any of the varied branches of the trade who took up their Freedom by purchase or redemption.

The cost of translation varied, and was in some cases very considerable. One or two Extracts, shewing early instances of the custom in connection with this Company, are here introduced :—

"1636-7. January 19. The following sum was laid out by Symon Hackett Renter-warden about the translation of Mr. Richard Masterson from the Clothiers to the Clockmakers.'

		£	s.	d.
Item.	Spent with Mr. Williams at two several times Mr. Masterson being then present		2	0
Item.	Paid to Mr. Williams Clarke		2	6
Item.	Paid to the Chamberlayne of London for his fee	1	2	0
Item.	Paid to the Towne Clerke		5	0
Item.	Paid to the Common Cryer		3	0
Item.	Paid to the Clothworkers Beadle to warn the Company		5	0
Item.	Given to the Clothworkers a Silver Cupp price	1	10	0
Item.	Given a watch . . . . . price	4	0	0
Item.	Given to Mr. Latham a Clock . . price	3	0	0
	Sum total	£10	9	6

' Company's Journal I.

THE CLOCKMAKERS' COMPANY. 113

"1636-7. February 20. These moneys following were allowed unto the Renter-warden Simon Hackett for the translation of Mr. Dawson and Mr. Durant from the Imbroderers to the Clockmakers.'

Item.	To the Beadle of the Imbroderers Company to warn their Company	£	s.	d.
			2	6
Item.	The Towne Clarkes fees for both		10	0
Item.	To the Common Cryer for his fees for both		6	0
Item.	To the Chamberlayne for his fees for both		2	4	0
Item.	To Mr. Dawson and Mr. Durant		2	1	6
	Sum total	£5	4	0

"1724. April 6. Mr. John Shirley appeared at this Court and consented to pay twenty pounds to the use of the Company pursuant to an order of the last Quarterly Court, on condition that this Court translate him to the Vintners Company, but desired this Court would take his bond for twelve months for the payment thereof which was agreed to, and the Clerk is ordered to prepare a bond for that purpose.²

"1811. November 4. James Masters, a free Clockmaker and a Member of the Livery, attended the Court for the purpose of requesting their permission to be translated unto one of the Twelve Companies, urging that he had very particular reasons which made him desirous of obtaining the freedom of the Goldsmiths' Company.

"Ordered—That the Clerk do inform James Masters that the Company cannot part with its Members, but with the utmost regret and reluctance, notwithstanding which the Court is induced, upon the representations made, to comply with his request upon payment to the Company of the sum of Fifty Pounds.

"1812. January 13. James Masters who had applied at the November Court for permission to be translated from this Company to the Goldsmiths' and to which this Court had returned their answer, again applied and declared himself willing to pay the sum of Thirty Pounds for such permission and hoped the Court would agree to the same.

"Resolved—That this Court do comply with the request of James Masters to translate him to the Goldsmiths' Company upon his payment of the sum of Thirty Pounds.

"1812. April 14. The Master accompanied by Messrs. Potter, Thwaites, D. Rivers, Jackson and Marriott, together with the Clerk and Beadle all clothed attended the Court of Aldermen this day at Guildhall and translated James Masters unto the Company of Goldsmiths, he having previous thereto paid unto the Renter Warden the sum of Thirty Pounds, conformable to the resolution of the last Christmas Quarter Court.

"1844. February 5. A letter was read from Mr. George Russell a Liveryman requesting permission to withdraw himself from this Company for the purpose of being translated to the Company of Salters.

"Resolved that his request be complied with on his paying a Fine of £30 together with £5 for calling a special meeting to attend the Members of the Salters Company to the Court of Aldermen.

---

¹ Company's Journal I.   ² Company's Journal III.

"The Master, Mr. Joseph Fenn, with several Members of the Court, attended the Court of Aldermen on his being translated."

By the Bye-Laws of the Company, made on the 30th November, 1631, and approved on the 11th August, 1632, in accordance with the Act of Parliament of the 25th January, 19 Henry VII, it was enacted that no person should use the Trade, Art, or Mystery of a Clockmaker, Mathematical Instrument Maker, Sun-dial Maker, Graver, Casemaker, or any thing otherwise peculiarly belonging to the same trade, unless he had served as apprentice for seven years; and the view, search, and survey of the goods of such trade were also given to the Company.

There is no reason to doubt that thenceforward the persons using the various branches of the trade enumerated in the Bye-Laws, who carried on business within the City of London and its liberties, were required to take up their Freedom in this Company, and from time to time were admitted as Members of the Fellowship.

In the year 1677 there is an entry on the Minutes of the Court of Assistants of the admission of a number of Mathematical Instrument Makers at one time, a fact which is a strong evidence in favor of the claim subsequently put forward by this Company in opposition to the Spectacle Makers, to which reference is hereafter made.

"1667. February 24. The persons whose names are hereunder subscribed being by trade Mathematical Instrument Makers and free of severall Companyes in London were admitted Brethren of the Company of Clockmakers of London, and all of them (except Helkiah Bedford, Robert Fole, Isaac Carver, and John Sellars, who in their judgements dissent from taking an Oath) did take the Oath of the Company ffor which their admission they altogether paid to Mr. Thomas Claxton, Renter Warden of the said Company the sume of twelve pounds for the use of the said Company, and have submitted and severally promised and obliged themselves to conforme and yield obeydience unto the Constitutions, Ordinances, Orders and Government of the same Company of Clockmakers'[1] :—

Walter Hayes		
Helkiah Bedford	John Marke	James Atkinson
John Browne	Phillip Smith	Edward Fage
Walter Henshaw	Joseph Wells	John Bell
William Howe	John Nash	Robert Starr
William Elmes	Isaac Carver	John Sellars
Robert Fole	Robert Cooke	James Griffith."

[1] Company's Journal I.

Others were subsequently admitted upon payment of a fine of Twenty Shillings each.

"1669. September 29. John Briggs a Cutter of Glasses for Watches, formerly a Soldier under the Duke of Albemarle, when the king was restored, produced the Act of Parliament 12° Car. II^d enabling Soldiers of the Army then to be disbanded, to exercise trades, and a certificate according to the said Act, and prayed to be admitted a Brother of the Company, who was thereupon admitted and sworn a Brother and for his admission did promise to pay to the Company twenty shillings within a week's time and to be conformable to the orders of the Company."[1]

"1719. September 29. It was ordered that the French Watchmakers and other Foreigners be informed that they may be admitted into the Freedom of this Company, but that none be admitted unless at a summoned Court."[2]

"1719. October 1. Paid by Mr. Warden Markwick at a Meeting at the 'Angell and Crowne,' with the Master elect, to consider of proper Frenchmen to be invited to take up their Freedome £0.8.0."[3]

The Court of Assistants tried for many years to obtain an Act of Common Council for regulating the Freedom of the Company, but they did not succeed until 1765.

The following Extracts refer to the various proceedings in reference to this object :—

"1694-5. January 14. It was ordered that the Company do endeavour to procure and obtain an Act of Common Council to oblige all persons for the future who have right to the Freedom of the City of London, and work in any branch or part of the Art of Clockmaking and Watchmaking, or either of them, to take the Freedom of this Company, and that all persons free of other Companies working in either of the said Arts shall bind their Apprentices to this Company for the future."[4]

"1696. April 6. Ordered that the Master and Wardens of the Company do endeavour to procure an Act of Common Council according to the order of the Court of the 14th January 1695 at the charge of the Company."[5]

The subject did not come before the Common Council until the 20th of April in the following year, when the Petition of the Company is found entered at length in the Journals of that Court, in the following terms :—

"1677. April 20. At this Court the Petition of ye Master Wardens and Assistants of ye Company of Clockmakers London was read wch follows in these words [6]

"To the Right Honõble ye Lord Mayor and Aldrẽn of the City of London and the Cõmons in Cõmon Councill assembled

"The humble Petition of ye Master Wardens and Assistants of the Company of Clockmakers London

---

[1] Company's Journal I. [2] Company's Journal III.
[3, 4, 5] Company's Journal II. [6] Journal of Common Council, No. 52, fol. 97.

"Sheweth—That whereas it hath been found convenient y^t persons of p̃ticular trades or mysteryes should be incorporated wth imunityes and powers to ye end y^t some expert and skillfull in each Art might take by search and inspection to suppress and regulate ye abuses daily com̃itted by ye ignorant and unskillfull y^t ye subject might not be imposed on, nor the creditt of such Arts or Mysteryes diminished.

"And whereas by y^r Petitioners Charter of Incorporaçõn dated ye 22nd day of August in ye 7th yeare of the reigne of King Charles ye first, inrolled amongst ye Records of this City, All p̃sons who shall use ye Art Trade or Mystery of makeing Clocks Watches and Alarums, Boxes or Cases for such, Mathematicall instruments, dialling and other worke p̃perly belonging thereunto wthin ye Limits of y^r Petitioners grant ought to be subject unto and regulated by ye rules and ord^{rs} of ye said Company.

"And whereas many psons useing ye said Arte or part thereof do daily endeavour to become Freemen, and are made free of other Companyes, not practizing any part of y^r Petitioners Art, who have no skill nor knowledge of ye goodness or insufficiency of any of ye worke belonging thereto, and such psons, beinge exempted from ye Governm^t of y^r Peticõners and the subjection to such orders as are needfull for ye reforming ye abuses com̃itted in ye said Art, do make up much bad and deceitfull worke both in ye materialle and workemanship to ye scandall of the said Arts and the abuse of the Citizens of this City and others.

"And for ye continuance of such practizes will tend to make ye constituçõns and priviledges, obteyned by y^r peticõners predecessors, rather a burthen y^n an advantage to such ingenious Artists as are conformable to good orders and rules both in respect of their worke and ye numb^r of their App^{n}tices.

"Your Petitioners therefore humbly pray this hoñoble Court will please to pass an Act of this Court in behalfe of y^r Petitioners that all persons now or hereafter using ye said Trade Art or Mystery of Clockmaking, Watchmaking, Mathematicall Instrument makeing, Dialling or any branch thereof that are Freemen of this City shall cause all their App^{r}ntices for the time to come to be bound to and made free of ye Company of Clockmakers, and that the App^{r}ntices now bound to the said Trade shall at ye expiraçõn of their App^{r}nticeshipps take their freedom of ye said Company, that in time they may be incorporated into one body whereby y^r Petitioners humbly conceive they may be enabled to regulate and reforme y^e abuses in y^e said Arts, and keep up y^e reputacon thereof att home and abroad.

"And y^r Petition^{rs} shall pray &c.

Edward Stanton,	Master.	Walter Henshaw
John Ebsworth	⎫	Henry Wynne
Rob$^t\cdot$ Williamson	⎬ Wardens.	Joseph Windmille
Rob$^t\cdot$ Halsted	⎭	Thomas Tompion
Edward Morris		James Markwick
John Harris		Charles Gretton
Nathan$^l\cdot$ Barrow		Thomas Hanconne
Nicasius Russell		William Speakman.

"And thereupon y^e consideration thereof was referred to y^e Committee for letting and demiseing y^e lands and tenements given to this City by Sr Thomas Gresham, Knight, deceased, who are to report their opinions thereof to this Court."

At a Meeting of the Court of Assistants on the 3rd of May, 1697, the draft of a Bill intended for an Act of Common Council, was read and approved, and the Master and Wardens were desired to prosecute the same with all care and dispatch, and to disburse what charges were necessary therein.

Before, however, the matter had proceeded further, the Blacksmiths' Company, from whom, as has been already shewn, the Clockmakers emanated, petitioned the Common Council against the Bill in these words :—

"1697. May 14. At this Court ye Petic̄ōn of ye Keepers or Wardens of ye Society of Blacksmiths London was read and follows in these words [1]

"To ye right hoñoble the Lord Mayor Aldermen and Comons of ye City of London in Comōn Counccll assembled

"The humble Petic̄ōn of ye Keepers or Wardens and society of ye Art or Mystery de Lez Blacksmiths London

"Sheweth—That ye Company of Clockmakers haveing lately petitioned y^t by an Act of this honōble Court all Clockmakers may be obleiged to bind and make free wth y^m (or to such like purpose) And forasmuch as ye same will be a great intrenchm^t upon your Petitioners and irreparably injurious to them—

"Your Pet^{rs} therefore most humbly pray y^t they may be heard by themselves or their Councill as need may require against ye subject matter of ye said Petic̄ōn and any Bill y^t may thereupon be brought in and may have a copy of ye said petic̄ōn and notice from time to time of y^r p̄ceedings therein.

"And y^r Pet^{rs} shall ever pray &c.

Thomas Day } Wardens. Francis Pound
Robert Blackett   Thomas Lee
John Webster   Macklin Green
Wm. Buck   John Whitehead
                          Richard Lidiard.

"And thereupon ye consideratc̄ōn thereof was referred to the Coh̄iitee app^{tcd} to consider of ye petition lately p̄sented to this Court by ye Company of Clockmakers London."

Whilst the Petition was before the Committee of the Common Council, the Blacksmiths appear to have taken very active measures in opposition to the Bill, and the following Extracts from the Records of that Company serve to elucidate the causes which led to a state of feeling between the two bodies, happily now only matter of history :—

"At a Meeting of the Court of Assistants of the Blacksmiths' Company 18th May 1697. This Court being acquainted with the petition of the

---

[1] Journal of Common Council, No. 53, fol. 99^b.

Clockmakers and their purpose to obtain an Act of Common Council to have all Clockmakers and others made free of them, Resolved that this Company will oppose the Clockmakers in their present designe and that the utmost endeavours be used to prevent their obteying the Act prayed for in their petition. That the management thereof be left to the Wardens.[1]

"1697. June 8. The Committee appointed by the Court of Common Council met, when the following reasons against the Bill were delivered in on behalf of the Blacksmiths' Company

"That one maine part of their Peticõn for having all Clockmakers bind in their Company (tho' free of others) is impracticable, the late Act of Parliament for releife of the orphans enjoyning every p̃son to bind in ye Comp^y whereof he is a member.

"That the reasons assigned for such Bill which are that p̃sons useing the s^d art or part thereof become free of other Comp^es not practising any part of their art and have no skill nor knowledge of any of the workes thereto belonging doe not at all concern the Blacksmiths, for it is well knowne that they are the originall and proper makers of Clocks &c. and have full skill and knowledge therein and that many of their employments are wholly in such worke Therefore hope the Clockmakers intend not to include the Smiths in such their Bill, nor can it be thought reasonable that all p̃sons exerciseing the Clockmakers art or any branch (part) thereof shalbe within the limitts or meaning of such act (as they pray) because it will necessarily take in the Artists in Smithery.

"That the Blacksmiths are Artists (yea the most curious) in such worke is undeniable matter of fact and doth plainly appear, not only in that ye most Artists therein at this day were Smiths in their originall, but it appears in that no Clockmaker can finish any Clocks &c. without the distinct and peculiar workmanship of ye Smith, yet the Smith can entirely do of himself because the whole (indeed) is but a branch of ye Art of Smithery and having been always so accompted the Blacksmiths Comp^y have therefore hitherto enjoyed all Clockmakers, Watchmakers &c. that were members of them, And highly just and reasonable it is That in regard the said Art of Smithery is not only of great antiquity and use but absolutely necessary it should be encouraged, And the ingenious improvers thereof permitted to continue in the society to which they originally and of a right, belong for the benefit and reputacõn thereof. And that all the Grants heretofore made to them by the Kings and Queens of this Realme should be construed to their greatest advantage, and that no subsequent Grant or Charter should be taken or interpreted to ye p̃judice or diminution thereof.

"The Clockmakers grand plea or allegation y^t abuses are committed in the Trade because p̃sons exerciseing it are made ffree of other Comp^es unskilled therein, and are exempted from Government is of no force with respect to the Blacksmith, who is as good if not a better and more competent judge thereof then they, and indeed it is but a specious pretence of theirs, for ye Clockmakers have never yet given any instance of their ability or care in that matter. Nor is it apprehended how they ever can, Whereas the Comp^y of Blacksmiths have (as need required) reformed the abuses of their trade and particularly a few months since expended a considerable sume for the publick good in detecting and punishing ye makers and owners of some bad and deceitful wares and workmanship apperteying to their Art, and while the Clockmakers work in

[1] Journal of Blacksmiths' Company X.

part of their Art of Smithery they must be subject to the Blacksmiths searches agreable to Charter and Ordinances of said Blacksmiths Comp[y] and antient Custome of this City.

"Such act will not only be injurious to ye Blacksmiths Comp[y] but highly p[e]juditiall to ye City in that it will incapacitate those who have and may be bound in a Livery Comp[y] from serving the Publick in many things in such a Comp[y] which they will be p[e]vented in doing when removed (contrary to their will and designe) to one that neither enjoys that priviledge nor is constituted of such members as ever yet shewed a willingness (tho otherwise able enough) to contribute (as such) to the support of the City Grandeur, and it must necessarily be injurious to the p̃sons so removed because then their dutys of Quarteridge &c. will be double and the ffines for Steward &c. as great and yet they deprived of an equell right with their fellow citizens and hindered in doing y[t] service for ye publick which otherwise they might have had and done.

"The Company of Blacksmiths have from antient times had a Livery, and as such have all along sustained great charges in contributing to ye grandeur of this hono[ble] City, have been at great costs in building a Hall, do pay considerable taxes to the Kings Maj[tie,] they also pay to the church and poor, and bear Armes in the Militia &c. none of all which is done by the Clockmakers Comp[y.]

"The said Company of Blacksmiths by meanes of the great charge they have been at in building their Hall, and other incident charges as a Livery, have been a long time and still are in Debt, and if such a Branch (w[ch] for so long time they have enjoyed) should be taken from them, and ye Clockmakers Watchmakers &c. (their members) prohibited ye making of their apprentices of them, especially at this time when the decay of Trade in generall and impoverishment of the said Blacksmiths' Art in particular is so great, they shall not be able to sustain their necessary charges.

"1697. June 10. The Committee of the Common Council met and some of the Wardens and Assistants appeared ag[st] the pet[rs] where the pet[rs] gave their reasons for the Bill but forewent our part of their peticõn, to witt that concerning binding, and then objected an agreement said by them to be made bet[w] their Comp[y] and ours and some other things as a barr to our opposicõn— Concerning which matter the Clerk in behalf of the Comp[y] denied their unacquaintedness, and being therefore altogether unprovided to give an answer thereto desired 14 days time to inquire and consider thereof, which was granted, and also craved that the Com[te] would order that they might have coppeys of these things the Clockmakers produced which was ordered wee paying therefore."[1]

COPY OF AGREEMENT.

"Item: That no p̃son or p̃sons now inhabiting or dwelling or which hereafter shall inhabit or dwell within the said City or within Four Miles of the same and there use or exercise either the s[d] Art or Mistery of a Blacksmith or a Spurrier (excepting those p̃sons free of the Comp[y] of Armorers London) nor no other p̃son being the s[d] Society De lez Blacksmiths London shall hereafter take any p̃son or p̃sons to be his or their Apprentice or Apprentices not being borne within the Kings obeysance nor shall by any Cullor or Device bind or cause to be bound his Apprentice or Apprentices to himselfe

---

[1] Journal of Blacksmiths' Company XI.

or to any other p̄son being free of any other Society or Comp^y whereby his said Apprentice and Apprentices may not be a ffreeman and ffreemen of the s^d Society De lez Blacksmiths London. But that all p̄sons useing the said Arts or Misterys or either of them and being free of any Society Guild or Fraternity whatsoever (except as afores^d) shall bind their Apprentices to some freeman of this Society to the intent they may become ffreeman of the same according to their Letters Patents in that behalfe granted, And excepted and provided alwayes That those that now are or hereafter shall be free of this Society and professe the Art and Trade of Clockmaking (so they be not great Church Clockmakers of Iron) may bind their Apprentice or Apprentices to some ffree Clockmaker of London to become ffreemen thereof, this Constitucõn notwithstanding, Nor shall any p̄son of the Society teach or instruct any other Man Servt or Apprentice above the space of one month unless he be presented and admitted by the Keepers or Wardens of this Society, Nor shall sett to worke any other man's Apprentice neither shall retain keep or sett to worke in the Art or Mistery which he useth any p̄son or p̄sons other then his owne child or children above the space of one month before he shall take and binde him to be his Apprentice by Indenture to be made by the Clerke of this Society for the terme of seven years at the least, And that if any p̄son shall offend in any point of this Ordinance That then he shall forfeit and pay to the s^d Keepers or Wardens and Society for every his offence Ten pounds of lawfull English money or such less sume of like money as by the s^d Keepers or Wardens and their Assistants or the more part of them for the time being (whereof two of the Keepers or Wardens to be two) shall be ordered and adjudged to be paid for every such offence.

Josyas Deveris } Wardens of ye	Sampson Shelton Master	} of ye
Robert Chaplin } Blacksmiths.	Richard Masterson } Wardens	} Clock-
The marke[RK] of Robt Kilborne	Richard Morgan	} makers.

"1697. June 29. The Warden Markham and Renter Warden and Mr. Briscoe and Ed. Freeman who had the manageing of this affair [met the Committee appointed by the Court of Common Council]. They desired that the Clockmakers might prove that which they had produced and called by them an agreement, wee apprehending it not to be any such thing as not having any date nor place expressed, no due confirmation, nor any witnesses, which they could not directly do but produced their Records which set forth that there had formerly been a contest between the two Companies, their plea and our answer, and then an order of my Lord Keeper about 1638 or 9 for both Companies to attend him in order to have the business settled whereupon they affirm'd this agreement was made and argued that it was in our books and thereupon the Courte asked for our books whereto was answered that we had no directions from this Court, therefore they were not brought, but should be ready to observe their ord^rs therein, the Courte seemed to take it for granted that it was in our Books whereupon the Clarke further objected that it could have no binding or conclusive force as an agreement being signed by the Wardens only and one other person when there were 4 Wardens always equall in power and trust and for that a thing of this nature ought to be done under the Comon Seale of the Company. The Court thereupon wav'd the consideration thereof and directed to proceed to the meritts of the case as now it stood that they might judge whether it were now fitt to be allowed of wch accordingly was done in substance much the same with what is herein before inserted and the comprehensive clauses in Charter and Ordinances relative to binding making free turning over &c. were read and urged. It admitted of a long debate in Committee and their Clerk informed us they had agreed upon a Report Speciall."[1]

The Report of the Committee of the Common Council on the subject was presented to that Court on the 8th October following, in which they recommended that the Petition of the Clockmakers should be complied with and a Bill brought in accordingly, which was done, but being still opposed by the Blacksmiths, it was recommitted and stood over for some time. Eventually on the Petition of the Clockmakers, a new Committee was appointed who brought in another Bill against which the Blacksmiths continued their opposition, both sides being heard by Counsel,[2] and the Bill was finally thrown out on the third reading, on the 31st November, 1698. The proceedings are given at length in the following Extracts:—

"At a Common Council held on the 8th October 1697, Clarke Mayor. This day the Com^tee to whom the Peticon of the Master and Wardens and Assistants of the Company of Clockmakers was referred did deliver into this Court a Report in writeing under their hands touching the same the tenour whereof follows, viz.

"To the Right Honoble the Lord Mayor Aldren and Comons in Comon Councill assembled.

"In obedience to an Order of this Honoble Court bearing date the 20th day of Aprill last past We whose names are hereunto subscribed being of the Com^tee appointed by the said Order to consider of the Peticon of the Master Wardens and Assistants of the Company of Clockmakers And also an Order of this honoble Court bearing date the 14th day of May last to consider of the Peticon of the Keepers or Wardens and Society of the Art or Mystery de lez Blacksmiths London have sev^all times mett and considered of the m^res sett forth in the said Peticons and have heard the Allegacons on both sides and have seen entries in the Bookes of the said Companies and a Report made and confirmed in Bromfeild's Mayoralty dated the 16th June 1636 purporting that such persons as used the Art of makeing watches and chamber clocks and would not be translated to the Society of Clockmakers or could not procure the Companies whereof they were free to give their consent thereto should notwithstanding bind their App^ntices to some freeman of the said Company of Clockmakers and be made free of the said Company And also an agreem^t made and signed by the then Master Wardens and Assistants of the Company of Clockmakers and the Wardens of the Blacksmiths purporting that those which then were or should hereafter be free of the Society of Blacksmiths and professe the Art or trade of Clockmaking (except great Church Clockmakers of Iron) might bind their App^ntice or App^ntices to some free Clockmaker of London to become free of the Clockmakers Company.

---

[1] Journal of Blacksmiths' Company XI.
[2] By the Company's Minutes of the 25th November, 1698, it appears that the Counsel selected by the Clockmakers were Sir Bartholomew Showers, Mr. Northey, Mr. Cowper, and Mr. Dee.

And being satisfied of the great losse of trade the said Company of Clockmakers have and may sustein by reason of the exportacōn of great quantities of badd goods both in Workmanship and Mr̃cialls made up and sold by sev͡all persons exerciseing the Trade or Mystery of Clockmaking and Watchmaking being free of other Companies and keeping more App^ntices then the said Company lawfully can, whereby the number of Clockmakers are extreamly multiplied and not well educated in the said Trade, and doe procure their freedomes in other Companies, by reason whereof they are not subject to nor under the governm^t views searches and correccōns of the said Company of Clockmakers, nor obliidged to observe the Rules Lawes and Ordinances of the same Company. For remedy whereof and to the intent that all freemen of this Citie using any of the said Arts or Trades of making Clocks Watches Larrums and Boxes and Cases for them and Mathematicall Instrum^ts Sunn Dyalls or other Workes belonging p͡perly to the said Art or Trade of Clockmaking may in time be compelled to be made free of the said Company of Clockmakers And that the Master and Wardens of the said Company for the time being may hereafter have lawfull power to make a more free and effectuall search inspeccōn and correccōn of all frauds deceipts and defaults com̃itted and done by persons useing the said Arts and Trades last mencōned within this Citie and Libt̃ies thereof then heretofore they have had whereby such frauds deceipts abuses and offences may be discovered and punished according to the Antient Lawes and Customes of this City, We are humbly of opinion That it may be enacted by this hono^ble Court that all and every person and persons using and exerciseing the Art Mystery or Trade of making Clocks Watches Larums Boxes and Cases for them Mathematicall Instrum^ts Sunndyalls or any other Worke properly belonging to the said Art Trade or Mistery or any part thereof (being free of other Companies) or the Clerkes of the Companies such persons are free of doe from and after the   day of   next immediately after the binding of any App^ntice or App^ntices, deliver the names of the App^ntice or App^ntices soe bound and the date of the indr̃es of such App^ntice or App^ntices soe bound to the Master, Wardens or Assistants of the said Company of Clockmakers for the time being or one of them to th'end such App^ntice or App^ntices soe bound may for the future be compeleable to take up their freedomes in the Company of Clockmakers And that all App^ntices already bound or hereafter to be bound to any person or persons useing or exerciseing the said Art Trade or Mistery of making Clocks or Watches Larums Boxes and Cases for them, Mathematicall Instrum^ts Sunndyalls, or any other Work properly belonging to the said Art Trade or Mistery or any parte thereof free of any other Company whatsoever And also that all and every person or persons whatsoever useing or exerciseing the Art Trade or Mistery last mencōned or any or either of them having any right to their freedoms of this Citie by Patrimony Redempcōn or otherwise be for the future oblidged to take up their freedomes and be made free of the said Company of Clockmakers only. All which neverthelesse is humbly submitted to the great wisdome and judgm^t of this hono^ble Court. Dated this 7th day of October, 1697

    Ric. Levett   O. Buckingham   Edw. Wills
    James Boddington   Tho. Pitts   John Harvey

Which being read and the Question being put Whether a Bill should be brought in upon the said Report It was carried in the Affirmative and referred to the said Com^tee to bring in a Bill pursuant to the said Report.[1]

---

[1] Journal of Common Council, No. 52, fol. 143 *et seq.*

"1697. October 27. Clockmakers' affair. The major part of the Committee favouring the Clockmakers' cause did agree upon a report after our hearing in June last and signed the same severally without having a Committee therefore which gave offence to some of the Committee and thereupon diverse Committees were summoned in the month of September but without effect and on the 7th of October was a Committee where were p'sent Sr Richard Levett Sr Owen Buckingham Sr Edwd Mills Col. Boddington Mr. Harvey and Capt Pitts when the Report was read, and it being our Quarter day Mr. Holland Mr. Markham and Mr. Clements only appeared who endeavoured to possess ye Court with the disadvantages upon y^t account but they required our reasons now against the Report; ye Clerk then endeavoured further to evince that allegation of Clockmaking was originated in ye Smith and that they were the sole makers thereof. The Clockmakers asserted the contrary and urged that they forged all ye ironwork. Mr. Harvey spoke much on our behalf and in vindication of those points but all availed nothing. The report was passed, and the next day a Common Council was held and the report read and a Bill ordered to be brought in.[1]

Additional Reasons against the Bill delivered in to the Committee by the Blacksmiths.

"The Blacksmiths Company yet willing to deal ingeniously and to conceal nothing within their knowledge concerning this matter doe therefore own That in certain By Laws by them heretofore made there is a clause of like import with that paper which the Clockmakers have urged as an agreement signed &c. concerning which it is humbly submitted to consideration.

"1. That it does not appear by the Company's Records to be any Act of theirs either in signing any such agreement (as before) or admitting any such exception in their By Laws and therefore have reason to suspect that it was obteyned by some indirect manner.

"2. That the said exception is but in one Clause of the By Laws, to wit that for takeing of Apprentices, but in those for presenting, turning over and makeing free of Apprentices &c. it is not inserted, whereas Armorors who were indeed designed to be excepted are so excepted in those aforesaid and all other clauses needfull thro'out both Charter and Ordinances, soe that this exception is directly contrary to the Blacksmiths' Charter and runs counter to the general scope of all their other By Laws.

"3. That the clause in which this exception is conteyned is but a part of the Blacksmiths' By Laws which they can revoke, alter &c. as need requires."[2]

"At a Common Council held on the 10th of November 1697. Edwin, Mayor. This day the Com^{tee} to whom the Report of the Master Wardens and Assistants of the Company of Clockmakers was referred to bring in a Bill pursuant to the said Report did in pursuance of the same deliver into this Court a Bill which being read and the Question put Whether the said Bill should be read a second time at the next Com͞on Councell it was carried in the Affirmative.

[1,2] Journal of Blacksmiths' Company XI.

"A Peticōn of the Keepers or Wardens and Society of the Company of Blacksmiths London was p̃sented unto this Court relating to the Clockmakers Bill which followes in these words, viz.

"To the Right Hoñoble the Lord Mayor Aldreñ and Coñions of the Citie of London in Coñion Councell assembled.

"The humble Peticõn of the Keepers or Wardens and Society of the Art or Mistery de lez Blacksmiths London,

"Sheweth—That the Com^tee to whom the Peticõn of the Company of Clockmakers was referred having been pleased to prepare a Bill in their behalfe ag^t which your Petitioners have many m̃reiall and weighty objeccõns and reasons to offer (besides what they in geñall offered to the said Com^tee ag^t the bringing in thereof) which will fully shew that the said Bill (should it pass into an Act) will be a great encroachm^t upon and very injurious to your Petitioners and which they humbly hope will prevaile with this hono^ble Court to set aside the same soe farr as it relates to the Blacksmiths Company.

"Your Petitioners therefore most humbly pray that they may be heard by Councill ag^t the said Bill at the Barr of this Hono^ble Court or otherwise.

"And your Petitioners shall ever pray &c.

Robert Blacket }
Thomas Lee   } Wardens.
Thomas Phillips }
William Buck   }

Thomas Bristoe
William Taylor
Robert Hoe
Henry Neale.

"Which being read and the Question being put whether they shall be heard by their Councell at the Barr of this Court according to the prayer of the said Peticõn It was carried in the Affirmative. And the Mr Wardens and Assistants of the said Company of Clockmakers are hereby ordered to have notice thereof and are at liberty to be heard at the same time by their Councell ag^t the said peticõn.[1]

"At a Common Council held on the 20th December 1697. Edwin, Mayor. This day being appointed for the hearing the Councell as well for the Blacksmiths as the Clockmakers Companies touching a Bill depending in this Court for the regulating the Art of Clockmaking they were accordingly called in And the said Bill was read a second time. And after hearing the Councell on either side and a long debate The Question was put Whether the said Bill should be recommitted And was carried in the Affirmative.[2]

"At a Common Council held on the 8th July 1698. Edwin, Mayor. A Peticõn of the Master Wardens and Ass^ts of the Comp^y of Clockmakers of London was presented unto this Court and read in these words

"To the Right Hono^ble the Lord Mayor Aldr̃en and Coñions of the City of London in Coñion Councell assembled.

"The humble Peticõn of the Mr Wardens and Assistants of the Comp^y of Clockmakers London,

"Sheweth—That a Bill for regulateing the Art of Clockmaking brought in by order of this hono^ble Court hath been twice read and recom̃itted and hath so stood ever since the 20th day of December last. That by reason of

---

[1] Journal of Common Council, No. 52, fol. 157.
[2] Journal of Common Council, No. 52, fol. 161.

THE CLOCKMAKERS' COMPANY.

the new Com̃on Councill and the alteration of some of the Members of the Com^tee to whom the said Bill was com̃itted your Petitioners Bill hath layn still ever since. They therefore humbly pray this honoble Court will now please to noĩate and appoint a Com^tee to consider of the said Bill. And your Petitioners shall pray &c.

J^no. Ebsworth, M^r.
Robt. Williamson
Robt. Halstead   } Wardens.
Charles Sutton
Nath. Barrow
Edwd. Stanton

James Parkwick
Thos. Tompion
Sam. Merchant
J^no. Finch.

"And upon the Question put Whether so many Members of this Court with an addition of two Comõners to be added in the roome of Mr. Scriven and Mr. Harvey as were a Com^tee to consider of a Bill formerly in this Court shall be a Com^tee to consider of the said Bill or noe It was carried in the Affirmative And thereupon Mr. Chitty and Mr. Greville were added to the said Com^tee. [1]

"At a Common Council held on the 26th October 1698. Edwin, Mayor. This day a Com^tee appointed to prepare and bring in a Bill for the regulateing the Art of Clockmakeing delivered in a Report with a Bill annexed into this Court wch being read the Question was put whether the said Bill should be read a second time the first thing the next Com̃on Councell or no. It was carried in the Affirmative." [2]

"At a Common Council held on the 18th November 1698. Child, Mayor. At this Court the Bill for regulateing the Art of Clockmaking was read a second time and upon the Question put whether it should be read a third time at the next Com̃on Council or no? It was carried in the Affirmative.

"This day the Master and Wardens of the Company of Blacksmiths London as well as the Master Wardens and Assistants of the Company of Clockmakers London were called in and their sev^all Petic̃ons being read for the passing of the said Bill and thereupon the Question was put whether Council for or against the said Bill shall be heard at the Barr of this Court at the reading the said Bill a third time or no, It was carried in the Affirmative and Ordered accordingly. [3]

"At a Common Council held on the 23rd of November 1698. Child, Mayor. The Bill for regulating the Art of Clockmaking was this day read a Third time. And the Counsel as well for as against the said Bill appointed to be heard at the barr of this Court were accordingly heard and afterwards withdrawing and a debate ariseing thereon the Question was put whether this Court would adjourne the debate of the said Bill to the next Com̃on Council or no, It was carried in the Affirmative and Ordered accordingly. [4]

"At a Common Council held on the 31st of November 1698. Child, Mayor. Att this Court the Bill for regulating the Art of Clockmaking was read a third time and the blanks being filled up and some amendments made thereto and also sev^all debates thereon were had, and upon the Question put whether the s^d Bill now read a Third time with the amendments made thereto

---

[1] Journal of Common Council, No. 52, fol. 213.
[2] Journal of Common Council, No. 52, fol. 221^b.
[3,4] Journal of Common Council, No. 52, fol. 227.

and the blanks filled up should pass into an Act and be a law of this Court or no, It was carried in the Negative and a Poll being demanded and granted there were Sixty for and Eighty-five against the passing of the said Bill. And the said Bill was thereupon ordered to be rejected."[1]

Upon the failure of this attempt on the part of the Company to procure the passing of the Act of Common Council the matter remained in abeyance for a lengthened period. In the year 1764, however, it was revived, and the following entries appear in the Minutes of the Court of Assistants :—

"1764. January 10. On a Motion made by Mr. Matthews that the Court of Common Council be applied to, to oblige all persons of the trade of a Clockmaker, hereafter applying for the freedom of this City to take it up of the Clockmakers' Company, It was ordered that the Clerk do inspect the Bye Laws, and enquire the expence of such application as well as he possibly can, and lay them before the Court that the same be argued and finally approved or disapproved of, at the next Court.[2]

"1764. July 2. Ordered that the Clerk do apply to the Court of Common Council for an act of theirs to oblige all persons using or exercising the Trade of a Watch or Clockmaker, hereafter applying for the freedom of the City of London, to take it up of this Company.[3]

"1764. October 11. The Master and Wardens presented a Petition to the Lord Mayor and Court of Aldermen and Common Council of the City of London, praying for the Bye Law of the City to be granted to them to empower them to oblige all persons exercising the business of a Clockmaker hereafter applying for the freedom of the City of London to take it up first of this Company."[4]

The following is the record of the proceedings in the Court of Common Council :—

"At a Common Council held on the 11th of October 1764. Bridgen, Mayor. The humble Petition of the Master Wardens and Fellowship of the Art or Mistery of Clockmaking of the City of London was this day presented unto this Court and read in these words

"To the Right Honourable the Lord Mayor Aldremen and Commons of the City of London in Common Council assembled.

"The humble Petition of the Master Wardens and Fellowship of the Art or Mistery of Clockmaking of the City of London,

"Sheweth—That his late Majesty King Charles the First by his Charter or Letters Patent dated the 22^d of August in the 7th year of his reign did will, ordain, constitute, and grant that all and singular the Clockmakers and other person and persons whatsoever as well Freemen of the City of London as also all other natural Free Born Subjects using the Art or Mistery of Clockmaking within the said City, Liberties or Suburbs thereof, or within any place

---

[1] Journal of Common Council, No. 52, fol. 227^b.
[2, 3, 4] Company's Journal IV.

within Ten Miles of the said City, as well within Liberties and places exempt as in other places, should be for ever thereafter one Body Corporate and politick by the name of the Master Wardens and Fellowship of the Art or Mistery of Clockmaking of the City of London, to the end that all frauds and deceits in the said Trade might be discovered and reformed, and for prevention of such abuses and evils as might occur therein.

"That notwithstanding the said Charter many Persons who exercise the Art or Mistery of Clockmaking have obtained their Freedoms of other Companies by redemption or otherwise, and many others who are Free of the said Company of Clockmakers do obtain people of other Companies to bind Apprentices for them, and afterwards turn them over to them, by reason whereof the said Company of Clockmakers is much diminished in its number of Members and may fall into decay.

"Your Petitioners therefore humbly pray this Honourable Court will be pleased to order that from henceforth no person or persons using or exercising the Art or Mistery of Clockmaking be permitted to take up his Freedom of this City by redemption or otherwise unless he be first Free of your Petitioners said Company. And that you will grant them such further or other relief in the premises as to you shall seem meet.

"And your Petitioners shall pray, &c.
"Signed by order of Court
"JASPER TAYLOR, Clerk.

"Whereupon it is referred to Sir Robert Ladbroke Knight, Marshe Dickinson, George Nelson, Esquires, Sir Francis Gosling Knight and Samuel Turner Esquire, Aldermen, Mr. Deputy John Skynner, Mr. Christopher Robinson, Mr. Deputy John Paterson, Mr. William Hussey, Mr. Deputy Robert Gamon, George Bellas Esquire, Mr. Henry Major, Brass Crosby Esquire, Samuel Freeman Esquire, Mr. Arthur Beardmore, Mr. George Maynard and Mr. Laurence Holker, Commoners, or any two of the said Aldermen and four of the said Commoners to be a Committee to examine the allegations thereof, and report their opinions thereon to this Court."[1]

On the 11th of December, 1764, notice was received from Sir Robert Ladbroke, Knight and Alderman, that he had summoned a Committee to sit at Guildhall on that day, and the Master with the Wardens and some of the Court attended the Committee, who, after the proper allegations in the Petition had been proved, stated that they were of opinion the said allegations were fully made out, and that they should so report to the next Common Council.

This appears to have been done, and in the Journals of the Common Council of the 7th February following, the Report of the Committee is entered, together with an instruction to the Committee to prepare a Bill. This Bill was introduced and discussed in July and October of that year, in which latter month it was passed into a law.

---

[1] Journal of Common Council, No. 63, fol. 203[b.]

"At a Common Council held on the 7th of February 1765. Stephenson, Mayor. The Committee appointed by this Court the 11th day of October last to examine the allegations of the Petition of the Master Wardens and Fellowship of the Art or Mistery of Clockmaking of the City of London did this day delivered into this Court a report in writing under their hands which was read in these words

"To the Right Honourable the Lord Mayor Aldermen and Commons of the City of London in Common Council assembled.

"Whereas by an order of this Honourable Court bearing date the Eleventh day of October last, It was referred to us amongst others to examine the Allegations of the Petition of the Master Wardens and Fellowship of the Art or Mistery of Clockmaking of the City of London praying for the reasons therein mentioned that this Court would be pleased to order that from thenceforth no person or persons using or exercising the Art or Mistery of Clockmaking be permitted to take up his freedom of this City by Redemption or otherwise unless he be first free of the Petitioners said Company, Now we whose names are hereunto subscribed do humbly certify that in obedience to the said order we have met and examined the allegations of the said Petition and likewise heard what the said Master Wardens and Fellowship had to offer in support thereof and we are of opinion that they have proved the same and may have a By Law under proper regulations and restrictions which we submit to this Honourable Court this 11th day of December 1764.

"CHRIS. ROBINSON." "SAM. FREEMAN.
"ROB. GAMAN." "HEN. MAJOR.
"ROB{T.} LADBROKE." "GEO. NELSON.

"And a Motion being made and Question put that this Court doth agree with the Committee in their said report the same was resolved in the Affirmative and it is referred back to the said Committee to prepare and bring in a Bill pursuant to the prayer of the said Petition. [1]

"At a Court of Common Council held on the 25th of July 1765. Stephenson, Mayor. The Bill for regulating the Master Wardens and Fellowship of the Art or Mistery of Clockmaking of the City of London, was this day presented unto this Court and read a first and second time, and referred back to the Committee who brought in the same to fill up the blanks therein and report the same to this Court. [2]

"At a Court of Common Council held on the 15th October 1765. Stephenson, Mayor. This day the Committee having pursuant to the order of this Court of the Twenty-fifth day of July last filled up the blanks in the Bill for regulating the Master Wardens and Fellowship of the Art or Mistery of Clockmaking of the City of London, did deliver the same so filled up into this Court and the same was read a third time, and a motion was made and question put, That the Bill as now read do pass into a law and become the act of this Court it was resolved in the Affirmative and ordered accordingly, which Act follows in these words

"An Act for Regulating the Master, Wardens and Fellowship of the Art or Mystery of Clockmaking of the City of London.

---

[1] Journal of Common Council, No. 63, fol. 244.
[2] Journal of Common Council, No. 63, fol. 302.

"Whereas the Master, Wardens and Fellowship of the Art or Mystery of Clockmaking of the City of London are and have been an ancient Company and Fraternity of this City and long since Incorporated into one entire body by the name of the Master, Wardens and Fellowship of the Art or Mystery of Clockmaking of the City of London, and whereas many persons who exercise the Art or Mystery of Clockmaking within the City of London have obtained their Freedoms of other Companies by redemption and otherwise by reason whereof the said Company of Clockmakers is much diminished and impoverished. For remedy whereof be it enacted, ordained and established by the Right Honorable the Lord Mayor, Aldermen and Commons of this City of London in this present Common Council assembled and by the authority of the same that from and after the Twenty-fifth day of December 1765 every person not being already free of this City using or exercising or who shall use or exercise the Art Trade or Mystery of Clockmaking within this City of London or liberties thereof shall take up his or her Freedom and be made free of the said Company of the Master, Wardens and Fellowship of the Art or Mystery of Clockmaking of the City of London, and that no person or persons now using or exercising or which shall hereafter use or exercise the said Art or Mystery of Clockmaking within the said City or Liberties thereof, shall from and after the said Twenty-fifth day of December be admitted by the Chamberlain of this City for the time being into the Freedom or liberties of this City of or in any other Company than the said Company of the Master, Wardens and Fellowship of the Art or Mystery of Clockmaking of the City of London, any law, usage or Custom of this City to the contrary notwithstanding. Provided always that all and every person and persons not being already free of this City and who now are or hereafter shall be entitled to the Freedom of any other Company within this City by patrimony or service and ought in pursuance of this Act to be made free of the said Company of the Master, Wardens or Fellowship of the Art or Mystery of Clockmaking of the City of London shall be admitted into the Freedom of the said Company upon payment of such and the like fine and fees and no more as are usually paid and payable upon admission of the Child or Apprentice of a Freeman of the same Company into the Freedom of the said Company. And be it further enacted and ordained by the Authority aforesaid that if any person other than and except such person who is already free of this City doth or shall at any time or times from and after the said Twenty-fifth day of December, occupy, use or exercise, the Art, Trade or Mystery of Clockmaking within this City or Liberties thereof not being free of the said Company of the Master, Wardens and Fellowship of Clockmaking of the City of London then every such person, other than except as aforesaid, shall forfeit and pay the sum of Five pounds for every such offence.

"And be it further enacted and ordained by the authority aforesaid that the forfeitures and penalties made payable by this Act shall and may be recovered by action of debt, bill or plaint to be commenced and prosecuted with the privity and consent of the Master and Wardens of the said Company for the time being in the name of the Chamberlain of the said City of London for the time being in any of His Majesty's Courts of Record to be holden within the said City, security being first given by the Master and Wardens of the said Company to indemnify the said Chamberlain against all costs, damages, and expenses that may happen or arise on account of commencing and prosecuting the said action, and that the said Chamberlain of the said City for the time being in all suits to be prosecuted by virtue of this present Act against any offender shall recover his ordinary costs of suit to be expended in and about the prosecution of the same, and that in case the said Chamberlain for the time being shall be nonsuited or discontinue the same action or judgement shall be given against the said Chamberlain in any such action to be brought by virtue of this Act that the defendant in such action shall and may recover his or her ordinary costs of such nonsuit discontinuance or judgement any Law usage or custom of the said City to the contrary, notwithstanding. And be it further enacted and ordained by the authority aforesaid that all penalties and forfeitures to be had and recovered by virtue of this Act, the costs of the suit for the recovery thereof being first deducted, shall after recovery and receipt thereof be divided into two equal parts, the one moiety thereof shall be paid to him or them that shall prosecute the suit in the name of the Chamberlain of the said City for recovery of the same, and the other moiety thereof to the Treasurer of the London Workhouse for the time being to be applied towards the maintenance of the Poor harboured therein.[1]

"RIX."

This Act came into force on the 25th of December, 1765, and soon bore fruit. On the 5th of May, 1766, John Fish, son of Wm. Fish, Citizen and Draper, of London, bound to his mother, Mary Fish, for seven years, was admitted to the Freedom of the Clockmakers' Company agreeably to the Act, being by Trade a Clockmaker. On the 7th July, 1766, James Scott, late Apprentice of John Jackson, Citizen and Carpenter, by indenture, dated September 1st, 1752, was admitted agreeably to the Act, being by Trade a Clockmaker; and Samuel Riddlesdon, Citizen and Joiner, was admitted by patrimony, being by Trade a Clockmaker.

Many more examples might be given, but these are sufficient to show the effect produced by the Act.

In the year 1812, the attention of the Court was directed to the necessity for some effectual means being taken to ensure a more complete observance of the provisions of the above Act, and after the following recital, viz.:—

"1812. August 13. The Court having taken into consideration the frequent evasions of the provisions of the Act of Common Council passed in the year 1765 and the means proper to prevent the recurrence thereof And it appearing that by a certain Ordinance of this Company made 7th day of October 1672 It was ordained that a Caveat should be entered in the Chamberlain's Office to prevent persons engaged in the practice of the Art and Mystery of Clockmaking from transacting business in the Chamber of London but as Citizens and Clockmakers only, And it appearing also that the said Caveat has proved ineffective as the persons usually attending in the said Chamber have not hitherto had any competent inducement to give full operation to the objects proposed to be attained by this Corporation."

[1] Journal of Common Council, No. 63, fols. 314—316.

it was Resolved that certain premiums should be paid to the Clerks in the Chamberlain's Office for stopping persons applying for the Freedom in other Companies who by right belonged to the Clockmakers, and obliging them to take it up therein, and also for each Apprentice to any person using the Art of Clockmaking, not free of the Company, applying to be enrolled or turned over in any other Company, provided an endorsement upon the Indenture and an entry in the Chamberlain's Books were made to secure his admission at the expiration of his servitude in this Company.

The Clerk of the Company was also ordered to prepare and keep perfect a Book containing the names, alphabetically arranged, with companies, residences, trades, and other needful information concerning all persons practising the Art of Clockmaking, but not free of the Company, or free of any other, and to lodge a copy of it, to be called the "Caveat Book," at the Chamberlain's Office, for the information of the Clerks, and to be used for the purposes above mentioned.

On the 29th September following, a form of Caveat was agreed upon by the Court, and ordered to be lodged with the Chamberlain, and on the 12th October it was duly sealed, and ordered to be presented in these words:—

"To the Right Worshipful Richard Clark Esquire
Chamberlain of the City of London.

"The Memorial of the Master Wardens and Fellowship of the Art or Mystery of Clockmaking of the City of London,

"Sheweth,—That by Letters Patent under the great Seal of England bearing date the 31st day of August 1631, His late Majesty King Charles the first was graciously pleased to grant and constitute that all and singular the persons engaged in the practice of the Art and Trade of Clockmaking in all and every of its various parts and branches should be and be incorporated into one Body Politick and Society by the name of The Master Wardens and Fellowship of the Art or Mystery of Clockmaking of the City of London.

"And whereas by a certain order bearing date the 25th day of May 1630 the Right Hon'ble the Lord Mayor and the Right Worshipful the Court of Aldermen of the City of London were pleased to ratify and approve the granting by his said Majesty King Charles the first of the said Charter of Incorporation.

"And whereas by a certain other order of the said Court of Lord Mayor and Aldermen bearing date the 11th day of October 1632 the said Charter was ordered to be entered upon Record that it might thenceforth be acted upon and carried into effect.

"And whereas by a certain other order of the said Court of Lord Mayor and Aldermen bearing date the 16th day of June 1636 it was ordered that all and every the Apprentice and Apprentices taken by or to any person practising the Art of Clockmaking shall be bound to some Free Brother of the said Company by the name of Citizens and Clockmakers of London only, conformably to the directions of the Charter for the Incorporation of the said Company of Clockmakers in the said order in part recited.

"And whereas by the said last in part recited order it further appears that previous to the granting of the said Charter for the Incorporation of the said Company so much thereof as requires that the Apprentice and Apprentices of every person whatsoever taken to practice or learn the said Art of Clockmaking shall be bound to some Free Brother of the said Company of Clockmakers only, that the said Company might in time be strengthened and become an able body of itself, was especially referred by the Lord Keeper of the Great Seal to Sir Henage Finch, Knight, Recorder of London, with directions that his Lordship should be satisfied of the legality and propriety of the said provisions for the binding of Apprentices as aforesaid and that the said Recorder did thereupon certify unto his Lordship that the said Charter had been carefully perused and approved by him, that the said clause was fit to be inserted therein, and he did not see any inconvenience that could result therefrom.

"And whereas by the said last recited order It is further ordered that the Chamberlain of this City for the time being shall receive, enroll, and, having served their terms, admit the said Apprentices into the Freedom of this city by the name of Citizens and Clockmakers of London, and further that the Chamberlain of this City shall take notice of and in all respects see the order duly executed.

"And whereas by a certain Act of Common Council of this City bearing date the 15th day of October 1765 entitled 'An Act for regulating the Master Wardens and Fellowship of the Art or Mystery of Clockmaking of the City of London;' It is among other things enacted That from and after the 25th day of December 1765 every person (not being then already Free of this City) using or exercising or who shall use or exercise the Art Trade or Mystery of Clockmaking within the City or the Liberties thereof shall take up his or her Freedom and be made free of the said Company of the Master Wardens and Fellowship of the Art or Mystery of Clockmaking in the City of London.

"And it is by the said part recited Act further enacted That no person or persons now using or exercising or who shall hereafter use or exercise the said Trade Art or Mystery of a Clockmaker within the said City or the Liberties thereof shall from and after the said 25th day of December be admitted by the Chamberlain of this City for the time being into the freedom of this City of or in any other Company than the said Company of the Master Wardens and Fellowship of the Art and Mystery of Clockmakers of the City of London.

"And it is by the said part recited Act further enacted That if any person other than except such persons who are already Free of this City doth or shall at any time or times from and after the said 25th day of December 1765 use occupy or exercise the Trade Art or Mystery of a Clockmaker within this City or the Liberties thereof and not being Free of the said Company of the Master Wardens and Fellowship of the Art and Mystery of Clockmaking of

London, then every such person, other than except as aforesaid, shall forfeit and pay the sum of Five Pounds of lawful money of Great Britain for every such offence.

"And whereas it appears to be expedient for the better performance and due execution of the several provisions and regulations by the said hereinbefore in part recited Charter and Act and Orders appointed and directed to be fulfilled, that the principal parts and branches of the said Art of Clockmaking should be set forth so that none hereafter may plead ignorance as to what persons properly appertain to and are liable to be and become free and take up their freedom of and abide by the Rule and Government of the said Company of Clockmakers, Your Memorialists therefore by this present Memorial take occasion to state for the information of your worship, That the Art and Mystery of Clockmaking consists of and in the making or construction of, selling and dealing in either in part or in the whole, of the Machinery, Instruments and Apparatus used or employed in Mensuration and to ascertain or set forth the several portions parts and divisions of Time and space, which Machinery, Implements and Apparatus are usually called Clocks, Watches, Larums, Sun-Dials and Mathematical Instruments of various kinds, and the several parts thereof, or by whatever other names the same may be known, and also all those persons practising as Clock or Watchmovement Makers, Dial Makers, Enamellers, Engravers, Gilders, Silverers, or Varnishers of Clock or Watch Work, Watch Jewellers or Escapement Makers, or Motion Makers, or Wheel or Pinion Makers, Clock or Watch Case Makers, Clock or Watch Spring Makers, Chain Makers, or Weight Makers, Watch Glass Makers, Watch Pendant or Key Makers, Secret springers or Liners or Coverers or other Ornamenters of Clock or Watch Cases, Clock or Watch Hand Makers and all other persons employed in the making ornamenting compleating and sale of Clocks, Watches, Larums, Sun-Dials and Mathematical Instruments or otherwise using the said Art are by the said Act of Common Council designated by and comprehended in the general name of persons using or exercising the Trade Art or Mystery of a Clockmaker, and have been always so considered by your Worship's predecessors in the office of Chamberlain of this City, and conformably with the said Act are to be and become Free and Freemen of the said Company and to be admitted as Citizens and Clockmakers of London, and not otherwise or contrary thereto.

" But so it is may it please your Worship further to be informed that the aforesaid Charter of Incorporation, Act of Common Council and Orders of the Court of Lord Mayor and Aldermen from time to time granted and made for the protection of the Public against fraud and deception, and to encourage the said Master Wardens and Fellowship in the exercise of their Art and Mystery of Clockmaking, are in a great degree rendered inoperative and fail to produce their intended effect, inasmuch as great numbers of the persons using and practising the said Art of Clockmaking or some or other of its parts or branches herein-before specified or set forth have by divers frauds and pretences contrived to obtain their freedom of this City in other Companies wherein they afterwards bind their apprentices and also such apprentices acting in the like manner contrary to the Charter and Act and Orders aforesaid such persons thereby evade the laws and proper government of the said Company of Clockmakers and His Majesty's subjects are left without protection from the frauds and abuses frequently practised by such illicit practitioners of the said Art, and the said Company is not only deprived of the natural flow of the growing increase of Members lawfully appertaining to its Body but is threatened with utter decay by the decrease of the number of the Freemen and cannot have redress but by the aid and assistance of your Worship. "Your Memorialists therefore trust that your Worship will be pleased to take such measures and to establish such orders in the office of Chamberlain of this City as may give practical effect and operation to the said Charter of Incorporation and Act of Common Council and Orders of the Lord Mayor and Court of Aldermen so that no person whatever now using or practising or that may hereafter use or practise the said Art of Clockmaking or any of its parts or branches as aforesaid may henceforth become free or be made a Freeman of this City or the Liberties thereof but as Citizens and Clockmakers of London only, And also that upon the Apprentice of any person using practising or following the said Art of Clockmaking either in the part or in the whole as aforesaid appearing or applying in the Chamber of this City for the purpose of being enrolled or entered as having been turned over That your Worship will be pleased to order and cause an Indorsement to be written upon the Indentures of such apprentice and a like entry to be made in the books of the Chamberlain that at the expiration of his term such Apprentice shall be admitted to the Freedom as a Citizen and Clockmaker of London and not otherwise, and that your Worship will be pleased to afford to your Memorialists such further and other relief in the premises as to your Worship shall seem meet.

"Sealed by Order of the Court this 12th day of October 1812

"Witness G. ATKINS, Clerk
35 Clements Lane, Lombard Street."

As a result of this action numerous opportunities of enforcing their rights in due course presented themselves to the Company, the following being a few of the instances :—

"1813. June 7. Samuel Joseph Bird of Little Compton Street, Soho, Watch Case maker, late apprentice of Jasper Swindells of Salmon and Ball Court, Bunhill Row, in the Parish of St. Luke's Old Street, Watch Case maker, Citizen and Goldsmith of London, having some time past contrived to procure his admission as a Free Goldsmith, contrary to the Act of Common Council for regulating this Fellowship, the said Jasper Swindells presented his said late apprentice at the Chamber of London in order to obtain his admission and the Copy of his Freedom as a Citizen and Goldsmith. The which Freedom was there stopped by virtue of the said Act of Common Council, he having been bound Apprentice to or served a Watch Case maker and all such are by the Charter of this Company required to become Free as a Citizen and Clockmaker only. And the Beadle of this Company then being present in the name of this Fellowship demanded possession of the Indenture by which the said Samuel Joseph Bird was bound, so that he might not obtain the Freedom of the City contrary to the said Act, which indenture being handed over accordingly by the Clerk of the Chamber, the said Samuel Joseph Bird was thereupon named to attend this Court in May last past which he did, but declined then to take up his Freedom of or in this Company. And the said Samuel Joseph Bird having been again warned for his appearance and being in attendance this day, stated that in consequence of this Company having claimed him to become a Member, he had applied at the Court of the Goldsmiths' Company for directions how he should act therein, that the said Company had relinquished all claim to him as a Member, had returned to him the money which he had paid for his admission therein, and likewise had absolved him from all connexion and obligation whatsoever as a Member of that Company. And the said Samuel Joseph Bird was this day by virtue of the said Act of Common Council admitted a free Clockmaker.[1]

"1813. June 7. Peter Patmore of Ludgate Hill, Pawnbroker, Citizen and having commenced trade to deal in, buy and sell watches and at the same time circulating printed Watch Papers or Shop Bills setting forth himself to the Public as a Watchmaker was summoned to appear at the Monthly Court in May last; but, not having attended thereon, was again peremptorily summoned to appear this day, and being in attendance accordingly before the Court, was required to show cause why he should not discontinue to practice in the Trade placed under the Government of this Company or forthwith take up his freedom of the same. And the said Peter Patmore on being questioned as to his practical abilities or skill in the Art of Clock and Watchmaking after some equivocation declared that he did not pretend to any such knowledge, and then pleaded that the Act of Common Council for regulating the Master, Wardens and Fellowship of Clockmakers was not obligatory on him to become a Member of this Company, which compliance he persisted to refuse saying he would continue so to do until he was informed of some stronger law to oblige him, and then he would conform to its provisions; the said Peter Patmore was then informed that in the case of John Allen, formerly of Barbican, Gold and Silver Watch Case maker, Citizen and Goldsmith, which was tried in the Mayor's Court in 1785 in which the said John Allen was condemned with costs and judgement given against him for trading in the said Art contrary to the Act of Common Council contemptuously refusing to become a Member of this Company, thereupon the said Peter Patmore declared that he was satisfied of the Jurisdiction and Authority of this Company in the case, and having consented to come under its Rule and Government was, by virtue of the said Act of Common Council and the Charter, admitted."[2]

It having been suggested to the Court of Assistants that it might conduce to the welfare of the Company if a Certificate, signed by the Master and Clerk, were given to each Member upon his admission to the Freedom, it was, on the 12th of October, 1812, determined to carry out the suggestion, and on the 1st of February, 1813, "A design for a Freeman's

---

[1,2] Company's Journal VI.

Certificate was produced and approved, and the Senior Warden was directed to have it engraved and executed in the best manner."

The proceedings at the Court of Assistants in the following June are of sufficient interest to be inserted *verbatim*, as follows :—

"1813. June 7. Whereas by an order made on the 12th October last directions were given for the preparation and engraving of a Copper Plate for a Certificate of the admission of certain persons as Members of this Company. And whereas the necessity for issuing such Certificates by this Corporation has been occasioned by the many persons who have of late pretended and attempted to carry on the Trade of Clock and Watchmaking without having served seven years as Apprentice or being otherwise in any respect qualified to practice the said Art whereby the fair course of Trade has been diverted from the hands of the real Artist and qualified Workman. And whereas Clocks and Watches from their complicated nature and intricate construction must ever be objects of confidential purchase and the public has not heretofore had any certain means whereby to know what persons are actual Clock and Watchmakers and so to distinguish the bona fide Artists from such mere pretenders who have often deluded and do not unfrequently defraud the unwary purchaser by boldly warranting and assuring as good Machines such Articles as are wholly insufficient and of which the purchasers being ignorant of the Art of Clock and Watchmaking could not in most instance be qualified to judge. And forasmuch as it is desirable to protect the public as much as possible from the recurrence of such frauds and abuses in future as also to give encouragement to those Members of this Corporation who are practical workmen in the Art of Clock and Watchmaking, and as such are entitled to the confidence and patronage of the public, and at the same time to prevent the issuing such Certificates to improper or unqualified persons. It is ordained and declared

"1st. That those Members of this Company only who have served Seven years as Apprentice or Journeyman to a Clock or Watchmaker, a Clock or Watch Movement maker, a Clock or Watch Finisher or a Repeating motion maker, shall be deemed eligible to receive Certificates of his or her qualification.

"2nd. That such Certificates shall not on any account be granted to any person using any other part or branch of the Art whatsoever other than is particularized in the first Item of this order.

"3rd. That every Member of this Company who may be desirous to obtain such Certificate shall if he reside within five miles of the Royal Exchange make his personal appearance in Court for that purpose.

"4th. That any Member of this Company who is resident at more than five miles distance from the Royal Exchange may make application for such Certificate by writing under his or her hand.

5th. That to prevent the granting of any Certificate improperly to any person who does not fully answer and come within the description of persons qualified as in the first Item of this present Order is specified, any Member

THE CLOCKMAKERS' COMPANY. 137

of the Court of Assistants may and shall be at his entire liberty to require the Applicant for such Certificate to produce his or her Masterpiece duly and lawfully made pursuant to the Seventeenth Bye Law of this Corporation, and in case of any Assistant so requiring, the said Bye Law shall be strictly enforced and no Certificate shall upon any consideration whatsoever be made out for such applicant until he or she hath in open Court produced his or her Masterpiece duly made as aforesaid.

"6th. That when any applicant has duly and satisfactorily set forth his qualifications without objection as aforesaid, he shall be deemed eligible to receive the said Certificate of his or her admission.

"7th. That no Certificate shall be made out for any person whatsoever but by the especial Order of this Court, and proof shall previously be given to the satisfaction of this Court that each applicant is duly qualified to receive such Certificate conformably to this present Order.

"8th. That for each and every such Certificate of Admission, and qualification previous to the same being issued to Members as aforesaid there shall be paid to the use of the Company the Sum of Ten shillings and sixpence, to the Clerk for filling up and entering the same Three shillings and sixpence, and to the Beadle one shilling."[1]

On the 11th October, 1813, in consequence of the decreasing number of Freemen admitted and Apprentices bound, the Court of Assistants appointed a Committee to investigate and ascertain the powers of the Company, and, if necessary, to endeavour to obtain additional powers, either by Act of Common Council, Order of Court of Aldermen, or otherwise.

On the 10th January, 1814, the Committee presented their Report, which was received and adopted by the Court, and which recommended that the Clerk of the Company should write to the Clerks of all the other Companies of the City stating the facts and requesting that their respective Courts would order that the irregularities hitherto prevailing might in future be avoided by their officers directing to this Company at once all persons applying to them to Bind or to make Free, who in anywise used the Arts, Trades or Mysteries placed under the government of this Corporation.

The Committee for the affairs of Freemen and Apprentices made a further Report on the 3rd April, 1815, in which they state as follows :—

"Your Committee herewith presents for the information of your Worshipful Court, the Copy of a Memorial which on the 20th day of February last past,

[1] Company's Journal VI.

your Committee addressed to his Worship the Chamberlain of this City, in support of the rights of the Company, and soliciting attention to the Memorial under Seal presented to him on the 12th day of October last.

"Your Committee has now prepared for the approbation of your Worshipful Court, a Petition in the name of the Company that the same (if approved) may, under the sanction of the Common Seal, be presented to the Right Honourable the Lord Mayor and Court of Aldermen of this City; your Committee having duly considered the same and in the present state of the business judged it necessary for the proper service of the Company.

" To the Worshipful Richard Clark Esq.
Chamberlain of the City of London.

" The Memorial of the undersigned being a Committee of the Company of the Master, Wardens and Fellowship of the Art and Mystery of Clockmaking of the City of London in support of the Memorial of the said Company presented on the 12th day of October 1812, and in reply to a Memorial of the Master, Wardens and Fellowship of the Spectacle Makers of London,

" Sheweth,—That in reference to the Memorial presented to your Worship by the Company of Spectacle Makers under date the 19th day of January 1815 your Memorialists have not denied that the Master, Wardens and Fellowship of Spectacle Makers of London are an Incorporated Company of this City.

"But your Memorialists confidently state that the Charter and Bye Laws of the said Company of Spectacle Makers do not mention or contain any notice of or allusion to any other Article, Ware, production or trade whatsoever but the making of 'SPECTACLES ONLY' of which your Worship may be satisfied by reference to their said Charter, and moreover it is important to the right understanding of the Question now at issue, that your Worship should observe that the words 'IN ALL ITS BRANCHES' introduced into the said Memorial of the said Company of Spectacle Makers are not contained in the Charter or Bye Laws of the said Company.

"Your Memorialists admit that the rights conveyed by the Charter of Incorporation to the Master, Wardens and Fellowship of the Art and Mystery of Clockmaking are extensive and properly so, inasmuch as the persons who practised the Art of Clockmaking were the only makers of Clocks, Watches and Mathematical Instruments, however various in their construction and use, and the practice thereof hath ever since been continued by their sucessors the Clockmakers in all parts of the kingdom.

" And your Memorialists are satisfied of the legality of the rights so granted to them by their said Charter and Bye Laws which (previous to the same being granted) were most strictly scrutinized and examined by the Lord Mayor Aldermen and Recorder of this Hon[ble] City and by His Majesty's Lord Keeper of the Great Seal of England and the Chief Justice of His Majesty's Court of Common Pleas, during more than three years that the said Incorporation was in progress, by whom respectively the said Charter and Bye Laws were approved and declared to be no infringement upon the rights or privileges of any other Body or Government then existing and thereupon the said Charter and Bye Laws were granted to your Memorialists and ratified and carried into effect accordingly.

" Your Memorialists have further to state that when in attendance in the Chamber of London on the 16th day of December, 1814, in pursuance of the summons of your Worship they did there shew that in consequence of the great number of persons who had unlawfully evaded their jurisdiction rule and government, the Act of Common Council of this City for regulating the Master, Wardens and Fellowship of the Art or Mystery of Clockmaking was in the year 1766 made for the protection of the 'Chartered Rights' of your Memorialists.

"And that in the first twenty years after the passing of the said Act (without reference to the instances which occur in the later periods) the law had been carried into effect as to eighteen branches of the Arts or Mysteries of Clockmaking, Watchmaking, Mathematical Instruments making and engraving placed under and within the Incoporation of the said Master, Wardens and Fellowship of the Art or Mystery of Clockmaking and that in the same period more than two hundred persons, who had intended to obtain their freedom and be recorded as of or in other Companies of this City were pursuant to that Act recorded as Citizens and Clockmakers of London.

" And further that in the instance of a Gold and Silver Watch Case maker who (pretending analogy of his trade to the Goldsmiths by the materials he worked upon) had unlawfully taken his freedom and become recorded as a Goldsmith although according to Law, he ought to have been recorded a Clockmaker, Your Memorialists upon suit in the Mayor's Court obtained judgement against him for the penalty and costs incurred by such his offence.

"That although your Memorialists have never been desirous to assume to themselves Rights that belong to others, they nevertheless are bound to maintain the 'Chartered Rights' to which their Body is lawfully entitled ; and however great the number of branches into which their Mathematical Art of making Clocks, Watches, Larums, Sundials, Boxes and Cases for the said trade, Art or Mystery of Clockmaking be they of what metal or of what nature, condition or fashion soever or any other Work particularly belonging to the said trade of Clockmaking, has in course of time been extended as well before as since the Incorporation of your Memorialists they most earnestly deprecate the doctrine now for the first time assumed by the Company of Spectacle Makers that any of such branches are to be abstracted from the Rule, Government and Incorporation of your Memorialists by which that Company has denominated 'Assimilation' or by any other means than by a new law to take such branches out of the Fellowship and from under the Government of your Memorialists. And however some persons, who by law ought to be members of this Company may have joined any other Fellowship, such Company has no rightful cause to complain when your Memorialists reclaim such persons into their proper jurisdiction so soon as they are discovered to have evaded the law on that behalf. And your Memorialists submit that this is the only way in which any other Company of this City can be affected by the claims of your Memorialists notwithstanding what the Company of Spectacle Makers has asserted on that head.

"That your Memorialists have further to complain that of late years the Company of Spectacle Makers has used every endeavour silently to withdraw ' Mathematical Instrument Makers' from the Incorporation and Government of your Memorialists nor can your Memorialists pass without· observing the unbecoming attempt now made to convert such unlawful aggressions into an assumption of right.

"Your Memorialists have to complain of a further aggression on their Chartered Rights by the Company of Spectacle Makers who have within these

Four or Five years last past unlawfully taken and assumed as Armorial Bearings and Crest in their Common Seal newly made about the year 1810 certain articles appertaining to the Art and Trade of Clockmaking and which has been so long since as the year 1672 duly granted to your Memorialists by Patent under the proper authority vested in Garter King-at-Arms, but which assumption on the part of the Company of Spectacle Makers might if suffered to pass unobserved be taken at a future period as a collateral proof of right to have the rule and government of the persons using the Art and Trade of Mathematical Instrument making. Your Memorialists are therefore obliged to state that the Armorial Bearings of the Company of Spectacle Makers as used on their Common Seal until this late period accorded with the nature of their Incorporation viz.: ARGENT THREE PAIR OF SPECTACLES VERT, GARNISHED OR ; TWO AND ONE, NO CREST the motto appropriate 'A BLESSING TO THE AGED,' sufficiently setting forth the sole object of their Institution.

"That your Memorialists have duly weighed the claims lately assumed and set up by the Company of Spectacle Makers whereby among other things they seek to deprive your Memorialists of the rule and government of the 'Mathematical Instrument Makers' which has always been and now is a branch of your Memorialists Art of Clockmaking and as such has been carried on by the Clockmakers as well Freemen of this City as Foreigners beyond the walls and liberties thereof both before their Incorporation and from thenceforward to the present day by a regular train of Artists as aforesaid.

"That your Memorialists in pursuance of their Charter and Bye Laws have always had and exercised the inspection, rule and government of the 'Mathematical Instrument Makers' and 'Mathematical Instrument Making' as practised by Freemen of this City as also by Foreigners not resident therein. And if some persons from time to time have fraudulently and unlawfully avoided to become free of your Memorialists Company or by living in concealed places have evaded their Bye Laws, your Memorialists confidently trust that such evasions cannot be received as precedents or allowed to affect or destroy their 'Chartered Rights' further explained and set forth in their Bye Laws drawn up together in the year 1628 and produced to the Court of Lord Mayor and Aldermen and the Recorder of the City of London on the 2nd March 1629 and by that Court approved before the Company of Spectacle Makers was incorporated.

"Moreover it may not be immaterial to remark that the same Attorney (Thomas Copley who was in both Charters created and named as the first Clerk to each of the said Companies) drew up the Charters and Bye Laws both of the Clockmakers and of the Spectacle Makers so that no doubt can arise concerning the original design and constitution of those Bodies.

"That your Memorialists have already set forth that every Member of their Fellowship using the Art, Trade or Mystery of a professed Clockmaker and taking an Apprentice is by their Bye Law bound to 'teach and instruct his said Apprentice and Apprentices in such manner and form as their predecessors formerly have done, which is to keep daily and duly him and them in his house, and there by himself or his sufficient Journeyman teach and instruct him in the making of Cases and Boxes of Silver or Brass, and likewise the several springs belonging to such Watches, Clocks or Larums, and likewise all other particular and peculiar things belonging to such Watches, Clocks, Larums, Mathematical Instruments and Sundials his or their said Master shall teach and instruct them in to the end they may in time make up their Masterpiece with sufficiency of credit and truly understand both the beginning and the ending of the work from time to time which they shall take in hand.

"And your Memorialists challenge contradiction when they assert that the best workmen in Mathematical Instrument making were, have been, and still are Clockmakers, as well Freeman of this City as Foreigners not residing therein, and that the most celebrated Clockmakers have been from time immemorial and yet are the inventors, improvers and makers of Mathematical Instruments, and such practical Clockmakers and their Workmen are constantly resorted to for such Instruments by the Spectacle Makers and other persons keeping Shops for the Sale thereof.

"Your Memorialists further deny the assumption of the Company of Spectacle Makers, that the trade of making Spectacles, and Mathematical Instrument making have ever been practically united, although there are persons who keep Shops wherein Spectacles as also Mathematical Instruments are bought and sold, the trade of grinding glasses and making Spectacles being to this day distinct from that of Mathematical Instrument making, moreover of such Sale Shop Trade that of selling Spectacles forms but one Article out of an almost infinite number of variety when compared with Mathematical and Philosophical Instruments and Apparatus prepared and made by the Clockmakers and their Workmen.

"Your Memorialists deny it to be true that the Spectacle Makers are resorted to by the Clockmakers for Mathematical Instruments it being a well known fact that no practical Spectacle Maker can make a Mathematical Instrument, the Grinding and forming of Glasses and setting them in Spectacle Frames being the sole and only rightful object of the Spectacle Makers' Art and trade.

"Your Memorialists are also constrained to deny that the Spectacle Makers teach their Apprentices the practice of 'Mathematical Instrument making' however such Apprentices may be taught how to take orders from a Customer for or to buy and sell 'Mathematical Instruments' in their Shops.

"And although the Company of Spectacle Makers assert that your Memorialists 'have never molested or claimed any person who was a recorded Freeman of the Spectacle Makers' Company' your Memorialists are prepared to prove that they have compelled persons using the Trade of 'Mathematical Instrument Making' who had been Apprenticed as Citizens and Spectacle Makers to become recorded Freemen as Citizens and Clockmakers of London.

"Your Memorialists therefore deny that the Company of Spectacle Makers are by Charter or by Assimilation, or by any other right or title, real or implied, entitled to claim or have the rule or government of the persons using the Art or trade of 'Mathematical Instrument Making.' And your Memorialists are bound to assert that by virtue of the Charter of the Company of Clockmakers and their Bye Laws at the same time duly made as aforesaid for the better and more full explanation of their said Charter, your Memorialists are lawfully and of right entitled to claim and have all persons using the Art or Trade of 'Mathematical Instrument making' to be recorded Freemen and Members of their Fellowship of the Art and Mystery of Clockmaking to which fellowship alone such persons lawfully appertain, since both trades are not only incorporated together but are carried on and accomplished by one and the same course of practical Workmanship.

"Your Memorialists now proceed to the particular case of Robert Brettel Bate whom in the year 1813 your Memorialists had discovered to have opened and set up a Mathematical Instrument Maker's shop in the Poultry within this City, he not being a Freeman thereof. Whereupon your Memorialists in pursuance of their Charter and Bye Law and the Act of Common Council on that behalf, summoned the said Robert Brettel Bate to appear on the 11th day of October 1813 and to take up his Freedom and be recorded as a Citizen and Clockmaker of London, but he not appearing as required your Memorialists lodged with the Clerk of the Chamber in the Guildhall of the City of London an especial caveat against the admission of the said Robert Brettel Bate to the freedom of or in any other Company or Fellowship of this City, and they again summoned him to appear at their Court for the purpose aforesaid on the 6th day of December 1813 but which he did not comply with.

"Your Memorialists did not hear any more of the Case of Robert Brettel Bate until the 30th day of March 1814 when your Memorialists were informed that on the preceding day the said Robert Brettel Bate accompanied by two Members of the Company of Spectacle Makers appeared in the said Chamber and then and there the said Robert Brettel Bate was by John Sewell (then a Minor) Clerk to the said Company of Spectacle Makers, sworn a Member of the said Company of Spectacle Makers alike contrary to the common law and to the Charter, as also the 30th 31st and 36th Bye Laws of the said Company of Spectacle Makers which require that the Oath to be taken by any person upon his admission to be a Freeman shall be administered by and in the presence of the Master and Wardens in a lawful Court of Assistants of the said Fellowship duly convened.

"Your Memorialists cannot pass from this part of the subject without protesting seriously against such illegal mode of administering the Oath to persons desiring to be admitted to the Freedom which as now appears hath of late been but too much practised by the Clerks and other Officers of several Companies of this City, because such persons so illegally sworn are not either in Law or fact Freemen of the Body to which it has been so pretended that they were admitted, such abuse therefore being subject to occasion the most injurious consequences not only to the Persons upon whom it is practised but also as it affects in secret the rights of all other Companies of this City ought to be suppressed.

"Your Memorialists further submit that they having in pursuance of their Charter and Bye Laws summoned the said Robert Brettel Bate, as the keeper of a 'Mathematical Instrument maker's shop,' to become a recorded Clockmaker at least six months before his name was known to the Company of Spectacle makers. And the trade of the said Robert Brettel Bate consisting almost entirely in the Sale of all sorts of Instruments and Apparatus usually denominated 'Mathematical Instruments' and composing part of the Incorporation and trade of your Memorialists whereas the sale of 'Spectacles' (for he doth not make any of the Articles sold by him) forms but one small article of his trade.

"Wherefore your Memorialists with all due deference claim by Law and Chartered Right that the said Robert Brettel Bate be recorded as a Citizen and Clockmaker of London, and they trust that upon reference to the authority given in and by the Charter, Bye Laws, Orders of the Court of Aldermen, and Act of Common Council made and contained for the protection of the Rights of your Memorialists, your Worship will be pleased to pronounce for them accordingly notwithstanding the assumption, and pretence of the Company of Spectacle Makers to the contrary, as it is not true in law or in fact that the said Robert Brettel Bate has ever been admitted a Member of the Company of Spectacle Makers, and even if he had been so admitted the Company of Clockmakers is upon every view of the Case entitled to claim and have as Members all the Persons using the Art or Trade of Mathematical Instrument making and to take the precedence of having the said Robert Brettel Bate as a recorded Clockmaker as well for the nature of his trade as the number of the productions of the Clockmakers Art in which he deals.

" And your Memorialists for all these considerations respectfully solicit that the protection of Your Worship may be afforded to the Chartered Rights and Privileges of the Art and Mystery of Clockmaking of the City of London which of late have been much encroached upon.

" And that Your Worship will be pleased to afford them such further and other relief touching the premises as to Your Worship shall seem meet.

" London, February 20th, 1815.

Wm. Robins, Master.
Jno. Jackson } Wardens.
John Thwaites }
Isaac Rogers } Assistants."
Henry Clarke }

" The which Report was read and together with the Copy of the Memorial therein referred to approved.

" The form of Petition referred to in the said Report was then read in the words following, viz.

" 'To the Right Honorable the Lord Mayor and
Court of Aldermen of the City of London.

" The humble Petition of the Master Wardens and Fellowship of the Art or Mystery of Clockmaking of the City of London,

" Sheweth,—That your Petitioners are an ancient Company of this City and were long time incorporated into one body or society with divers rights, privileges, powers and immunities and amongst other things to make Bye Laws for the better order, rule and government of all and singular person and persons now using or who hereafter shall use their several Arts and Mysteries, as by their said Charter and Bye Laws doth more fully appear.

" That long previous to their incorporation their Trade consisted of and in the making and sale of the various Articles of Workmanship, Machinery, Instruments and Apparatus used or employed in Mensuration and to ascertain or set forth the several parts, portions and divisions of matter and space which Mathematical and Mechanical contrivances are usually called Clocks, Clockwork, Watches, Larums, Sundials, Mathematical Instruments and Apparatus, Engraving, Gilding, Silvering and Varnishing of their several kinds and the various parts thereof, or by whatsoever other names the same may be known. And which several Arts and Mysteries (however the same may at this date be divided and sub-divided in the modern divisions of labour) were at the time of their said Incorporation used and carried on by the same individual and were all included under the generic name or appellation of Clockmaking, the name by which your Petitioners are incorporated.

"That for a considerable period after the Incorporation of your Petitioners the Clockmakers were the only makers of Mathematical Instruments and at this day every practical Clockmaker is by the nature of his Mechanical Education, Tools and Employment equally qualified to, and in fact does work at or upon making Clocks or making Mathematical Instruments as his occasions may require.

"That in the flux of time, your Petitioners said several Arts and Mysteries respectively have in divers instances been sub-divided into different branches and parts whereunto at this day Apprentices are separately taken as distinct Trades.

"That persons using or practising such branches and parts of the several 'Arts and Mysteries' as aforesaid had by divers evasions sought to obtain their freedom and be recorded of or in other Companies and Fellowships contrary to the Charter and Bye Laws of your Petitioners, whereby the Company of your Petitioners was so far injured as to induce an application to be made for remedy of such abuses, and an Act of Common Council of this Honorable City was passed in the year 1765 'for regulating the Master Wardens and Fellowship of the Art or Mystery of Clockmaking of the City of London' whereby amongst other things it is enacted 'That no person or persons now using or exercising or who shall hereafter use or exercise the said Art, Trade or Mystery of Clockmaking within the said City or Liberties thereof shall from and after the said 25th day of December (1765) be admitted by the Chamberlain of the said City for the time being into the Freedom or Liberties of this City of or in any other Company than the said Company of the Master, Wardens and Fellowship of the Art or Mystery of Clockmaking of the City of London, any law, usage or custom of this City to the contrary notwithstanding.'

"That the said Act of Common Council at the time it was passed was considered beneficial and proved in some degree beneficial for the proper recording in the Chamberlain's Office, upon their admission to the Freedom of the said City, of the persons using the said several Arts and Mysteries of your Petitioners and the various parts and branches thereof and during several years thereafter many persons were reclaimed and recorded as Citizens and Clockmakers pursuant to the said Act notwithstanding they had endeavoured to procure their freedom to be recorded of or in other Companies of this City.

"But the said Act of Common Council not mentioning any one of the parts or branches of the 'several Arts and Mysteries of Clockmaking' but only the generic name by which the said Artizans your Petitioners are incorporated, which generic name was justly considered to and in fact does include the whole of the branches of the said Art, the evasions of the provisions of the said Act had become so great as to oblige your Petitioners to present on the 12th day of October 1812 a Memorial and claim the protection of his Worship the Chamberlain of this Honorable City on that behalf and to which Memorial, whereof a Copy is annexed, your Petitioners crave leave to refer.

"That your Petitioners sometime in the year 1813 discovered that one Robert Brettel Bate, a Foreigner not of the freedom of this City, had opened in the Poultry a Mathematical Instrument-Maker's shop wherein he sells Sundials and various other Instruments of the Clockmaking Art whereon his own name is engraven as the maker, and they caused him to be summoned in the accustomed manner to take up his freedom and be recorded as a Citizen and Clockmaker pursuant to the said Act of Common Council.

"But that instead of appearing and taking his freedom as a Citizen and Clockmaker as by Law he ought to have done, your Petitioners were some months thereafter informed that the said Robert Brettel Bate had petitioned your Worshipful Court to be admitted to the freedom of this City and recorded as of the Spectacle Makers Company, and that the progress of the said Freedom according to the said Petition had been suspended in the Chamberlain's Office upon the Caveat of your Petitioners, who by virtue of their Charter and Bye Laws further enforced by the said Act of Common Council claim that the said Robert Brettel Bate should be recorded as a Citizen and Clockmaker only.

"That his Worship the Chamberlain having called before him the said Robert Brettel Bate and the Master and Wardens of the Company of your Petitioners as also the Master and Wardens of the Company of Spectacle Makers respectively for the purpose of investigating the claim of each of the said Fellowships to have the said Robert Brettel Bate as a Recorded Freeman, your Petitioners produced an attested Copy of their said Charter, Bye Laws and Ordinances, also of divers Orders of this Honourable Court and Act of Common Council made on their behalf as aforesaid, as also such other persons as they conceive are conclusive of the right of your Petitioners to have and maintain the rule and government of the persons using any and every the parts and branches of their said 'several Arts and Mysteries' respectively and Mathematical Instrument making in particular and that all such persons should be recorded as Citizens and Clockmakers only.

"That finding that the said Company of Spectacle Makers had presented to the Chamberlain a Memorial claiming to exercise rights which are adverse to the rights of your Petitioners and not consonant with either the Charter or Bye Laws of the said Company of Spectacle Makers, which are restrictive to the Art and Trade of Spectacle Making only, and do not refer to or take cognizance of any other branch or article whatsoever, your Petitioners by their Committee on the 20th day of February last presented to his Worship the Chamberlain a further Memorial in support of their Chartered Rights and Privileges to which they crave leave to refer by a Copy of the same hereunto annexed.

"That your Petitioners upon the further hearing of the Case on the 23rd day of March last past were much surprised to hear his Worship the Chamberlain declare his opinion that 'Mr. Robert Brettel Bate is entitled to take his Freedom of the Spectacle Makers' Company,' And the Master of the Company of your Petitioners found it necessary thereupon to give notice of the intention of Your Petitioners to make the present appeal and application to your Worshipful Court for protection in the exercise and enjoyment of their Chartered Rights and Privileges further assured to them by the several grants of this Honorable City and the Act of Common Council on their behalf, his Worship the Chamberlain having kindly consented to suspend further proceedings in the Case of Mr. Bate pending the opinion and order of your Worshipful Court touching the same.

"Your Petitioners therefore humbly pray that your Worshipful Court taking consideration of the premises will be pleased to make such order as every person and persons using or practising the 'several Arts and Mysteries' of your Petitioners in or by the making or construction of, selling or dealing in, either or part or in the whole, of Clocks, Watches, Mathematical Instruments and Engraving, or any part or branch of their said several Arts or Mysteries whatsoever, and being hereafter admitted or to be admitted by the Chamberlain of this City for the time being to the freedom and liberties of this City, may be recorded as Citizens and Clockmakers only, pursuant to the said Act of Common Council passed for the protection of the Company of your Petitioners in the enjoyment of their Charter, Rights and Privileges, and that the obvious intentions of the said Charter and Bye Laws and Act of Common Council for the good government of their said Arts and Mysteries so incorporated in and with the Company of your Petitioners, or intended so to be, may not hereafter be evaded upon any pretence whatsoever.

"And further that the said Robert Brettel Bate whose chief trade consists in the making or sale of Sundials and divers Mathematical Instruments so included in and with the Company of your Petitioners as aforesaid may not be admitted into the Freedom and Liberties of this City of or in any other Company than the said 'Company of the Master, Wardens and Fellowship of the Art or Mystery of Clockmaking' and also the Chamberlain of this City under direction of your Worshipful Court may cause the said Robert Brettel Bate to be recorded as a Citizen and Clockmaker accordingly.

"And that your Worshipful Court will be pleased to afford to your Petitioners such further and other relief in the premises as to your Worships shall seem meet.

"And the same being approved the Common Seal was thereunto put and the Committee were authorized to take measures for causing the same to be in due form presented unto the Court of Lord Mayor and Aldermen.

"1815. May 1. The Master reported that the petition to the Court of Lord Mayor and Aldermen had been presented in due form, and that a Committee of Aldermen had been appointed to consider the same and to report thereon.

"It was Resolved,—That the Master and Wardens do from time to time take out of the Chest of this Company the Charter, Bye Laws, Patent for Armorial Bearings, Records, and other documents according as the same may be necessary in order to their being produced by the Committee for the affairs of Freemen and Apprentices in or towards the support of the petition of this Company."

The final decision of the Court of Aldermen upon this question was not given until the 4th of November, 1817, when a report from their Committee was presented, in which the decision of the Chamberlain of the 3rd March, 1815, was recommended to be affirmed; this was accordingly adopted by the Court. This decision was in favour of the Spectaclemakers, upon the ground that Bates was a maker of Spectacles, and was therefore entitled to take up his Freedom in that Company, that he neither made or sold Clocks or Watches, or professed the Trade of Clockmaking, and was therefore not compellable to take up his Freedom in the Clockmakers' Company; but as he sold Mathematical Instruments he subjected himself to the penalties inflicted by the Clockmakers'

Bye-Laws (if good in Law), unless he also became a Freeman of the Clockmakers' Company; that if any Mathematical Instruments he made or sold were within the intent and meaning of the Charter and Bye-Laws, as peculiarly belonging to the Trade of Clockmaking, the Company might prevent the dealing therein by enforcing the penalties of the Bye-Laws.

This opinion was reported to the Court of Assistants on the 1st of December following, and ordered to be entered on the Company's Journal, no further action being taken in the matter.

QUARTERAGE.

The payment of Quarterage by the Freemen was long a vexed question, which the Court of Assistants again and again tried to solve. Members refusing to pay were proceeded against; but this leading to much ill feeling, a scale of payments for redemption of such Quarterage was agreed upon in the year 1820, the particulars of which are contained in the following Minute:—

"1820. April 3. The Court of Assistants having taken into consideration the desire expressed by many of the Members of this Fellowship for permission to redeem their Quarterage, has Resolved: 'That such of the Members of this Fellowship as may be inclined to redeem their Quarterage *(being four shilllings per annum during life)*, be permitted so to do, upon payment of the sums set forth in the following table: first having paid and discharged all arrears due up to the time of such redemption.'

TABLE.

					£ s. d.		
Members of 30 years of age and under 35 to pay					2 8 0	being 12 years' purchase.	
,,	35	,,	,,	40	2 0 0	10	,,
,,	40	,,	,,	45	1 16 0	9	,,
,,	45	,,	,,	50	1 12 0	8	,,
,,	50	,,	,,	55	1 8 0	7	,,
,,	55	,,	,,	60	1 4 0	6	,,
,,	60	,,	,,	65	1 0 0	5	,,
,,	65	,,	,,	70	0 16 0	4	,,
,,	70	,,	,,	75	0 12 0	3	,,
,,	75	,,	,,	80	0 8 0	2	,,

ADMISSION OF JEWS, &c., TO THE FREEDOM.

On the 10th of December, 1830, an Act of Common Council was passed, enabling persons not professing the Christian religion to be admitted to the Freedom of London, which Act is in these words:—

"A Common Council holden in the Chamber of the Guildhall of the City of London on Friday the 10th day of December 1830.

"An Act for enabling all persons born within this kingdom, and all natural born subjects whatsoever not professing the Christian Religion but in other respects duly qualified, to be admitted to the Freedom of the City of London upon taking the Freeman's Oath according to the forms of their own religion.

"Whereas it is expedient that all persons born within this kingdom, and all natural born subjects whatsoever, not professing the Christian Religion but in other respects duly qualified, should be entitled to be admitted to the Freedom of the City of London upon taking the Oath of a Freeman of the said City according to the forms of their own religion.

"Be it therefore enacted ordained and established and it is hereby enacted, ordained and established by the Right Honorable the Lord Mayor, the Aldermen his Brethren and the Commons in this Common Council assembled, and by the authority of the same, that from and after the first day of January now next ensuing it shall be lawful for any person born within this kingdom, and for any natural born subject whatsoever not professing the Christian Religion but in other respects duly qualified, to be admitted to the Freedom of the City of London upon taking the following Oath of a Freeman of the said City according to the forms of his own religion and in such manner as is binding upon his own conscience."[1]

[*Here follow the words of the Oath.*]

On the 10th of October, 1831, it was determined by the Court of Assistants that in consequence of the passing of the above Act of Common Council permitting the admission of Jews, etc., to the Freedom of the City, the proceedings of the last Lady-Day Quarter Court, respecting the admission of John Grafton *alias* Solomons to the Freedom of this Company, should be stopped.

The following entry records the admission of the first Jew to the Freedom of the Company:—

"1831. December 5. Jonas Levy (a Jew) of Bevis Marks, St. Mary Axe, Watchmaker, admitted a Free Clockmaker by Redemption.[1]

CITY FREEDOMS.

On the 17th day of March, 1835, the Court of Common Council passed a Resolution in the following terms:—

"Resolved that in the opinion of this Court persons should be admitted to the Freedom of this City without the intervention of the Trading Companies."

The effect of this Resolution was speedily felt by the various Companies. Many persons to enable them to carry on their business within the City took up their Freedom under the terms of the order; and to this cause may doubtless be attributed the gradual weakening of the connexion of the various Companies with the Trades over which they had previously exercised such extensive and useful powers of control and government, although in some instances, notably in the case of the Goldsmiths, Vintners, Brewers, Clockmakers, Stationers, Coachmakers, Gunmakers and others, they are still associated therewith, and a great many of their Members carry on the Trades with which the Crafts are identified.

Fees now payable on taking up the Freedom of this Company:—

By Servitude   £6 3.
„ Patrimony   .   . £6 13.
„ Purchase [2]   .   £20 0.

---

[1] Company's Journal VIII.

[2] Increased 1st January, 1876, from £8 12 0.

APPRENTICES.

 HE Company's Bye-Laws, Nos. XV, XVI, and XVII, provide that every Freeman, being a Master Workman, may take one Apprentice, and the Master, Wardens, and Assistants two, but, in order that he may not be left destitute of an Apprentice, every Master may take another at the expiration of two years after the binding of the former one.

Bye-Law XIV, however, provides for the taking of Turnover Apprentices, with the consent of their former Masters, or of the Master, Wardens, and Court of Assistants.

An Apprentice having truly served his Master for seven years, and having been admitted to the Freedom of the Company, was required to serve as a journeyman for two years, at the expiration of which period he was to make his MASTER-PIECE, and submit the same to the Master, Wardens, and Assistants. If the work was allowed and approved, he was then admitted to be a Work-Master of the Company.

The following Extracts will explain this trade custom :—

"1632. October 23. This daye the Court have thought fit that Edward Buck shalbe allowed of and admitted after he hath performed seven years service and made his *Maisterpece*. And the said Court will consider of his fine for his admittaunce.'

¹ Company's Journal I.

"1654. April 2. This Court day Francis Bowen, Apprentice to Mr. Bowyer, brought his *Masterpiece*, having served his Master 7 years, and was admitted and sworn a free Clockmaker and paid 20s to the Company.

"1656. April 14. This day was admitted a free brother of this Company James Lello. He shewed his *Masterpiece* or Watch with the day of the month with his own name, attested to be of his handy work by Mr. Samuel Betts, and he promised conformity to the orders.[1]

"1681. January 16. Ordered that each person who shall hereafter come to be admitted into this Company shall before their admission shew to the Court assembled a *Masterpiece* of his own making as heretofore hath been used.[2]

"1639. April 1. John Drake, for not binding his Apprentice to some free Brother of this Company according to the Charter and Ordinances of Law under the Judges' hand, and likewise an order from the Court of Aldermen, and confessing that he had bound him to the Blacksmiths, is fined by this Court £10 to be leavied and recovered as is directed by the Ordinance of Law.[3]

"1646. December 7. This Court day it is ordered by reason of many abuses that do arise that every Member of this Company before he maketh any Apprentice free of the City that hath been bound to any other Company he shall first bring him to be admitted and sworn a brother of this Company before he makes him free of the City or else forfeit the sum of £5."[4]

The question of the number of Apprentices to be taken by each Member of the Company was one which occasioned much trouble. Some, defying the authority of the Bye-Laws, took several. On the 25th of February, 1656, Thomas Loomes was charged before the Lord Mayor with having five, when the following order was made:—

"Tichborne Mayor. The 25th day of February 1656. Upon complaint made to his Lordship by the Company of Clockmakers against Thomas Loomes, for keeping of five Apprentices contrary to the orders of the said Company—It is ordered by his Lordship that the said Thomas Loomes shall forthwith put away three of his said Apprentices and keep only but two, and his Lordship doth likewise declare that all persons that use the said Trade of a Clockmaker shall observe the orders of the said Company concerning their number of Apprentices.

"THOMAS LATHAM.

"On July 5 1658. Thomas Loomes was fined 40s. for taking an Apprentice without the consent of the Company."[5]

Shortly afterwards Ahasuerus Fromanteel and his son were charged with keeping more Apprentices than the Law permitted. The case was brought by the Master, Wardens,

---

[1] Company's Journal I.   [2] Company's Journal II.
[3,4,5] Company's Journal I.

and Court of Assistants, under the notice of the Lord Mayor, who heard both parties, when it would appear from the following letter addressed by Mr. Fromanteel to the Court of Assistants, that strong words had been used on either side, but the Lord Mayor ordered Mr. Fromanteel to comply with the Law. The Letter runs as follows:—

"Gentlemen,—Upon serious consideration of what passed before my Lord Mayor on Wednesday last I find that, in the managing of that business, there were such things uttered that did not become Christians nor Civil men, and forasmuch as the law of God commands us as much as in us lay to live in peace with all men, and that an account must be given as well for words as actions to the Lord, I do in order to the discharge of my duty towards God and man lay myself open before you, and that with all plainess, for the clearing of my conscience, and desire this one thing from you, that is, that prejudice may be laid aside, that you may be the better able without partiality to consider of what I write; and I begin with myself, whereas I said that my journeyman could do that in the Trade that no five of the Assistants could do, I do confess I spake rashly, and it savoured most of vain boasting, and I resolve by the help of God for time to come to be more cautious how I express myself, but withal I must desire you to consider how vainly I was charged by some of you, nay I must say falsely, for so it is, and that in several things—one thing was that I taught Mr. Creek the Trade—another was that my son Louis had three prentices more than the Company allowed him, and was by my means—a third was that I had taken a mere smith that was never trained up in Clockwork and taught him the trade, all which are as opposite to truth as light to darkness, upon which I was provoked and said what I said, and what I said is true, but not seasonable then to be spoken; I can but admire how it could be affirmed with so much confidence that my man was never trained up in Clockwork, forasmuch as several of the Court of Assistants know that two men that had known him long came to the Clockmakers' Court, and testified that he had served one five years in the country that made Jacks and Clocks and Guns and Locks and several sorts of work beside, and these men were not strangers but Citizens of London.

"I wonder also what reason you have to send me word that I should put him away which you must not expect as long as I have employment for him; now I desire of you, which is but reason, that you see me righted in those charges that were laid against me, either in the clearing of me or else to prove those things I am charged with, for till that be done I am much wronged; and concerning my son Louis I wonder why he should be so faulted by you for multiplying apprentices more than any of the Company, he employs none but such as are bound by the Company, if there be any multiplying of apprentices it is your own doing, for he doth not employ any but as are bound and approved of by the Company, or by your officer, he never entertained any other. Now the reason why he employs other men's prentices as well as his own you may know if you will enquire of their Masters, And if he detains them wrongfully from them they have a clear way against him, and may recover them again. If all that have prentices had done as he have done, take none till they have been 4 years out of their time theere would not have been so many as are and where others have three apiece bound to them for their own use as Mr. Irland, Mr. Davis, Mr. Miller, and others all with them at one time, he never had but two and one turned over to serve the remnant of his time, and therefore I pray consider how prentices are multiplied and by whom; but forasmuch as I find you cannot endure to have your actions questioned I shall be willing to wait and see what you will do for our release and reforming the whole Company, but in case of oppression I must relieve myself as well as I can, in the meantime I shall expect that you will make an appearance of that reformation you promised before my Lord Mayor, and so I shall leave you to the Lord that will one day judge righteous judgement upon all mens words and actions.

"AHASUERUS FROMANTEEL.

"Moses Alley 3rd of March 1656."

The following Resolutions have been passed by the Court of Assistants from time to time for the management and control of Apprentices :—

"1634. October 13. It was ordered by this Court that Edward Ambrose, Apprentice unto Elias Voland, upon the complaint of Josias Cuper shall work with the said Josias untill ye watch be finished which he is about, and that no man shall set him at work during that tyme.[1]

"1676. November 6. This Court, taking into consideration the great inconvenience arising to the Company by the multiplicity of the Apprentices taken, have ordered the Clarke to issue out ticketts to all and every the Members, of the Company to give notice to them That henceforward noe Apprentice will be allowed to be bound unto, or taken by any Member of the Company otherwise then according to the ordinances of the Company.[2]

"1681. January 16. It was ordered that all Members of the Company who hath or have unduly taken and bound any Apprentice or Apprentices, or who shall hereafter unduly take and bind any Apprentice or Apprentices to any other Company than this Company to which they are sworn shall be therefore prosecuted by the Master Wardens and Assistants of this Company, as the Company's Charter and Ordinances and the Laws of the Land enableth them."[3]

"1684. September 29. Whereas for some years past there hath been some restraint upon the Members of the Company as to the time when they might first bind an Apprentice, and when a second, and so successively, and by reason thereof divers Members have by secret shifts and undue means procured Apprentices to be bound to other Companies, and to be turned over or committed to themselves contrary to the Company's Ordinance in that behalf, whereby this Company hath been, is and will be much damaged, and a great increase made of Artists or Clockmakers and Workers in the Art, which are or will be freemen of these other Companies to which they are bound. This Court therefore thought fit and ordered that before they do take off the restraint, or make any alteration therein they will advise with good Counsell whether they may not legally prosecute those persons who have so transgressed, or shall so transgress and how and in what manner it best may and ought to be done. And the Master and Wardens and Mr. Gregory, Mr. Bell,

---

1, 2, 3 Company's Journal I.

Mr. Barrow and Mr. Jones are appointed a Committee in this behalf and that they or any 5 or more of them the Master and one or more of the Wardens or 2 or more of the Wardens without the Master being of the number are to act therein accordingly, And to report their proceedings and success to the Court.'

"1684. December 11. The matter relating to binding Apprentices to other Companies, which, at the Court of the 29th of September last, was by order referred to this Committee was debated, but, upon consideration of the unsuitableness of the present time for punishing such transgressions as are intended in that order of reference, nothing was done or concluded therein save that it was left to the consideration of the next quarter Court.[2]

"1685. March 1. Some complaints were made against Jasper Harmer, Ironmonger, neer Smithfield Bars (against whom the Company hath formerly had suit) he exercising the Art of Clockmaking not having served seven years Apprentice in the Art of Clockmaking, and doing things to the discredit of the Art and prejudice of the good Artists, It was thought fit that the Company should by all legal means endeavour to suppress or punish him therefore, But first that Mr. Henry Jones should ask the advice of the Recorder how it may be best performed.[3]

"1688. April 2. Ordered that William Whittingham shall be prosecuted at Law for exercising the Art or Trade of Clockmaking, he having not served seven years in or to the same Art or Trade.[4]

"1691. July 6. Whereas at a Court holden the 6th of November 1676, the then Master Wardens and Assistants of this Company for good reason and cause them moving thought fit to put some restraint upon the Members of the Company, in the time and manner of their taking of Apprentices from which time it hath hitherto been practiced and insisted upon as a Rule, That no Member having one apprentice might take a second till his former should have served full five years of his time. Now forasmuch as it hath appeared and by many and frequent examples it doth appear That many great inconveniences have arisen, and will further arise to this Company, if that restraint, practice, and rule be not ceased, wholly taken off and nulled, this Court therefore for the prevention of those or any other inconveniences which may hereafter happen by or from that restraint, practice, rule, Did and do by their vote and order cease, wholly take off and null the said restraint, practice, and rule, for and concerning binding of Apprentices, And did and do leave and refer each Member of the Company in and as touching the binding his Apprentice or Apprentices to the rule, time, manner and method prescribed, and ordeined in and by the Ordinance entered fol. 48 of the Company's Book of Ordinances, by which ordinance this Court was sensible and did and doth judge that he who hath one Apprentice bound for seven years may bind a second when his first hath served two years and he who hath one bound for 8 years may bind a second when his first hath served three years, the first Apprentice in either case having five years to serve.[5]

"1691. July 22. Memorandum, That the Master Wardens and Assistants together with William Young and William Speakman two of the Members of the Company of Haberdashers appeared before the Chamberlain of London upon occasion of a complaint by the said Master and Wardens by promotion of the said Wm. Young That one Andrew Strachan a Scotchman

---

[1, 2, 3, 4, 5] Company's Journal II.

accompted to be between 30ly and 40ly years of age, and no Freeman, hath for several years past worked in the Art of Clockmaking within the Limits of this Company's Charter of Incorporation, not submitting to the Charter Ordinance Search and Rule of this Company, hath in order to his prosecution been served with Exchequer Writs, to avoid which he hath shifted from place to place and at last by the contrivance of the said Thomas Warden and Abraham Strachan, he the said Abraham Strachan hath upon the 10th day of this last July bound himself Apprentice by Indenture unto the said Thomas Warden for the term of seven years thereby intending under his Countenance, and as his Apprentice to carry on without control a Trade for himself in the Art of Clockmaking, and gain a freedom of this City. Upon hearing of the matter It was by the Chamberlain adjudged and ordered by consent of the said Thomas Warden that the said Indenture of Apprenticeship should be cancelled (which was forthwith accordingly done) and he declared that as it was illegal and contrary to the Custom of the City of London that any person being under the age of 14 years should be bound Apprentice So was it also that any person above the age of 21 years should be bound Apprentice.[1]

"1692. April 4. It was resolved voted and ordered that the Master, with such as he shall think fit of the Wardens and Assistants to concern therewith, shall endeavour to obtain an Act of Common Council in favour of this Company of like nature as the Company of Spectacle Makers have relating to binding Apprentices to Freemen and committing them to Foreigners to be taught."[2]

FEMALE APPRENTICES.

In the year 1715, it appears that the Company recognized and sanctioned the taking of Female Apprentices, and the following among numerous other instances are to be found in their Records :—

"1715. January 27. Mariane Viet was bound Apprentice to her Father Claude Viet for seven years from this date.[3]

"1715. April 28. Rebeckah Fisher was bound Apprentice to George Taylor and Lucy his wife for seven years from this day.

"1725. October 4. Charlotte Hubert bound to James Hubert and Elizabeth his wife for 7 years.

"1730. April 6. Catherine Cext Apprentice to James Hubert and Elizabeth his wife.

"1733. January 3. Anna Maria Shaw, bound to Isaac Loddington and Ann his wife for seven years.[4]

"1734. February 3. Elizabeth Askell bound to Elinor Mosely.[5]

"1747. July 18. Susanna Smith to Hannah the wife of James Wilson.[6]

---

[1] Company's Journal II.   [2] Act of Common Council, 1st July, 1650.
[3] Company's Journal III.   [4, 5, 6] Company's Journal IV.

ADVICE TO APPRENTICES.

"1827. October 8. The Clerk having laid before the last Court a printed circular from the Rev. H. G. Watkins, M.A., Rector of St. Swithin's London Stone, containing a small pamphlet entitled 'Affectionate Advice' which he requested to submit to the consideration of this Company (it having been adopted by several of the Corporations of this City) to present to youths on being bound Apprentice, whereupon the Master directed that, for perusal, each Member of this Court should be furnished with a Copy of the same previous to taking the sense of the Court this day on the propriety of its being adopted by this Company, and the same being taken into consideration it was on the motion of Mr. Harris and seconded by Mr. Ganthony [1]

"Resolved unanimously,—That the pamphlet entitled 'Affectionate Advice to Apprentices' by the Rev. H. G. Watkins be adopted by this Company, and that the Clerk do procure One Hundred Copies thereof stitched in a cover bearing the Company's Arms and stating its having been presented on the day the Apprentice was bound in this Company."

On the 3rd of July, 1865, it was resolved that the fee to be paid upon binding an Apprentice, "The consideration being Faithful service only," should be reduced from two Guineas to one, and on July 8th, 1867, it was

"Resolved unanimously—That in future all Apprentices serving seven years to the satisfaction of their Masters and where the consideration is 'Faithful Service' only, who shall take up their Freedom within 12 months after being out of their time shall be admitted at half the usual fees." [2]

Charges for binding Apprentices :—

						£	s.	d.
"Charity Indentures			...	...	...	1	5	0
If no Premium		...	...	...	...	0	17	6
" any sum under £10			...	...	...	3	11	0
" £10 and under £20			...	...	...	3	16	0
" 20	"	30	...	...	...	4	1	0
" 30	"	40	...	...	...	6	1	6
" 40	"	50	...	...	...	6	6	6
" 50	"	100	...	...	...	8	6	6
" 100	"	200	...	...	...	13	6	6
" 200	"	300	...	...	...	19	6	6
" 300	"	400	...	...	...	27	16	6
" 400	"	500	...	...	...	37	16	6

" Fee to the Clerk in each case 3s. 6d."

---

[1] Company's Journal VII.   [2] Company's Journal X.

BIOGRAPHICAL NOTICES

OF

MEMBERS OF THE COMPANY

WHO HAVE

Distinguished Themselves,

IN CONNECTION WITH THE TRADE,

OR WHO HAVE FILLED MUNICIPAL OFFICES.

A LIST

OF SOME OF THE

CELEBRATED CLOCKMAKERS

ADMITTED

MEMBERS OF THE COMPANY

DURING THE

SEVENTEENTH CENTURY,

Not included in the succeeding Biographical Notices.

Date of Admission.

1633.	September 9.	Timothy Gray.
1633.	October 3.	Richard Masterson.
1640.	October 12.	Peter de Laundre.
1649-50.	January 14.	Thomas Loomes.[1]
1651.	December 18.	Solomon Bouquett.
1655.	January 10.	Ahasuerus Fromanteel.[2]
1668.	January 18.	Nathaniell Delander.
,,	,, ,,	James Delander.
1669.	November 1.	James Gibson,
		A great Clockmaker.
1670-1.	March 9.	Jame Clewes,
		A great Clockmaker.
1671.	July 3.	John Hunt,
		A Clockmaker, and Brother of the Society of Tobacco Pipe Makers of London.
,,	,, ,,	Ignatius Huggeford,
		Clockmaker, and free of the Company of Haberdashers.
1671.	September 4.	Thomas Grimes,
		A great Clockmaker.
1671.	September 29.	Joseph Windmills.
		A great Clockmaker.

---

[1] He resided at the "Mermayd," in Lothbury, and was charged before the Lord Mayor, by the Company, for keeping more than two Apprentices. A specimen of his workmanship is in the Company's Collection.

[2] Ahasuerus Fromanteel, admitted November 29th, 1632, was probably the father of the above.

1671. January 15. William Million,
A great Clockmaker, and Free of the Merchant-taylors.
1672. January 20. John Howes,
A great Clockmaker.
1674. September 29. William Dent,
A great Clockmaker.
1675. March 29. Gabriell Stubbs,
A small Clockmaker.
1675. February 7. John Delaunder,
Watchcase Maker.
1678. September 30. Gerard Overzee,
Clockmaker. A naturalized subject.
1687. September 29. Charles Le Febuce,
A Frenchman, and a great Clockmaker.
1691. September 29. John Heerman,
A Dutchman. A Watchmaker.

CELEBRATED MEMBERS OF THE TRADE.

JOHN ARNOLD.

Born at Bodmin, Cornwall, in 1744, and apprenticed to his Father, a Watchmaker there. Some family disagreement arising, he went to Holland and obtained employment at The Hague, where he remained for several years. On returning to England, he earned a scanty livelihood as an itinerant mechanic. A gentleman, whose repeater he repaired, was so struck with his superior talent, that he assisted him to establish himself in London, where he commenced business as a Watch and Clockmaker in Devereux Court, Fleet Street, and afterwards removed to Cornhill. His patron having introduced him to the notice of George III, the King gave him £100 to enable him to commence experiments for the improvement of Chronometers. He was subsequently assisted by the Board of Longitude. In 1764, he made the smallest repeating Watch ever attempted, which he presented on the 4th of June as a birthday gift to George III; it was set in a ring, and was less in size than a silver twopenny piece; it contained one hundred and twenty different parts, and weighed 5 dwts. $7\frac{3}{4}$ grains, including the first ruby cylinder ever made. The King was so pleased with it, that he presented the donor with five hundred guineas. The improvements introduced by this ingenious Mechanician are too numerous to particularize. In 1775, Arnold obtained[1] a patent for a helical or cylindrical spiral spring. He was employed by the East India Company to make Chronometers for use in their ships. He made two, which were supplied to Captain Cook, one for the "Adventure."

---

[1] See Patent No. 1113, Dec. 30, 1775.

and the other for the "Resolution." In 1782,[1] he patented the Epicycloid scape-wheel. Admitted a Free Clockmaker by redemption April 7, 1783, and chosen on the Livery October 27, 1796. Was one of the competitors for the reward offered by the Board of Longitude, under the Act of Parliament, 12 Anne, cap. 15, passed in 1713, which promised £20,000, upon certain conditions, to those who should submit the best instrument for determining the Longitude at Sea, and, although he did not gain the prize, the Board in 1805 awarded his son, John Roger Arnold, £3,000 for the improvements his father had made in Chronometers. In 1780, he published by permission of the Board, an account of the going, during 13 months, of a pocket chronometer of his manufacture, deposited at the Royal Observatory; the greatest difference from mean time shown in one day had never amounted to four seconds. He died August 25, 1799, and was buried at Chislehurst. In the Company's Horological Collection are several specimens of his work presented by Messrs. Charles Frodsham and Co., in 1875. In the Library will also be found several works upon the Chronometers constructed by him.

CHARLES CABRIERE,

Watchmaker, of Broad Street; made Free of the Company in 1726, chosen on the Court of Assistants, 4th October, 1750; served the office of Warden in 1754-56; elected Master, 29th September, 1757.

On the 7th of July, 1777, Mr. Cabriere attended and acquainted the Court of Assistants that he had entered a prosecution against sundry persons for putting his name, without his knowledge or consent, to Watches which they had made up, and prayed their assistance and advice, which was unanimously promised.

The case Cabriere v. Anderson,[2] recorded in the Annual Register of 3rd December, 1777, was tried before Lord Mansfield, in the Court of King's Bench, and was considered a remarkable cause, the first of its kind. The defendant was sued for putting the plaintiff's name to five Watches made by

---

[1] See Patent No. 1328, May 2, 1782.
[2] Volume 20, page [212] Gents' Magazine, vol. 47, p. 608.

the former, and thereby hurting the reputation of the plaintiff. A verdict was given for £100, being £20 for each Watch, agreeably to an Act of Parliament of William III.

This led to a Meeting being called by the Master, Wardens, and Court of Assistants of the Company, who passed a Resolution that the Bye-Law XLVI, together with an Extract from the Act of the 9th and 10th of William III, cap. 28, paragraph 2, be printed in the Gazette and the Public Newspapers, etc., etc. *See* Trade, etc.

The Company have in their collection of Watch movements, three by this maker.

PETER DE BAUFRE,

Watchmaker, admitted to the Freedom of the Company, 1st July, 1689. He in conjunction with his brother Jacob, and Mr. Nicholas Faccio, of Duiller, a Member of the Royal Society, obtained from Queen Anne a grant of letters patent for the sole use in England, etc., for 14 years, of a new art, invented by them, of figuring and working precious or common stones, crystal or glass, and certain other matters different from metals, so that they might be employed in Watches, Clocks, and many other engines, etc. The Inventors were not satisfied with their 14 years' patent, and therefore applied to Parliament for an extension of the term, and also for an Act for the sole monopoly. This application met with the strenuous opposition of the Company, and was defeated. For full particulars, *see* Patents and Inventions. The Company have in their Collection a Silver Watch, made by him, with original lever escapement, and with a small crystal at back to show the balance. It beats half-seconds, and has stop-work, etc.

SIMON DE CHARMES,

Whose ancestors came over to England upon the revocation of the Edict of Nantes, was admitted to the Freedom of the Company, 6th of April, 1691, and became eminent in his profession. A Gold Repeater and two Movements, made by him, are in the Company's Collection of Watches. He purchased an Estate at Hammersmith, and built a house subsequently called Grove Hall. His son David De Charmes resided there, and was buried in Hammersmith Churchyard in 1783.

THOMAS EARNSHAW.

Born at Ashton-under-Lyne, Lancashire, in 1749. He resided in High Holborn, and was summoned before the Court of Assistants of the Company for carrying on the trade of a Watchmaker without paying quarterage to the common fund. He appeared before them May 2, 1796, and the law relating thereto being read to him, he declared himself fully convinced of the power of the Company, and paid the amount claimed. In 1781, he began to use the improved spring detent. In 1802, he made a great improvement in Chronometers by employing a single balance instead of two combined as used by Arnold. He succeeded in making Timekeepers so simple and cheap, that they were within the reach of private individuals. There is a curious transit Clock at the Greenwich Observatory, made by Graham, but greatly improved and simplified by Earnshaw. He was one of the unsuccessful competitors for the rewards offered by the Board of Longitude; the Commissioners voted him £500 in 1800, but upon an application being made to them they again considered his claims, and on the 3rd of March, 1803, came to the following Resolution:—

"Resolved,—That the Board are convinced that Mr. Earnshaw's Watches have gone better than any others that have been submitted to trial at the Royal Observatory, and therefore are of opinion that he deserves a reward equal at least to that given by Parliament to Mr. Mudge, provided he will disclose the construction of his timekeepers in such a manner as shall satisfy the Board that other Watchmakers will be enabled to construct them with equal accuracy, etc.

"That the President of the Royal Society be desired to wait upon the Chancellor of the Exchequer, and request him to consent to the additional grant intended for the reward of Mr. Earnshaw."

This was done, and on the 27th December, 1805, he received £2,500, making £3,000.

His appeal to the public, stating his claims to the original invention of the improvements in his Timekeepers, is in the Company's Library. They also have his portrait, engraved by Bellin, from a painting by Sir Martin Archer Shee, R.A.

EDWARD EAST,

Watchmaker to King Charles I. One of the ten original Assistants appointed by the Charter of Incorporation in 1632.

He was a Watchmaker of great repute, and resided in Pall Mall, near the Tennis Court. It is reported of Charles II, when Prince of Wales, that he frequently played at Tennis, the stakes being an "Edwardus East," as His Royal Highness called it; that is, a Watch of East's making.[1] It would appear that East afterwards removed to Fleet Street.

"Another night His Majesty (Charles I) appointed Mr. Herbert to come into his Bed Chamber an hour sooner than usual in the morning; but it so happened that he overslept his time, and awaken'd not untill the King's Silver Bell hasten'd him in. Herbert, (said the King) you have not observ'd the command I gave last night. He acknowledged his fault. Well (said the King) I will order you for the future; you shall have a Gold Alarm-Watch, which, as there may be cause, shall awake you; write to the Earl of Pembroke to send me such a one presently. The Earl immediately sent to Mr. East, his Watchmaker in Fleet Street, about it; of which more will be said at his Majesty's coming to St. James's . . . . The Earl delivered to a Military Officer who was going to St. James's the Gold Watch that had the Alarm desiring him to give it to Mr. Herbert, to present it to the King . . . . . The King commanded his Gold Watch to be given to the Duchess of Richmond."[2]

He was Warden of the Company in 1638 and 1639; elected Master 29th of September, 1645, and again 4th of October, 1652. He was also appointed Treasurer 11th of October, 1687, and was the only occupant of that Office.

JOHN ELLICOTT, F.R.S.,

Clockmaker to King George III. Resided in Sweeting's Alley, Cornhill, and was a Mathematician of considerable ability. Elected a Fellow of the Royal Society in 1738. In .1752, invented the compensated pendulum (*see* his work in the Company's Library)- He had also submitted an improved Pyrometer to the Society in 1736. In the proceedings of the Royal Society for 1762 (page 534 *et seq.*) are printed some observations, by Charles Mason, concerning the going of Mr. Ellicott's Clock at St. Helena. His portrait, engraved by Dunkarton, from a painting by Nathaniel Dancel, is in the Company's Collection.

[1] In the Company's Museum is a specimen of one of the small Oval Hunting Watches, and a Clock with an Alarum, by the same maker.
[2] Memoirs of the two last years of the reign of King Charles I, by Sir Thomas Herbert, Groom of the Chambers to his Majesty, edition 1815, pages 148 and 173.

WILLIAM JAMES FRODSHAM, F.R.S.,

Of Change Alley, Cornhill, admitted a FreeClockmaker, October 11, 1802; and to the Livery of the Company, 7th October, 1811; chosen on the Court of Assistants, January 12, 1824; served the office of Warden, 1833-35; twice elected Master, 1836-1837. He published several works, among them one in 1838 on the results of experiments on the vibration of pendulums. Two Chronometers, made by Frodsham, were tested at Greenwich in 1830, and after a twelve months' trial one varied 86-100 of a second, and the other 57-100 parts of a second. He died June 28, 1850, and left a legacy of £1000 to the poor of the Company.—[*See* Charities.] His portrait, by Miss Ada Cole, is preserved in the Collection.

AHASUERUS FROMANTEEL,

The elder, a great Clockmaker, admitted and sworn a Free Member of the Company, November 29, 1632. He resided in Mopes Alley, Southwark, on the Bankside, and also at the sign of the Mermaid, in Lothbury. Noted for his Steeple-clocks. Evelyn in his Diary, May 3rd, 1661, says, "returned from Fromantil's ye famous Clockmaker to see some pendules." He took an active part in the Trade disputes between the Freemen and the governing body of the Company.

GEORGE GRAHAM.

Born in the parish of Kirklinton, Cumberland, July 7, 1673, of parents who were members of the Society of Friends. In 1688, he came to London, and was apprenticed to Henry Aske, Clockmaker, July 2 in that year. During his apprenticeship he made the acquaintance of the family of the celebrated Thomas Tompion, Watchmaker, of Fleet Street, who ultimately received him into his employ. He married Elizabeth, the daughter of Tompion's brother James, and at his master's decease in November, 1713, succeeded to the business. Made Free of this Company July 2, 1715; chosen one of the Court of Assistants April 2, 1716; Warden 1719-21; Master September 29, 1722. He died November 20, 1751, and was buried by the side of his friend and benefactor, Tompion, in Westminster Abbey.

He was acknowledged to be the greatest Horologist of his day, and a most ingenious Mathematical Instrument-maker. In 1715, he applied a compensating power to counteract the effects of heat and cold upon the length of the pendulum. He also invented the repose or dead escapement. In 1724, he greatly improved the horizontal escapement invented by Tompion, and also constructed a great mural arch at the Greenwich Observatory, as well as the sector, by means of which Dr. Bradley first discovered two new motions in the fixed stars. When the French Academicians were sent to the north, to make observations for ascertaining the figure of the earth, Graham was selected to supply them with instruments. The first Planetarium made in England was the work of his genius; it was made for *Lord Orrery*, whose name has ever since been given in this country to all machines of this description. He was elected a fellow of the Royal Society, March 9, 1720, and communicated to that Society several very important discoveries. He greatly improved the horizontal or cylinder escapement which was used in most of the best watches of his day, while his mercurial pendulum and dead-beat escapement are still used in the best regulators and astronomical time-keepers.

By his will, dated 23rd June, 1747, he left to the poor of the Company, twenty pounds.

The Company have in their Collection a long Eight-day Clock and a Watch-movement of his work, and also his portrait, engraved by Faber, from a painting by T. Hudson.

JOHN GRANT.

John Grant, the elder, was a Watchmaker of considerable repute, who carried on business for many years in Fleet Street. He was apprenticed to his uncle, Alexander Cumming, F.R.S., an honorary Freeman of the Company, and the author of several valuable works upon Horology, and ultimately succeeded to his business. Grant himself was also admitted añ honorary Freeman April 2, 1781, and was called to the Livery April 6, 1789. On October 9, 1809, he was elected to the Court of Assistants, and was chosen Junior Warden January 8, 1810, but died on May 4th in that year. Four curious and valuable examples of his workmanship the gift of his son, are in the Company's Collection. His son and

Elève, the subject of the present notice, who succeeded to his business, was admitted to the Freedom February 3, 1817, and to the Livery March 3 in the same year. On the 8th January, 1827, he was chosen one of the Assistants of the Company, and served the office of Warden from 1833 to 1837, again in 1845, and from 1855 to 1857. He has five times filled the office of Master, viz., in 1838, 1839, 1846, 1858, and 1867, and is now the Father of the Company. His portrait, painted by order of the Court of Assistants in 1880, when in his 84th year, is among the Company's Collection.

CHARLES GRETTON.

Apprenticed to Lionel Wythe, 30th of June, 1662; admitted to the Freedom, June 3, 1672; chosen on the Court of Assistants, July 1, 1689; served the office of Warden, 1697-99; elected Master 30th September, 1700. On the 1st September, 1701, he gave upon trust to the Company the sum of £50, to pay fifty shillings a year to apprentice the sons of deceased Freemen of the Company, to the trade of Watch and Clockmaking. Two specimens of his workmanship are in the Company's Museum.

HENRY JONES.

Apprenticed to Edward East, 22nd August, 1654; admitted to the Freedom, July 6, 1663; served the office of Warden, 1687-1689; elected Master, September 29, 1691. He resided in the Temple. In the "London Gazette," No. 2499, for October 21st to 24th, 1689, appears the following advertisement:—
"Lost, the 21st instant, between the Haymarket, near Charing Cross and the Rummer in Queen Street, near Cheapside, a round Gold Pendulum Watch of an indifferent small size, shewing the Hours and Minutes, the Pendulum went with a straight Spring, it was made by Henry Jones, Watchmaker in the Temple, the Out-case had a Cypher pinn'd on it, and the Shagreen much worn off. Whosoever gives notice of it to the said Mr. Jones, or Mr. Snagg, a Goldsmith in Lombard Street, shall have 2 Guineas Reward."

Charles II, according to tradition, gave to Mrs. Jane Lane a Clock, in memory of her services, after the battle of

Worcester. On the Clock was engraved the name " Henricus Jones, Londini."

> "1673. January 19. Mr. Henry Jones, Clockmaker, acquainted the Court of the Company that he had made for The King (Charles II) a Clock of the value of £150 whereon was engraven HENRICUS JONES LONDINI, and which stood in His Majesty's closet for about seven years, but being by his Majesty given unto a Lady it came into the hands of ROBERT SEIGNIOR, Clockmaker, of Exchange Alley, to be repaired, and he caused Edward Staunton, Clockmaker, or some other person to take out the maker's name and inserted his own."[1]

This was doubtless the Clock above referred to. After some inquiry, no further action appears to have been taken by the Company.

In North's Life of the Lord Keeper Guildford, vol. II, page 203, it is stated that Barometers were first made and sold at his suggestion, by one Jones, a Clockmaker in the Inner Temple Gate.

In the Company's Collection is a Vertical Watch by this maker, in a metal covered case, presented by Miss Butter to the Company in 1876.

THOMAS MUDGE,

Second son of The Rev. Zachary Mudge, a learned divine and master of the Grammar School at Bideford, Devon. Born at Exeter about 1716. At the age of 14 he was apprenticed to George Graham, then the most famous of Watchmakers, May 4, 1730. Whilst in his apprenticeship he became known far and wide as one of the best authorities upon Timekeepers. He succeeded to his Master's business, carried on at the " Dial and One Crown," opposite the " Bolt and Tun," Fleet Street. Admitted a Free Clockmaker, January 15, 1738. In 1750 he entered into partnership with Mr. William Dutton, and in 1763 published " Thoughts on the means of improving Watches, and particularly those for use at Sea." In 1760 he was introduced to Count de Bruhl, envoy extraordinary from the Court of Saxony, a great admirer of the Art, who became his friend and patron. He made a Watch with a compensation curb for Smeaton, the Engineer, and also several

[1] Company's Journal I.

Timekeepers for Ferdinand VI, of Spain. He was the inventor of the Lever Escapement, the first instrument to which this improvement was applied, being made in 1770 for Queen Charlotte. In 1771 he retired from active business, and turned his attention to Chronometers. In 1789 he, with several others, competed for the reward offered by the Board of Longitude for the most accurate Timekeeper for determining the longitude at sea, but was unsuccessful. In 1793, a Select Committee of the House of Commons, assisted by several men of science, reported that Mr. Mudge was one of the first Watchmakers this country had produced, and recommended the Parliament to give him a reward of £3,000 for his improvements in the construction of Chronometers. He died at his Son's house in Walworth, November 14, 1794. Several specimens of his work are preserved in the Company's Collection.

They also possess Portraits both of him and his Father, the Rev. Zachariah Mudge.

DANIEL QUARE,

"A great Clockmaker," admitted a Brother, April 3, 1671; chosen on the Court of Assistants in 1697; Warden 1705-1707; Master September 29, 1708. In 1676, he invented the repeating movement in Watches, by which they were made to strike at pleasure, and in 1687 gained well-deserved credit for placing the minute hand concentric with the hour hand in Clocks. Upon an application by Mr. Barlow for a patent for the sole making of Repeating Clocks and Watches, the Company petitioned the King in Council against the grant, and at the hearing of the case in March, 1687, the Council having tested the merits of Mr. Barlow's Repeaters with those of Mr. Quare, refused to grant the patent.

In the bedroom of William III, at Hampton Court Palace, is a Clock standing at the head of the bed, made by Daniel Quare, it goes 12 months without winding up.[1]

A patent was granted to him, August 2, 1695, for the invention of a portable Weather Glass or Barometer, which in the words of the patent, "may be removed and carried to any

---

[1] Wood's "Curiosities of Clocks and Watches," edition 1866, p. 64.

place, though turned upside down, without spilling one drop of quicksilver, or letting any air into the tube."

A description of the identical Watch, made by him for King James II, was given in a letter to the "Morning Chronicle," dated December 11, 1823, re-printed in Wood's "Curiosities of Clocks and Watches," edition 1866, page 295.

He died in 1724, and was buried in the Quakers' burying ground at Bunhill Fields, March 30, 1724. Most of the Watchmakers in London attended his funeral.[1]

DAVID RAMSEY,

Clockmaker to King James the First, and the First Master of the Company. He was the friend of Master Heriot, "Gingling Geordie," Jeweller to James I, and was an eminent Scotch Artificer. In 1610-12, he made three Watches for Henry, Prince of Wales, son of James I. Wood, in his "Curiosities of Clocks and Watches," edition 1866, pages 266-7, says :—

> In "The Accompte of the money expended by Sir David Murray K$^{t.}$ as Keeper of the Privie Purse to the late Noble Prynce Henry, Prynce of Wales, from the first of October 1610, to the sixth of November 1612 (the daye of the decease of the said Prynce) as likewise for certaine paymentes made after the deathe of the said Prynce in the monethes of November and December 1612."

In the Audit Office, Somerset House, is the following entry :—

"Watches, three bought of Mr. Ramsey the Clockmaker lxi$^{li.}$ (£61). In the list of Guyftes and Rewardes in the same account will be found, Mr. Ramsey the Clockmaker, xjs."

The following Particulars and Extracts from the Calendars of the State Papers, give some interesting details of his history :—

He held the appointment of Groom of the Bedchamber to the Prince, and in 1613 a Pension of £200 per annum was granted to him. In 1613, King James gave him a pension of £50 per annum.[2] In the grant he is styled Clockmaker Extraordinary. In [3] 1616, a warrant was signed to pay him £234 10s. for the purchase and repair of Clocks and Watches for the King. November 26, 1618, he was appointed to the Office of [4] Chief Clockmaker to His Majesty, with fees and allowances for workmanship. [5] On July 27, 1619, a grant of denization was passed to David Ramsay, the King's

---
[1] Wood's "Curiosities of Clocks and Watches," edition 1866, pp. 64-297.
State Papers (Domestic) 1611-18, [2] p. 211. [3] p. 419. [4] p. 598. [5] 1619-23, p. 67.

Clockmaker, born in Scotland. [1] March 30, 1622, a warrant was signed to pay him £113, for work for the late Prince Henry, and for Watches and Clocks for the King. [2] September 30, 1622, he received £232 15s for repairing Clocks at Theobalds, Oatlands, and Westminster, and for making a chime of bells adjoining to the Clock at Theobalds. [3] January 25, 1626, a warrant to pay to David Ramsey £150, for coins to be given by the King (Charles I) on the day of his Coronation was signed.

1627. March 17 Warrant to David Ramsay, Page of the Bedchamber and Clockmaker £441 3s. 4d. for work done for his late Majesty; and £358 16s. 8d., in lieu of diet and bouche of Court.[4] 1628. July 10. A warrant was signed to pay him £415 for Clocks and other necessaries, delivered for the king's service.[5] In 1632 £219 was paid to him on his bills for one year.[6]

He appears to have been a man of considerable ability, from the number of inventions for which he sought, and in several cases obtained, grants of Patents.

Although no official grant to him from King Charles I, as his Clockmaker, has been found, yet from the entries in the State Papers he seems to have continued the office he held under his father. His appointment by the king as first Master of the Company tends to confirm this. He was sworn into office as Master by Sir George Whitmore, Lord Mayor, on the 12th of October, 1632. He did not, however, take an active part in the affairs of the Company, Henry Archer, who was appointed Deputy-Master, having presided at the several Courts held during his term of office.

Sir Walter Scott, in the *Fortunes of Nigel*, thus speaks of Ramsey : " Memory Monitor, Watchmaker and Constructor of Horologes to His Most Sacred Majesty James I." The novelist then goes on to say :

"Although his profession led him to cultivate the exact sciences, like many at this period, he mingled them with pursuits which were mystical and fantastic. David Ramsey risked his money on the success of the vaticinations, which his researches led him to form, since he sold Clocks and Watches under condition that their value should not become payable till King James was crowned in the Pope's chair at Rome."

State Papers (Domestic) 1619-23, [1] p. 365. [2] p. 451. [3] 1625-26, p. 558. [4] 1627-28, p. 97. [5] 1628-1629, p. 202. [6] 1631-1633, p. 484.

ISAAC ROGERS,

Son of Isaac Rogers, Citizen and Baker, a Levant Merchant and Watchmaker. Born in White Hart Court, Lombard Street, 13th of August, 1754. Upon the completion of his education at the Rev. Dr. Milner's School, Peckham, he was apprenticed, and in 1776, succeeded to his father's business. On the 2nd of September, 1776, he was admitted to the Freedom of the Clockmakers' Company by Patrimony, and on January 11, 1790, became a Liveryman. Like his father, he was a member of the Levant Company, and carried on an extensive trade with Turkey, Smyrna, Philadelphia, and the West Indies; and although thus occupied with business, he devoted considerable attention to scientific pursuits, Chemistry and Mineralogy being his favourite studies. He designed and constructed two Regulators, one with a mercurial pendulum, and the other with a gridiron pendulum. The improvement of Naval Architecture was also a project in which he took an active part ; he was one of the projectors of a Society for that purpose, many of its meetings being held at his residence. In 1799, he was appointed the Treasurer of the Society. Later in life he became largely engaged in mining operations both in Cornwall and Wales. The best method of lighting the streets with gas also occupied his attention, and upon the establishment of the Imperial Gas Company, in 1818, he was elected one of the Directors, and subsequently became Chairman of the Board.

Reverting to his connection with this Company, on the 9th of October, 1809, he was chosen one of the Court of Assistants, and served the office of Warden, 1810-12, and again in 1823. On the 29th of September, 1824, he was elected Master. Whilst serving the office of Renter Warden, his attention was directed to the state of the Company's finances, and with the able and zealous co-operation of his friends, Mr. Henry Clarke, and Mr. George Atkins the then Clerk, he projected a well-digested and sound plan for the resuscitation of the Company upon a good financial basis ; and on the 30th of September, 1811, laid the same before the Court of Assistants, when, after mature consideration, it was adopted, and the thanks of the Court were presented to him for his attention to the finances of the Company, and the plan devised for insuring its future prosperity.

With his friends, Mr. Clarke and Mr. Vulliamy, he was ever ready to defend the interests of the Trade before the Ministers of the Crown or the public, and he helped to direct public attention to the pernicious system of affixing the names of the best English Watchmakers to foreign work, and then exporting them as English made; and also to the method of stamping Gold and Silver Cases at Goldsmiths' Hall. He died in December, 1839, at the age of 85, the Father of this and also of the Levant Company.

A Portrait of him is preserved in the Company's Collection in the Guildhall Library.

THOMAS TOMPION,

Called the "Father of English Watchmakers," was a native of North-hill, Bedfordshire, and is said to have been originally a Blacksmith. He resided at No. 67, Fleet Street, at the corner of Whitefriars Street. He was made free of the Company, 4th September, 1671; chosen one of the Court of Assistants, 7th September, 1691; served the office of Warden, 1700-3; Master 29th September, 1704. He died 20th November, 1713, and was buried in Westminster Abbey. His will, dated 21st October, 1713, was proved by his friend and successor, George Graham, one of the Executors. He made a Watch with a spiral balance, or pendulum spring, for King Charles II. One end of the spring was made fast to the arbor of the balance wheel, whilst the other was secured to the plate, the oscillations being rendered equal and regular by its elastic force. He invented the cylinder escapement, with horizontal wheel, in 1695, and greatly improved Striking Clocks (*see* Patent for Watch and Clockmaking, No. 344, dated September 23, 1695).

The monumental stone over the grave of Tompion and Graham was removed by the authorities of the Abbey about 1838. Mr. George Atkins, then Clerk of the Company drew attention to this act of desecration in the following letter, which was inserted in the newspapers :—

"Previous to 1838, visitors to Westminster Abbey may remember to have read on a slab in the nave of that Church the following inscription :—

"' HERE LIES THE BODY
OF MR. THO TOMPION
WHO DEPARTED THIS LIFE THE 20TH OF NOVEMBER 1713 IN THE
75TH YEAR OF HIS AGE.'

HERE LIES THE BODY
OF M.^R THO TOMPION
WHO DEPARTED THIS
LIFE THE 20TH OF
NOVEMBER 1713 IN THE
75TH YEAR OF HIS AGE.

ALSO THE BODY OF
GEORGE GRAHAM OF LONDON
WATCHMAKER AND F.R.S.
WHOSE CURIOUS INVENTIONS
DO HONOUR TO Y^E BRITISH GENIUS
WHOSE ACCURATE PERFORMANCES
ARE Y^E STANDARD OF MECHANIC SKILL
HE DIED Y^E XVI OF NOVEMBER MDCCLI
IN THE LXXVIII YEAR OF HIS AGE

"'ALSO THE BODY OF
GEORGE GRAHAM OF LONDON WATCHMAKER AND F.R.S.
WHOSE CURIOUS INVENTIONS DO HONOUR TO YE BRITISH GENIUS
WHOSE ACCURATE PERFORMANCES ARE YE STANDARD OF
MECHANIC SKILL
HE DIED YE XVI OF NOVEMBER MDCCLI IN THE LXXVIII YEAR OF HIS AGE.'

"*Now*, all that remains to commemorate the 'Father of Clockmaking,' Thomas Tompion and 'Honest George Graham,' is this inscription, cut upon a small lozenge-shaped bit of marble :—

'Mr. T. Tompion 1713.
'Mr. G. Graham 1751.'

"I presume the Very Reverend the Dean and his Chapter consider it *infra dig.* to allow a tablet to the memory of two Watchmakers to remain amongst the monuments of the mighty dead which adorn the walls of their Cathedral. Death is said to level all distinctions. It appears these holy men have forgotten that axiom.
"Yours obediently,
"A DETESTOR OF INTOLERANCE.
"*June 2nd 1842.*"

The following notice appears in the Historical Memorials of Westminster Abbey, by Dean Stanley, 1869, page 348 :—

"In the centre of the Nave, in the same grave, were laid master and apprentice—Tompion and Graham, the fathers of English Watchmakers. The slab over their grave, commemorating their 'curious inventions and accurate performances' was removed at the beginning of the century. This change called forth many an indignant remonstrance from the humble but useful tribe who regarded this gravestone as their Caaba. 'Watchmakers,' says one of them, 'the writer amongst the number, until prevented by recent restrictions, were in the habit of making frequent pilgrimages to the sacred spot : from the inscription and the place they felt proud of their occupation ; and many a secret wish to excel has arisen while silently contemplating the silent resting place of the two men whose memory they so much revered.' Their memory may last, but the slab is gone." [1]

Dean Stanley, with commendable good taste, had a search made for the missing stone ; happily it was found unimpared, and has since been restored to its place.

---

[1] Thompson's Time and Time Keepers, p. 74. The passage was pointed out to me by a friend in consequence of the strong irritation expressed on the subject by an obscure Watchmaker in a provincial town. The gravestone happily had not been destroyed, and has since been restored.

The inscription on the stone and accompanying sketch shewing the exact position in which it is placed, have been kindly furnished by Thomas Mills, Esq., whose drawings of Westminster Abbey are well known.

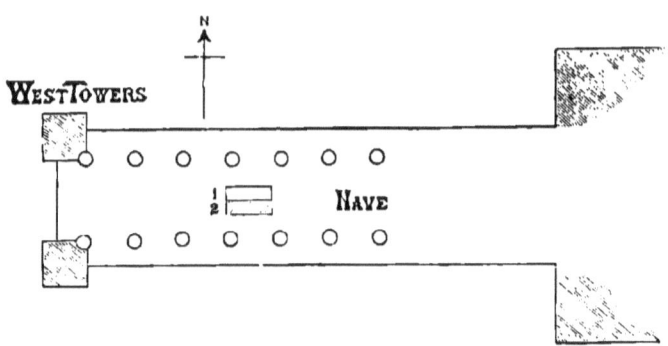

BENJAMIN LEWIS VULLIAMY, F.R.A.S., F.R.G.S.,

Watch and Clockmaker to the Queen. Son of Benjamin Vulliamy, Clockmaker to the King; he resided in Pall Mall; was made a Free Clockmaker by Redemption, December 4, 1809; admitted to the Livery, January 8, 1810; chosen on the Court of Assistants, April, 1810; served the office of Warden, 1815-20, and again in 1843-6; and that of Master five times, viz., 1821, 1823, 1825, 1827, and 1847. On the 2nd July, 1849, a presentation of plate was made to him by the Court, on which the following inscription was engraved :—

"Presented to Benjamin Lewis Vulliamy, Esq., F.R.A.S., F.R.G.S., Associate of I.C.E., &c., &c., by the Master, Wardens and Court of Assistants of the Company of Clockmakers of the City of London in token of the high sense they entertain of the eminent services rendered by him as a member of the Court during the long period of Forty years with a degree of zeal and ability which have greatly advanced the interests and character of the Corporation."

He was the first Clockmaker in this country to employ a two-seconds pendulum. In 1827-8, he effected great improvements in the make of large public Clocks. He died January 8, 1854, aged seventy-four, leaving to the Company, by will, three portraits of members of his family, and one picture, see Catalogue 1875, p. 97.

JOHN HARRISON.

This celebrated Horologer and Mathematician, who has been aptly called the Father of Chronometry, not having been enrolled as a Member of the Company, his name for that reason is not included amongst the preceding Biographical Notices of distinguished Men connected with the Trade.

The Company, however, having in September, 1879, determined to undertake the restoration of his tomb in Hampstead Churchyard (previous efforts to obtain the necessary funds by public subscription having failed), have thus identified themselves with the desire which was felt to perpetuate the memory of so great a benefactor to mankind in general, and the navigator in particular.

The following particulars, collected from various sources, with respect to Harrison's career, seem, therefore, to find an appropriate place in this volume, in which reference is made to so many of the members of a Craft with which his name must ever be associated :—He was born at Foulby, near Pontefract, Yorkshire, in the year 1693, his father, Henry Harrison, a carpenter at that place, having been married in the month of July, 1692, at the parish church of Wragby, to Elizabeth Barber, of the same parish, where John, their eldest son, was baptized, it is said, on March 31st in the following year. The father was in the habit of repairing Clocks, indeed much of the mechanism of the larger Clocks being, in those days, frequently made of wood, the carpenter was very often called upon to repair them. In the year 1700, his parents removed to Barrow, in Lincolnshire. Here he attracted the attention of a clergyman, who lent him a MS. copy of the lectures of Nicholas Saunderson, the blind Lucasian Professor of Mathematics at Cambridge, which he copied with all the diagrams. His early devotion to mechanical pursuits led him to give his attention to the improvement of Clocks, and in 1726 he had constructed two, chiefly of wood, in which he applied the escapement and compound, or, as it is called, gridiron pendulum, of his own invention. Stukeley, in his manuscript Journal, 1728, says, " I saw his famous Clock last winter at Mr. George Graham's. The sweetness of the motion, the contrivances to take off friction, to defeat the lengthening and shortening of the pendulum, through heat or cold, cannot be sufficiently admired." In the year 1726, he made his first

Timekeeper, which Dr. Hutton asserts did not err a second in a month. In 1713 an Act of Parliament, 12 Anne, cap. 15, was passed, the preamble of which recites as follows: " Whereas it is well known by all that are acquainted with the art of navigation, that nothing is so much wanted and desired at sea as the discovery of the longitude for the safety and quickness of voyage, the preservation of ships, and the lives of men; and whereas in the judgment of able mathematicians and navigators several methods have already been discovered, true in theory, though very difficult in practice, some of which, there is reason to expect, may be capable of improvement, some already discovered may be proposed to the public, and others may be invented hereafter; and whereas such a discovery would be of particular advantage to the trade of Great Britain, and very much to the honour of this kingdom." A commission was appointed under the Act, upon which a large number of officers of state, and men distinguished as mathematicians, mechanics, and navigators, were appointed, and a reward of £20,000 was offered to any one who could discover a method whereby the longitude at sea could, within certain stated limits of exactness, be ascertained. Harrison came to London in 1728 with drawings of an instrument for the purpose, hoping to get assistance from the Commission for its construction, but the Astronomer Royal referred him to the then great Watchmaker, George Graham, a member of the Company, who advised him to make his machine first, and then apply to the Commission. He returned home, and in 1735 again came to London with his first Timepiece, which was examined by several members of the Royal Society (Halley, Graham, and others), who certified its excellence to the Board of Longitude; and in 1735-36 Harrison was sent with it on a voyage to Lisbon and back to test its performance. In this voyage he is said to have corrected the dead reckoning nearly a degree and a-half. In 1737 the Commissioners presented him with £500, and encouraged him to proceed in his improvements.

In 1739, he produced a second instrument, and in 1749 a third, which erred only three or four seconds in a week. For this he obtained the annual gold medal of the Royal Society. Some time afterwards, practising improvements upon Watches, he was induced to make a fourth machine in the form of a

Pocket Watch, about six inches in diameter, which he finished in 1759. Trial of its accuracy was made during two voyages, when his son William went in charge of it; one to Jamaica, in 1761-2, and the other to Barbadoes, in 1764, in H.M.S. "Tartar," Captain Sir James Lindsay. In both voyages it corrected the longitude within the nearest limits required by the Act of Queen Anne, and entitled him to the reward of £20,000. At a meeting of the Board of Longitude, held on February 9, 1765, it was unanimously determined that the performance of Harrison's Timekeeper had been such as to entitle him to the offered reward, part (£10,000) being shortly afterwards paid to him, and in 1773 the other £10,000. In later years he made a fifth instrument which, on a ten weeks' trial at the King's Private Observatory at Richmond, was found, it is said, to have erred only four and a-half seconds. His invention of the Metallic Compensation, his Remontoir, and his addition of a secondary spring as an equivalent substitute for the maintaining power during the time of winding up, which is an essential requisite in producing permanent motion, may fairly entitle him to be considered as the parent of Chronometry. As will be seen by his works in the Company's Library, he had a musical ear, and made experiments on sound with a curious monochord of his own invention, from which he constructed a new musical scale or mechanical division of the octave, according to the proportion which the radius and diameter of a circle have respectively to the circumference. He died at his house in Red Lion Square.

Harrison, as has been already stated, was buried in Hampstead Churchyard, and the Company, at the instigation of Mr. J. G. C. Addison, a Member of the Court, determined to restore his tomb, which was of a Corinthian character, and of Portland Stone with marble panels. It was found, however, on examination, to have so far succumbed to the influences of time and weather, that this was impracticable. Its entire reconstruction was therefore determined upon, and, with the sanction and concurrence of the Vicar, the Rev. S. B. Burnaby, M.A., the work was entrusted to Messrs. W. Cubitt & Co., by whom it has been carefully performed. In form it is an exact reproduction of the original, but it has been executed in Ketton Stone, with Sicilian marble panels, the plinth being of Spinkwell Stone.

The inscription on the tomb, which has been preserved in its entirety, is as follows :—

" In memory of Mr. John Harrison, late of Red Lion Square, London. Inventor of the Timekeeper for ascertaining the Longitude at Sea. He was born at Foulby, in the county of York, and was the son of a builder at that place, who brought him up to the same profession. Before he attained the age of 21 he, without any instruction, employed himself in cleaning and repairing Clocks and Watches, and made a few of the former, chiefly of wood. At the age of 25 he employed his whole time in chronometrical improvements. He was the inventor of the gridiron pendulum and the method of preventing the effects of heat and cold upon Timekeepers by two bars of different metals fixed together ; he introduced the secondary spring to keep them going while winding up ; and was the inventor of most, or all, of the improvements in Clocks and Watches during his time. In the year 1735, his first Timekeeper was sent to Lisbon, and in 1764, his then much-improved fourth Timekeeper having been sent to Barbadoes, the Commissioners of Longitude certified that it had determined the longitude within one-third of half a degree of a great circle, having erred not more than forty seconds in time. After near sixty years' close application to the above pursuits, he departed this life on the 24th day of March, 1776, aged 83. Mrs. Elizabeth Harrison, wife of the above Mr. John Harrison, departed this life, March 5th, 1777, aged 72."

On the reverse side of the tomb is left a similar panel, on which it is intended to recut the original inscription, if it can be ascertained, recording the death of his son, Mr. William Harrison, F.R.S., who died April 24, 1815, at the ripe age of 88, at Caroline Place, Guildford Street. He was a Deputy-lieutenant of the Counties of Monmouth and Middlesex, and in his earlier years had materially assisted his father in his great undertakings, and especially in making voyages to sea in charge of his instruments whilst in process of trial. On the edge of the upper stone of the tomb are inscribed these words :—" Reconstructed at the expense of the Worshipful Company of Clockmakers of the City of London, 1879. William Parker, Master."

The tomb having been completed, was formally uncovered in the presence of the Master, Wardens, and Court of Assistants, and the Vicar of Hampstead, on the 16th January, 1880.

The following works relating to Harrison and his discoveries, some of which are written by himself, are preserved in the Company's Library, whilst their Museum also contains two of his early achievements in the shape of two long Eight-day Clocks, the works being almost entirely of wood, and one of them having his gridiron-pendulum attached :—

" The principles of Mr Harrison's Timekeeper, with plates of the same. Published by order of the Commissioners of Longitude. London : Printed by W. Richardson and S. Clark. 4to. 1776." The preface and the following

chapter, entitled "Notes taken at the Discovery of Mr. Harrison's Timekeeper," are written by the Rev. Nevil Maskelyne, F.R.S., Astronomer Royal.

"An Account of the going of Mr. John Harrison's Watch at the Royal Observatory, from May 6th, 1766, to March, 4th 1767, together with the original Observations and Calculations of the same. By the Rev. Nevil Maskelyne, Astronomer Royal. Published by order of the Commissioners of Longitude. London : Printed by W. Richardson and S. Clark. 4to. 1767." Thereto is added an "Appendix, containing observations of Equal Altitudes of the Sun, taken at Portsmouth, Jamaica, and Barbadoes, according to the time of Mr. Harrison's Watch, upon the two voyages made to the West Indies for the trial of the same." Published by order of the Commissioners of Longitude.

"A description concerning such mechanism as will afford a nice or true mensuration of time, together with some accounts of the attempts for the discovery of the Longitude by the Moon ; as also an account of the discovery of the Scale of Music. By John Harrison, Inventor of the Timekeeper for the Longitude at Sea. London: Sold by T. Jones, No. 138, Fetter Lane. 8vo. 1775."

An engraved Portrait, by Reading, of "Longitude Harrison," as he was called, appeared in the *European Magazine;* another, by P. L. Tassaert, was also published in Knight's *Portrait Gallery*, a copy of this is in the Company's Collection.

MEMBERS OF THE COMPANY WHO HAVE FILLED IMPORTANT CIVIC OFFICES.

Sir JOHN BENNETT, Knight,

The son of Mr. John Bennett, Watchmaker, of Greenwich. Born in 1814. Educated at Colfe's Grammar School, Lewisham. Upon the death of his father, he successfully carried on the business. In 1846, he commenced business in Cheapside, and in 1862 was chosen by the inhabitants of the Ward one of their representatives in the Court of Common Council. Admitted a Freeman and Liveryman of the Company, November 6, 1871; served the office of Sheriff of London and Middlesex during part of the year 1871-2, on the decease of Richard Young, Esq ; received the honour of Knighthood on the occasion of the visit of Her Majesty to St. Paul's, upon the National Thanksgiving for the recovery of His Royal Highness the Prince of Wales, February 27, 1872. He was elected a member of the London School Board in 1872. In 1877, he was three times elected Alderman of the Ward of Cheap, but the Court of Aldermen refused to ratify his election.

JOHN CARTER, F.R.A.S., Alderman,

The son of William Carter, of Tooley Street, Southwark, Watchmaker. Bound apprentice to Boys Err Burrill, of Great Sutton Street, Clerkenwell, January 13, 1817; admitted to the Freedom and Livery of the Company, October 14, 1829; chosen on the Court of Assistants in 1852; elected Alderman of Cornhill, March 10, 1851; served the office of Sheriff of London and Middlesex, 1852-3; Warden of the Company in 1852-5, and again in 1862-3; served the office of Master three times, viz., in 1856, 1859, and 1864; chosen to the exalted office of Lord Mayor in 1857. He died May 5th, 1878.

COLONEL A. ANGUS CROLL, C.E.,

Son of George Croll, of Perth. In 1849, he was appointed Engineer to the Great Central Gas Consumers' Company, which had then been started for supplying Gas at a cheap rate and with greater illuminating power. Through his scientific skill and energy many difficulties were overcome, and a new era in the manufacture and supply of Gas began, which brought about great advantages to the consumers. In 1852 he was chosen one of the Sheriffs of London and Middlesex. On the 10th of October, 1859, he was admitted to the Freedom and Livery of the Company; chosen on the Court of Assistants, October 10, 1870; served the office of Warden, 1874-6; and was elected Master in 1877. One of the great projects with which his name will ever be associated is that of the establishment of the United Kingdom Electric Telegraph Company, founded for carrying messages to every part of the United Kingdom at one uniform rate of one shilling a message. He was elected Chairman of the Company in 1860, and by his skill and determined energy he carried the project to a most successful issue in spite of all difficulties. In 1868, he was presented with a very flattering Testimonial by his Brother Directors, and on March 22, 1871, at the conclusion of the negociations for transferring the Company to Her Majesty's Postmaster General, the Shareholders also presented him with a Testimonial of the value of a Thousand Guineas.

Sir ROBERT DARLING, Knight,

Sheriff of London in 1766. Admitted on the Livery of the Company, September 16, 1766, and on the same day chosen on the Court of Assistants. On the 29th of September he was elected Master, but was excused serving the office upon payment of a fine of £10. In 1770, he gave £100 to the poor of the Company, and his friend, Mr. Nathanael Styles, gave £10.

RICHARD HARTLEY KENNEDY, M.D. F.R.A.S.,
Alderman.

Served more than 30 years in the East Indies. Was Physician-General and President of the Medical Board of Bombay, and chief of the Medical Staff of the Bombay division of the Army of the Indus during the campaign in Sind and Kaubool in 1838-9. He was the friend of Sir Jamsetjee Jejeebhoy, the first Baronet. Returning to London he entered into public life, and was admitted to the Freedom and Livery of this Company, April 26, 1851; chosen on the Court of Assistants, April 4, 1853; elected Alderman for the Ward of Cheap in 1854; served the office of Warden of the Company in 1854-6; elected Sheriff of London and Middlesex in 1855. He resigned his Aldermanic Gown, March 30, 1858. Died July 24, 1865. His portrait is in the Company's Collection.

He was the Author of a Narrative of the Campaign of the Army of the Indus, in Sind and Kaubool, in 1838-9; published in 1840; and Notes on the Epidemic Cholera, written in 1826, and re-published in 1846.

Sir GEORGE MERTTINS, Knight, Alderman,

Son of . . . Merttins, of Cornhill, Goldsmith and Jeweller. Admitted to the Freedom of the Company . . . Served the office of Warden, 1711-12; chosen Master, 1713; elected Alderman of Bridge Ward, December 9, 1712; knighted, April 11, 1713. Translated by permission to the Skinners' Company, June 16, 1713. Appointed Treasurer to Christ's Hospital in 1716. In 1721, he was elected to the office of

Sheriff, and in 1724 to that of Lord Mayor. He became President of Christ's Hospital in 1727, but did not long occupy that distinguished office, dying November 11, 1727. He was buried in the South Cloister of Christ's Church, Newgate Street.

HONORARY FREEMEN.

The desire which the governing body of this Company has ever evinced to maintain the closest possible relationship with the Trade, and to gather into its ranks men whose practical knowledge of the Art would be valuable in the protection of the rights and privileges of the Craft, and whose social position would enable them to render useful service in the defence of its interests, especially in its opposition to the deceits practised by the importation of Foreign Watches, etc., probably induced the Court to pass the following Resolution, by which a number of gentlemen, many of whose names are still familiar to us, were enrolled amongst the Fellowship as Honorary Freemen, some of whom also subsequently became active and most useful Members of the Company :—

"1781. January 8. Resolved that a Special Court be summoned to meet on Monday the 5th of February next at 9 o'clock in the morning in order to admit a number of Gentlemen of the trade and profession into the Freedom of this Company.

"Ordered that Mr. Martin who attended be acquainted with the foregoing resolution for the information of the Gentlemen of the Trade who meet at the Devil Tavern.

"1781. April 2.

Benjamin Vulliamy	John Leroux	Robert Storer
John Fladgate	James Tregent	Paul Hobler
James McCabe	George Allen	George Philip Strigil
William Frodsham	John Grant	William Carpenter
John Dwerrihouse	John Jardin	John Bittleston
William Storr	Joshua Rigby	John Melvill
Alexander Wilson	Christopher Pinchbeck	Thomas Laidlaw
Willm. Ellison Simpson	Thomas Langford	John Devis
Josiah Emery	John Wightwick	John Coleman
James Vigne	Benjamin Webb	John Rooke
Alexander Hare	John Scott	John Baker
Charles Haley	James Wilson	Samuel Bishop.
Robert Twyford	Henry Baker	

"1781. July 2.

John Wright	William Hughes	Francis Perigal
Alexander Cumming	James Smith	John Perigal "

A LIST OF GENTLEMEN ENROLLED HONORARY MEMBERS OF THE COMPANY.

HENRY CLARKE,

Son of John Clarke, Citizen and Goldsmith. Born 4th November, 1780. Admitted to the Freedom of the Goldsmiths' Company, 3rd March, 1803. Upon the decease of his Father he was taken under the paternal care of Mr. Isaac Rogers, and continued closely associated with him throughout a long active life. Under his auspices he had every opportunity of acquiring a thorough practical knowledge of many branches of Science, the run of a good Laboratory, and a well-selected Library. He became associated with him in mining operations in Cornwall and Wales, and they succeeded in introducing several improvements in smelting, etc. While thus engaged he became acquainted with Richard Trevithick, the subsequently celebrated Engineer, whom he assisted in carrying out some important scientific investigations. His business connection with the Levant Trade brought him into association with the principal men of Smyrna, Turkey, etc.

In 1810-11, he aided Mr. Rogers and Mr. George Atkins in an examination of the affairs of the Company, and helped materially in the preparation of the scheme of a permanent Accumulation Fund, the result being that on the 6th of July, 1812, the Court of Assistants passed the following Resolution:—

" The Court having taken into consideration the voluntary and gratuitous services rendered to this Company on various occasions by Mr. Henry Clarke Citizen and Goldsmith. It was thereupon

" Resolved unanimously,—That the thanks of the Court be given to Mr. Henry Clarke for the essential Services rendered by him to this Corporation, and that the Freedom and the Livery thereof be presented to him, as a mark of the sense the Company entertains of his exertions in its behalf."

He attended on the 3rd of August following, and was duly clothed and sworn.

On the 12th of October, 1812, the following Resolution was passed :—

" The Court having taken into consideration the continued services rendered by Mr. Henry Clarke to this Corporation and a motion thereon having been made and seconded pursuant to notice given it was

" Resolved,—That Mr. Henry Clarke be summoned to take his oath and his seat as an Assistant and he was duly elected an Assistant accordingly."

In 1818, he founded the Imperial Gas Company, which became one of the most successful in the metropolis. In 1820-21, in connection with several friends, he took active measures and had preliminary surveys made for promoting the Atlantic and Pacific Ship Canal for connecting the two Oceans by the Lake of Nicaragua.

He served the office of Warden of the Company in 1822-26.

His sympathy with the Portuguese in their misfortunes led him to spend much of his time on the Continent, assisting the Emperor Don Pedro, Generals Lafayette, Mina, Saldanha, and others, with his great experience and advice at that critical juncture. He subsequently visited the United States.

He died in 1865, the Father of the Company, aged 84, a Portrait of him is preserved in the Company's Collection.

ALEXANDER CUMMING, F.R.S.

An ingenious Scotch Mathematician, born at Edinburgh. Carried on business in Fleet Street. He made a Clock for George III, which registered the height of the barometer during every day throughout the year. It cost nearly £2,000 : he was allowed £200 a year to attend to it. In 1766 he published " The Elements of Clock and Watch Work." His works are in the Company's Library. They also have an engraved Portrait of him, from a painting by S. Drummond, A.R.A. Made an Honorary Freemen of the Company July 2, 1781.

Dr. THOMAS SIMPSON EVANS, F.L.S.

Master of the Royal Mathematical School, in Christ's Hospital, from 1813 to 1819. Admitted an Honorary Freeman, November 2, 1813.

" Resolved unanimously,—That the Freedom of this Company be presented to Thomas Simpson Evans, Esq., Master of the Royal Mathematical School in Christ's Hospital, London, and Fellow of the Linnæan Society, as a permanent mark of the sense, in which this Fellowship views his exertions towards the improvement of the Art of Chronometry in this kingdom, and in the general promotion of the Mathematical Sciences."

SIR JAMSETJEE JEEJEEBHOY, 1ST BARONET.

Born in Bombay July 15, 1783; married March 1, 1803, Awabaee Framjee, daughter of Framjee Pestonjee, of Bombay. His public endowments were said to be nearly £300,000. Her Majesty conferred upon him the honour of Knighthood, accompanied by the gift of her Portrait, set in Diamonds, March 2, 1842. The following is a copy of an inscription on the Foundation Stone of the Medical College which he founded in Bombay in 1842 :—

THIS EDIFICE

WAS ERECTED AS A TESTIMONIAL OF DEVOTED LOYALTY TO

THE YOUNG QUEEN OF THE BRITISH ISLES

AND OF UNMINGLED RESPECT FOR THE JUST AND PATERNAL

BRITISH GOVERNMENT IN INDIA;

ALSO IN AFFECTIONATE AND PATRIOTIC SOLICITUDE FOR THE WELFARE OF

THE POOR CLASSES OF ALL RACES AMONG HIS COUNTRYMEN THE

BRITISH SUBJECTS OF BOMBAY,

BY

SIR JAMSETJEE JEEJEEBHOY, KNIGHT,

THE FIRST NATIVE OF INDIA HONOURED WITH BRITISH KNIGHTHOOD,

WHO THUS HOPES TO PERFORM A PLEASING DUTY

TOWARDS HIS GOVERNMENT, HIS COUNTRY, AND HIS PEOPLE,

AND IN SOLEMN REMEMBRANCE OF BLESSINGS BESTOWED

TO PRESENT THIS HIS

OFFERING OF RELIGIOUS GRATITUDE TO

ALMIGHTY GOD,

THE FATHER IN HEAVEN,

OF THE CHRISTIAN, THE HINDOO, THE MAHOMEDAN AND PARSEE,

WITH HUMBLE EARNEST PRAYER

FOR HIS CONTINUED CARE AND BLESSING UPON

HIS CHILDREN, HIS FAMILY, HIS TRIBE AND HIS COUNTRY.

The Freedom of the City of London was also tendered to him on the 14th of April, 1855, when the following Resolution was passed by the Common Council :—

"Resolved unanimously,—That the Freedom of this City be presented to Sir Jamsetjee Jeejeebhoy, of Bombay in the East Indies, Knight, as a testimonial of the high estimation entertained of him by the Corporation of the City of London, and from respect for his justly renowned character as a princely benefactor of his Country and mankind, a noble example of blameless private life and public worth as a Citizen of Bombay, and of spotless commercial integrity as a most eminent British subject and Merchant in India.

"Ordered,—That the said Resolution be ornamentally written on vellum, signed by the Town Clerk, properly emblazoned, framed and glazed, and presented to Sir Jamsetjee Jeejeebhoy."

He was unanimously elected to the Honorary Freedom and Livery of this Company, July 2, 1855. He presented £250 to the poor of the Company, and a Pension has been founded, called after his name. Created a Baronet of the United Kingdom, August 6, 1857. Died April 14, 1859. A portrait of him is in the possession of the Company.

Sir CURSETJEE JAMSETJEE JEEJEEBHOY,
2nd Baronet,

Eldest son of Sir Jamsetjee. Born October 9, 1811; married first, Deenbaee, daughter of Dinshaw Corvarjee, of Bombay; second Ruttonbaee Cursetjee, November 29, 1835. He succeeded his Father as second Baronet, April 14, 1859, and, by a Special Act of the Legislative Council of India, (passed with the sanction of Queen Victoria in 1860,) he assumed the name of the First Baronet, and by this Act all future holders of the title are to relinquish their own names and to assume that of the First Baronet. He was elected an Honorary Freeman and Liveryman of the Company, July 2, 1855. He died July 11, 1877. Photographs of him are in the Company's Collection.

RUSTOMJEE JAMSETJEE JEEJEEBHOY,

The second son of Sir Jamsetjee Jeejeebhoy, Bart., was born January 23, 1824. Married Sonabaee Murcherjee, January 24, 1836. Died April 13, 1872. He was elected an Honorary Freeman and Liveryman of the Company in October, 1864.

He presented £200 to the Company for the benefit of its poor, and a Pension has been established therewith, called after his name.

SIR JAMSETJEE JEEJEEBHOY, 3RD BARONET.

Succeeded to the title on the death of his Father, July 11, 1877. He was born March 3, 1851, and married Terball, daughter of Sapoorjee Dhunjeebhoy, February 8, 1869. Elected an Honorary Freeman and Liveryman of the Company, January 7, 1879.

WILLIAM HENRY OVERALL, F.S.A.,

Librarian to the Corporation of London, was elected to the Honorary Freedom and Livery of the Company on the 2nd of July, 1877.

"Resolved,—That the Honorary Freedom and Livery of this Company be presented to Mr. W. H. Overall, the Librarian of the City of London, in recognition of his valuable services in connection with the Company's Library and Museum."

JOHN POND, F.R.S., ASTRONOMER ROYAL.

Born about 1767. Educated at Maidstone Grammar School, from which he proceeded to Trinity College, Cambridge.

In 1800, he made a journey to Lisbon and Malta, to pursue his observations on the fixed Stars. The researches then made were published in the "Philosophical Transactions of the Royal Society" in 1806, and attracted the attention of Astronomers and scientific men, by their accuracy and clearness of detail. He became a Fellow of the Royal Society, and in 1811 was chosen to succeed Dr. Maskelyne as Astronomer Royal. In 1813, the Company passed the following Resolution:—

"1813. October 11. Resolved unanimously,—That John Pond of the Royal Observatory, Greenwich, in the County of Kent, Esquire, Astronomer Royal and Fellow of the Royal Society be, and he is hereby elected a Member of this fellowship That he be requested to accept and take upon him the Freedom of this Corporation as a mark of the sense this Court entertains of his exertions for the promotion of Science."

He retired from his high office in 1835; died September 7, 1836; and was buried at Lee, Kent, in the same tomb, with Dr. Edmund Halley.

As a practical Astronomer Mr. Pond had no superior; few, if any, equals. His perception of the capabilities of instruments generally, and of the mode of using them, and his sagacity in detecting and avoiding error, placed him in the front rank of observers. The numerous folio volumes of his observations, so highly appreciated by scientific men in every part of the globe, are alone sufficient to show the extent and utility of the work performed at Greenwich during the time the establishment was under his direction. He finished his catalogue of 1,113 stars in 1833. His skill has been admitted by Astronomers of all nations.

THOMAS REID, Esq.,

Of Edinburgh, was presented with the Honorary Freedom of the Company, October 10, 1825.

"As a testimony of the estimation in which this Court holds his exertions for the advancement of the Arts placed under its Government."

He dedicated to the Company his work, published in 1826, entitled a "Treatise on Clock and Watch-making, Theoretical and Practical."

An engraved Portrait of him, presented by Messrs. Charles Frodsham and Co., in 1874, is in the Company's possession.

MEETING PLACES.

HIS Company have never been the fortunate possessors of a Hall or permanent Place of Meeting, but have been wanderers since their incorporation. They have usually met at one or other of the Livery Companies' Halls, and sometimes, especially during the last century, at Taverns. Since the removal of the London Tavern, they have held their Meetings at Guildhall. The following Extracts from their Records show the different Meeting Places, etc. :—

"1642. September 29. The day aforesaid the Company of Clockmakers delivered and gave to the Company of Paynter-Stayners as a free Guift according to the agreement of both Companies unto their first propositions One Chamber Clock for the which they were to have the use of their Hall for some Meetings as occasion should require.'

"1653. January 20. At this Court were opened and perused the writings and papers that were in the Company's Chest in Paynter-Stayners Hall for the standing of which Chest several years we did pay unto the Company of Paynter-Stayners three pounds, which the Master and Wardens and Court of Assistants of the Paynter-Stayners at a Court of theirs did order we should pay unto them.[2]

"1654. January 8. Mr. Warden Hill and Mr. Warden Pennock and Mr. Coxeter were ordered by the Company to treat with the Company of Imbroderers for the use of their Hall,[3] and agreed for one year at the rate of four pounds and if we use it at the general feast to give twenty shillings more, and if there be any mislike to give half-a-year's warning at any time to each other.[4]

"1655. July 12. It is this day ordered that the Quarter Court shall be held at the Imbroderers Hall in the afternoon the 16th of this month at 3 o'clock in the afternoon.[5]

[1,2] Company's Journal I.   [3] In Gutter Lane.   [4,5] Company's Journal I.

"1671. October 16. Ordered that for the space of the yeare next ensuing Monthly Courts shall be kept upon the first Monday in each month at the sign of the Catt in Long Lane betwixt the houres of ten and twelve and that for the three next Quarterly Courts the Master Wardens and Assistants shall be summoned to appear by Nine of the clock and other Members of the Company be summoned to appear at two in the afternoon.[1]

"1680. September 29. It was discoursed That the Company might have the use of Blacksmiths' Hall for eight pounds a year And it was thereupon appointed and desired that six of the Assistants will go and judge of the conveniences and give their report at the next Court."[2]

No further entry on the subject appears.

"1684-5. January 19. This Company having for some time past kept their Courts in Goldsmiths' Hall this Court referred and left it to the discretion and liberty of the Master and Wardens and Mr. Jeremy Gregory (being of the Goldsmiths' Company) to give them (the Goldsmiths) what satisfaction for it they (the Referees) shall think fit.[3]

"1685. September 10. Resolved that a piece of Plate of the value of £10 shall be presented and delivered to the Goldsmiths.[4] (A Silver Tankard was presented to the Goldsmiths 2nd October 1685.)"

How long the Company continued to use the Goldsmiths' Hall does not appear, the next entry on the subject of their place of Meeting occurs on the 31st August, 1698, when the Master moved that instead of the "George" in Ironmonger Lane, some other convenient place in the City might be found for the Company to keep their Courts in. Founders' Hall being proposed as a proper place, a Committee was appointed to treat with the Founders' Company for the purpose, and to agree with them for the use of their Hall for one year, on such reasonable terms as they might think fit.[5]

On the 5th September, 1698, the Master reported that an agreement had been entered into with the Founders' Company for the use of their Hall, for all the meetings of this Company for one year, for £5 10s. to the Company, and £2 to the Clerk.[6]

"1701. January 19. Ordered that the Master and Wardens with such of the Assistants as they shall from time to time call in to their assistance shall inquire into the nature and quality of Fishmongers' Hall in Thames Street (which it is said is to be sold) and also to look out some other Hall or convenient place for hire for the Company's Meeting and report their proceedings therein to the next Court.[7]

"1701. February 2. The Master reported that he with the Wardens and one or two Assistants had viewed Saddlers' Hall and found the same convenient for this Company's use, but the rent thereof they could not tell what it would be. Ordered that they do inquire the rent, &c.[8]

[1,2] Company's Journal I.   [3,4,5,6] Company's Journal II.   [7,8] Company's Journal III.

"1702. August 2. The Clock Makers' Company to have the use of the Parlour (at Founders' Hall) for their meetings, at a rental of ten pounds per annum.[1]

"1702. September 29. Ordered that the Master and Wardens for the time being with such Assistants as they shall think fit to call in, do consider of continuing at this (Founders') Hall, or do find out some other hall, or other convenient place.[2]

"1706. February 3. Committee of the Founders' Company appointed to confer with the Clock Makers' Company, concerning their continuing in the Hall, and to raise the rent, or give them warning, as they shall think fit.[3]

"1706-7. April. The Master acquainted the Court that the Company of Founders, by their Master, had given him warning to leave their Hall at Midsummer next, and had acquainted them that they expected more rent if this Company continued the use of their Hall, Thereupon the Court thought fit to put the two Questions following, viz. :—

"1st, Whether the Company shall advance any more rent for the use of the Hall. This was carried in the negative.

"2nd, Whether this Company shall not advance any more rent, and shall accept the warning. This was carried in the affirmative.

"Ordered that the Master of the Founders be acquainted that this Company do not think fit to advance any more rent for the use of their Hall.

"Ordered that the Master and Wardens and such Assistants as they shall call in be a Committee to provide a convenient place for the Company to meet in at next Quarter Court.[4]

"1707. July 7. The Master and Wardens reported the matter about finding a convenience for the Meeting of this Company and the terms they had agreed upon for the use of this (Cutlers') Hall vizt Ten Pounds p Annum and 5s. p Quarter for cleaning the Hall and that the Cutlers' Company had proposed a method by Lease between the Master and Wardens of each company for certainty of terms. Ordered that this Company will indemnifie the Master and Wardens from any damage they may sustain by their entering into the said lease in trust and for the use of the said Company.[5]

"1708. November 1. Paid for the Lease from the Cutlers' Company to this Company for the use of their Hall £2 7s. 6d."[6]

In 1710, negotiations were opened with the Merchant Taylors' Company for the use of their Court Room and Hall, and it was subsequently reported—

"That the Company might have the use of their Court Room, Hall, Kitchen and other conveniences for the business of this Company for the Sum of £20 a year and not under."

[1,2,3] Annals of the Founders' Company, William M. Williams, p. 201.
[4,5] Company's Journal III.
[6] This Lease, dated 7th July, 1707, and signed by John Finch, John Pepys, Daniel Quare and George Etherington, was purchased at an old bookseller's and presented to the Company in 1877, by Sidney Young, Esq.

In 1712, the Master, Wardens, etc., were authorized to treat with the Master and Wardens of the Stationers' Company, about the use of their Hall.

In 1713, it was proposed to remove the Courts from Cutlers' Hall to Weavers' Hall, and inquiries were directed to be made as to terms, etc.; and the Clerk of the former Company was to be applied to as to the use of the Room next the Court Room, which the Company formerly enjoyed. The Master stated at the next Meeting that the Clerk of the Cutlers' Company had directed the little Room to be cleared when this Company met.[1]

This arrangement seems to have satisfied all parties for some years, but in 1741 it was determined to remove to Leathersellers' Hall, and to give notice of leaving Cutlers' Hall at the ensuing Lady-day.[2] The cost of Meeting at Leathersellers' Hall was £10 a year.

In 1757 it was agreed to leave Leathersellers' Hall at Michaelmas, but on acquainting their Clerk with the order he offered the use of it without rent, which was referred for further consideration.[3] No rent appears to have been paid after this date.

Their Meetings ceased to be held at Leathersellers' Hall in 1764. At the close of that year the Court met at the " Paul's Head Tavern," Cateaton Street. In November, 1772, it was resolved that for the future the business of the Company should be transacted at the " Queen's Arms Tavern," St. Paul's Churchyard, but this place not being found convenient, the Court returned to the " Paul's Head Tavern."

In September, 1800, the " Paul's Head Tavern," being closed, the Company met at the " London Tavern," where they remained until 1802, when they removed to the " King's Head Tavern," Poultry, which was their permanent abode until 1851. In 1811, an attempt was made to purchase or rent premises in Garlick Hill for the Meetings of the Company, but it failed. The " King's Head Tavern," being taken down, they returned to the " London Tavern " in November, 1851. In May, 1876, this property having been disposed of, the Court of Assistants resolved that their future Quarterly Meetings should be held at the Guildhall, where they still continue.

[1,2,3] Company's Journal III.

SEARCH COURT MEETINGS.

It was the custom for the Members of the Search Courts, with the Master and Wardens, to hold their Meetings in the district where they intended to carry out the powers granted by the Charter and Bye-Laws—viz., to search, survey, and view the making or working of any wares or merchandizes, or other works belonging to the Trade, Art, or Mystery of Clockmaking. The following list of old City Taverns, where such Meetings were held, will be interesting to many :—

1660.	The "George Inn," Ivy Lane.
1663	The "Feathers Tavern," St. Paul's Churchyard.
	The "Three Sugar Loaves," in Lothbury.
1664.	The "Dolphin," in Abchurch Lane.
1666.	The "Castle Tavern," Fleet Street.
	The "Crown Tavern," Smithfield.
1667.	The "Cat," Long Lane, Smithfield.
1692.	The "Bull Head Tavern," Gracechurch Street.
1693.	The "Half Moon Tavern," Cheapside.
	The "Swan," Old Change.
	The "Swan," Exchange Alley, Cornhill.
1696.	The "Rose Tavern," Birchen Lane.
1698.	The "Angel and Crown," Threadneedle Street.
1699.	The "Swan," in Old Fish Street.
	The "Bell Tavern," St. Nicholas Lane.
1700.	The "Greyhound," in Fleet Street.
1701.	The "Crown Tavern," Fleet Street.
1702.	The "Half Moon Tavern," Cheapside.
	The "Sun Tavern," Threadneedle Street.
	The "Globe," in Hatton Garden.
1712.	The "Angel and Crown Tavern," Ludgate Hill.
1718.	"Sarah's Coffee House," Cheapside.
1722.	"Peele's Coffee House," in Fleet Street.
	The "Sun Tavern," behind St. Paul's.
1723.	The "Castle Tavern," Lombard Street.
1725.	The "King's Arms," by Temple Bar.
	The "Naggs-head Tavern," Cheapside.
1726.	The "Crown and Cushion," in Bread Street.
1727.	The "Mitre," in Fenchurch Street.
1728.	The "Sun," in Fish Street Hill.
	The "Fleece," Cornhill.
1730.	The "Feathers Tavern," Cheapside.
1732.	The "Globe Tavern," in Stocks Market.
1733.	The "Fountain Tavern," in Bartholomew Lane.
	The "George Inn," George Yard, Lombard Street.
1734.	The "Globe Tavern," Moorgate.
	"Steele's Coffee House," in Bread Street.
	The "Pope's Head Tavern."
1735.	The "Ship Tavern," in Bartholomew Lane.
	The "King's Arms Tavern," Lombard Street.

1735. The "Salutation Tavern," Budge Row.
1736. The "Runner's Tavern," Queen Street.
       The "Globe and Sceptre," Old Bailey.
1743. The "White Hart," Bishopsgate.
1760. The "White Lyon Tavern," Cornhill.
       The "Sun Tavern," Milk Street.
1771. The "Dog Tavern," Garlick Hill.
1772. The "Queen's Head," St. Paul's Churchyard.

FEASTS.

THE social meetings of this Company were originally few, and were held at different Companies' Halls, mostly at that of the Leathersellers. Prior to the Master's Feast-day, it was the custom to elect from among the Members not on the Court of Assistants, three or four to the office of Steward, the distinction entailing upon them the payment of certain fees or fines, which went towards the expenses of the Feast. This custom, however, has long since fallen into disuse.

The following entries from the Journals of the Company, give some interesting particulars as to the arrangements made for the Feasts, and the places at which they were held :—

"1639. October 7. At a Court holden the 7th day of October, 1639, were chosen Stewards for the Master's feast Oswell Durant and Thomas Dawson for the year ensuing, and willingly did accept of it, and then it was ordered that the Master Wardens and Assistants should pay for them and their wives 4 shillings and the rest of the Company to pay for themselves 2 shillings a piece and the Assistants that brought not their wives to pay but 2 shillings and sixpence.[1]

"1656. July 23. The same day Mr. Fromantle voluntarily and freely promised £5 by way of fine to be paid to the Company the next feast day to be excused for holding Steward."[2]

[1,2] Company's Journal I.

"1664. July 22. The feast appointed to be held at the Mitre Tavern Wood Street and the order of the 23rd July 1663 to be observed and that none but the Court of Assistants and their wives and such as have passed the degree of Stewards and their wives to come to the feast this year, and that for the prevention of disorder and exception the Clerk shall make a list in writing of the Assistants and Stewards according to their priority according to which they and their wives shall be called by the Clerk and placed at the table.[1]

"1672. July 3. Edward Norris having been summoned appeared and being acquainted that he was next in course to be one of the this year's Stewards, accepted of the place and was content to hold it with Mr. Richard Jarett, whereupon it was appointed that the dinner shall be kept on Thursday the 8th of August, at the George Inn Ironmonger Lane, And that the Master, Wardens, and Assistants, present Stewards, and those that have served or fined for the office of Steward and their wives, and those only shall be invited, and each couple to pay to the present Steward 4/o and each single person 2/6, upon receipt of their ticketts of Invitation.[2]

"1673. July 23. Ordered that the annual feast be held at Cooks' Hall Aldersgate Street on Thursday the 14th of August.[3]

"1674. July 6. Ordered that on the next Michaelmas Quarterly Court day and on all Michaelmas Quarter Court days for the future only the Court of Assistants and such as have served or fined for Stewards and such as shall be made free upon those respective Michaelmas Quarter Court days shall dine at the dinner for that day.[4]

1677. July 26. The Feast held at Goldsmiths Hall

"1678. July 1. Ordered that whatsoever Member of the Company or his wife or person representing her shall at the Company's feast take upon him or her the liberty to set him or herself at the Table above his true degree in the Company or above the degree of her husband or of the wife she represents, the Member who, or whose wife or wife's representative shall so do shall therefore forfeit and pay 5/o to the use of the poor.[5]

1693. August 3.
"1696. September 17. } The Feasts held at Cooks' Hall without Aldersgate.

"1701. April 7. Ordered at the Stewards' feasts of this Company the Masters' friends shall always sit next him and the Wardens' friends with and next them at the tables they are placed at, and not to be displaced upon any account, and this to be a standing order.[6]

1701.-3.-4. The Stewards Feasts were kept at Stationers' Hall.

"1705. August 29. Paid by Mr. Warden Finch for the use of Leathersellers' Hall for the Stewards' Feast this year £2 and more £1 which the Company allowed Mr. Wareham the Cook, &c.[7]

In 1707-8 and 9 The Stewards' Feasts were kept at Leathersellers' Hall.

In 1710 At Mercers' Hall Cheapside.

[1, 2, 3] Company's Journal I.
[4] At this time the Dinner was provided for out of the Stewards' fines, a fourth part of the expenses only being defrayed by the Company.
[5, 6, 7] Company's Journal III.

In 1711-1712 and 13 At Stationers' Hall.
In 1714-1715 and 1716 at Leathersellers' Hall.
In 1717 at the same Hall. The entry records that Mr. Davies (a Quaker) performed the Cookery thereof but very indifferently."[1]

For some years afterwards, the Feasts were annually held in the month of August, at Leathersellers' Hall.

In the years 1743 and 1757, the following Resolutions were passed:—

"1743. September 29. Resolved that the custom of treating the Stewards after their Feast be wholly laid aside, and instead of it that the sum of Eight pounds be continued by quarterly payments to the poor.[2]

"1757. January 17. It was agreed that the Ladies' Feast should be discontinued."[3]

In 1804, several regulations were made limiting the expenditure for the Company's Festivities, which were further modified in 1807, and again in 1812.

In 1829, it was determined to invite a portion of the Livery in rotation according to seniority to dine with the Court of Assistants, 20 being selected each year. In 1843, the whole of the Livery were ordered to be invited, which practice has since been continued, and they are now entertained twice a year; with the occasional privilege of bringing a friend.

To commemorate the completion of the second century of the incorporation of the Company, the Members dined together on Monday the 22nd of August, 1831.

On the 8th of June, 1860, a special banquet was given in honour of the Right Hon. John Carter, F.R.A.S., then Lord Mayor and Master of the Company; and on the 2nd of July, 1866, a banquet was held to celebrate the First Centenary of the Company's existence as a Livery Company.

It is customary in this Company, when the Junior Members of the Court of Assistants reach the number of eight, that they should invite the Court of Assistants and their Ladies to a banquet at their expense. This is called the "Colts Dinner." The last was given at Greenwich on June 14, 1866. The "Colts" being C. Frodsham, Mr. Alderman Carter, W. Rowlands, G. W. Adams, J. Addison, W. Lawley, and G. Moore.

---

[1] Company's Journal III.   [2,3] Company's Journal IV.

ARCHIVES.

THE Company having no Hall, it was the custom for the Master for the time being to have the charge of the Records, together with the Plate and any other valuables, these being deposited for safety in the Company's Strong Chest. It will be seen from the following Extracts that the Chest was frequently conveyed from one end of the City to the other, yet, in spite of its vicissitudes, the Archives and Documents are still perfect.

" 1658. April 5. This Court and quarter day the Assistants before named being present, It being put to the vote concerning the removing the *great Chest* wherein is the Charter and ordinances in the hands of Mr. Edward East, he desiring it may be removed; Now it is agreed with the consent of Mr. Robert Grinkin to be removed to the said Mr. Grinkin's House in Fleet street but because it would not enter into his house, It is set up to be kept in St. Dunstan's Vestry house, there to remain till further order be taken.[1]

" 1659. November 9. Memento that the Keyes of the ould Chest which is in St. Dunstan's church are in Mr. Hill's hands.[2]

" This Court day Mr. Hill delivered to Mr. Hackett all the Plate, the Charter, Mr. East's bonds one of £100 and another of £10 with ye chest and both the Wardens Bonds with severall Books of Records of the Company, all which are put into the chest and sent unto our Master's house, which our Master is to give a Bond of £200 to give a true account of, when he shall be required to it by ye Company, casualty with Fier excepted only.

" 1660. October 8. This Court day the Plate, the Chest, with the Charter and ordinances and other things were delivered to the New Master and Wardens and they did give bond to make a true account, The Wardens, bonds are put into the Chest, The Master's bond is in Renter Warden Gregory's hand and the schedule is with the bond.[3]

" 1663. October 15. Mr. John Pennock now Master of the Company received from Mr. Nicholas Coxeter the last Master of the Company all the Plate, the Charter and ordinances, and all other things lately in his possession and keeping as Master, the which were locked up in the Chest and carried to Mr. Pennock's house in Loathbury, the particulars whereof are mentioned in a Schedule annexed to the Bond now given by Mr. Pennock according to the order of the last Court.[4]

[1, 2, 3, 4] Company's Journal I.

"1672. October 7. Mr. Samuel Horne the new Master was thereupon sworn and tooke his place, and Mr. Nicholas Coxeter the late Master, delivered up to him the Company's Books, Chest, Charter, Ordinances, Plate, and other things usually kept therein, and also the Pattent for the Company's Coat of Armes, the Hatchment upon Wainscott, and the three brass Standards.¹

"1676. October 9th.

"DIRECTIONS TO UNLOCK AND LOCK THE COMPANYES CHEST.

'It hath 3 Locks and 3 Keyes, the Locks are marked or numbered from the Left hand to the Right, 1. 2. and 3. and each key hath a labell of Parchment fixed to it marked or numbered according to the Lock which it serveth.²

"'To unlock the Chest the Key 3. must be put into the Lock 3. and the Lock unlocked and the Key to remayne in it, next the Key 2. into the Lock 2. and that unlocked, and the Key to remayne in it, And last the Key 1. into the Lock 1. and that unlocked and the Key to remayne in it. Then will the Chest open.

"'To lock it, turne towards the left hand the Key 1. and take it out, next the Key 2. soe, and next the Key 3. soe, Then is the Chest fast.

"'The Master is to keepe the Key—3.

"'The Upper Warden the Key—2.

"'The Renter Warden the Key—1.'

"1688. February 4. The Chest was this day removed from the Clerk's House to the Master's house and the £500 paid by the Goldsmiths' Company locked up in the said Chest.³

"1701. June 2. Ordered that there be a book provided for the use of the Company wherein to enter all cases, orders and proceedings of this Company in relation to any advice of counsel had or to be had upon the Charter or Bye Laws of the Company or any suit of law begun or prosecuted or upon any of them, and the original Papers to be lockt up in the Chest."⁴

There is no evidence of what became of the Old Chest, but in 1766 a new one was provided made of Oak. It has the following inscription on a brass plate on the lid.⁵

"THE CHEST OF THE
WORSHIPFUL COMPANY OF
CLOCKMAKERS,
August 2, 1766.

Mr. THOMAS HUGHES, MASTER.
Mr. DANIEL FENN, }
Mr. PETER HIGGS, } WARDENS."
Mr. BOYER GLOVER, }

---

¹,² Company's Journal I. ³ Company's Journal II.
⁴ Company's Journal III. ⁵ Company's Journal IV.

It has four Locks,[1] The Keys being labelled : 1.—The Master. 2.—The Senior Warden, 3.—The Renter Warden. 4.—The Junior Warden.

October 30th, 1766. Paid for Chest £11 8. 0.

On the 13th of October, 1873, the Court determined to have this Chest properly repaired before depositing it in the Guildhall Library.

In 1803 several Members of the Court of Assistants expressed a desire that the Records of the Company should be examined, and a list made of their various official and other documents, and on the 9th of January, 1804, a Committee was appointed for the purpose. Subsequently, a lengthened report was presented in which they stated in detail the property belonging to the Company and then contained in the Chest.

Most of the documents enumerated in the report with many others have since been arranged, catalogued, and bound in volumes under the following heads :—

Charter, Bye-Laws, and Act of Common Council, for establishing and regulating the Company.

Apprentices. The Payment of Quarterage, Watch Papers, Petitions to Parliament, &c., relating to the importation and exportation of Watches, Clocks, &c., Gifts to the Company for the Poor, &c., *see* the printed Catalogue of the Library, pages 40 to 61.

Also, a volume entitled, " The Charter, Bye-Laws, Grant of Arms, Charitable Bequests, and other Official Documents illustrating the History of the Company."

On the cover is an engraved brass plate, with the Arms of the City of London and the Company, bearing the following inscription—

"Death could not cause my love to dye;
My love doth live though dead am I."

"The free guift of Richard Morgan to the Clockmakers of London. Symon Hackett, Master, 1647; Thomas Allcock, Onesiphorus Helden, wardens. Engraved by I. Droeshout, 176½.[2]

A volume containing the Copy of the Charter and Bye-Laws, with several other matters connected with the history

---

Vide Bye Law XLIX. Page 42.
A relative, doubtless, of Martin Droeshout, who engraved the Portrait of Shakespeare or the first edition of his works.

of the Company, also a list of the Masters from 1632 to 1716; Wardens from 1632 to 1712; Assistants from 1632 to 1697.

"NOTE.—This book is all that I had of Mrs. Goodwin, after her husband's disease, for my nine years' service in assisting him in the Clerkship of the Clockmakers' Company. The collection was made for his private use and no ways belongs to the Company; when I die it will be worth to my successor (whomsoever he shall be) twenty guineas, which I charge them whose hands it shall fall into not to part with it under. Witness my hand, this 20th day of February, anno dñi. 1717. FRANCIS SPEIDELL."

"1st April, 1745.—The Renter Warden was desired to give a guinea to Mr. Shuckburgh for a Book, now produced, which appeared to be of the handwriting of Mr. Goodwin, a former clerk, containing copies of the Charter, Bye Laws, and other things relating to the Company."

A Copy of the Charter incorporating the Company, with the Bye-Laws, examined by Tutet and Howse. The Act of Common Council for Regulating the Fellowship authenticated by Sir James Hodges, Knt., Town Clerk, 1765.

Copy of the Charter, Bye Laws, Act of Common Council, &c., with Index.

The Roll of Apprentices, with the date of their Apprenticeship, to whom they were bound, and when they were admitted to the Freedom, from the time of the incorporation in 1632 to 1694, alphabetically arranged. The names of the Stewards from 1639 to 1696 (some years, however, are wanting), also a List of 246 persons carrying on the trade in or near the City in 1782.

The series of Records, called the Journals of the Company, begin in 1632, and are continued to the present time:—

		FROM		TO	
Journal	1.	12th October,	1632	6th December,	1680.
,,	2.	13th January,	1680	27th October,	1699.
,,	3.	27th October,	1699	23rd October,	1729.
,,	4.	23rd October,	1729	22nd October,	1778.
,,	5.	2nd November,	1778	29th October,	1804.
,,	6.	5th November,	1804	9th October,	1815.
,,	7.	26th October,	1815	2nd June,	1828.
,,	8.	7th July,	1828	4th January,	1845.
,,	9.	13th January,	1845	5th January,	1864.
,,	10.	11th January,	1864	3rd January,	1878.

The first 5 volumes were repaired in 1813.

FREEDOM BOOKS.

	FROM		TO	
1.	5th July,	1736.	1st December,	1777.
2.	12th January,	1778. ...	4th December,	1809.

These books were signed by the Freemen upon admission. The first volume has an Alphabetical Index.

STAMP BOOKS.

3. 3rd November, 1712. ... 7th October, 1723.
4. 5th September, 1720. ... 5th September, 1757.

These have no Indexes.

5. 7th November, 1757. ... 6th March, 1786.
6. 3rd April, 1786. ... 2nd December, 1811.

These are both Indexed.

7. A Record of the admissions to the Freedom from 1775, down to the present time. Arranged alphabetically.

8. The Livery Admission Book, 7th July, 1766, to the present time, Indexed.

LIBRARY.

The difficulty of acquiring a general knowledge of the various inventions and improvements which had been made, from time to time, in the Science of Horology, was long felt by the Members of the Court of Assistants, as well as by some of the prominent Trade Members of the Company. The few works of value written in English, relating to the theory and practice of the Art of Clock and Watchmaking, made them desirous of securing several treatises of great interest and importance written in French.

It was also thought that much valuable time might be saved to the practical mechanic, and even to the amateur, if an opportunity could be given them, of seeing what advancement had been made in this very important branch of industry.

The Court of Assistants, on the 2nd of November, 1813, Resolved—

"That it is expedient that this Company should possess, and from time to time procure such Books, Pamphlets and Tracts as have been written and published respecting or appertaining to the subject of the Art placed under the government of this Corporation.[1]

"1814. January 10. Resolved unanimously That a permanent Committee be appointed and empowered to carry this object into effect. That the said Committee do report progress at every Midsummer and Christmas Quarterly Court respectively. That the said Committee do meet at the expense of its several Members and that the Junior Member of the said Committee from time to time in attendance do write the Minutes of its proceedings in a Book to be kept for that purpose.

"That the said Committee do consist of Dr. Robert Hamilton Benj[n.] Vulliamy, Henry Clarke, John Jackson Jun[r.] Fred[k.] Barraud, and Justin Vulliamy."

Valuable additions were, from time to time, made both by presentation and by purchase, and in 1830 a Catalogue of the Library was completed, printed, and issued to the Members.

The difficulty of granting access to the Library, and also to the collection of specimens of Chronometers, Clocks, Watches, and Watch Movements, possessed by the Company, the want of space for properly arranging the specimens, etc., led to the following communication being addressed to the Senior Member of the Court of Assistants, by Mr. Deputy Atkins, then Clerk of the Company :—

"Cowper's Court, Cornhill,
"*December 5th, 1871.*
"My Dear Mr. Grant,
"I am reminded by the near approach of the coming year, that in January next I shall have completed the 30th year of my service, as Clerk of our Company, and I cannot ignore the fact, that in the ordinary course of events, circumstances may occur, and that at no very lengthened period, when my connection with the Company, so far as relates to the official position I occupy, must cease. I may say that I have no present intention to resign a position I have held for so many years, and one in which it has been my privilege to make so many friends, but I feel it is not out of place to make this communication to you as the Senior and only surviving Member (with one exception) who was on the Court at the time of my appointment.

"The more immediate object, however, of my writing to you, is upon the subject of our Library and Museum, which in former years occupied so much of your attention, but which, as you are aware, has now become almost a dead letter, and I should very much like before the time arrives, when

---
[1] Company's Journal VI.

I may cease to have any active interest in the affairs of the Company, to see them placed upon a more solid and secure foundation. I have thought a great deal on this matter, and as to the best way of making them not only useful, but to place them in a position where by free access on the part of the Public, and thereby becoming better known, they might form the nucleus of a much larger and more important collection. You are doubtless aware that the Corporation of London are building a magnificent Library and Museum which is fast approaching completion, and which I believe will be second to none in the kingdom, and my proposition is, if it meet with the concurrence of the Court, to open negociations for their reception by the Corporation, upon terms hereafter to be agreed, whereby they would be at all times open to the Public, and those interested in Horological matters. I of course do not for a moment, mean that the Company should part with a single iota of their right or interest in their property, it should still be theirs and called by their name, and subject to removal, on proper notice, at the pleasure of the Court. Being a Member of the Library Committee of the Corporation, and knowing the great desire they have to avail themselves of every opportunity of extending its usefulness, I feel sure almost that such a proposition would be gladly received, and that in the event of arrangements being come to for their transfer to Guildhall, they would have the greatest possible amount of care and attention bestowed upon them.

"I enclose a few suggestions which have occurred to my mind as to the regulations under which they might be deposited, should the Court be willing to negociate for their transfer, and the Corporation agree to accept the responsibility of their care.

"As you are the only remaining Member of our Library Committee, I have ventured to address you on this subject, and should what I have shadowed forth coincide with your views, and be thought worthy of being entertained, I should feel greatly obliged if you would kindly bring the matter formally before the Court at an early opportunity.

"I am, my Dear Mr. Grant,
"Yours very truly,
"S. ELLIOTT ATKINS, Clerk."

The foregoing letter having been laid before the Court of Assistants by Mr. Grant, at their Meeting on the 8th of April, 1872, and the suggestions contained therein having been duly considered and unanimously approved, the Court passed the following order :—

"Resolved unanimously. That the Clerk be requested to communicate with the Corporation of the City of London so as to ascertain upon what conditions they would undertake the charge of the Company's Library and Museum maintaining the same in proper order and finding suitable accommodation therefor in their new Library subject to removal by either party on proper notice, and to report to this Court.

"1872. July 8. The Clerk reported that the Library Committee of the Corporation had presented a report to the Court of Common Council recommending the acceptance of the offer made by this Company to deposit its Library and Collection of Ancient Watches in the New Library and Museum of the City of London and that the report had been referred back to the Committee to prepare a deed upon terms mutually to be agreed upon.

"1873. April 7. The Deed of Trust conveying the Company's Library and Museum to the Corporation of London was read, and it was unanimously Resolved That the Corporate Seal of the Company be affixed thereto which was accordingly done in open Court."

The City's seal having been attached by the Corporation to the Deed of Trust, shortly afterwards the transfer took place, the Library being deposited in the new Committee Room of the Guildhall Library, and the Collection of Ancient Watches, Clocks, etc., in the Museum.

On the 6th of April, 1874, it was—

"Resolved unanimously That the Master and Wardens, together with such Members of the Court as may desire to accompany them, do visit the Company's Library and Museum at the Guildhall of the City of London some time during the month of March in each year, and that they do report the state and condition thereof at the Lady-day Quarter Court then next ensuing.

"It was also ordered That a new Catalogue of the Books in the Company's Library be compiled by Mr. W. H. Overall, the Librarian to the Corporation, the said Catalogue to contain the MSS. recently arranged by him and also the Watches and Watch Movements and all other articles belonging to the Company recently deposited in the Guildhall Library and Museum of the City of London." [1]

PLATE.

IN the troublous period of 1643-48, many of the Companies were compelled to part with their Plate to meet the heavy demands made upon them, first by the King, and then by the Parliament. In 1643, Parliament passed an ordinance for a weekly assessment throughout the Kingdom,

---

[1] This was completed and issued in the following year.

the City of London's share being £10,000 per week. The Common Council, on the 18th of July, 1643, passed an Act to provide a Loan of £50,000, and on the 11th of August following, another for the same amount; each Company had to provide a certain proportion according to its position. On November 30th, 1648, the Lord Mayor and Common Council received a Letter from Sir Thomas Fairfax, informing them of the approach of the Parliamentary Forces, and directing the City to raise an immediate supply of £40,000, when more Plate was sacrificed. This Company had several pieces of Plate presented by different Members, which escaped the melting pot.

Numerous entries referring to gifts of Plate, etc., by Members, some in part payment for their admission, and others to be excused serving Offices, etc., are to be found in the Company's Journals.

In 1652 the Plate was described and weighed, but a few years afterwards the whole, with the exception of a Silver Gilt Cup and Cover, the gift of Mr. William Petit, was sold, the proceeds being devoted towards the purchase of two large Silver Tankards.

Some additions have, however, been made in recent years, amongst others a valuable Cup, used on festive occasions, to which further reference is made hereafter.

"1635. October 26. Received of Mr. Almond the 26th of October being a Court and Quarter day a Silver Incase and Outcase to the value of XXs. which he gave to the use of the Company.

"1636. January 18. Mr. Henry Barraud presented a silver and gilt spoon.

"1642. July 25. Mr. Bowyer did present to this Fellowship one great chamber Clock desiring in consideration thereof hereafter to be freed from all Offices in this Fellowship with which this Company are contented, and do order that the said Mr. Bowyer shall for ever hereafter be exempted from place, office, and service except in case he be willing thereto, and except only his usual quarterage, and search money, formerly paid and hereafter to be paid to this fellowship, and binding his Apprentices thereto according to his oath.[1]

"1651. April 7. Robert Grinkin delivered up to the Renter Warden Mr. Robert Smith one Silver Dish being the gift of David Moody one Silver Wine Cup being the gift of Robert Whitwell and three Silver Spoons with gilt heads.[2]

[1, 2] Company's Journal I.

"1652. October 4. Mr. John Pennock did give unto the Company a fine House Clock of his own making, in consideration of his fine, being an Assistant.[1]

"1652. November 20. There severall peeces of plate followinge were weighed being then in the hands of Mr. Edward East, Treasurer of the Company.

"Imprimis one silver flatt Cupp being the guifte of John Whitlach, Clockmaker weighing 7 ounces 4 pennyweight.

"One ovall chast sugar dish being the guift of Jacob Hulst, Clockmaker weighing 7 ounces 7 pennyweight.

"One round chast sugar dish of silver weighing 6 ounces and a halfe being the guift of David Moody.

"One silver Wyne Bowle weighing 6 ounces 10 penny weight being the guift of Robert Whitwell, Clockmaker.

"One silver Beere Bowle weighing 9 ounces one penny weight being the guift of Abraham Beckner, Clockmaker.

"Likewise foure silver spoones weighinge 6 ounces 14 penny weight being the severall guifts of severall other Clockmakers.

"Likewise two Silver and guilt spoones, one of them the guift of William Partridge, Clockmaker, having the figure of a Bishopp on the topp.

"Likewise there is in Mr. East's hands one flat Silver Cupp weighing 4 ounces 14 pennyweight which Mr. Jeremy Gregorye gave unto the Company the 4th of April 1653.

"1653. April 4. Mr. Jeremy Gregory presented a silver dish to the Company weighing 4 ounces 14 penny weight, which was the gift for his admittance.[2]

"1654. July 3. Mr. Paul Lowell the elder did deliver to the Renter Warden one Silver Wine bowl weighing   in full of all demands due to the Company.[3]

"All which severall parcells of Plate doe weigh in all fifty foure ounces and thirteene pennyweight.[4]

"1656. June 2. This Court day Mr. Grinkin did deliver to the Master, John Nicasius, one Silver Boale being the guift of Mr. Guiliam Petitt."[5]

It bears the following inscription :—

"'Dono datum Horologicorum Societati a Guillielmo Petit, 1655.'

"1959. July 28. This Court day Mr. Nicholas Sparkes presented the Company with a piece of plate being a charge in lieu of his fine for not holding Steward.[6]

"1660. November 12. This Court day all the Plate was weighed particularly and it was found to be all right and never a piece missing.[7]

"1664. October 3. William North presented the Company with a Silver Chased drinking Cup marked W. N. and weighing 7 ozs. and 2 dwt. being his fine to be excused from serving Steward.[8]

1, 2, 3, 4, 5, 6, 7, 8 Company's Journal I.

PLATE OF THE COMPANY.

"1686. March 7. All the pieces of plate belonging to the Company which have been usually kept in the Chest and expressed in a Schedule annexed to the Bond given by each Master upon his coming into his Mastership were brought to and seen at this Court, And upon consideration all the pieces (except the Gilt Cup and Cover the Gift of Mr. Wm. Petit and the Tankard the Gift of Mr. Thomas Whaplett) are small pieces useless or unfit for the Company. It was determined and ordered That all of them except the said Cup and Cover and Tankard shall be weighed and disposed of by the Master and Wardens and that therewith they cause *Two Tankards* of the same or a fitting value to be made with the Companys Arms engraven thereon for the credit and service of the Company at such times and upon such occasions as shall be thought fit.

"1687. April 4. In pursuance of the order of the Court of the 7th of March last all the pieces and parcels of plate belonging to the Company (except the Cup and Cover the Gift of Mr. William Petit and the Tankard, the gift of Mr. Thomas Whaplett) having since been weighed and found to weigh together 85 ozs. which at 5s. 2d. the oz. amounts in Money to £21 19s. 2d. And two New Tankards having been since made which are reported to weigh together 100 ozs. 19 dwt.

	£	s.	d.
"And the same at 6s. 4d. the ounce amounts in money to ¹	31	19	5
And that the Engraving of the Companys Coat of Arms on both of them	1	0	0
And the Two Cases for them Cost	1	0	0
In all	33	19	5
Deducting the value of the old plate	21	19	2
It appears That the Company are debitor to Mr. John Harris the Upper Warden who provided the New Tankards and their Cases ²	12	0	3

"1872. July 8. Mr. G. W. Adams returned the two recently discovered Tankards which he had sent to Goldsmiths' Hall for verification of the Hall Mark which proved to be of the year 1686. The Clerk having looked through the Records of the Company at that period, found the entry containing full particulars relating to them, the weight 100 oz. 19 dwts. exactly agreeing with the original weight when manufactured.

"It was Resolved unanimously That the best thanks of this Court be presented to Mr. George William Adams for having restored the Company's Loving Cup and provided a Case for its better security in future.

"1861. January 7. W. Rowlands, Esq., Master, presented to the Company, a Silver Salver, bearing the Company's Arms, together with a Silver Alms Dish and a large Glass Jug and two Goblets engraved with the Company's Crest and the initials of the Donor.

---

¹ Company's Journal II.
² These two Silver Tankards were missed for some years, but upon examination of the old Plate Chest in 1872, they were discovered beneath a false bottom of the Chest.

"1863. April 6. The Clerk placed before the Court a handsome and elaborately finished Silver Gilt Cup and Cover emblematical of the Company and of the Trade, which had been forwarded to him by the late Master, G. W. Adams, Esq., with a request that he would beg the Court's acceptance of the same on his retiring from the Chair.

"DESCRIPTION OF THE FOREGOING CUP.

"The design of engraving is to represent the various stages of time. Around the foot is entwined a fillet, inscribed with the twelve hours of the day, the stem, an hour-glass, indicating the early method of measuring time. On the body, an artizan is depicted at work: on his bench is seen the entire work of a Turret Clock shewing the great improvements of the present age; on the reverse, the Arms of the Company. Figures of Time with his desolating scythe form the handles. On the cover, the four quarters of the day. Morning represented scattering flowers and odours from a Vase. Noon in a Chariot surrounded by the full rays of the Midday Sun. Evening shrouded in flowing drapery with the evening star and flitting bat. Night with a sleeping child reposing at her feet keeping watch in the spangled firmament. The whole surmounted by the celestial globe being the Crest of the Company.

"Resolved—That the best thanks of this Court be and are hereby presented to George William Adams, Esq., the late Master, for the very handsome and unique present, he has this day made to the Court, which they trust will be preserved for generations to come as a Memorial of its kind and liberal donor.

"It was also further resolved that a short inscription, stating under what circumstances it was presented, together with the date, be engraven on the interior of the cover."

The inscription is as follows :—

"The Gift of George William Adams, Esq., to the Worshipful Company of Clock Makers, on his retiring from the Chair, January, 1863."

CHINA BOWLS.

"1848. November 6. Mr. Williams, of Baldwin Street, St. Luke's, a Liveryman, presented a handsome large China bowl which had been in his possession 46 years, which was accepted with Thanks.

"1876. July 3. The Clerk informed the Court that a large old China Bowl belonging to the Company, which had been lost for some years, had come to light on the sale of the effects of the London Tavern Company, Limited, and had been restored to the Company by Mr. Bathe, one of the late proprietors, the description of which is as follows :—

"Chinese Porcelain Bowl painted in Colors with gilding between each Compartment.

"In one compartment an Acrobat is balancing a female who is performing with a dagger in either hand—the band consisting of six performers are playing in concert, the instruments being, the Tambour, Cymbals, Flute, Guitar, Hand Bells, and Dulcimer. The next compartment represents the Mansion of a Mandarin whose family are witnessing the performance from the Balcony and Casement.

ADAMS'S CUP.

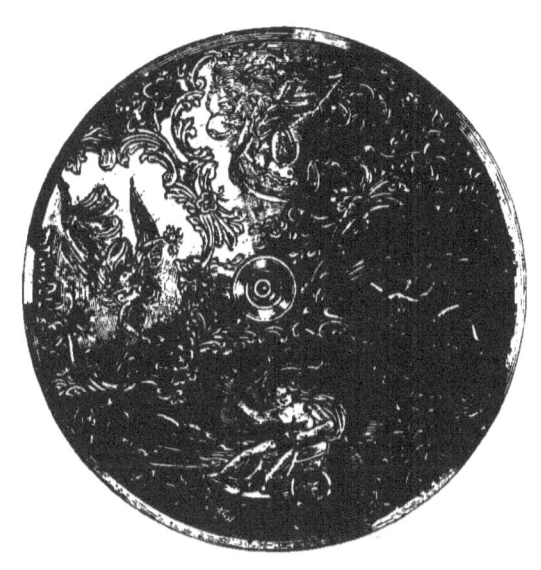

ADAMS'S CUP.

ADAMS'S CUP.

"In another compartment is a procession through the City—The Emperor of China accompanied by the Empress and their Court mounted, preceded by Attendants carrying banners.

"At the bottom of the Bowl is a grotesque figure of a Chinaman attended by his Flappers."

The Company also possess three large China Punch Bowls, of Lowestoft manufacture, with their Arms and those of the Donors, on the sides.

At the Audit in 1877, it was reported by the Clerk that the following Articles of Plate belonged to the Company, viz. :—

2 Loving Cups.
2 Covered Tankards.
1 Salver.
1 Alms Dish.
1 Snuff Box.
1 Beadle's Staff Head.

PORTRAITS, &c.

A descriptive list of the Portraits, etc., belonging to the Company has been included in the recently-published Catalogue of the Library, etc., pages 97—103.

FUNDS.

This Company cannot be classed among the wealthy Guilds of the City, and this may in some measure be accounted for from the fact that they did not obtain a grant of Livery from the Court of Aldermen till 1766. The following Extracts from their Journals afford evidence of their early care in the disposal and investment of their funds, which, as may be seen, were very limited.

"1663. July 6. Warden Taylor received of Mr. Edward East 39 shillings for one quarter of a years interest ending at Midsummer last for the £130 by him owing to the Company, and in regard he hath declared that he will not keep the money longer. It is ordered that endeavours shall be made that the same may be lent to the Company of Goldsmiths, and to be made up to £150.[1]

"Memorandum That this £150 was accordingly lent unto the Company of Goldsmiths for which they have given their Bond to this Company of the penalty of £300 dated 24 July 15 Charles 2 1663 for the payment of £153. 15[s] the 26th of January next at Goldsmiths Hall in Foster Lane.

"1665. February 9. The Goldsmiths Company paid £7—10. for a 12 months interest on the £150 borrowed of the Company.[2]

"1667. May 6. The sum lent to the Goldsmiths increased to £205 and a new bond given.[3]

"1671. October 16. £100 was lent to Sir Robert Viner at 3 per cent.[4]

"1674. May 4. It was ordered that £50 should be lent to the Goldsmiths' Company making £250 at 5 per cent.[5]

"1675. January 17. Ordered that £50 more be lent to the Goldsmiths' Company making £300 at 5 per cent.[6]

"1676. February 5. Ordered that another £100 be lent to the Goldsmiths' Company making £400 at the same rate of interest.[7]

"1678. April 27. It was resolved to accept an assignment upon the Exchequer of £100 owing by Sir Robert Viner to the Company.[8]

"1681. January 16. It was consented and ordered that the Clark shall endeavour to get two or more Talleys as he shall think fit for the five quarters payment due at Christmas last of the £6 per annum payable out of the Exchequer.[9]

[1, 2, 3, 4, 5, 6, 7, 8] Company's Journal I.   [9] Company's Journal II.

THE CLOCKMAKERS' COMPANY.

"1681. July 4. The Goldsmiths' Company agreed from this date to pay 4 per cent. for the £400 they have belonging to the Company.'
1682. September 19. Another £100 lent to them on the same terms.[2]
1685. November 2. The Goldsmiths' Company increased their interest upon the £500 lent to them to 5 per cent.[3]
1688. February 4. The Goldsmiths' Company repaid to the Company the £500 lent by them.[4]
"1689. January 20. Order, that £300 of this money be lent to King William upon the security of the late Act of Parliament at 7 per cent. Carried into effect by the Master and Wardens 22 Jan. 1689.[5]
1690. July 28. The £300 was transferred into the Chamber of London at the same rate of interest.[6]
1690. November 19. £150 added to the above £300 at the same interest in the Chamber of London."[7]
"1692. July 11. Resolved that the sum lent to the King upon the security of the Land Tax at seven per cent. be increased to £500.[8]
1693. December 4. The £500 was re-invested as follows.[9]

"Received the 19 day of December 1693, of the Master Wardens and fellowship of the Art or Mystery of Clockmaking of the City of London the sum of £500 by them lent on credit of a vote passed on the 18th of November 1693 in the Honorable House of Commons where it was resolved that whosoever should lend any money (not exceeding £400,000) on the Exchequer in general towards the maintenance of the Fleet for the year 1694 the House would take care to see them repaid with interest after the rate of £7 per cent. per ann. out of the next Aids to be granted to their Majesties for the Fleet next after moneys borrowed on the clause of credit on the *Million Act* and the Act for review of the Quarterly Poll.

"I say received,
"LEN ROBINSON Chamberlain.

"1694. January 15. It was resolved to invest the £200 given by Mr. Edward East and Mr. Henry Jones on the security of the first Act of Parliament passed to raise money for the King."[10]

"Received the 31st day of January 1693, of the Master Wardens and Fellowship of the Art or Mystery of Clockmaking London the sum of Two hundred Pounds by them lent on credit of an Act of Parliament entitled an Act for granting to their Majesties an Aid of 4 shillings in the pound for one year for carrying on a vigorous War against France. To be repaid with interest for the same after the rate of £7 per cent. per Annum.

"I say received,
. "LEN ROBINSON Chamberlain.

"1694. October 23. Notice being given to the Company that the £200 which was lent the King at Guildhall on the 31st of January would be repaid, it was resolved to continue it on loan to the King upon the credit of the Poll Tax at the same rate."[11]

1, 2, 3, 4, 5, 6, 7, 8, 9, 10, 11 Company's Journal II.

"£500 and £200 invested at the Chamber of London for the King.

"1697. June 9. This Court was summoned concerning the Company's Money lent to the King at Guildhall, And upon the Master and Wardens giving an account to this Court how far the £500 that was lent upon the 10th of March 1695 upon the 4 shillings in the pound Land Tax was behind in the deficiency upon that fund and also upon proposing, that £500 may be subscribed to the additional stock of the Governor and Company of the Bank of England as a readier or more likely means to come into the money sooner, and also upon, discoursing what way to raise £125 in Bank bills or notes to add to that subscription pursuant to the intent of the Act of Parliament, And upon discourse and debate of the whole matter, It was voted and ordered That the sum of £500 should be subscribed to the additional Stock of the Governor and Company of the Bank of England. And upon debate which way to raise part of the £125 in Bank bills or notes There were three following ways proposed

"1. By calling in some persons on the Court of Assistants and by their paying their fines.

"2. By borrowing so much money as should be wanting.

"3. By each Member of the Court of Assistants lending £5 a piece for the present.

"And it was voted and ordered that there should be a choice of 6 new assistants.

"It was also ordered that the Master and Wardens are desired to take care of subscribing the money and procuring the Bank Bills, and the money now in the Company's Chest is ordered to be applied to that use, &c.[1]

"1697. July 5. At this Court 6 New Assistants were chosen.

William How.	Samuel Marchant.
Robert Webster.	John Finch.
Benjamin Graves.	John Pepys.

"1697. July 9. The six Gentlemen above named attended and accepted office with the exception of William How who was excused, James Atkinson being chosen in his room, and sworn.

"1701. January 19. Ordered that with the Money (now in the Company's Chest) be bought: £200 stock in the Bank of England.[2]

"1702. May 4. The Master acquainted the Court that notice was given from the Chamber of London that £200 the Company's Money lent some time past at Guildhall on the Act for Births, Burialls and Marriages &c. was become payable at the Exchequer the 29th of April last. Ordered that the same be received and invested in Capital stock of the Bank of England.[3]

"1704. November 6. A motion made that £200 of the Company's Money in the Chest and Renter Warden's hands might be lent at Interest at £5 per cent. upon small remote Tallys on the Two shillings Aid and some debentures to a friend of the Master's who made the Motion, Ordered that £300 of the Company's Money be put into the Bank on their sealed Bills at 2$^{d.}$ per cent. per diem, or such Bills bought till further order concerning the same.[4]

"1720. July 19. It was resolved to invest £200 in South Sea Stock.[5]

---

[1] Company's Journal II.   [2, 3, 4, 5] Company's Journal III.

"1730. January 18. £400 was invested in the South Sea Stock.[1]

"1781. November 5. An order was passed to invest the funds of the Company in Bank of England Stock."[2]

In 1811 the then Renter Warden, Mr. Isaac Rogers, in conjunction with his friends Mr. Henry Clarke and Mr. George Atkins, prepared with much skill and labour, a well-matured plan of a *Permanent Accumulation Fund*, whereby a sum of money was to be invested in Government Stocks, and a fixed proportion of all moneys received by the Company added thereto. This was adopted by the Court of Assistants, and has been continued down to the present time. Payment of Quarterage was thereby abolished, and in lieu thereof each person upon his admission to the Freedom, was required to pay an equivalent to the credit of this Fund. Upon the binding of every Apprentice, and the admission of each new Member on the Court of Assistants, portions of the fees payable were also to be devoted to the same purpose. In order to form a nucleus for the Fund, a number of new Liverymen were made, and the proceeds and fines were invested, half the dividends thereon being from time to time added to the corpus. The result has been materially to improve the financial position of the Company, and to enable them from time to time to vary the number of Pensioners, and increase the amounts given to them. In 1860 a scale was agreed upon regulating in future the sums to be added to the Accumulating Fund from fines, etc., received for admission to the Court, Livery, Freedom, Apprentices, etc. On the 8th of October, it was Resolved unanimously—

"That in future the uniform sum of £150 being part of the interest arising from the 'Accumulating Fund' of this Company be annually added to such fund—such amount being £30 per ann. in excess of the average investment from that source during the last 10 years.

"That the whole of the present Pensions of £8 ℔ ann. (twelve in number) be augmented to £10 per ann.

"That 2 new Pensions of £10 per ann. be created and paid out of the ordinary funds of the Company to be open at the discretion of the Master, Wardens and Court of Assistants either to Freemen, Widows or unmarried daughters of Freemen subject to such rules and regulations as the Master Wardens and Court of Assistants for the time being may deem expedient.

"That in future the sums to be invested and added to the 'Accumulating Fund' from Fines &c. received for admission to the Court, Livery, Freedom,

---

[1] Company's Journal IV.   [2] Company's Journal V.

Apprentices &c. be continued as heretofore such amounts to be invested together with the aforesaid sum of £150 arising from the interest of the 'Accumulating Fund' in new 3 per ct. Annuities.

"That all the foregoing resolutions take effect as from the next January Quarter Day Court.

"And it was also Resolved That such Freemen, Widows and unmarried daughters of Freemen who may be Candidates for the foregoing two new pensions of £10 per annum be respectively not under the age of Fifty years except such as by reason of mental or bodily infirmity are prevented obtaining their own livelihood."

CHARITIES.

One of the first duties of the Livery Companies has ever been the care of their poor, decayed Members and their Widows; this Company has not been behind in this respect. The first gift recorded in their Archives is that of Sampson Shelton in 1650. He was one of the first Wardens, being named in the Charter, and was chosen Master in 1634.

"1649-50. January 14. The same day Mr. Richard Broughton paid the Legacy of Mr. Sampson Shelton which he bequeathed to this Company amounting to the sum of £50 and the Master and Wardens of the said Company gave their acquittance under their hands and seals.[1]

"1650. March 25. This Court day it was agreed by the Court of Assistants that the parish of Annes' Aldersgate should have Mr. Shelton's Legacy at the rate of £7 per centum and the Churchwardens bonds to be taken for six months for the said sum of £50.[2]

"1650. November 8. This Court day it was ordered that the half years interest of Mr. Shelton's Legacy should be distributed as followeth: To the widdow of Richard Child 10ˢ To the widdow of Daniell Howell 10ˢ To the widdow of Jasper Lowart 10ˢ and to the widdow of David Elson 5ˢ which was paid accordingly by the Renterwarden."[3]

In 1680, John Freeman left to the poor of the Company £10.

"1680. April 16. Warden Bell received from Mr. John Freeman's Executors a Legacy of £10 which the deceased had left to the poor of the Company."[4]

1693. Edward East and Henry Jones each gave £100 to the Master, Wardens and Fellowship of the Company in trust, to pay to five Freemen, or their Widows, twenty shillings annually by two half-yearly payments. East was one of the first Assistants appointed by the Charter.—[*See* Biographical Notices, pages 164 and 168.]

1, 2, 3. Company's Journal I.

"1692. October 20. Mr. Henry Jones the present Master this day acquainted the Court That Mr. Edward East formerly Master was pleased to give £100 now in his lifetime to this Company for the benefit of the poor. And the said Mr. Jones after the charitable example of his said Master having promised to give one hundred pounds more for the benefit of the poor likewise in such manner as shall be hereafter appointed and declared by the said Mr. East and Mr. Jones. Whereupon and in consideration that security could not be yet had nor the Money disposed at present as is desired, Therefore it was agreed voted and consented by this whole Court (not one dissenting) that for the reasons aforesaid the said Mr. Jones shall have free liberty for one year to enter or caused to be entered a Memorial in the Charter Book or other Book or Books of the Company of Mr. East and himself as done in the year when he was Master. [1]

"1693. June 20. Mr. Edward East gave the £100. Ordered that it be put into the Company's chest and that the Master and Wardens do go to Mr. East and give him hearty thanks for this his charity.[2]

"1693. July 18. Mr. Henry Jones did give the £100 promised to the Company and it was resolved to place the same in the Chest and to thank Mr. Jones."

1701. Charles Gretton gave by deed of Gift dated the 1st of September, 1701, to the Master, Wardens and Fellowship upon trust, the sum of £50, to pay yearly the sum of fifty shillings to apprentice the sons of deceased Freemen of the Company to the trade of Watch and Clock making.

"1701. April 7. At this Court the Master (Charles Gretton) declared his intention and will of giving £50 to this Company upon condition that they will allow 50^s p ann. for such purposes as he shall appoint in a deed for that purpose which this Court thankfully accepted to do.[3]

"1701. July 7. At this Court the draft of a Deed of Settlement for distribution of 50^s p ann. for £50 the gift of Mr. Charles Gretton the present Master was read and approved and ordered to be engrossed against such time as the Master shall appoint for sealing thereof and paying in the £50 which he now again said should be before Michaelmas day next.[4]

"1701. September 1. Mr. Charles Gretton paid the £50 and the Deeds were signed.[5]

"1719. October 5. Ordered that whenever five pounds or more is in the Company's hands notice be thereof given in the next Quarter Court bills and in every succeeding Quarter Court bills till the money be disposed of according to the intent of the donor."[6]

1701. Mrs. Russell's Gift of Ten Pounds to the Poor of the Company.

[1, 2] Company's Journal II.   [3, 4, 5, 6] Company's Journal III.

"1701. January 19. At this Court Mr. Cornelius Russell Son of Captain Nicasius Russell [1] deceased a late Member of the Court of Assistants came from the widow Russell his mother and brought as her gift to the poor of the Company £10, which was left to the distribution of the Court of Assistants, amongst such of the poor of the Company as they should see fit, which Mr. Warden Tompion received, and is to be distributed at another time."

1736. Richard Hutchinson, a Freeman of the Company, left the interest of a sum of money to the Poor.

"1736. July 5. At this Court Mr. Richard Hutchinson made an offer of giving the Company £100 to be allowed an annuity during his and his Wife's lives, which the Court took into consideration, and after some debates the Question was put to allow them Six pounds per annum and after their deaths what appeared to be in the Company's hands the interest of it to be given to the poor at the discretion of the Master and Wardens and Assistants for the time being and the Master and Wardens were then empowered to meet and fix the Company's seal to a Bond."

The Bond was sealed on the 15th, and the Renter Warden received the Money.

1747. George Graham, by his Will, dated 23rd June, 1747, left to his Wife one-half of his personal Estate, etc., and to the Poor of the Company Twenty pounds. He died in 1751.—[*See* Biographical Notice, page 166.]

"1752. January 18. Mr. George Graham, an Assistant, late deceased, having left the sum of twenty pounds to be given to the poor of the Company, the same was paid by his Executor Mr. Barkley." [2]

1769. Benjamin Gibbons, a Member of the Company, left £110 to the Poor.

"1769. February 6. Mr. Cundee the executor of Mr. B. Gibbons deceased, attended and produced the probate of the will of the said testator, wherein was the following bequest.

"To the poor of the Clockmakers' Company, not on full pension, the sum of One Hundred and ten pounds Bank Stock.

"And the said Executor will call on Mr. Jas. Brown the Renter Warden and transfer it accordingly." [3]

1770. Sir Robert Darling, Knight, a Member of the Court of Assistants, gave £100, and also induced his friend

---

[1] He was apprenticed to William Rogers on the 3rd of July, 1653, and admitted to the Freedom 6th of July, 1663; was chosen on the Court of Assistants, and served the office of Warden from 1688 to 1690; elected Master in 1692.
[2,3] Company's Journal IV.

Mr. Nathaniel Styles to give £10.—[See Biographical Notice, page 183.]

"1770. September 3. On the 6 November 1769, Sir Robert Darling Knt., of his own kindness and generosity offered to pay into the hands of Mr. Jas. Brown of Lombard Street, Banker, the sum of One Hundred Pounds if Mr. Nath¹· Style of Wood Street would pay into the same hands the sum of Ten Pounds, which the said Mr. Nath¹· Style cheerfully and generously accepted to do. And the said One Hundred Pounds from Sir Robert Darling and the Ten Pounds from Mr. Nath¹· Style making together One Hundred and Ten Pounds were paid into the hands of Mr. Jas. Brown and laid out in the purchase of Seventy Three Pounds Bank Stock, in Trust to the Worshipful Company of Clockmakers, the Interest thereof for the use of the Poor of the said Company for ever, to be paid quarterly at every Quarter Court, agreeable to the order and design of the said benevolent Sir Robert Darling Knt. and Mr. Nath¹· Style." [1]

1770. September 3. Mr. Jasper Taylor, Clerk of the Company, left £10 for the Poor.

"Ordered that the Renter Warden do wait on the Executors of Mr. Jasper Taylor the late Clerk, deceased, to receive the legacy of Ten pounds left by his will bearing date 3 March 1770, unto the poor Pensioners of the Clockmakers' Company, and that at the same time, he pay his Salary &c. which was due the 25th March last to the Executors.

"1770. September 29. Mr. Jasper Taylor the late Clerk by his last will and testament bearing date 3 March 1770, left the sum of Ten pounds unto the poor of the Clockmakers' Company to be paid to the Renter Warden at Christmas next after his decease, which Ten pounds were paid on the 25th of this instant September by Thos. Taylor his Executor to Mr. Dan¹· Aveline, the Renter Warden." [2]

1773. Devereux Bowly, a Freeman and Liveryman, chosen on the Court of Assistants, October 16, 1754, served the Office of Warden 1756-1758, elected Master of the Company in 1759, left a legacy of £500 for the benefit of the Poor Freemen and their Widows.

"1773. April 5. The Clerk reported from the Commons, that Mr. Devereux Bowly deceased had by his will bearing date 17 July 1772, left to the Master, Wardens and Court of Assistants of the Clockmakers' Company for the time being the sum of Five Hundred Pounds 4 per Cent. Bank Annuities, the Interest and Dividends thereof for the benefit of so many poor Freemen and the Widows, as they shall deem worthy, and to be distributed twice a year." [3]

1773. September 6. The Master reported that the Upper and Renter Wardens had received the sum of Five Hundred Pounds, Four per Cent. Bank Annuities, from the Executors of the late Devereux Bowly.

1, 2, 3 Company's Journal IV.

1795. Benjamin Sidey, Watchmaker, of Moorfields, a Freeman and Liveryman, left by his Will Three Hundred Pounds for the relief of the poor Members of the Company. He was chosen one of the Court of Assistants, October 16, 1754; served the office of Warden in 1758-1760, elected Master in 1761. Again served the office of Upper Warden in 1788. Elected a second time Master of the Company in 1789. He was a most active Member in everything affecting the interest of the Trade.

"1795. September 7. The Renter Warden informed the Court that he had received of the Executors of the late Mr. Benjamin Sidey deceased the sum of Three Hundred Pounds which he had left by his last will to the Company of Clockmakers, to be invested in the public funds, in their names, the interest thereof to be applied to the relief of their poor Members, in their accustomed manner." [1]

The Renter Warden also informed the Court that he had, in compliance with Mr. Sidey's Will, purchased £400 in the Three per Cent. Reduced Annuities, at 70¾ per Cent., which, with the Commission and some other necessary expenses, amounted to £288 1s. 6d.

1819. Robert Atchison apprenticed to Robert Hardin, Watchmaker, July 2, 1753, and admitted to the Freedom, September 9, 1760, left a legacy of £10 to the Company.

"1819. June 7. The Renter Warden reported that he had received from the Executors of the late . . . . Atchison deceased, a Member of the Fellowship, the sum of Ten pounds, the same was directed to be invested in the Funds and the interest applied to the poor of the Company." [2]

1828. Samuel Fenn, the son of Daniel Fenn, the celebrated Tool Manufacturer, of Newgate Street, left a Legacy of £200 Bank Stock for the poor Members of the Company. He was admitted to the Freedom and Livery of the Company by patrimony, March 2, 1767; chosen on the Court of Assistants in 1789; served the office of Warden 1790-1792, and was elected Master in 1793.

"1821. October 8. The Clerk laid before the Court a letter he had received from the Executors of the late Mr. Fenn, of which the following is a copy:—[3]

"'Mr. Joseph Fenn respectfully informs the Master and Court of the Worshipful Company of Clockmakers that his late uncle Mr. Samuel Fenn has bequeathed Two Hundred Pounds Bank Stock to the Company to be transferred to them at the decease of Mrs. Fenn his late uncle's widow.

"'Newgate Street, Sept. 29th, 1821.'

---

[1] Company's Journal V. [2] Company's Journal VII.

"Whereupon the Clerk was directed to acknowledge the receipt of Mr. Joseph Fenn's letter and to thank him for the communication.

"1828. May 5. The Clerk reported that he had received from the Executors of the late Mr. Samuel Fenn a Stock Receipt for £180 Bank Stock transferred by them to this Company in trust for its poor Members, being the amount of a Bequest of £200 Bank Stock, after deducting £10 per Cent. Legacy duty on the sterling value thereof. Also that he had received from the same parties the sum of £4 3s. 7d. for 119 days Interest from 12th December 1827 to 9th April 1828 on the above named Stock after deducting 14/3 being the charge for Stamps and Commission on transferring the same."[1]

1850. William James Frodsham, F.R.S., Watchmaker, of Exchange Alley, Cornhill, an active Member of the Company for many years, left by his Will a Legacy of £1000 for poor, decayed Members of the Company, and their Widows. Two Pensions of £15 10s. each, designated the Parkinson and Frodsham Charity, are bestowed annually upon decayed Members, or their Widows. [*See* Biographical Notice, page 166.]

"Extract from the Will.

"'I bequeath to the Worshipful Company of Clockmakers in the City of London the sum of One Thousand Pounds to be invested in the Three Pounds per Cent. Consolidated Bank Annuities to the intent that the dividends and annual income thereof may be from time to time for ever applied in aiding and assisting decayed Workmen, Freemen of the said Company or their Widows in such manner as the Master and Wardens for the time being of the said Company shall from time to time think fit, and I declare that the said Master and Wardens shall be the sole judges as to the intent and meaning of the expression 'decayed Workmen.' And I further declare that the receipt of the said Master and Wardens for the time being or other the Officer or Officers of the said Company competent in that behalf shall be a conclusive discharge to my Executors for the said sum of One Thousand Pounds and fully exonerate them from seeing to the investment or due application thereof. And out of respect to the memory of my late Partner William Parkinson, I direct that the said bequest shall be for ever known and distinguished by the name or description of Parkinson and Frodsham's Charity. And I further direct that the Legacy to the said Clockmakers' Company shall be paid free of Legacy Duty out of such part of my personal estate as may by Law be applicable to that purpose.'"[2]

1855. Sir Jamsetjee Jeejeebhoy, Baronet, of Bombay [*see* Honorary Members, page 187], on behalf of himself and his son Cursetjee Jamsetjee, presented through his friend, Richard Hartley Kennedy, Esq., Alderman, a Member of the

---

[1] Company's Journal VII.   [2] Company's Journal IX.

Court of Assistants, £200, which the Court applied to the formation of a Pension of £10 per annum, entitled, The Sir Jamsetjee Jeejeebhoy Pension. Sir Jamsetjee Jeejeebhoy, the second Baronet, visited this country in 1860, and prior to his return to India, placed in the hands of the Lord Mayor (Alderman Carter) a further sum of £50, which was invested to increase the Pension. It has since been further augmented and now amounts to £13 2s. 6d., which is given to a poor Freeman, or the widow of a Freeman.

1861. Charles Rawlings, Watchmaker and Silversmith, of Brook Street, Holborn, admitted to the Freedom in September, 1818, and to the Livery, July 3, 1826, gave £100, the interest thereof to be given annually to the poor of the Company; and left by his Will a further sum of £100, to be appropriated in augmenting the Casual Relief Fund.

"1861. April 8. The Clerk reported that Charles Rawlings Esq. of Cheyne Walk, Chelsea, one of the Gentlemen of the Livery has presented to the Company the sum of One hundred Pounds to be invested in the new Indian 5 p ct. Loan, the dividends arising therefrom to be annually given in one sum of Five Pounds to such deserving object connected with the Company as the Court should deem worthy to receive it, whereupon it was Resolved unanimously, That the best thanks of this Court be given to Charles Rawlings Esq. for the munificent donation of £100—this day communicated to the Court by the Clerk of the Company, and that the same be gratefully accepted and the interest arising therefrom be placed at the credit of the Casual Relief Fund and dispensed in accordance with the expressed wish of the benevolent donor. [1]

"1864. July 4. The Renter Warden informed the Court that he had received the Legacy of One Hundred Pounds bequeathed by the late Charles Rawlings Esq. whereupon it was Resolved,—That the same be invested in the India 5 p ct. Stock in addition to the Accumulating Fund and that the interest arising therefrom be carried annually to the Casual Relief Fund." [2]

1864. William Rowlands, Gold Watch-case maker, of Smith Street, Clerkenwell, presented £1000, the interest to be devoted for the benefit of the inmates of the Clock and Watchmakers' Asylum, Colney Hatch, and the poor of the Company. He was admitted to the Freedom of the Company, by servitude, October 9, 1820; to the Livery, November 4, 1820; chosen on the Court of Assistants, July 3, 1854; served the office of Warden, 1856-1859, and was elected Master in 1860.

[1, 2] Company's Journal IX.

"1864. July 4. On the conclusion of the business of the day William Rowlands Esq. a Member of the Court of Assistants, placed in the hands of the Master a Bond of the value of One Thousand Pounds of the Imperial Ottoman Loan of 1862 bearing interest at six p ct. p ann. together with Thirty Pounds being half a year's interest due 30th June last. The said Bond to be held upon trust by the Master, Wardens and Fellowship for the joint benefit of the Clock and Watch Makers' Asylum and the Company.

"Resolved unanimously That this Court gratefully accepts the Trust imposed upon it by William Rowlands Esq. and authorizes the present custody of the Bond of £1000 so munificently placed in its hands—to be committed to the Master and Wardens.[1]

"1864. October 10. The following communication accompanied the Turkish Bond for £1000 presented at the last Quarter Court by William Rowlands Esq.

"The Gift of William Rowlands, of Smith Street Clerkenwell, Gold Watch Case Maker, in trust to the Master, Wardens, and Fellowship of the Worshipful Company of Clockmakers of the City of London the sum of *One Thousand Pounds* in a six p ct. Bond for that amount of the Imperial Ottoman Loan of 1862 with full power and control to receive and apply as follows, that is to say, they shall on the 27th day of August of each and every year pay to each Male and Female Pensioner in the Clockmakers' Asylum Colney Hatch the sum of *Twenty Shillings*, but if any Pensioner be a Freeman of the Company of Clockmakers or a Widow of a Freeman of the said Company the sum to be given shall be *Thirty Shillings*, but if a Liveryman, or the Widow of a Liveryman, then the sum to be given is to be increased to *Forty Shillings*.

"The Clerk of the Company is to receive annually the sum of *Five Pounds* for keeping the accounts, the Beadle is to receive *Forty-two Shillings*, for paying and taking receipts for the amounts of the payments as above specified, out of which sum of Forty-two Shillings he is to defray any expenses he may incur.

"The Secretary of the Clock and Watchmakers' Asylum Colney Hatch who shall render to the Clerk of the Clockmakers' Company annually at the end of June a list of Pensioners in said Asylum, shall receive for his trouble the sum of *Twenty Shillings*.

"The residue after payment of the above is to go to an Accumulating Fund from which the Court of the Clockmakers' Company is to have the power of appropriating the sum of *Ten Pounds annually* to be distributed at their full discretion among the Poor Applicants of the Company, and if at any time the Clockmakers' Company should become possessed of any Alms Houses the Pensioners therein are to receive the same amounts as if they had been Pensioners in the Clockmakers' Asylum.

"(Signed) W. Rowlands,

"23rd January 1864.

"Witnessed by Jno. Cragg }
and Chris^{r.} Rowlands." }

[1] Company's Journal X.

THE CLOCKMAKERS' COMPANY. 225

" Referring to the above it is to be understood, that if at any time the Thousand Pound Bond be paid off in full, the Trustees shall in such case have full control and power to reinvest the amount in such manner as they may deem best for the purpose of carrying out the objects above specified.

"1864. 10th October. The Master reported that he had, in his official capacity, in conjunction with several members of the Court of Assistants, attended on the 27th of August last, the day appointed by W. Rowlands, Esq., to distribute for the first time the gift of that gentleman to the inmates of the Clock and Watchmakers' Asylum, Colney Hatch, on which occasion a handsome entertainment was given by the aforesaid benevolent donor to the friends of the Institution, including the inmates, in the grounds of the Asylum."

The Court of Assistants have since annually voted the sum of Five Pounds for entertaining the Pensioners in the Asylum on Founder's day, the 27th of August.

1864. The Hon. Rustomjee Jamsetjee Jeejeebhoy, Member of the Legislative Council of Bombay *(see* Honorary Members, page 188), presented £200 to the Funds of the Company. The Court of Assistants passed a resolution establishing a Pension, amounting to £10 per annum, to be called after the generous Donor.

"1864. October 10.
"71, Old Broad Street,
"31st August, 1864.

" Dear Sir,—My friend the Honorable Rustomjee Jamsetjee Jeejeebhoy Member of the Legislative Council of Bombay has requested me to offer a contribution of £200 to the funds of the Clockmakers' Company of which his father the late Sir Jamsetjee Jeejeebhoy was for some years a member.

" I have the pleasure to hand a Cheque for the amount in question the receipt of which I shall be obliged by your acknowledging.'
" I am Dear Sir,
" Yours faithfully,
"(Signed)   R. W. CRAWFORD.

" Mr. S. E. Atkins,
"Clerk to the Clockmakers Company."

"It was Resolved unanimously That the Honorary Freedom and Livery of this Worshipful Company be, and is hereby presented to the Honble. Rustomjee Jamsetjee Jeejeebhoy of Bombay as a tribute of respect to the private virtues and public character of a highly distinguished British subject and native merchant of India.

"That the sum of £200 so generously presented by the Honble. Rustomjee Jamsetjee Jeejeebhoy to this Company, through the medium of R. W. Crawford Esq. M.P. for the City of London, be invested, and the interest arising therefrom be applied to the formation of a pension to be entitled "The Rustomjee Jamsetjee Jeejeebhoy Pension" for the benefit of needy Freemen of the Company or their Widows.

GIFTS TO THE COMPANY.

1779. Conyers Dunlop, a Freeman and Liveryman of the Company, was chosen on the Court of Assistants September 29, 1750; served the office of Warden 1755-1757; chosen Master in 1758. He left by Will £50 to the Company to purchase a piece of Plate; but it appears from the Records that his estate was thrown into Chancery by his relatives, and the Company did not receive the Legacy.

> 1779. March 1. "The Clerk reported that Mr. Stubbs of Suffolk Street, Charing Cross, Attorney, had acquainted him in writing that Mr. Conyers Dunlop is dead, and by his Will gave some freehold Estates in London and Westminster to the Master and Wardens of the Clockmakers' Company upon Trust, to receive and divide the moneys accruing by such sale among several persons in his Will mentioned. And he gave the Company Fifty Pounds to purchase a piece of Plate. Mr. Stubbs is concerned for the representatives of Mr. Dunlop and will send Mr. Hughes a copy of the Will."

1845. John Berryhill Cross, Watchmaker, of Jewin Street, Cripplegate, admitted a Freeman by redemption April 4, 1831, and chosen on the Livery October 13, 1834, presented Ten Guineas to the Company.

> "1845. November 3. John Berryhill Cross, Esq., a Liveryman of the Company, presented a Donation of Ten Guineas to be applied to such purpose as the Court might see fit. Resolved that the same be invested."

1866. William Henry Warre, of Skinner Street, Snow Hill, Silversmith, was admitted to the Freedom and Livery of the Company by redemption April 6, 1857; chosen on the Court of Assistants January 12, 1863. He left a Legacy of £100 for the use of the Company.

> "1866. January 9. Mr. William Lawley, as Executor of the late Wm. Henry Warre, Esq., Member of the Court of Assistants, handed to the Court a Cheque for One Hundred Pounds being the amount of a legacy left by that Gentleman to the Corporation."[1]

---

[1] Company's Journal X.

A list of the Company's Pensioners, being Freemen, Widows, &c., with the Amount of their respective Pensions, 1880.

PARKINSON AND FRODSHAM CHARITY.

WHEN ELECTED.	AGE.		AMOUNT. £ s. d.
1865-70	76	William John Lloyd, Clock & Watch Makers' Asylum, Colney Hatch	15 10 0
1866-77	84	Martha Hoskins, 183, Holloway-road, N.	15 10 0

SIR JAMSETJEE JEEJEEBHOY CHARITY.

1874-77	83	Ann Elizabeth Pretty, Ann's-place, Creek-road, Deptford	13 2 6

HONOURABLE RUSTOMJEE JAMSETJEE JEEJEEBHOY CHARITY.

1873	79	James Martin, 40, Gerard-street, Colebrook-row, Islington ...	10 0 0

ORDINARY PENSIONS.

1871-73	84	Richard Musgrove, Providence House, College-st., Highbury, N.	20 0 0
1871	70	Samuel Taylor, 151, Keppell-street, King's-road, S.W.	12 0 0
1876	70	William Henry Bagnall, 12, Lenham-road, Lee, Kent	12 0 0
1860	80	Sarah Margaret Keel, 84, Fetter-lane	12 0 0
1863	79	Mary Neale. 18, Mayton-street, Hornsey-road, N.	12 0 0
1874	69	Hannah Mitchell, 164, St. Paul's-road, Camden Town ...	12 0 0
1875	69	Mary Ann Ely, Colney Hatch...	12 0 0
1875	67	Ann Elizabeth Bond Doorey, 33, Queen's-row, Walworth... ...	12 0 0
1877	76	Eleanor Ellis, 37, Ferndale-road, Brixton	12 0 0
1877	85	Lydia Hale, 29, Packington-street, Islington	12 0 0

EXTRA PENSIONS TO UNMARRIED DAUGHTERS OF FREEMEN.

1872	53	Elizabeth Jane Hicks, 211, Marylebone-road	10 0 0
1879	75	Jane Bagnall, 10, Park-road-terrace, Forest Hill	10 0 0

£202 2 6

THE TRADE.

♣

THE TRADE.

REGULATIONS OF WORKMEN, SEARCHES, &c.

The powers of control over the workmen, and articles manufactured by them, or imported from foreign parts, given to the Company by their Charter and Bye-Laws, were very extensive, and for some time were strictly enforced.

The Master, Wardens, and Assistants, or any two of them, the Master or one of the Wardens being one, had power to search and view all productions of the Art made within the Realm or imported for sale, and to seize and break work unlawfully made. or composed of bad or defective materials, or in any way faulty; to carry the same to the Company's Hall or meeting place, to be adjudged, and, if condemned, to be broken; to break open any place, if refused admission, to search it, and to seize work and tools therein concealed; to prevent aliens or strangers from working except with an allowed and professed Clockmaker, and also all persons who had not served a seven years' apprenticeship to the trade.

The authority thus exercised had the effect of bringing them into frequent conflict with members of the trade, but they seem to have carried out what was sometimes a difficult duty with moderation and firmness, thus protecting the public from being imposed upon, and the manufacturer from unfair and ruinous competition.

The following extracts selected from numerous instances to be found in their records, explain the steps taken to give effect to their powers :—

"1632. October 23. This daye John Townsend covenaunt servaunt to Mr. Clarke is forbidd the working at the trade either with him or any other using the Arte of a Clockmaker.[1]

---

[1] Company's Journal I.

"This daye Mr. Lawe was prohibited from working hereafter in the Trade of a Clockmaker being never bound to the Arte, but to the Arte of a Graver.

"This daye Mr. Bisse was prohibited in the like manner for using the Arte any longer and likewise for keeping an Apprentice contrarie to the Statute.¹

"1632. November 29. This day Mr. Peto was forbidden to work any longer in the trade of a Clockmaker.

"This day James Beraud was admitted to be the servant and journeyman of Mr. Charlton.²

"1646-7. January 18. It was ordered, Forasmuch as divers abuses come by imploying of journeymen and chamber-workers that deceive the Masters of their Boxes, Watches and Money to the damage and scandall of the profession, It is therefore ordered by full consent that if any Master hereafter shall give any Box or trust any journeyman or chamber-worker with any Watch to mend or Money beforehand, and hee shall fraudulently make it away or pawne it, and then take worke of any other man before satisfaction be given to the former Master that imployed him, the party wronging the former Master having warning given him by the Beadle of the Company to make satisfaction, and he not appearinge at the next Court to give an account why hee hath so done, then by order of the Company the Beadle shall print upon the next Bills for warninges of Watches lost and stolen, the dishonest dealing of that man, that every Master may take notice of his deceite, and if any Master shall imploy him before satisfaction be given to the former Master complayning, hee shall be lyable to the penalty of the ordinances.³

"1654. May 2. The same day it was ordered by general consent that Henry Creeke having been sued by the Company for using the Clockmakers' trade contrary to the statute, in regard he is a poor man he is content to submit to the rules and orders of the Company, and promiseth to present the Company with a new house clock and larum and 20s. of money the next quarter day, and Thomas Loomes promiseth likewise to see it performed.⁴

"1656. July 7. The same day John Wyeth shewing a Watch and Box made of a Spelter Mettle being utterly disliked by this Court and counted fraudulent in regard it may deceive the good people of this land, being in imitation of Gold, It is ordered by this Court that from henceforth there be noe more of that Mettle wrought in the fashion of Watch Boxes or Cases on the penalty for the first offence 40s. and for the second £5 sterling and the officer to give notice to the Boxmakers of this order.⁵

"1657. April 20. This Court day Mr. Fromantle being called to account for having a Journeyman without orders was fined 40s.⁶

"1668. January 18. A petition was presented to the Court by several Members of the Company shewing that sundry Aliens do work in and about the City of London contrary to the Laws of the Kingdom and the Charter of the Company, and the petition prayed that the Company would speedily take a legal course for finding out and prosecuting such Aliens so working, which petition was publickly read, and in regard the petitioners have not named what Aliens or where or when any such Aliens have so worked, the Court

1, 2, 3, 4, 5, 6 Company's Journal J.

did give to the petitioners for answer to their petition, That when they shall make known to the Master Wardens and Assistants of the Company the names of the Aliens so working, and the time and place thereof, by sufficient proofs which they will make good, the Company will take such legal course therein as they are enabled by the Laws of the Kingdom and the Charter and ordinances of the Company.[1]

"1668. February 8. Leave was given by the Company to five of the Petitioners to prosecute at their own charge, but in the name of the Company, Nowell Paul and Jaques Swale, two Aliens who worked at the trade of Clockmaking within the liberties of the grant of the Charter of the Company.[2]

"1682. April 3. Whereas special summonses have been sent out to divers persons members of the Company, some being much in arrear of Quarterage, some having unduly and irregularly taken and bound apprentices, and others exercising the Art of Clockmaking or some branch thereof within the extents and limitts of the Company's Charter, and are not admitted into the Company, and some of them have appeared at this Court and given satisfaction, but others have neglected and seeme to slight all fair meanes used to bring them to a conformity, It was thereupon thought fitt and ordered that there shall be sued and prosecuted in the Exchequer for undue taking and bindeing of apprentices these following, viz.[3]

        John Martin in White Gate Alley
        Samuel Steevens in Grub Street
        Thomas Spencer in the Strand
        Thomas Fletcher in St. Martins

And for exercising the Art not being admitted these following

        Eysum Perkins of Rederiffe the end of Love Lane
        Richard Blundell
        William Whittingham
        William Kenney
        James Meniall, Frenchman

And for the effectual management and carrying on of the suites and prosecutions against them, this Court did Nominate and Appoint the committee following viz.

    The Master   Mr. Henry Winne
    The 3 Wardens   Mr. Henry Jones
    Mr. Jeremy Gregory Mr. Nicasius Russell
    Mr. Nathan Barrow and Mr. William Knottsford

who, or so many of them as shall appear, are desired and authorized to meet consult, advise and determine of and concerning the same as the case shall require, at such times and places as the Master shall appoint.

"1682. May 1. The following appeared and acknowledged they were wrong after being served with an Exchequer writ

"John Martin, fined thirty shillings, ten being subsequently returned to him.

"Samuel Stevens did not appear.

[1,2,3] Company's Journal I.

"Thomas Spencer appeared and paid his share of the charges, and promised to take up the Freedom the next Quarterly Court.

"Thomas Fletcher appeared and he could not come to any certaine issue.

"Eysum Perkins promised to take up his Freedom at the next Quarterly Court.

"Richard Blundell paid his fine, and promised to take his Freedome the next Quarter Court.

"Richard Whittingham appeared, but the Court and he could not come to any certaine issue.

"William Kenney appeared, but the Court and he could not come to any certaine issue.

"James Mesniell appeared, paid his proportion of the Exchequer charge, and was admitted to the Freedom.[1]

"1682. June 5. Thomas Fletcher submitted himself and was fined £5.[2]

"1688. April 2. Ordered that William Whittingham shall be prosecuted at Law for exercising the Art or Trade of Clockmaking, he having not served seven years in or to the same Art or trade.[3]

"1698. May 2. This Court being summoned in pursuance to the order of the last Quarter Court touching the Members of this Company imploying Foreigners, Aliens and others not Freemen of this Company contrary to the ordinances thereof, which each Member is sworn to observe, And it being at this Court seriously debated and considered that if those ordinances or Bye Laws were duely observed by the Members of this Company, it would tend very much not only to the advantage thereof but be for the good of the Art and Artists in generall, It is therefore ordered That for the future no Freemen of this Company doe employ, trade or deale with any such Foreigners, Aliens or Unfreemen as they tender their Oaths, and will avoid the penalties which by the said ordinances are to be and will be inflicted upon them in case of the contrary, to the intent that all Members of this Company may be incouraged and imployed, and other persons useing the Art be induced to take their Freedoms of this Company, for the good thereof and preservation of the Art in esteem of posterity.[4]

"1787. December 3. The Master produced two letters which he had received since their last meeting purporting that various attempts had been making for some time past, to entice our Artists out of the Kingdom contrary to the Laws of the Realm; that a Bill had been preferred to the Grand Jury, against the person attempting to seduce them, but the most material witnesses not being produced, the Bill was thrown out and the person enlarged; but a workman named John Abbott who had made an agreement to go to St. Petersburgh in Russia, to work at Clockmaking, was now in custody, to be tried for the offence; and the writers of the letters requested the assistance of the Company, to produce the necessary witnesses; upon which a motion was made seconded and carried unanimously.

"That the Master and Wardens be desired to wait on the Solicitors for the Treasury to know the state of the Action, against the said John Abbott, and that they be empowered from the information they receive, to give such directions as they shall think necessary in support of the prosecution.[5]

[1, 2, 3, 4] Company's Journal II.   [5] Company's Journal V.

"1788. February 4. Ordered that the Company do give two Guineas, to John Vincent, and Thomas Leach, in consideration of their loss of time in attending the trial of John Abbott a Clockmaker who was convicted at Hicks's Hall of having made an agreement to go to Russia to follow his said business of a Clockmaker contrary to 'Act of Parliament.'"

SEARCHES.

In order to carry out practically the powers given them of searching for deceitful or bad work or materials, the Court of Assistants divided the City into walks, viz.:—The City walk—South-west walk—North-west walk—Eastward walk. To meet the necessary expenses of attending the several Searches, every Member of the Fellowship was required to pay quarterly, the sum of fourpence.

Even with this small fee, the Searches produced a revenue in the year 1708 of over twenty-eight pounds.

"1634-5. January 19. Memorandum: That the 17th of January our Master going a general search Westward there was a Cross Cristal Watch garnished with Brass, and a silver Watch and 2 boxes seized upon by the Master and Wardens and some of the Assistants of the Company, which had been brought from beyond the seas, and not brought to our Common Hall or meeting place to be approved or allowed, therefore according to the Charter of Incorporation granted to this Society, this Court ordered that such course should be taken by law for the condemnation thereof as ye Company shall be advised by their learned counsel, and this to be the Master and Wardens discharge in that behalf.'

"1635-6. January 18. The same day Thomas Hill a dyall maker at the Tower had 4 pocket dyalls cutt and did affront Mr. Allen with opprobrious words.

"The Court day aforesaid Thomas Kellett paid a fine of 5s. and had his Watch delivered to him again.[2]

[1,2] Company's Journal I.

"1652. November 3. Whereas at a general search by the Master and Wardens the 24 of October there was a Chamber Clock seized by Mr. Thomas Holland, Warden, according to the orders of our Charter, being the work of Samuel Davis dwelling in Lothbury, London, the work being found very unserviceable and deceitful by the Court aforesaid. It was therefore adjudged to be defaced and broken that it might not be put to sale to deceive the people, which was done accordingly, Samuel Davis being present gave his consent thereunto and was fined forty shillings according to the orders and he submitted thereunto.

"1657-8. March 24. This search day a contrate second wheele of a dyall wheele being taken from Thomas Battin was viewed by the said Company and adjudged to be so bad as not fitting to be put into any worke, and he was fined according to the orders of the said Company.¹

"1661. July 18. This day a movement being seized, present Mr. Warden Gregory, Mr. Hill, Mr. Claxton, Mr. Jones and Mr. Daniel did seize a movement which was judged not merchantable ware nor fit to be sold until made good and mended, and he is ordered to be summoned to answer the defects of the worke, Mr. Fromantel being upon the view at the time.

"1661. August 19. The movement of John Marston, which was seized on the late search for deceitful work, was by this Court condemned, and for his not appearing, being warned, he is by the Court fined forty shillings.

"1668. April 15. At a search there being present the Master and Wardens 4 Assistants and 3 *Mathematical Instrument Makers* being Assistants.

"There was seized by them who went the Western part of the Search where Hilkiah Bedford, Mathematical Instrument Maker was present and carried the Standard Measure, these Rules and Measures following which were found disagreable to the Standard (vizt.)²

"In the shop of Samuel Morris, Ironmonger, at the sign of the Dripping pan near Charing Crosse, 3 yards and 2 joynted 2 foot rules.

"In the shop of —— Byfield, Ironmonger, near the Chequers Inne in Holborne one plaine Joynt rule.

"In the shop of —— Bagge Ironmonger att Holborne Bridg 3 plaine Joynt Rules and one brassed Joynt rule.

"In the shop of —— Walker, Ironmonger, at the Dripping pan in Smithfield Six Rules.

"All which are delivered into the Custody of Warden Claxton.

"1668. May 4. Samuell Morris —— Byfield and Walker, Ironmongers, from whom severall faulty Rules and Measures were seized at the last search appeared at this Court, and being convinced, by proofe of the Standard, that the said Rules and Measures were faulty, each of them received back what was seized from them and each broak one and promissed the others should be amended before they be exposed to sale.

"1668. July 6. Bagge, Ironmonger, from whom some faulty Rules and Measures were seized at the last search, appeared and pleaded his ignorance of their faultyness, and it was consented that Warden Claxton deliver them

---

¹, ² Company's Journal I.

both to him soe as he break one; which he promised to doe and the rest shall be amended before they be put to sale [1]

"1671. September 4. Three Brass Standards received from the Court of Exchequer under the Statute 12 Hen: VII. [2]

"1671-2. February 21. At a search made the 21st day of February 1671, upon and for the concerns onely of the Mathematicall instrument Makers [3]

Present
Nicholas Coxeter Master
Samuell Horne } Wardens
Jeffery Bayley
John Nicasius, John Browne } Assistants
Walter Hayes—Richard Ames

"There was seized in Shopps, within the limitts of the search of the Company, of severall Tradesmen who buy and sell and severall persons who make Mathematical measures and instruments, the workes and measures hereafter particularly expressed for that they are (as the said Walter Hayes, and John Browne, who are Mathematicall Instrument Makers and carried with them the company's standards [4] sealed in his Majesties Exchequer to trye and prove the same, doe finde and affirme them) not agreeable to the said standards and the rules and proportions of art, but are faulty and therefore not fitt to be put to sale (vizt.)

"Of Mr. Samull Gadlingstock a seller of canes &c. in Exchange Alley seized one Joynted Yard Rule

"Of Mr. John Sellars, a seller of Globes, Mapps instruments and other like wares, in the same place seized one 2 foot Rule and one yard Rule.

"Of Mr. James Noakes a seller of Canes in Popes head alley seized two foot Rules of three joynts.

"Of Mr. Frewen, a seller of Canes &c. next the signe of the Naked Boy in Cheapside, seized two sun dialls for posts, affirmed by him to be made or sold to him by the Widow Cater in Moorfields.

"Of Joseph Silvester, Ironmonger, at the signe of the Frying pan within Ludgate, seized thirteene streight Rules and ten two foot Rules joynted, affirmed by him to be made or sold to him by William Elmes.

"Of Mr. Robert Jole, Mathematicall Instrument Maker in Fleet street, seized two 2 foot Rules affirmed by him to be made by William Elmes or Joseph Wells.

"Of Mr. Mercer, a seller of Canes &c. at the signe of the Feathers in Fleet street, seized one yard Rule or Measure affirmed by him to be made or sold to him by John Nash.

"Of Mr. Charles Danley, a seller of Canes &c. at the signe of the Grapes in Fleet street, seized two Sun Dialls for Posts, affirmed by him to be made or sold to him by the aforesaid Widow Cater.

"Of Mr. Piggott, a seller of Canes &c. in Fleet street over against Chancery Lane, seized three 2 foot joynted Rules, affirmed by his servant to be made or sold to his Master by the aforesaid William Elmes.

1, 2, 3, 4 Company's Journal I.

"Of Mr. Francis Hewitt, a seller of Canes &c. at the signe of the Blew Bell in the Strand near Charing Crosse, seized one 2 foot joynted Rule affirmed by him to be made or sold to him by the aforesaid Robert Jole.

"Of Mr. Faulkingham, a seller of Canes &c. under the south East corner of the Royall Exchange, seized six plane joynted Rules of 18 Inches, ffive plaine joynted 2 foot Rules, foure the like tipped with brasse, two the like being brasse joynted and 2 yard rules in three joynts, all affirmed by him to be made or sold to him by the aforesaid John Nash.

"Of Mr. Anthony Poole, Ironmonger in Foster Lane, seized two plaine joynted two foot Rules and five plaine two foot Rules foure of them being tipped with Brasse and one untipped.

"Of Mr. Jesson, an Ironmonger, neer the Barrs without Aldgate, seized two plaine joynted 2 foot Rules and one Brasse joynted tipped.

"Of Mr. Clarke in the Minories seized two plaine joynted two foot Rules.

"And upon the same day the said Mr. Anthony Poole appeared at the Court then holden and being fully satisfied upon tryall and proofe by the standards that the measures which were seized from him were faulty, one of them the most faulty was then broken by him and the rest were delivered back to him upon his promise not to put them to sale till made perfect.

"Likewise the said Mr. John Nash, the maker of the Measures which were seized from Mr. Faulkingham, appeared and being fully satisfied upon tryall and proofe by the Standards that they were faulty did promise to make good to him so many true measures of like sort as those seized, and that those seized should not be put to sale untill made perfect, whereupon they were delivered to Mr. Faulkingham's servant, who, on behalfe of his Master, appeared with Mr. Nash as to this concerne. And all other things so seized and not broaken or redelivered as aforesaid were committed to the custody of Mr. Nicholas Coxeter the present Master.

"The rest were given up upon promise that they were to be made perfect.

"1672-3. March 3. There was seized in the Shopp of Mr. Harris, an Ironmonger at the sign of the May-Pole in the Strand, three two foot Rules tipped with Brass which tryed by the standard were found to be too long, about the tenth part of an Inch, the which were committed to the custody of the Master.[1]

"At a search and Court the 3rd day of June 1672,

"Seized in the shopp of Mr. Robert Markham, Cane seller over against St. Dunstan's Church in Fleet Street, seven one foot Rules Two 2 foot Rules of Brasse Joynts, One two foot Rule plaine, and one Joynted Rule of Three foot, all which compaired with the Standards were found to be faulty.

"Seized in the shopp of Mr. Butlin, Ironmonger, at the Crosse Keys within Newgate, 2 two foot Rules which being compaired with the Standards were found to be faulty, but Mr. Butlin did afterwards appeare and promise that they should not be exposed to sale till they were made perfect, and thereupon they were redelivered to him.

---

[1] Company's Journal I.

THE CLOCKMAKERS' COMPANY. 239

"Seized in the Shopp of Mr. Richard Wilson, Ironmonger, within Newgate, Two 2 foot Joynt Rules which being compared with the Standard were found to be faulty.

"Seized in the Shopp of William Birchmore, Ironmonger, without Newgate, Two 2 foot Joynt Rules tipped with brasse, which being compared with the Standard were found to be faulty.[1]

1676-7. March 13. The Master haveing lately seized a new Movement of a Watch proffered to him in his shop to be sold by an Apprentice, which he found to be very faulty and insufficient work, and which watch as the Apprentice affirmed belonged to —— Howse but hath been since challenged by Richard Hamlin, the said Watch was viewed at this Court and found to be very bad and not capable to be made fitt to be exposed to sale, which the Master hath in his hands, with a note of those faults and defects which were found in it.

"1677. April 2. The movement formerly seized by the Master and owned by Richard Hamlin, was again viewed at this Court, and such parts of it as were faulty were broaken, and such of it as were useful were delivered to John Pinson, Apprentice of John Parker, on behalf of Hamlin.

"1677. April 2. Another Movement lately seized by the Master made by one —— Jackson of Newington, Surrey, was viewed at this Court and judged to be so insufficient that it was fitt to be broaken, but remayned yet in the Masters hands unbroken.[2]

1677. [May 19. It appears by an entry of this date that Mr. Thomas Bennett claimed the above Movement; such parts of it as were faulty were broken and afterwards handed by consent to Mr. Savage.][3]

"1681-2. January 16. Ordered that more frequent and strict view and search then hath heretofore been shall hereafter be made of all such Clocks, Watches and Works belonging to them, as well those made in England, as those imported into England by way of Merchandize, And if upon view they be found sufficient and approved they shall, before being exposed to sale, receive a Mark by the Master Wardens and Assistants of the Company to be ordained, testifying their allowance of the same, And those persons that deny to show their work or ware to be viewed shall be presented by the Master Wardens and Assistants of this Company as the Companies Charter and Ordinances and the Laws of the Land enableth them.[4]

"1682-3. March 5. Mr. Bell, Master, with some of the Assistants having lately seized in the shop of Robert Halsted in Fleet street two very bad or insufficient unfinished movements for Watches, the same were at this Court produced and exposed to a view in the presence of the said Robert Halsted. The Court referred the further view of them to some more convenient time by open daylight. The Master with some of the Assistants haveing also lately seized at the house, shop or workroom of some workmen or persons working or using the art of Clockmaking or some part or branch thereof four unfinished Movements, two whereof have engraven thereon (Ambrose Smith, Stamford, and William Burges, Fecit, and Jaspar Harmar, London, another) all which names are greatly suspected to be invented or fobbed, a Committee was appointed to take proceedings therein and Mr. Peter Bridger, of Freeman Yard Cornhill was appointed Attorney."[5]

1, 2, 3 Company's Journal I.   4, 5 Company's Journal II.

"1683. September 29. Mr. Robert Halsted's movements seized about six months since being viewed were judged to be absolutely insufficient, and uncapable of amendment and were therefore in their severall parts either broken or defaced soe as that they could never be usefull and in that condition were delivered to the Beadle that he should deliver them to Mr. Halsted.

"1687. August 1. It was ordered that Mr. Francis Stamper be prosecuted in the Exchequer for refusing to admit the Master and Wardens into his Work Room when they were upon a search.[1]

1687. [November 7. He attended the Court and submitted himself and was fined 20s and 7s for the Law expenses.][2]

"1688. April 2. Some Watch or Pockett Clock chaines having been before that time seized at the house or shop of Mr. Henry Harper, Watchmaker, and judged to be insufficient ware, It was ordered that the said Mr. Harper shall be warned to appear before the Lord Mayor to answer the complaint of the Master and Wardens as to this matter.[3]

"1688. July 26. The twelve steel chains for watches heretofore seized as insufficient at the house or shop of Mr. Henry Harper in Cornhill, concerning which a jury hath been impanelled and a hearing in the Mayor's Court, which jury gave verdict that they were insufficient, and thereupon judgement was given that they should be broken and spoyled, were at this Court broken and spoyled, and in such condition delivered to one Thomas Tom whome the Court appoynted to deliver them to Mr. Harper, and he accordingly forthwith went to Mr. Harper's house, and upon his return acquainted the Court that he had delivered them to Mr. Harper.[4]

"1688. September 13. In this (days) search there was seized by the Master with Mr. Wheeler and Mr. Russell, two of the Assistants, in the Shop of Benoni Tebbatt, Watchmaker, in Little Old Bailey, a Gold Watch case both for that it was made of coarse and unwarrantable Gold, as less in value then the legal Standard, and also of soe little weight and consequently soe extreamly thinn as that it was insufficient in the strength thereof, and great fraud would be put upon ye person who should happen to buy it, and an abuse and disparagement redound to the Art, and all good and honest Artists, The which watchcase was by ye person then in the said shop affirmed to belong unto —— Brafeild as made by him.[5]

"1688. September 29. At this Court William Brafeild attended and admitted his fault and was fined 5s., the Case being broken up."[6]

"RECEIPTS AND EXPENDITURE.

"1708. At a search the 25th day of August 1708 in 5 Walks.

"Present John Pepys, Master, Mr. Quare Mr. Etherington and Mr. Taylor, Wardens.

Mr. Hancorn   Mr. Speakman
Mr. Henshaw   Mr. Windmills
Mr. Stanton   Mr. Graves
Mr. Shaw   Mr. Barrows
Mr. Gibbs, and the last Stewards.

[1, 2, 3, 4, 5, 6] Company's Journal II.

THE CLOCKMAKERS' COMPANY.

		£	s.	d.
"Received by Mr. Warden Etherington as followeth from the	City Walk	8	14	5
	South West Walk	8	8	1
	North West Walk	5	3	4
	Eastward Walk	1	15	8
	New Walk	4	7	8
		£28	9	2
"Paid by him the charges for the day		8	13	7

Entries of a similar nature to the above appear in subsequent years, the results only of which are given below.

Year	Date	Type		£	s.	d.
"1709.	July 1.	Receipts	...	25	18	10½
		Expenditure	...	5	9	6
"1710.	June 16.	Receipts	...	20	4	0½
		Expenditure	...	11	16	4
"1712.	September 17.	Receipts	...	26	16	0
		Expenditure	...	6	9	6
"1713.	September 11.	Receipts	...	27	2	9
		Expenditure	...	6	16	6
"1714	May 28.	Receipts	...	23	19	1
		Expenditure	...	6	2	6
"1717.	September 12.	Receipts	...	28	6	5
		Expenditure	...	6	1	6
"1718.	September 24.	Receipts	...	34	6	7
		Expenditure	...	6	13	6
"1721.	September 21.	Receipts	...	24	9	10
		Expenditure	...	3	10	0
"1722.	September 12.	Receipts	...	38	8	3
		Expenditure	...	4	11	9
"1723.	September 19.	Receipts	...	27	4	1
		Expenditure	...	4	14	11
"1724.	September 17.	Receipts	...	25	6	5
		Expenditure	...	2	11	4
"1725.	September 15.	Receipts	...	27	15	8½
		Expenditure	...	3	8	6
"1726.	September 15.	Receipts	...	22	11	1
		Expenditure	...	3	17	0
"1727.	September 28.	Receipts	...	26	5	11½
		Expenditure	...	3	7	7½
"1728.	September 12.	Receipts	...	23	14	2
		Expenditure	...	6	3	6
"1729.	September 18.	Receipts	...	24	18	4
		Expenditure	...	5	2	0
"1730.	September 17.	Receipts	...	23	19	9
		Expenditure	...	5	4	3
"1731.	September 16.	Receipts	...	18	8	6
		Expenditure	...	4	4	0
"1732.	September 14.	Receipts	...	21	18	0
		Expenditure	...	3	15	9

			£	s.	d.
"1733. September 20.	Receipts	... ...	29	1	9
	Expenditure	... ...	4	8	0
"1734. September 18.	Receipts	... ...	19	7	4
	Expenditure	... ...	5	17	0
"1735. September 18.	Receipts	... ...	27	7	5
	Expenditure	... ...	5	6	10½

Soon after this date the Searches were discontinued, as interfering with the liberty of the trade.

PATENTS AND INVENTIONS.

The entries in the Company's Records on these subjects are not numerous, nor indeed could they be so, seeing that applications for Patents for improvements in Time measurers were themselves but few before the year 1755, since which date no active steps against such applications appear to have been taken by the Company.

In their opposition to Patents, moreover, it is but fair to observe that they do not seem to have been actuated by a desire to stifle invention, but rather to prevent the granting of monopolies to individuals for so-called improvements, which were not in themselves novelties, and which, if granted, would have precluded the trade at large from manufacturing the articles sought to be patented; in fact, as a public body, fully cognisant with all the details of their profession, they rather sought to render assistance and advice to the Crown upon matters of a technical character connected with the craft, for the oversight, government, and protection of which they had been incorporated.

In the prosecution of these objects they spent considerable sums of money out of their Funds, and though their attempts were not always rewarded with success (in one instance apparently owing to notice of the intended application for a Patent having been brought to their knowledge, only after it had actually been granted, and of the details of which, as appears from their Minute, they were but imperfectly acquainted), they at least seem to have been undertaken for the benefit of the Trade when it appeared in their judgment to be imperilled by the Patents sought for.

"1687. February 8. Whereas it was intimated at the Court of the 6th of February that some person or persons as Inventor or Inventors were endeavouring to obtain from the King a Patent for their sole making and managing of all Repeating Clocks and Watches, which Patent was then accounted would be both discreditt and damage to the whole Company, It was then thought fitt that a petition should be speedily presented to his Majesty praying his leave to enter a Caveat that the Patent should not pass the Seale till the Company have given their reasons against it, and although their was but a slender appearance of the Assistants at the said Court, a Petition was accordingly presented on the 7th to his Majesty by the Master and Wardens, who granted them leave to enter their Caveat, and told them they should be heard, and they forthwith entered the Caveat; Now this Court (which was summoned only upon this occasion) did not only allow and approve of such the actings and proceedings of the Master and Wardens, but did also desire and order them, with such of the Assistants or others as they shall think fitt to concern therewith, to pursue the same matter, according to their discretions, or advice of Counsel in such manner as they best may and the nature thereof will admit, the charge whereof is to be borne by the Company."[1]

"1687. March 5. The Master acquainted the Assistants present with the good success of the endeavours by him, the Wardens, and others, pursuant to the order of the Court of the 8th of February last, for prevention of passing the intended Patent relating to. pulling repeating pockett Clocks, which was that upon a hearing before the King and Council it was determined that the Patent should not be passed and that the same was utterly quashed and annulled.

[The disbursement by the Renter Warden with regard to the proceedings amounted to £25 4s.]

The following is the Order in Council in relation to the intended Patent referred to :- -

"At a Court at Whitehall 2nd March 1687
" Present
" The Kings most excellent Maj'y in Councill.
" Whereas on the 24th of February last his Maj'y thought fitt to appoint this day to hear the Master Wardens and Assistants of the Fellowship of the

[1] Company's Journal II.

Art or Mistery of Clockmakeing of the City of London against Edward Barlow, in whose name a Patent is passing for the sole makeing and manageing all pulling Clocks and Watches, usually called Repeateing Clocks, And both parties attending accordingly were called in and heard by their Councill learned.

"His Majesty in Councill haveing fully considered what was alleadged on either side, Is pleased to Order and it is hereby ordered, That no Patent be granted to the said Edward Barlow or any others for the sole makeing and manageing of pulling Clocks and Watches as aforesaid, The same being now made by severall Clockmakers, whereof all persons concerned are to take due notice.

"1688. October 12. Be it remembered That in pursuance of the order of the Court of the 8th of February 1687 and according to the Report at the Court of the 5th of March 1687, the Patent endeavoured to be obtained by one Mr. Edward Barlow (a Priest) and to be granted to him by the King's Majesty for his sole making and manageing of all pulling repeating pockett Clocks and Watches (he pretending to be the *True* and *first Inventor* of that Art, or Invention) was by the diligence and endeavours of the Master and Wardens of this Company, and divers others of the Assistants, Members and Officers of the Company, and with great Charge and Expence (which was borne by and out of the stock and income of the Company) very successfully prevented, and upon the second of March 1687 ordered by the King in Councill not to be granted, the copie of which intended Patent with the Petitions, Reasons, Testimonies, Orders and other things relating thereto are tyed together in one bundle and put into the Company's chest.¹

"1695. June 3. Upon a motion and discourse concerning Daniell Quare and his endeavouring to obtayne a Patent for the sole makeing of portable Weather-Glasses, It was resolved and ordered that the Company doe forthwith endeavour to put a stop to the passing of that Patent.²

"1695. September 30. The Master and Wardens made a report of their proceedings against Mr. Quare's Patent for portable Weather-glasses, and that the patent was passed, and there may be suits of law or trouble to some Members that make or sell those Weather-glasses, It was unanimously voted and ordered that the Company will defend any Members of the Company or their servants, and also Mr. John Patrick (who assisted the Company) in any actions or suits that may be brought against them on that account.³

"1704. December 11. This Court was called upon the occasion of Nicholas Facio and Peter Debaufree and Jacob Debaufree having petitioned the House of Commons for an Act for the sole applying precious and more common stones in Clocks and Watches and for enlarging the term in their patent.

"A Paper called their reasons for such an Act was read,

"And reasons of several Members of the Court were heard by way of answer.

"Ordered that the Master and Wardens with such of the Court of Assistants as they shall call in from time to time shall be a Committee to meet from time to time and employ a fit person or persons to be Solicitor or

---

¹ ² ³ Company's Journal II.

Solicitors, and to retain Counsel to draw a petition to the Parliament and to give and pay all necessary fees charges and expences, and do all other matters in order to stop the said bill."[1]

The following Extracts from the Journals of the House of Commons, and the Company's Records, explain the proceedings taken against the application, and show the success of the opposition, which was grounded on the fact that the supposed invention was not new, evidence in support thereof being submitted to the Committee of the House in the shape of a Watch, made at an earlier date, in which the principle was introduced. This Watch is still in the Company's possession.

"Mecurii 6° die Decembris 3° Annæ Reginæ 1704

"A Petition of Nicholas Facio, Gentleman, and Peter and Jacob Debaufree, Watchmakers, was presented to the House and read setting forth as follows :—

"To the Honoble. the Comons of England in Parliamt. assembled

"The humble Petition of Nicholas Facio, Gent". and Peter Debaufree and Jacob Debaufree, Watchmakers

"Sheweth,

"That Her most Gracious Majety. was pleased by Letters-Patents dated 1 May in the 3rd Year of her Reign to Grant to Your Petrs. the sole use and exercise within the Kingdoms of England and Ireland & Dominions thereunto belonging of a Certain new Art or Invention or working & Figuring precious or more comon stones & certain other matters different from Mettals, so that they may be imployed and made use of in Clock work or watch work and many other Engines, not for ornament only, but as internall and usefull part of the work or engine itself, in such manner as have not heretofore been used, and very much conducing to the greater perfection of Watches and Clocks, together with the advantages arising thereby for the space of fourteen yeares from the date of the said Letters Patents.

"That your Petrs. by their great pains and expenses, both before and since the granting the said Letters Patents, have greatly improved the said inventions which are likely to be of great use and advantage to the publick, but the same will require a far greater expense, whereby your Petrs. may deserve a better encouragemt. by having a longer term of years allowed, than by the sd. Letters Patents is granted them, otherwise they will not be able to prosecute the same effectually.

"Yor. Petrs. therefore humbly pray your Honrs. to give them leave to bring in a Bill for granting them such further term for the sole use of their said Inventions, after the expiration of the said Letters Patents as to your Honrs. in your great wisdom shall seem meet.

"And yr. Petrs. shall ever pray &c.

"Nicolas Facio   Peter Debaufree   Jacob Debaufree.

[1] Company's Journal III.

"Ordered,—That leave be given to bring in a Bill according to the prayer of the said Petition and that the Lord Marquis of Hartington and Sir Mathew Dudley do prepare and bring in the Bill.

"Sabbati 9° die Decembris 3° Annæ Reginæ 1704.

"The Lord Marquis of Hartington (according to order) presented to the House a Bill for the further encouragem[t] of the new Art or Invention of working and applying of precious & more common Stones for the greater perfection of watches clocks and other engines, And the same was received and read the first time.

"Resolved that the Bill be read a 2nd time.

"Jovis 14° die Decembris 3° Annæ Reginæ 1704.

"A Bill, for the further encouragement of the new Art or Invention of working and applying of precious and more common Stones, for the greater perfection of watches, clocks, and other engines, was read a Second time.

"Resolved,—That the Bill be committed to Mr. Foley, Lord Marquis Hartington, Sir Math. Dudley, Mr. Bridges, Lord Orrery, Sir Godfrey Copley, Mr. Woollaston, Mr. Stanhope, Mr. Hysham, Mr. Winnington, Lord Coningsby, Mr. Palmes, Mr. Freeman, Mr. Crosse, Sir Jos. Jekyll, Mr. Cesar, Mr. Pagit, Mr. Brett, Mr. Roberts, Sir Chr. Hales, Mr. Pitfeild, Lord Cutts, Mr. Grevill, Lord Edw. Russell, Sir Fra-Massam, Sir Gerv. Elwes, Mr. Nicholas, Mr. Yates, Mr. Bridgman, Mr. Vaughan, Mr. Comyns, Mr. Harley. And they are to meet this afternoon at Five a Clock, in the Speaker's Chamber.[1]

"Veneris, 15° die Decembris 3° Annæ Reginæ, 1704.

"Ordered,—That Sir Gilbert Heathcot, Sir Jeffry Jefferyes, Sir Robert Clayton, Mr. Moncton, Sir John Thorold, Mr. Wentworth, be added to the Committee, to whom the Bill, for the further encouragement of the new Art of applying precious, and more common Stones, for the greater perfection of Watches, Clocks, and other Engines, is committed.[2]

"Lunæ, 18° die Decembris 3° Annæ Reginæ, 1704.

"A Petition of the Clock-makers and Watch-makers in and about the Cities of London and Westminster, and Liberties thereof, on behalf of themselves, and all the Watch-makers and Clock-makers throughout the Kingdom, was presented to the House and read, setting forth, that the Bill depending in the House, for the further encouragement of the new Art or Invention of working and applying of precious and more common Stones, for the greater perfection of watches, clocks, and other engines, is founded upon false pretences, and, if it should pass, will greatly predjudice the Petitioners Trades in general: and praying to be heard by Counsel against the said Bill.

"Ordered,—That the consideration of the said Petition be referred to the Committee; to whom the said Bill is committed and that the Petitioners be heard by their Counsel, if they think fit, before the Committee, thereupon[3]

"A petition of the Jewellers, Diamond-cutters, Lapidaries, Seal-cutters, Engravers in Stone, and others dealing in Jewels, and precious Stones, and more common Stones, in and about the Cities of London and Westminster, was presented to the House, and read; setting forth, that they conceive, the Bill now in the House for the further Encouragement of the new Art or

---

[1,2,3] Journal of the House of Commons, pages 458, 459 and 462.

Invention of working and applying of precious and more common Stones, for the greater Perfection of Watches, Clocks, and other Engines, will, in a great measure, infringe upon the Petitioners in their several Arts and Trades, and abridge them of working and applying Jewels, and Stones in many Things : And praying, that they may be heard by Counsel against the said Bill.

"Ordered,—That the Consideration of the said Petition be referred to the Committee, to whom the said Bill is committed.[1]

"1704-5. January 15. The Master reported that pursuant to the orders of the last Court there has been a constant application and diligence used in obstructing the Bill in Parliament for the sole applying of precious and more common Stones in Clocks &c. (viz.) That the Parliament had been petitioned and ordered that the petition should be referred to the Committee to whom the bill was committed. That the petitioners had been twice heard by Counsel and themselves against the bill, and that the Committee had made such amendments that they thought best to destroy it, and therefor had therefore struck out all the parts of the bill but these words, 'Be it enacted,' and directed a report to be made accordingly.'

"The Master also acquainted the Court that in the proofs brought against the Bill, there was an old Watch produced, the maker's name Ignatius Huggerford, that had a stone fixed in the cock and balance work, which was of great use to satisfy the Committee.

"Ordered,—That the Renter Warden do buy the said Watch (if he can) to be kept for the Members of the Company's use to defend them in case the Patentees should commence any suit.

"Memorandum,—The said Watch was bought of Henry Magson for £2 10s. and the Watch was left with the Master of the Company.[2]

"Ordered,—That ten shillings be given to Mr. Wm. Seale who attended to prove his having the Watch above mentioned before the date of the Patent, and that he sold it to Mr. Magson.[3]

"1705. 16th October. Paid all ffees charges and expences in and about obstructing the Bill in Parliament for makeing jewell Watches, viz. :—

"Under Clerk in Parliament ...	...	...	£11	16	6
Clerks Fees at Committees &c.	...	...	17	10	6
Mr. Lawton Sollicitor 50 Guin	...	...	53	15	0
Mr. Harvey Sollicitor 10 Guin	...	...	10	15	0
Clerke of the Company for Copys &c.	...	...	20	0	0
Beadle of the Company for his pains	...	...	5	0	0
Fees to Council at severall times	...	...	8	11	0
To severall Witnesses for their Attendance	...	...	13	17	6
For Printing Reasons and paper	...	...	7	3	6
Messengers Charges and Expences &c.	...	...	20	19	9
Paid in all on this occasion	...	...	£169	9	9

---

[1] Journal of the House of Commons, 21st December, 1704, p. 467.

[2] It is a Silver Watch (still preserved in the Company's Museum), with tortoiseshell outside case, mounted and studded with silver, silver dial, with rotary day of the month circle. Ignatius Huggerford was a Freeman of the Haberdashers' Company. He was admitted and sworn a Brother of this Company July 3rd, 1671.

[3] Company's Journal III.

"1711. November 5. The Master acquainted the Court that one Mr. Hutchinson had been with him and offered to discover a new Invention or Improvement (as he called it) in Watchwork to preserve and keep Watches from dust and that the same (as he alledged) would be of great use to the trade in general, if the Company would consider him for his Invention. Ordered that the Master and Wardens with such Assistants as they shall call in, shall be empowered to discourse with Mr. Hutchinson about his Invention and report the same and their opinion thereon to next summoned Court.[1]

"1711. January 14. The Master reported that he with several of the Court of Assistants had met Mr. Hutchinson and discoursed with him upon his pretended invention, which is to keep dust out of Watches, and the Master and several others present giveing their opinions that the same did not deserve the notice of the Company so as to give him anything, and it being alledged that something to the like purpose had been done before:— The Question was put whether Mr. Hutchinson should have anything from the Company for his showing his Invention? It passed in the Negative.

"Ordered,—That a Caveat be entered with the Attorney and Solicitor General against any Patent to pass to Mr. Hutchinson for his pretended Invention.[2]

"1712. May 16. The Printed Votes of the House of Commons of Wednesday the 14th inst. were produced to this Court and part thereof, in the following words, read

'A Petition of John Hutchinson was presented to the House and read praying that leave may be given to bring in a bill for securing to him a new Invention of a portable movement with what improvements he shall make thereof to measure time, by such powers and for such (time) as shall be thought meet; Ordered That leave be given to bring in a bill according to the prayer of the said petition And that Sir William Windham, Mr. Auditor Harley, Mr. Foley and Mr. Lownds do prepare and bring in the same.'

"Whereupon this Court made the following order viz. Ordered That the Master and Wardens do take care to get a copy of the said petition forthwith and communicate the same to the Members of this Court and also a copy of the said Bill as soon as they can and acquaint the Court of Assistants with the same in order to their speedy opposing the passing such Bill."[3]

The following is the text of Hutchinson's Petition above mentioned :—

"To the Honorable the Commons of
Great Brittain in Parliament assembled.

"The humble petition of John Hutchinson,

"Sheweth,—That your Petitioner having invented and brought into Practice a portable movement to measure Time, which instead of the severall cross Motions, hollow Wheels with Teeth paralel to their Axes, used in former Movements, hath all the Axes paralel and streight, all the Wheels, the Plates, and the Ballance paralel and flat, all the Teeth streight in the Lines of the Diameter of the Wheels: The Axes, or Spindle of the Ballance,

[1,2,3] Company's Journal III.

moved by two Wheels alternately, and traversing equall Distance in equal Time, without Pause: in such sort that none of its moveing Parts can move nearer to, or farther from each other: Whereby in the Opinion of the greatest Mathematicians, and the best Judges of such Movements it is capable of moveing more equally, and less lyable to be disturbed by external motion, so that it may be of great Use to the Publick for finding the Longitude, and in several other respects. Besides what is here set forth your petitioner can make severall further additions, and Improvements. And has likewise a contrivance to wind up this, or any other Movement without an aperture in the Case through which anything can pass to foul the movement. Now your Petitioner is advised that the time granted by a Patent, the ordinary reward of such Inventions, cannot be sufficient in a thing of this nature, because it will require much time, contrivance, and nicety of workmanship to bring it to the perfection it is capable of before your Petitioner can be reimbursed the great expence he has and shall be at therein, and that Patents are also defective in never describing the Essentiall parts of the Invention to secure it, and the Improvements thereon, to the Inventor; and that for want of assigning a Penalty, the damages to be recovered for makeing a thing of this value will not be worth sueing for, and that for want of power to discover the Maker or Seller these things may be made, and carried away, privately and so used at sea.

"Your petitioner therefore humbly prays, that this Honorable House will be pleased to give leave, That a Bill or Clause may be brought in for securing these inventions and the improvements therein to your Petitioner by such powers and for such term of Time as to your Honours in your great wisdom, and justice shall seem meet.

" And your Petitioner shall ever pray, &c.

"JOHN HUTCHINSON."

1712. May 21. A copy of the Bill was read, Mr. Charles Lawton and Mr. Harvey Solicitors in Parliament were ordered to oppose its passing.

" Petition of the Master Wardens and several Assistants praying to be heard by counsel or otherwise against the Bill was agreed to and signed.

" Ordered,—That the Master, Wardens, and such Assistants as they shall call in do take care to get the said petition presented and to draw up Reasons against passing the Bill, and do all other Acts necessary thereunto, and the Renter Warden is to pay and defray all charges and expenses relating to and concerning the same."[1]

The Petition, which was presented to Parliament on the 22nd May, and referred to a Committee, was in the following terms :—

" To the Honorable the Commons of
Great Britain in Parliament assembled.

" The humble Petition of the Master Wardens and Assistants of the Company of Clockmakers of the City of London in behalfe of themselves and all other Members of the said Trade,

" Sheweth,—That your Petitioners are informed that there is a Bill now depending in this honorable House entitled A Bill for securing to

---

[1] Company's Journal II.

Mr. John Hutchinson the Property of a Movement invented by him for the more exact measuring of time both in Motion and at Rest.

"That your Petitioners humbly conceive that they shall be able to prove that in case the said Bill should pass into a Law, it would be highly prejudicial and destructive to their Trade, as well as a very great discouragement to all farther Improvements of their Art.

"Wherefore your Petitioners humbly pray they may be heard by their councill or otherwise against severall matters conteyned in the said Bill.

"And your Petitioners shall ever pray &c.

(Signed) Tho. Gibbs Tho. Tompion
John Barrow Robt. Webster
George Merttins Benjⁿ Graves
Robt. Halsted Geo. Etherington
Charles Gretton Tho. Taylor
Joseph Windmills John Pepys."

Reasons for and against the Bill were also printed and circulated amongst the Members of Parliament.

The following account of the proceedings in Committee on the Bill is taken from the Records of the Company:—

"1712. July 7. The Report of the proceedings in opposing Mr. Hutchinson's Bill in Parliament was read in Court and approved, and the same with the severall Reasons and other Papers therein mentioned were ordered to be put into the Book where Counsel's opinion upon several matters are entered or else put into the Company's Chest.

(Fees and expences for opposing the same - £143 13s. 4½d.)

"1712. June 2. The Committee sat and heard both parties; the Counsel for the Company produced a movement made by Mr. Charles Goode about 14 years ago, and Mr. Hutchinson's movement was also produced to the Committee and several questions were asked Mr. Goode and Mr. Graham, and they also asked Mr. Hutchinson severall questions, to which he could make little or no answer, but confest Mr. Goode's movement was made as his. So the Committee seemed satisfied that Mr. Hutchinson's movement was not a new invention and adjourned till this day fortnight.

"June 14. The Master, Mr. Warden Shaw, and Mr. Harvey the Solicitor attended Sir William Windham, the Chairman of the Committee, to know if it was his pleasure to proceed further upon the said Bill, and he gave for answer that he would not proceed further therein.

"1712. November 3. A proposal in writing of Mr. Samuel Watson's about an instrument to discover the hour of the day at Sea and several other useful Mathematical matters, which he therein offered to deliver and sell to the Company on certain conditions therein specified was read and considered, And the result was that this Court do not concern itself therein.

"1716. February 18. The Clerk acquainted the Court that he had received a Letter from the Attorney General's Clerk giving notice that a Petition of Charles Clay for a Patent for a Machine to answer the end of a Repeating Watch or Clock was referred by His Majesty to the Attorney General to consider of, and that the Company may be heard if they think convenient, And thereupon this Court came to the following Resolutions (viz.)

"That Mr. Gretton, Mr. Renter Warden, Mr. Jackson and the Clerk do forthwith go to Mr. Attorney General's and desire a time for the Company to be heard, and also that they fee S[r] Robert Raymond to be of Council for the Company in this Case.

"And that the Master and Wardens or any of them with such Assistants as they shall call in shall be a Committee to meet from time to time to draw up Reasons and oppose the said Patent, And the Renter Warden is to lay out such sums of money for Fees and expences as shall be advised necessary therein."[1]

The following is a Copy of Clay's Petition above referred to :—

"To the King's most excellent Majesty

"The humble petition of Charles Clay of Flockton in the County of York, Watchmaker,

"Sheweth,—That your petitioner hath lately invented a Machine that repeats the hours and quarters either upon a single Bell or upon more bells by changes or tunes from the communication of a pocket Watch, without taking off the outward case or fixing the same on the Fuzee of the said Watch or any way obstructing or hindering the motion; which Machine is very small and portable and wholly answers the end of a Spring Clock or Repeating Watch or Clock as to repeating the hours and quarters, and may be put into the machine with no more trouble than laying the Watch out of one's pocket.

"That your Majesty's petitioner hath spent several years and considerable sums of money by separate trials and alterations to bring the said Machine to perfection and is the first and only inventor thereof (which when seen may be easily made by other Artists) and will be a great discouragement to rare and new inventions.

"Your petitioner therefore humbly beseeches your Majesty to be graciously pleased to grant him a patent, as the first and only inventor of the said Machine, for the sole making and selling thereof for the term of 14 years, with prohibitions to the making using or selling such Machines, or any other of the like nature or use proceeding from the said inventions, within your Majestys dominions &c.

"And your Petitioner as in duty bound shall every pray &c.

'CHARLES CLAY."

Both parties were heard by the Attorney-General on the 25th of February, when the Master of the Company left a series of Reasons against the proposed Patent. On the 20th March they again attended, and Mr. Quare produced a Watch and Machine to answer the same end as Mr. Clay's, but the Attorney-General reported in favour of Clay.

---

[1] Company's Journal III.

1717. January 20. The Clerk read a report of the Company's proceeding against Clay's Patent from the beginning, which was approved, and ordered to be entered in a book for that purpose, for the better direction of the Company in like Cases for the future, By which Report it appeared That the Lords of the Council were of opinion, That the Patent sued for would be prejudicial and a discouragement to our Trade.

1717. February 3. The Clerk acquainted the Court that he had received a Letter from the Council Chamber that His Majesty was unable to hear Clay's affair in Council; the Letter was read and thereupon the Court ordered the Clerk to take out a Copy of the said Order if any was made relating thereto.

"1717. April 8. A Petition to his Majesty against Mr. Clay's Patent was agreed upon and Ordered to be signed by the Clerk on behalf of the Company and carried to the Secretary's Office.

"To the King's most Excellent Majesty

"The humble Petition of the Master Wardens and Assistants of the Fellowship of the Art or Mystery of Clockmaking of the City of London as well on behalf of themselves and many hundred Artists of your Maj^{tys} antient Company of Clockmakers London as of all others of that Trade within your Maj^{tys} Domin$^{ns.}$

"Sheweth,—That whereas one Charles Clay, of Stockton in the County of York, Watchmaker hath presented his Petition to your Maj^{ty} Praying a Patent for the term of 14 Years for the sole making, using, and selling within your Maj^{tys} Dominions of a small portable Machine, which he alledges repeats the hours upon and quarters upon one or more bells by Changes or Tunes from the communication of a pocket Watch, without fixing the same on the Fuzee of the said Watch or any way obstructing or hindering its motion, and of any other of the like nature or Use proceeding from his Invention which he affirms to be new, And your Maj^{ty} having been pleased to refer his said Petition to Mr. Attorney Gener^{ll} who hath reported in favour of the said Charles Clay.

"And your Pet^{rs} humbly conceiving the said Machine is not a new invention and that a Patent for the same will be prejudicial and inconvenient to the Public both at home and abroad as they can make appear, if your Maj^{ty} will be graciously pleased to vouchsafe them a hearing as your Predecess^{rs} have indulged them upon like unreasonable applications for such Patents. Wherefore your Pet^{rs} most humbly beseech your Maj^{ty} to be graciously pleased to hear what Reasons by themselves and Councill they have to offer against a Patent for the said Mr. Clay's Machine.

"And your Pet^{rs} as in duty bound shall ever pray &c.

"Signed by order of the Pet^{rs} this 8th day of Aprill 1717 in the 3rd year of your Maj^{ys} Reign by Fra. Speidell, Clerk of the said Company.

"SOME REASONS AGAINST PASSING A PATENT FOR CHARLES CLAY'S PRETENDED NEW INVENTION.

"That Mr. Clay's Machine is not a new Invention may appear from the following Reasons:—

"1st.—It being only a pockett watch, and the work of a repeating watch or clock that have communication one with the other and repeats the Houres & Quarters upon one Bell, or upon more Bells, by changes or tunes,

"2nd.—Watches have been made time out of mind and are therefore not his Invention and the Repeating Watch or Clock, has been made in great numbers and by variety of Ways and Motions; Repeating the Houres & Quarters on one Bell or upon more Bells by Changes or Tunes as the Maker thought fitt, and have been made by most of the Watchmakers & Clockmakers in London, and all over England between 30 & 40 yeares last past and therefore cannot be his invention. Now Mr. Clay alledges his invention is from the communication of a pockett watch without taking off the outward case or fixing the same on the Fuzee of the said watch or any way obstructing or hindering its motion.

"All the Repeating Pockett Watches or Clocks that have been hitherto made have had the work of a pockett watch, and the work of a Repeating pockett watch made to them; and those two separate pieces of work have communication one with the other, so that they do not interfere or obstruct one the other; And are so well and artificially contriv'd that they are no bigger & as portable as an ordinary pockett watch; and less trouble than Mr. Clay's Machine, and are not of his Invention; But he has rather borrowed or taken his Machine from them; his, having the same works that are in them.

"All Table repeating Clocks have two separate pieces of work to them, the one to show the hour and minute and any other motion that the maker thinks fitt to make to them, and is called the going or watch part, and the other is called the striking or repeating part that strikes the houres and repeats the quarters and if required are made to play severall Tunes on Bells to great perfection and have communication one with the other so that they do not obstruct or hinder one the other, as most gentlemen by experience have found that have bought them.

"3rd.—Had Mr. Clay been better acquainted with the many new inventions and improvements that have been made by members of the Clockmakers' Company in Watches & Clocks, and the many and various ways of communicating the severall parts of work one with the other within 40 years past which has made their work famous through most parts of the world, yet none of them ever had a Patent for the greatest Invention they have made, Mr. Clay would have been so modest as not to desire a patent for what he has now done, since what has been done before apparently exceed his.

"If this Patent should pass it would create great disturbance and Law suits between the Patentee and the other workmen of London, and all over the King's Dominions; And it is impossible to see at present the mischief it may do. And every man that makes the least alteration for the time to come, that has not been done his way before will think himself entitled to a Patent as much as Mr. Clay was for his; and then Patents will soon be innumerable as the alterations have been within 40 years past."

The following Letter was received by the Company, intimating that upon the Attorney-General's report, a Warrant had been prepared for the King's signature for passing Clay's Patent:—

"Whitehall *6th June 1717.*

"Sir,—In pursuance of a Report from the Attorney General in favour of Charles Clay, who pretends to have invented a Machine, that repeats hours and quarters from the communication with a pocket Watch.

a Warrant is prepared for His Majesty's signature for the passing of a Patent to secure to the said Charles Clay the benefit of his said invention, for fourteen years pursuant to the Statute in that behalf, but there lying also in this office a petition of the Master and Company of the Clockmakers against the said invention, My Lord Sunderland being desirous that if they have any further objections against the said patent than what they produced to the Attorney General, they might have an opportunity of setting them forth, will delay offering the said warrant to be signed till they have been heard before his Majesty's Privy Council, I have therefore transmitted the said petition of the Company of Clockmakers to the Clerk of the Council in waiting and give you notice of it (being informed it was brought by you to the Secretary's office) that you may acquaint the persons concerned therewith, to the end they may apply to the Council Office for a hearing, otherwise it will be unreasonable to delay passing of the patent above mentioned.

"Your most obedient humble Servant

"CH. DELAFAYE."

The Master, Wardens and Assistants immediately petitioned the Lords of the Privy Council to be further heard against the proposed Patent. And at a Meeting of the Council, held on the 15th of July, it was determined to refer the matter to a Committee of the whole Council to hear objections against the Patent, and to report their opinion thereon.

The Report being unfavorable, the Patent was not granted. The opposition cost the Company £74 17s. 11d.

"1719. December 7. The Master having reported to this Court that Mr. Clay had petitioned his Majesty for a rehearing of his affair in order to obtain a Patent for his pretended new invention, and that he had caused a Petition to be lodged at the Council Office at the Cockpit in opposition to Mr. Clay's, This Court did approve thereof and doth Order that all proper means be used by this Court to hinder the said Clay's Petition from taking effect."

No further steps, however, were taken by Mr. Clay, and the subject dropped.

"1729. January 19. Upon reading a Petition of John Hoddle and John Stafford, Watch Engravers, on behalf of themselves and the rest of the Watch Engravers, setting forth that one Mr. Griliat is upon a project of stamping Dial Plates for Watches which, if carried on, will be very destructive to the business of Watch Engraving:—It was upon the question put, voted and resolved that this Court will not only discourage the said undertaking themselves, but will also use their utmost endeavours to persuade others of the trade to discourage the said undertaking.[1]

[1] Company's Journal IV,

"1755. March 6. This Court was called to consider of a Patent lately applied for by Joseph Bosley, Watchmaker, of Leadenhall Street and said to be for an improvement in the making of Watches.

"Resolved,—That the Master and Wardens be desired to call to them such of the Assistants as they think fit, and enquire into the proceedings relating to it, and take proper measures to prevent it being carried into operation, and the Renter Warden to defray the charges of such an application."[1]

The Patent was granted by His Majesty March 1, 1755.

"1st.—For increasing the number of teeth in small pinions throughout the whole movement of repeating and other Watches, The pinions consequently become larger and the wheel that leads them goes farther from the centre, A wheel and pinion more than commonly used, is necessary to prevent the Watch going down before the usual time, but each wheel leading its pinion so much farther from the centre lessens the friction. The balance wheel goes the contrary way.

"2nd.—A new-invented slide, which slide has no wheel attached to it. The Index turns upon a brass socket, and points to an arch of a circle, divided with the word faster on one end, and the word slower on the other, and the Index may be made with a cock to keep it down, or with screws or with springs."[2]

"1755. April 7. The Renter Warden was desired to buy one of the Watches made according to the new Patent."[3]

IMPORTATION AND EXPORTATION, FALSE MARKING AND ENGRAVING, HALL-MARKING, ETC., ETC.

IN dealing with this branch of the subject, it must be premised that it is not within the scope of the present work to enter upon an inquiry as to the Trade generally, or the development of the "Arts or Mysteries" embraced within the

---

[1] Company's Journal IV.
[2] Abridgments of specifications of Patents relating to Watches, &c., 1858, p. 3.
[3] Company's Journal IV.

sphere of the Company's oversight, but rather to record the action taken by the Court of Assistants in the interest of the public, to prevent the sale of articles of inferior workmanship at home, and to prohibit the importation of foreign goods of a like character, which, in addition to bearing the name of some celebrated English Watch or Clockmaker, also had counterfeit Goldsmiths' Hall-marks, and were offered to the public as of English manufacture.

In the Chapter on Searches, it has been shewn that from a very early period of their existence the Company availed themselves of every opportunity to protect the public and the trade from the fraudulent and deceitful practices of some of the more unscrupulous workers in the Art, whether English or Foreigners, who were to be found within the limits of the jurisdiction assigned by the Charter.

There were, however, other methods by which the public were defrauded and the English maker injured, to which much attention was devoted. Amongst these may be enumerated the exportation of English Cases, Dial Plates, and other parts of Watches and Clocks, to be fitted to Foreign Works of inferior quality, and re-imported as of English manufacture; the pirating of the names of well-known makers, the fraudulent imitation of the English Goldsmiths' marks, Hall-marks, etc., etc.

The entries in the Company's Records concerning these and similar proceedings, which brought great discredit upon English work and great distress upon the workmen, are very numerous, and too lengthy to be given *in extenso*. Moreover, owing to the close connection which these matters of trade regulation necessarily have with each other, and the circumstance that the Company, in many instances, dealt with several of them by the same operation, it is impossible so to classify them as to shew separately the results obtained in respect of each grievance for which a remedy was sought. It has therefore been deemed desirable to arrange chronologically, and in a condensed form, some of the proceedings of the Court of Assistants having reference to these objects.

"1657. October 1. Mr. John Smith was fined and paid 10s. for putting Estme Hubert's name upon a watch.'

' Company's Journal I.

"1682. November 16. The Company of Goldsmiths having lately convened before them Mr. Nathaniel Delaunder Watch Case Maker upon pretence of a Gold Case made by him which upon their Assay[1] made is found not to be of the fineness appointed for Goldsmiths' work by an Act made in the 18th year of Queen Elizabeth (which was Anno 1576, entitled an Act for Reformation of Abuses in Goldsmiths[2]) this Court was called only upon this occasion, and it being judged that not only Mr. Delaunder but the whole Company, and especially Case Makers and small Clockmakers, were or would be concerned in this matter;—the sense and resolution of the Court was that Mr. Jeremy Gregory (who is of the Company and Court of the Goldsmiths) should endeavour that the Goldsmiths would admit of some persons of this as a Committee to meet with some of their Company to discourse them, and if they can to take them off from any their intended prosecution by making them sensible of the great unfitness inconveniency and insufficiency of their works for the end they are made, if they should be made of the fineness in the aforesaid Act, which is conceived relates only to Abuses in Goldsmiths not Clockmakers or any professing any branch of that Art. A Committee was thereupon nominated 'to apply to such Counsell learned in the Laws and acquainted with the customs and usages of the City and Corporation therein as they might think fit for advice. The charge thereof to be borne out of the Company's stock.'"[3]

In January, 1697, a Bill was ordered to be brought into Parliament permitting the exportation of Watches, Sword-hilts, etc. The Company thereupon considered the desirability of obtaining the insertion of a Clause in the Bill, for prohibiting the exportation of Dial Plates and empty Boxes and Cases for Clocks and Watches, and for preventing other than Freemen of London from putting "London" on their Watches and Clocks, and authorized the Master and Wardens to employ legal assistance to accomplish these objects.

---

[1] According to Chaffers, the first instance on record of an attempt to reduce Goldsmiths' work to a certain standard was in the reign of Henry III, A.D. 1238. The assaying of the precious metals was a privilege conferred upon the Goldsmiths' Company by a Statute of the 28th Edward I, cap. 20, A.D. 1300, by which it was enacted that no Goldsmith should use any gold which was worse than the touch (or assay) of Paris, or any silver inferior to the alloy of *Sterling*; that no vessels of gold or silver were to be delivered from the hands of the workman until they had been assayed by the Wardens of the Craft, and marked with the leopard's head. The Wardens were empowered to go from shop to shop and see if the gold was good, and, if not, they were to break it up, and such gold was forfeited to the King.—(*Vide* "Hall-marks on Plate," by W. Chaffers, F.S.A., 1863.)
The ordinances of the Goldsmiths' Company for 1336 direct the following marks to be put upon all assayed work:—1. The Goldsmith's Mark (his initials). 2. The Assay Mark (probably a letter of the alphabet). 3. The Mark of Goldsmiths' Hall (a leopard's head, crowned). By an Act of Parliament, 17th Edward IV, cap. 1, 1477, the standard of gold wares was fixed at 18-carats, and silver at the same as sterling; and in 1576, the 18th of Elizabeth, cap. 15, it was fixed at 22-carats. In 1798, by an Act of Parliament, 38th Geo. III, cap. 69, the standard of gold wares was again fixed at 22-carats.
[2] 18th Elizabeth, cap. xv. By this Act, it is enacted that no Goldsmith's work should be less in fineness for gold than "twenty-two *carrottes*, and that he use noe Sother, Amell or other stuffinges whatsoever in anye of their workes more then ys necessarie for the fynyshing of the same . . . . for the ownce of Golde." For silver, the standard of fineness is set, at not less than "11 ownces 2 penye waightes . . . . for every Pounde waighte of Plate or Wares of Sylver."
[3] Company's Journal II.

In February following they submitted Clauses for the purpose, and also a Clause requiring all makers of Clocks and Watches to put their own names, and the City, Town, or place, of which they were free, on articles of their manufacture.

Reasons in favor of the Clauses were approved and adopted, and directed to be distributed to Members of Parliament.

The Company were successful in their endeavours, as may be seen from the Extract from the Act, 9th and 10th William III, cap. xxviii, quoted in the Advertisement issued by them in December 1777.—(*Vide* pages 260-1.)

In April, 1699, the Court directed an abstract of this Act to be prepared and printed, and to be distributed to the Trade for their information.

In July, 1704, it was reported by the Master that certain persons at Amsterdam were in the habit of putting the names of Tompion, Windmills, Quare, Cabrier, Lamb, and other well-known London makers, on their works, and selling them as English. A Committee was thereupon appointed to determine what course could be pursued for the prevention of such abuses, but the results of their exertions do not appear.

On the 6th June, 1709, the Court were informed by the Master that he had been desired by the Lords Commissioners for Trade and Plantations to submit reasons for insisting upon the French King taking off the prohibition on the importation of Clocks and Watches into France. The reasons so prepared by him were read, and after modification approved and ordered to be signed by the Clerk and presented.

In March, 1717, a Bill was before Parliament to prevent the clandestine running of goods, and it is recorded in the journals of the House of Lords that the Clockmakers' Company promoted the insertion of a Clause therein relating to the exportation of Clocks and Watches, which Clause was opposed by the Goldsmiths' Company. The Bill, however, does not seem to have become Law that year.

In January, 1718, there is another entry in the Court Minutes upon the same subject, which shows that the object of the Clause was to get rid of the Oath required to be made on exporting Watches as to the quality of the gold or silver used therein. The Bill imposing the Oath was read and debated, and eventually a modified Clause, as framed by the Goldsmiths' Company, was adopted. The Act became Law in 1719 (5th George I, cap. xi.), but, as it contains no Clause to the effect desired, the Company's efforts do not appear to have been successful.

In July, 1777, Mr. Charles Cabrier, having obtained evidence that his name had been falsely used upon foreign Watches, brought the subject before the Court, when the following entry was made in the Minutes :—

"1777. July 7. Mr. Charles Cabrier attended and acquainted the Court that he had entered prosecutions against sundry persons for putting his name to Watches which they had made up without his knowledge or consent, praying their assistance and advice, which was unanimously promised whenever he applied again, if he would indemnify the Company from every expense that may arise from the prosecution of this business." [1]

The following paragraph upon the subject appears in the Annual Register, 3rd December, 1777 :—

"Was tried before Lord Mansfield in the Court of King's Bench, a remarkable case the first instance of its kind, Cabrier against Anderson, for putting his (Cabrier's) name to 5 watches made by the Defendant, and thereby hurting the reputation of the plaintiff. A verdict was given for £100, being £20 for each watch agreeable to an Act of Parliament of William III." [2]

Upon the result of Mr. Cabrier's case being made known to the Company, a special meeting of the Court was convened for the purpose of determining as to the desirability of issuing some public notification, by way of caution, to offenders, and for the protection of the purchaser. The following is the Minute in relation thereto :—

"1777. December 18. The Master acquainted the Court that the occasion of the present Meeting being summoned was in consequence of an application made to him by several of the Business in order to consider of some method to prevent the illicit practices carried on by sundry persons of putting the names of respectable Watchmakers without their consent on Watches not made by them. Ordered that the Clerk do read the Bye Laws which concern the manufacturing of Watches and the Act of Parliament of the 9th and 10th of William the Third. On a motion it was unanimously resolved that the Bye Law page 23,[3] together with the extract from the Act of the 9th & 10th of William the Third, Chapter 28 and paragraph the 2nd be printed in the Gazette and in the several Public Morning and Evening Papers with a declaration that the Court of Assistants are determined to prosecute all persons offending against the same." [4]

---

[1] Company's Journal IV.
[3] Bye Law 46.
[2] This is the Act before referred to.
[4] Company's Journal IV.

In consequence thereof the following advertisement was published :—

"London *18th December 1777*.

"Whereas the Worshipful Company of Clockmakers of London have lately discovered that for a long time past illicit practices have been made use of by several persons here, in making up base and bad Watches and putting thereon the names of the most respectable and known London Watchmakers to the great prejudice and discredit of the said Watchmakers and contrary to an Act of Parliament and Bye Law of the said Company. Therefore that no Person or persons may hereafter plead ignorance of the said Act and Bye Law, the said Company have hereby caused the said Act and Bye Law to be published with notice that if any person or persons shall hereafter be found offending therein, that the said Act and Bye Law shall be put in force against such offender or offenders by the said Company.

"Signed by order of Court

"THO. HUGHES, Clerk.

"THE BYE LAW.

"Item,—Whereas there hath formerly been divers and great abuses offered to divers expert and sufficient workmen in the said Art or Trade of Clockmaking, as well by importing from beyond the Seas as by making within the Realm faulty and deceitful work upon which have been set the names or marks of some other workmen who made it not, to the discredit and disgrace of them the said wronged workmen, whereby the others dishonesty and deceit is not discovered.

"It is therefore ordained that whosoever hereafter shall be found by the Master Wardens and Assistants of the Fellowship of Clockmakers, or by any of them or their lawful deputy or deputies, to have imported such work from beyond the Seas falsely marked to sell or exchange by way of merchandizing, or to have set any man's name or mark upon any work made within this kingdom or dominion of Wales other than the name or mark of the true maker or finisher thereof, shall forfeit the said work or works to the King's Majesty, his heirs and successors and also be fined to the use of the said Master, Wardens and Fellowship of Clockmakers for every time so offending, and for every piece of work which he or they shall be found to offend in the sum of Forty shillings or other greater or lesser sum according to the nature and quality of the said offence, to be taxed by the Master Wardens and Court of Assistants of the said Company.

"THE ACT OF PARLIAMENT.

" And whereas great quantities of empty boxes, cases and dial-plates for Clocks and Watches have been exported without their movements, and in foreign parts made up with bad movements, thereon some London Watchmakers Names engraven, and so are sold abroad for English work; and also there have been the like ill practices in England by divers persons, as well by some professing the Art of Clock and Watch making as others ignorant therein, in putting counterfeit names as also the names of the most known London Watch makers on their bad Clocks and Watches, to the great prejudice of the buyers and the disreputation of the said Art at home and abroad. For the prevention therefore of all such ill practices for the future.

"Be it enacted by the Authority aforesaid that no Person or persons whatsoever shall after the said 24th day of June export or endeavour to export, or send out of this kingdom of England, dominion of Wales or Town of Berwick-upon-Tweed any outward or inward box case or dial-plate of Gold Silver, Brass or other metal for Clock or Watch without the movement in or with every such box case or dial-plate made up fit for use, with the Clock or Watchmaker's name engraven thereon, nor any person whatsoever after the said 24 day June shall make up or cause to be made up any Clock or Watch without engraving or putting or causing to be engraven or put his or her own name and place of abode, or freedom, and no other name or place on every Clock or Watch he or she shall so make up or caused to be made up under the penalty of forfeiting every such empty box case and dial-plate, clock and watch not made up and engraven as aforesaid and also for each and every such offence the sum of Twenty pounds, one Moiety whereof to be to His Majesty his heirs and successors, and the other Moiety shall be to him, her or them that shall sue for the same in any of His Majesty's Courts of Record by Action of debt, bill, plaint or information, wherein no essoin, protection or Wager of Law shall be allowed, or more than one imparlance; anything herein contained or any Law or Statute to the contrary thereof in anywise notwithstanding."

Published in the *Gazette* 30 December in the *General Advertiser* 23 December, in the *Morning Chronicle* 5 January; in the *London Evening Post* 8 January 1778.

An influential meeting of the trade was held in October, 1780, at which the subject of the grievances sustained by the English makers was discussed, and a Deputation appointed to confer with the Court of Assistants. The Court received them on the 6th November following, when they pointed out the great grievances sustained in the Watchmaking profession by the importation of foreign Watches, and requested the Court's advice and assistance in putting a stop to the same. Several Clauses in the Charter and Bye-Laws relative to foreign Watches were read, and it was determined by the Court to carry into execution the powers vested in them for preventing the clandestine importation of foreign Watches.

On the 21st May, 1781, an advertisement was ordered to be published in the *Daily Advertiser, Morning Chronicle,* and *Morning Herald,* in the following words:—

"CLOCKMAKERS COMPANY.

"Whereas the Company of Clockmakers of the City of London are assured that for a considerable time past great numbers of Watches and Clocks have been illegally brought into this kingdom from France, Geneva and other foreign parts, to the great detriment of His Majesty's subjects, and which being contrary to the Charter and Bye Laws of this Company and to the Law of this kingdom, The Master, Wardens and Court of Assistants do hereby give notice that if any person or persons shall hereafter be found offending, that the said Charter and Bye Laws shall strictly be put in force against any such offender or offenders. And the said Master, Wardens and Court of Assistants do hereby further offer a reward of Ten Guineas, to be paid on conviction, to any one who shall give information to them or their Clerk of the person or persons carrying on such illegal trade.'

"Signed by order of the Court,

"THO. HUGHES, Clerk."

On the 3rd June, 1782, another Deputation from the Trade attended, and solicited the assistance of the Court to enable them to pursue some methods for putting a stop to the great number of Watches illegally brought into the Kingdom from foreign parts.

A Committee was appointed to consult with the Deputation on the most proper methods to be taken for such purpose.

On the 11th December, 1786, the Master reported that some members of the Trade had informed him that they had received a letter containing seven questions, proposed by the Lords of Council for Trade, which related to opening the trade with France, and desired their answers on the 13th instant, and that they requested the assistance of the Company in framing proper answers to the said questions. A conference was therefore held with a Deputation who were in attendance, at which the questions were fully debated, and answers thereto agreed upon, as follow :—

"Question 1.—Do you think that upon an equal duty of Ten per cent. or lower, the Trade may be opened with France, in the articles of Clocks and Watches to the advantage of this country; and will you state your opinions respecting those made of Gold, Silver and Metal distinctly?

"Ans.—We think it would be of disadvantage respecting Clocks, as well as Gold, Silver and Metal Watches.

"Question 2.—Upon what circumstances do you found your opinion?

"Ans.—We think the Trade to France would be disadvantageous to us because first, in the article of Clocks, we cannot manufacture them so cheap as the French, from the different principle on which they are made in the two countries, notwithstanding the same principles are known in both, the French trusting only to appearance, while the English depend upon the performance of theirs, which insures our Trade in Clocks; the Gold Watches would be disadvantageous to us because we cannot make them so cheap as the French, from the standard of our Gold and the quality of our workmanship, both of which we think necessary to continue in their present state, to maintain our credit, which we consider as the principal, and perhaps the only support to

---

' Company's Journal V.

this branch of Trade. The Metal and Silver Watches not being of the same general use in France as in other Countries, and we believe scarcely used at all, we do not foresee any probability of those Watches being introduced from this country into France; for although we think we can make them as cheap as they can, yet we do not think that the appearance or quality of our cheap Silver Watches would induce the French to purchase ours, when they can have Gold ones (or Silver or Metal ones if they prefer them) of their own.

"We therefore think it of the greatest consequence to the manufacture of this Country to preserve the difference as great as possible betwixt the real and ideal difference of this branch of Trade in the two Countries, which we apprehend could not be united in one of the branches of Gold, Silver, or Metal Watches without endangering the uniting the whole, which could not, from the above reasons, but be the ruin of this branch of manufacture.

"Question 3.—To what Countries do you now export Clocks and Watches?

"Ans.—We export Clocks and Watches to all commercial Countries except France; and particularly to Holland, Flanders, Germany, Sweden, Denmark, Norway, Russia, Spain, Portugal, Italy, Turkey, East and West Indies, China, &c.

"Question 4.—Do you not suppose that the Clocks and Watches you export to Flanders are conveyed from thence into parts of France?

"Ans.—By enquiry of Merchants who have resided in Flanders, and who now trade considerably to that Country, we find that the Clocks and Watches exported from hence to Flanders, are not any of them afterwards conveyed into France; but on the other hand France, Geneva and Switzerland, have the whole of the Flanders trade in Gold Watches, while ours is confined wholly to the Silver Trade; some of our Manufacturers have made attempts to introduce our Gold Watches into that Country, but without success, having been underworked by the French, Genevans &c.

"Question 5.—In what does the export of Watches chiefly consist, in those of Gold, Silver or Metal, and to what Countries are they exported respectively?

"Ans.—To East India, chiefly Gold, to China, chiefly Metal, to Holland, many Gold, few Metal and a great many Silver; to other Countries, some of each, principally Silver, though to Spain, a great many valuable Gold Watches accompany the Silver ones.

"Question 6.—What number of Watches do you conceive to be the whole of the exports to different parts of the World?

"Ans.—It is very difficult to determine the number of Watches exported from this Country, but by the nearest calculation we are able to make we presume about Eighty Thousand per annum.

"Question 7.—Are there many French Watches brought into this Country?

"Ans.—Great quantities of Gold Watches very detrimental to the Manufacture of this Kingdom, which numbers are greatly increased by the late duty of eight shillings per oz. on wrought Gold plate.

"The Answers being thus agreed to, it was determined that they should be prefaced by the following resolution viz. At a Special Court of the Master, Wardens and Assistants of the Worshipful Company of Clockmakers holden on Monday the 11th of December 1786. It was resolved unanimously that the following answers to the several questions delivered by order of the Lords of the Committee of Council for Trade to Mess[rs.] Vulliamy, Upjohn, Jackson and Potter for their answers in writing, be fairly copied and signed by the Master and Wardens of the said Company, and presented by the aforesaid Gentlemen to the Lords of the Council on behalf of the trade at large, which being done the above Gentlemen concluded as follows.

" We therefore pray your Lordships will, in consideration of the above reasons, continue the duty upon French Clocks and Watches as it has hitherto subsisted between the two Countries, and, if we might be permitted, we would endeavour on a future day, to propose a plan to prevent the illicit trade herein complained of."

On the 8th January, 1787, it was reported to the Court that the Questions and Answers had been submitted to the Lords of the Committee of Council for Trade, who received them favourably, and intimated that they would be happy to consider any plan the Company and the Trade might submit, which they would communicate to the Treasury, to whose department the matter appertained.

On the 5th February following, the Court, after further consultation with a Committee of the Trade, unanimously resolved, that, in their opinion, it would be advantageous to the Trade in general to enforce the Duty upon all Clocks and Watches imported into this Kingdom.

A Committee was appointed to endeavour to carry the resolution into execution.

The Committee met on the 9th February, and determined that representations should be made to the Lords of the Treasury, and also to the Lords of the Committee of Council for Trade, desiring that the Company might, agreeably to their Charter, put a mark upon all Foreign Clocks and Watches, to certify that they had paid the Duty.

At a subsequent Meeting of the Committee, a Report to the Court of Assistants was agreed upon, which was adopted by the Court on the 19th February, when the following Representation to the Lords of the Committee of Council for Trade was ordered to be presented :—

" *To the Lords of the Committee of Council for Trade.*
" My Lords,

" The Master, Wardens, and Assistants of the Fellowship of the Art or Mystery of Clockmakers of the City of London, beg permission to offer the copy of a Representation drawn up for the purpose of presenting to the Lords Commissioners of His Majesty's Treasury, stating certain grievances their Trade labours under; and humbly to request your Lordships' assistance in obtaining the desired redress.

"In the first instance, we humbly conceive it our duty to inform your Lordships, that great numbers of Foreign Clocks and Watches have been, for some time past, clandestinely brought into this country, and exposed to sale, which numbers are daily increasing, to the great detriment of His Majesty's Revenue, and very injurious to the manufacture of those articles in this country; for which reason we presume it has become highly necessary to enforce the Duties which are by Law prescribed, on the importation of such goods, and which are at this time generally evaded.

"By inquiry at the Custom-house, it appears very few, if any, such Foreign Clocks and Watches brought into this country, are there entered; and from the facility of introducing such goods, by reason of their being so very portable, it will be difficult to oblige the importers of such articles to make regular entries of the same.

"Since the Treaty with France has been generally known to the public, the Clock and Watchmaking branches are thought to be in most danger of suffering: this opinion we consider as founded upon such just grounds, and is of so much consequence to our Manufacture, that it requires the most serious attention of the Legislature; for if those Foreign articles should continue to be brought into this country without paying the said Duties, it must be inevitable ruin to our Manufacture of Clocks and Watches, as such illicit trade will increase, when the intercourse between the two countries becomes more frequent, without any method of discovery.

"With submission to your Lordships, we are of opinion, if the following Regulations were to take place, they would in a great measure remedy the evils complained of; be truly beneficial to the Revenue, and of important service to this Manufacture:

"The Master, Wardens, &c., of the said Company for the time being, to be empowered to strike or affix a certain mark on all Foreign Clocks and Watches imported; and if found necessary or expedient, to be farther empowered to receive the Duties thereon, for the benefit of His Majesty's Revenue, under such restrictions and limitations as your Lordships may hereafter prescribe.

"That it shall not be lawful for any person to expose such articles to sale, without the said Duty-mark being first struck or affixed thereto, and the Duties paid thereon, under the penalty of   or forfeiture of the goods.

"If such Clocks and Watches shall at any time be brought to the Clock or Watchmaker, or any other person, to repair, it shall not be lawful for them to amend or repair the same, until the said Duty-mark is struck or affixed thereto, under the penalty of

"The present possessors of such Clocks and Watches, to be allowed a convenient time to bring or send such articles to the place appointed, to be there marked, in order to distinguish they were imported previous to such Regulations, or that their Clock and Watchmaker may be allowed to get such goods marked for the said time, free of expence.

"If it should be considered such Regulation would affect Foreigners travelling in this country, the remedy is easy, by giving power to the said Masters and Wardens to grant Licenses to Foreigners to get such Watches repaired during their stay here, for their own use; but it shall not be lawful for them to expose to sale such Clock or Watch, until it has received the Duty-mark, and paid the Duty thereon.

"A given power to the Master, to change the said mark once a year, or oftener, if found necessary, and to appoint Deputies in different districts, for the purposes before mentioned, subject to the control of the Revenue Officers in that district.

"Authority to seize all such Foreign articles before named, if it shall appear such Duty-mark is copied or imitated; which goods shall be forfeited for the benefit of the State; and provision made to free the Company of any expence attending the execution of such Regulations.

"As the Duty on the articles above mentioned is laid *ad valorem*, it is humbly presumed that the Clockmakers' Company are more competent to detect any fraud that may be offered to the Revenue, by an under value of such goods, than any other persons, as their experience in the various branches of this Manufacture, renders it wholly improbable that such frauds can or may be put in practice.

"The disadvantage the manufacture of this country labours under, in the article of Watches, is great; the Duty of Eight Shillings per ounce on our wrought Gold Plate, gives the Foreign article the superiority in our market, which we consider as a substantial reason why the Duty on such articles should be enforced, particularly as the great influx of Foreign Watches herein complained of, consists chiefly of Gold; farther, it appears reasonable to us, a countervailing Duty of Eight Shillings per ounce should be laid on all Foreign-wrought Gold, and Sixpence on Silver Plate, as an addition to the reduced Duty of $27\frac{1}{2}$ per cent.

"The foregoing Regulations, if considered as calculated to remedy the evils complained of, could not be offensive to the Court of France, as we understand they are in the practice of a similar mode of marking all Foreign Clocks and Watches brought into that country.

"The following Extract from the Ordinances made in pursuance of the Charter of this Company, ratified and confirmed by

THOMAS LORD COVENTRY, Lord Keeper of the Great Seal; Sir THOMAS RICHARDSON, Knight, Lord Chief Justice of the King's Bench; and Sir ROBERT HEATH, Knight, Lord Chief Justice of the Common Pleas:

"SHEWETH,

"Article 34th. 'Item, It is also ordained, that all Clocks, Watches, Larums, and all Cases for Clocks, Watches, and Larums, plaine or graven, made of Mettals, or of any other nature, condition, or fashion whatsoever, or any other work or works, as Sun-dials, Mathematical Instruments, or any other work peculiarly belonging to the Art of Clockmaking, be it for great or small, brought into the Realm of England, or Dominion of Wales, from the parts beyond the seas, to be put to sale, shall be first customed, and then brought to the Hall of the said Clockmakers of London, or their meeting-place, and there presented to the Master, Wardens, and Assistants, to be viewed and approved of, according to the said Letters Patent of Incorporation ; and upon the approbation of the Master, Wardens, and Assistants, or the great part of them, shall, according to the usual custom of the said Company in such cases, receive the mark or allowance of the said Company, before the same be offer'd or put to sale, upon pain of such reasonable penalties as by the said Master, Wardens, and Court of Assistants, or the more part of them (whereof the Master, and one of the Wardens for the time being, to be two), shall in such case appoint and ordain.'

"Notwithstanding the powers granted by the above-recited Ordinance, we find it totally ineffectual to answer the purposes intended, as it is thereby directed, such goods shall be first customed, which, for the foregoing reasons, and the want of regulations to enforce obedience to the same, such Law never has or can be enforced without the interposition of the Legislature.

"From all which premises we would conclude by observing, with humble submission to your Lordships, that the manufacture of Clocks and Watches in this country, is entitled to every possible encouragement and protection, as a very great part of its value consists in labour, and appertains to the employing many thousand artists in its various branches, to the great benefit and advantage of the State.

"The great attention your Lordships constantly pay to the manufactures and commercial interest of this country, emboldens us to hope, this our Representation will be considered as entitled to your Lordships' countenance and support."

An interview with the Secretary of the Treasury, on the subject of the Representation, was afterwards had by a Deputation of the Court, who were informed that Mr. Pitt would consider it.

In September, 1789, a Committee was appointed to present a Memorial to the Commissioners of Customs, on the subject of the evil effects upon the Revenue, and to the English Manufacturers, caused by the illicit importation of Foreign Clocks and Watches, and the following Memorial was adopted by the Court, but the desired relief was not obtained:—

"*The Memorial of the Master, Wardens, and Court of Assistants of the Worshipful Company of Clockmakers:*
"SHEWETH,
"That your Memorialists have certain information, that a great number of Foreign Gold Watches have of late years been imported into this country, though very few have paid the duty prescribed by Law; and that a considerable number of such Watches were lately seized, and taken to His Majesty's Warehouse at the Custom House.

"'That this practice is carried on to such an extent, as must materially affect the Revenue, and prove greatly injurious to your Memorialists, and others concerned in the Watch Manufacture.

"Your Memorialists beg leave to observe that the Manufacture already labours under very great disadvantages in this country, from the restraints imposed upon it, and the Duty to which it is liable.

"That the Gold employed in the Cases, is required to be of a standard worth Eighty-one Shillings per ounce, on wrought Gold, whereas the Gold employed by Foreigners is of a quality greatly inferior; pays no Duty in manufacturing; and being rendered much harder by the great quantity of alloy, need not be of that substance requisite for Cases when made of purer Gold.

"That from these circumstances, they cannot stand the competition with those who have already such great advantages over them; and they have to apprehend, that the evil of which they complain, will, unless checked by a due execution of the Laws, increase to the utter ruin of your Memorialists, and others concerned in the Manufacture; by which Government will suffer a considerable loss of Revenue, not only from the Importation Duty being evaded, but also by the loss of the Duty on wrought Plate. This country will lose a valuable Manufacture, which now employs a vast number of hands, and many thousand persons will be reduced to poverty, be deprived of all means of supporting themselves and families, and become burthensome to the community."

"They therefore humbly pray, that your Honors will please to protect the Watch Manufacture, by carrying into effect the Laws, and by prosecuting to condemnation, the present and all future seizures.

"And your Memorialists, as in duty bound, will ever pray."

In the year 1790, the aid of the Company was invoked by the Trade for the purpose of obtaining an amendment of the Act of Parliament of the 9th and 10th William III, cap. xxviii, regulating the exportation of Watches, manufactured Silver, etc., which the Trade were of opinion, though adapted to the infancy of the craft, was not sufficiently stringent in its provisions; and they desired a considerable increase in the penalty for putting false names on Watches and Clocks, viz., £100 instead of £20, and costs, with forfeiture of the goods; they likewise suggested that a Public Register should be kept by the Company, in which the names and places of abode of all Clock and Watchmakers in Great Britain should be entered alphabetically, a number being assigned to each, which should be and remain his or their distinguishing mark, a penalty being enacted in case of non-registration.

These propositions received the careful attention of the Court, but in the result they advised the Trade that the relief sought was to be obtained rather by the strict enforcement of the existing Law than in any increase of Penalties or keeping of Registers, whilst to enable them to compete with the foreigner, the standard of gold should be reduced for Watch Cases.

In 1797, it was proposed by Mr. Pitt, then Chancellor of the Exchequer, to impose a Tax on the wearing and use of Watches and Clocks, viz., 2s. 6d. per annum for a Silver or Metal Watch, 10s. for a Gold Watch, and 5s. for every Clock, and the Trade again approached the Company, by whom a Representation on their behalf was prepared and submitted to the Minister, in which the workers in the Art in the Metropolis are stated to number 20,000 persons. The duty on Wrought Gold is quoted in this document as 16s., and Silver 1s., per oz., in addition to which License was requisite to enable persons to carry on the trade, for which they paid annually £2 6s. 0d. It was suggested that the Tax, which would be a perpetual yearly expense to the wearers and users of Watches and Clocks, would ruin the trade; and advantage was taken of the opportunity again to insist on the necessity for a reduction of the standard of gold, in Watch Cases, then 22 carats per oz., to 18, or even 14 carats, for which purpose a comparison of the cost of English and Foreign-made Cases was inclosed, viz. :—

"A GOLD CASE MADE IN SWITZERLAND.

	£	s.	d.
2 ozs. of Gold 18 carat fine at 66s. 3d. per oz. ...	6	12	6

"A GOLD CASE MADE IN ENGLAND.

	£	s.	d.
2 ozs. of Gold 22 carat fine at £4. 1s. per oz. ...	8	2	0
Duty 16s	1	12	0
	£9	14	0

" But in addition to the above 15 dwts. of Gold at 18 carat fine, will expend in any manufacture as far as 1 oz. of Standard Gold of 22 carat, the fair statement will stand as under :—

	£	s.	d.
1½ ozs. of Gold, 18 carat fine	4	19	4½

	£	s.	d.
2 ozs. of Gold, 22 carat fine	8	2	0
Duty	1	12	0
	£9	14	0

The Act (37th George III, cap. cviii),[1] notwithstanding the opposition made to it, was passed, only however to be repealed in the year following.

The Court were subsequently favored by Mr. Pitt with several interviews, in which they submitted to him undoubted evidence as to the distressed condition of the trade, in consequence of the passing of the Act, and at one of such interviews they left with him a Memorial which was also accompanied by the following statement, shewing the relative numbers of Gold and Silver Watch Cases marked before and after the passing of the Act.

" The following Account of Cases marked was left with Mr. Pitt, viz. :—

		Number.	Ozs.	Dwts.	Grs.	
" 1796	May	442	522	16	...	Gold Cases.
,,	June	533	661	2	9	,,
,,	July	557	673	16	22	,,
,,	August	603	692	13	4	,,
,,	September	577	653	17	23	,,
,,	October	589	635	14	10	,,
		3,301	3,840	...	20	

		Number.	Ozs.	Dwts.	Grs.	
" 1797	May	318	388	14	8	Gold Cases.
,,	June	302	359	9	15	,,
,,	July	335	360	...	12	,,
,,	August	268	305	13	4	,,
,,	September	168	205	10	14	,,
,,	October	169	206	8	4	,,
		1,560	1,825	16	9	

A pair of Cases is considered as two.

		Number.	Lbs.	Ozs.	Dwts.	
" 1796	May	12,692	1,188	3	19	Silver Cases.
,,	June	16,172	1,447	8	5	,,
,,	July	16,341	1,343	...	18	,,
,,	August	15,358	1,337	8	7	,,
,,	September	16,179	1,342	5	19	,,
,,	October	16,734	1,421	6	12	,,
		93,476	8,080	10	...	

---

[1] Many persons rather than pay the duty had their Gold and Silver Cases melted, and Metal Cases substituted.

THE CLOCKMAKERS' COMPANY. 271

		Number.	Lbs.	Ozs.	Dwts.	
"1797	May	14,801	1,222	4	7	Silver Cases.
,,	June	13,608	1,275	7	3	,,
,,	July ...	13,198	1,078	10	7	,,
,,	August ...	12,389	1,008	3	2	,,
,,	September	10,780	985	8	7	,,
,,	October...	9,543	783	10	13	,,
		74,319	6,354	7	19	

Upon the strong remonstrance of the Company, backed by Petitions from the Provincial Centres of the Trade— Coventry, Bristol, Leicester, Prescot, Newcastle-on-Tyne, Liverpool, Derby, Edinburgh, etc., and from the Workmen employed in its different branches in the Metropolis, shewing that the Tax had reduced the operatives to the verge of starvation, a Committee of the House of Commons was appointed, who after sitting several days and hearing evidence in support of the Petitions, presented their Report. This was considered by a Committee of the whole House, who on the 23rd March recommended the repeal of the duties, which was effected by the Act, 38th George III, cap. xl; whilst the Company's representations with respect to the duty on Gold and Silver used in Watch Cases were so successful, that in the same year an Act was passed (38th George III, cap. xxiv), by which such duties were wholly repealed. The Court also, doubtless, hailed with satisfaction the passing, during the same session, of the Act, 38th George III, cap. lxix, in which practical effect was given to the opinion they had expressed to the Trade in 1790, as to the necessity for reducing the standard of gold.

By the last-named Act, two standards were permitted to be used, viz., 22 and 18 carats per oz., respectively. This result, however, was not obtained until another forcible Memorial had been submitted to Mr. Pitt.

The combined effects of these Acts, by which the Tax on the manufactured articles and the Duty on the Gold and Silver in the Cases were repealed, and a lower standard of metal introduced, soon exercised a beneficial influence, so much, indeed, that in reply to a memorial from the Trade to the Company in 1802, the Court stated that they had placed them on the best footing to increase the home and foreign consumption.

In October, 1808, the Court appointed another Committee to consider the best means of preventing the practice of pirating names of known makers of Watches and Clocks. In March, 1809, they brought up a Report which was agreed to, and the following Memorial to the Lords of the Treasury and to the Lords of the Committee of Council for Trade, in which their recommendations are embodied, was on the 5th May following adopted by the Court :—

"*The Memorial of the Master, Wardens, and Court of Assistants of the Worshipful Company of Clockmakers of London:*

"HUMBLY SHEWETH,

"That your Memorialists deeply impressed with the just cause of complaints which have been made to them by many of their Members of the present state of the Trade, arising from various innovations which have obtained much to its prejudice, feel themselves called on in duty to state the same for your consideration, in a firm reliance on your Lordships' assistance in procuring for the Trade such relief as Parliament in its wisdom may judge proper to afford.

"Your Memorialists, in proceeding to set forth the evils complained of, conceive it necessary to a clear understanding of a true state of the Trade at this time to take a retrospective view of it, and to trace from their origin in as concise a manner as the subject will admit the causes which have led to its present situation.

"As the Art of making a good Clock or Watch may be justly considered an achievement of human skill and industry superior to many and inferior to none of those mathematical and mechanical professions or arts which tend alike to the advantage of the public and of the individuals engaged in them, and as it is not to be obtained without a considerable period of labour and study being devoted to the attainment of a competent knowledge both of its theory and practice, and as persons brought up to this Trade are in general qualified from their habits and information to perform almost every description of mechanical operation, which has been most fully and incontestibly confirmed by the improvements which have taken place in the Silk, Cotton, Woollen and various other manufactures, by the introduction of machinery, whereby great benefit has accrued to the Nation ; and as most of those improvements have been made by persons brought up to the Trade of Clock and Watchmaking, and as in the construction and reparation of those machines such workmen have been generally employed,—Your Memorialists therefore trust your Lordships will not consider the Watch and Clockmaker in the abstract, but hold in regard the services which he is capable of rendering the community in a more extensive scale, inasmuch as by protecting this class of society a succession of practical and excellent workmen is secured to the kingdom, equally beneficial to arts and manufactures as men engaged in the fisheries and the Coal Trade are to foreign commerce and navigation, to the latter of which the Watch and Clockmaker may be fairly allowed to claim the merit of having introduced considerable facilities by the perfection of Chronometers, whereby the Longitude has been so accurately ascertained, and in the construction whereof the Artists of this Country stand unequalled.

"Your Memorialists, feeling the importance of supporting and encouraging such persons as perfect themselves in the qualifications necessary to the proper exercise of their profession, conceive some particular advantage should be afforded them by the Legislature as a just reward for their expence, labour and study, and that the exclusive right of exercising their own Trade appears to be the most equitable remuneration. That this opinion is well founded has been evinced by the Grant of a Charter for the incorporation of the Trade in the year 1631, thereby acknowledging and confirming the exclusive right of exercising the same to the Members of the Corporation.

"That your Memorialists observe that, in the infancy of this Trade, it was the uniform practice of every Maker to engrave his own name and place of abode upon all the Clocks and Watches he made, which was as natural as it was political, for on the one hand it gave to the public, with the verification of the Maker's own act, a pledge of his honest dealing, and the direct means of redress in the event of misconduct, and on the other it secured to himself the reputation which his works merited, together with the assurance of obtaining benefit by the increasing demand of his productions. This was formerly the state of the Trade, and to which your Memorialists most ardently hope it may again be restored, as far as relates to the mode in which it shall hereafter be conducted.

"Your Memorialists perceive that in proportion as the utility of Watches and Clocks (thus made by Artists who considered their reputation as inseparable from their interests) was experienced, the demand for them increased both at home and abroad, and the Trade was in consequence considerably extended, but as this extension became apparent many persons ignorant of the Art, and in no respect qualified, insinuated themselves into it, and, being incapable of constructing Watches and Clocks either just as to theory or perfect as to workmanship, they adopted the practice of placing upon their bad machines the names of makers who had deservedly acquired reputation by the excellence of their performances, and were enabled, through these fraudulent means, to sell such spurious productions both at home and abroad; and to so great an extent has this pernicious practice prevailed that it became necessary for an application to be made to the Legislature for its suppression, and in the year 1698 an Act was passed prohibiting such practices in future (*vide* the Act of 9th and 10th of William 3rd).

"That your Memorialists have great cause to lament that the provisions in the said Act have not been found adequate to the prevention of the evil complained of, partly from its not being sufficiently explicit,—from the facility with which the offence is committed, the difficulty of detection,—the penalties being too small, and the time for prosecution too limited, owing to a subsequent Act of Queen Anne whereby the time for bringing penal actions is limited; and the evil has increased to such a degree that it has considerably reduced the credit of the Trade.

"As it is obviously the interest of the *bonâ fide* Watch and Clockmaker to place his name on all the Watches and Clocks he makes, it may be enquired, what are the inducements for persons to make use of other names than their own? which though well known to the Trade require some explanation to convey an idea of them to others. For this purpose the subject may be considered under three distinct heads, viz:—

" 1st.—That of one Maker assuming the use of the name of another Maker.

" 2nd.—That wherein the Maker puts on his Watch or Clock a name that is neither his own nor that of any other known maker, with which may be also taken the practice of omitting to engrave any name whatever.

" 3rd.—The practice of Dealers who are not Makers procuring Watches and Clocks to be made with their names engraven thereon, instead of the names of the *bonâ fide* Makers thereof.

" The great object of persons who engage in the practice first above mentioned is, as aforesaid, to usurp the Trade of Makers of established reputation by using their names, whereby the public is much injured by inadvertently purchasing spurious articles, instead of what were intended to be bought, and the person whose name is forged suffers both in property and reputation.

" And further, the making use of the names of deceased Makers is highly prejudicial to the Public, for, if the Machine be badly constructed, not the maker of it, but a dead man is substituted to be made answerable for the deception, which of course escapes punishment, and should the Machine be fit for the purpose intended, the credit of a good performance would not attach to the person entitled to it:—so that in the perpetuation of dead men's names, the rising Artist is depressed from the encouragement being withheld which would stimulate him to exertion.

" With respect to the second head, in principle it is a direct fraud towards the Public, because those who practise the use of other names than their own in this way, or omit to put any name whatever, generally do it with a view to avoid the responsibility that should in all cases attach to the Maker of the Clock or Watch for the honest performance of his duty to his Employer, or from pride that will not allow them to put their names to a Watch or Clock below certain prices.

" In practice it is illusory, and no permanent benefit can accrue to those who follow it, as at best they are only endeavouring to raise a precarious Trade on a false foundation, and pursuing a phantom which constantly eludes their grasp; for in proportion to their exertions in the establishment of such illicit trade (having no legal property in the use of any other name than their own) it follows as a consequence that other persons engage in a competition ruinous not only to the original promoter of such Trade, but also to the quality of the Machines, whereby such trades are inevitably destroyed by the same means as were used to establish them, and the working class of the community are alike consigned to poverty with their inconsiderate employers.

" As to the third head, the dealers in Watches and Clocks have their own names engraven on the articles they sell with a view to engross the whole trade, by endeavouring to place themselves in the situation of the maker in addition to that of the seller; but as such persons are ignorant of the art or incompetent to make Watches and Clocks, and are averse to purchase them from and bearing the names of the *bonâ fide* Makers thereof for the reason aforesaid, they have recourse to the improper practice of seducing the workmen from their employments under the actual Watch and

Clockmaker, and as the workmen know that such shopkeepers are not judges of the work, it is seldom executed in a proper manner, whereby the public are deceived in the purchase of such articles from the badness of their quality, and the Watchmaker is doubly injured, first by the loss of a portion of his trade, and then in being deprived of his workmen to execute the remainder.

"In foreign Countries the value of Watches and Clocks is very often estimated according to the name they bear, and therefore many persons who export them endeavour to procure bad and low-priced Watches to be engraven with the names of Makers whose works are in repute, by which means they gain the advantage of selling the same at superior prices, and at the same time, as they prejudice the reputation and trade of the persons whose names they forge, the kingdom also suffers in the diminution of the trade, which goes into the hands of foreigners and those practices with other frauds have been carried on to such an extent that the trade in Watches and Clocks from this Country to China, Russia, Turkey, &c., which was formerly very lucrative and extensive has been considerably reduced.

"That your Memorialists beg leave further to remark that from the extensive importation of foreign Watches and Clocks into these kingdoms, the internal manufacture has been materially injured; for although the duty on their importation is high, yet, from their portability, very few of the many imported pay any duty, most of them being smuggled; and whenever they are seized or stopped at the Custom House by His Majesty's officers they are sold for home consumption, by which means the same injury arises to the trade as if they were allowed to be imported free of duty, and moreover they serve as a colour to those which have been smuggled.

"Your Memorialists therefore venture with great diffidence to suggest to your Lordships that such foreign Watches and Clocks as may be seized hereafter may be sold for exportation only, and that dealers in foreign Clocks and Watches may be subjected to the regulation of the Excise as the only effectual check upon smuggling, short of a prohibition of the articles.

"Your Memoralists have also to remark that the above causes having long operated on the trade have occasioned such a scarcity of good workmen from the want of encouragement to initiate youth into it, that some of the material branches of the manufacture are nearly lost to the Country, and at present many unfinished Machines are imported into these Realms from foreign parts, particularly Repeating Watches, which being completed here are sold as English work, and on which English Makers' names are placed, which they conceive a strong proof of the serious injury the trade of these kingdoms sustains, and renders a prohibition of the import of such articles (whereby this practice can alone be checked) absolutely necessary.

"Your Memorialists further remark that the making of Watches and Clocks is not always carried on in the house of the Manufacturer, as many of the workmen pursue their respective avocations at their own residences, and as the work must under such circumstances be entrusted to them, much loss and many inconveniences have accrued to their employers in consequence of some of those workmen occasionally pledging the same, and notwithstanding an Act of Parliament was passed in the year 1754 to prevent the recurrence of such abuses, the practice still continues.

"Your Memorialists therefore hope that a further provision may be made to prevent Pawnbrokers from having in their possession any unfinished part or parts of Watches and Clocks on any pretence whatever.

"Your Memorialists having thus stated the causes and consequences of the irregularities and innovations under which the Trade now labours, humbly request that your Lordships will be pleased to afford them your assistance in obtaining such relief as Parliament in its wisdom may think proper to grant."

In this endeavour to improve the condition of the Trade, the Court do not seem to have achieved any material success.

In the next year, however, they renewed their efforts, and addressed to the Prime Minister, Lord Liverpool, the following letter, in which they endeavoured to acquaint him with the various objects for which they sought his assistance :—

"Office of the Clockmakers' Company,
"No. 35, Clements Lane, Lombard Street,
"*April 13, 1813.*

"My Lord,

"As the Master and Wardens of the Worshipful Company of Clockmakers who had the honor to be introduced to the attention of your Lordship by three of the Representatives in Parliament of the City of London, We avail ourselves of your liberal invitation and briefly represent—

"1st.—The evils of which, on the part of 30,000 Manufacturers of Clocks and Watches, we complain.

"2nd.—The causes to which those evils may be attributed, and

"3rd.—Some of the remedies by which those evils may be mitigated or removed.

"As preliminary to that statement we take the liberty to remind you

"1st.—That the art or science of Manufacturing Clocks and Watches had been cultivated in this country with great private and great consequent public advantage for at least 250 years and had attained unequalled excellence.

"2nd.—That 120,000 Clocks and Watches had therefore been annually made, whereby the sum of at least £600,000 had been produced by British Labour, on materials principally of British produce, and that many thousand Artisans were constantly and usefully employed.

"3rd.—That to a 'Maritime, Manufacturing, and Commercial Country the extent and consequences of this productive source of domestic industry had been incalculably beneficial, as the perfection of Chronometers, &c., aided Navigation :—as the principles and ingenuity of Clockmakers enabled them to invent and to improve all the Machines of which in the silk, woollen and cotton trades labour has been diminished and Manufacturers have been supported :— and as the reputation and superiority of the workmanship of British Artisans had ensured to their articles universal preference, and constituted an object of commercial attention, and were extensively, increasingly, and profitably exported.

"4th.—That on the accuracy of these Machines their value and ultimately their sale must depend; such accuracy cannot be immediately distinguished by persons ignorant of their construction:—that they must be therefore subjects of confidential purchase:—that all frauds which injure that confidence must suspend, diminish, and eventually destroy that manufactory:—that the practice of those injurious, even if unintentional, frauds cannot be prevented unless the Manufacturer possess that competent knowledge which practical experience only can confer, and be responsible for its exertion:—and that purchasers and honest Manufacturers are equally interested that such competent knowledge should be possessed and manifested by every person who professes to be a maker of these Machines valuable but intricate and therefore presenting motives and affording facility for the exercise of successful frauds.

"5th.—That the British Statesmen and the British Legislature long and wisely desired to encourage that Manufactory, by increasing public respect for real Manufacturers indicated by the Patent for the Incorporation of the Clockmakers' Company in 1630, and by preventing the rivalry of other Nations, for which purposes the countervailing duties were imposed in 1786-7, and have been since increased: by endeavouring to restrain fraudulent Manufacturers manifested by the Act of 9th & 10th William III, c. 28, sec. 2, prohibiting the exportation of a Box Case or Dial Plate for a Clock or Watch without the movement with the Clock or Watchmakers' name engraved thereon, and also forbidding any person from making up a Clock or Watch without engraving his own name and place of abode and no other on such Clock or Watch, on pain of forfeiting such article and paying a penalty of £20 recoverable only however by action and therefore unavailing. By other statutes, 5th Geo. I, 23rd Geo. II, 27th Geo. II, c. 7, 25th Geo. III, c. 64, 38th Geo. III, c. 24, c. 40 and 69 for additionally regulating the trade, preventing embezzlement by servants, prohibiting pawnbrokers from receiving unfinished watches as pledges, and for other purposes, and which although ineffectual for all the objects designed are sufficiently indicative that the Legislature has regarded the Trade as sufficiently important to deserve such frequent and well intended protection from the state.

"Having made these preliminary remarks we proceed to the first topic which we propose to introduce and intimate the evils private and public which at present exist.

"1st.—The progressive decline of the Manufactory and the consequent impoverishment and misery of the Manufacturers: as the parishes of Clerkenwell, St. Lukes, and other places, near the Metropolis, and throughout the country, where they chiefly reside, and being destitute of employment, depend upon parochial relief, can unfortunately attest.

"2nd.—The Emigration of the most ingenious Artisans to America, France, and other places in great numbers, thirty Manufacturers, collected by public advertisement, having embarked in one vessel to America.

"3rd.—The institution and improvement by those emigrants of foreign Manufactories in those Countries which this Country formerly supplied.

"4th.—The increasing incompetence, from decreasing practice and encouragement, of the remaining Manufacturers to execute repeating Watches and other Chronometers either curious in construction or accurate in effect.

"5th.—The investment of the capital devoted to this national object in speculative and transitory pursuits, and

"6th.—The individual suffering, parochial distress and national disadvantage, which are the effects of these evils, which are so profusely sown, and which flourish with a luxuriance mournfully productive.

"From this imperfect and unexaggerated sketch of the evils which now exist, we invite your attention to the causes of these calamitous effects, being the second topic which we propose to discuss; they may be considered as twofold,—

"1st.—The importation and exportation of Watches without the payment of the Duties which the Law has imposed, and

"2nd.—The frauds which individual avarice and necessity have invented to the impairment of the confidence essential to the prosperity and even to the existence of the Trade, and for the preservation of which no law adequately remedial has been hitherto provided.

"The first cause divides itself into two points, resulting, 1st, from fraudulent importation, and, 2nd, from exportation, equally fraudulent. To prove the existence and operation of those causes, innumerable facts might be adduced and many observations might be made, but we will only repeat and remark.

"As to Importation,—

"1st.—That the comparative cheapness of articles of the first necessity, and of labor on the Continent has enabled its inhabitants not only to create a foreign competition but to undersell our Manufacturers in our own Markets.

"2nd.—To prevent this effect the countervailing duties have been progressively increased until they now amount to 50 per cent., and that even if they were invariably collected they would now scarcely countervail.

"3rd.—That they are not collected and that the duty is not paid on one hundredth part of the Watches which are imported.

"4th.—That the facility of disposing of them when imported from their relative cheapness, and the impossibility of detecting and restraining the importer under the existing laws encourages smuggling which has so perpetually and progressively increased that the delivery of any quantity of smuggled Watches will be insured for 10 p cent., and the British Manufacturer is therefore compelled to require £40 p cent. more for his goods if equally excellent than the fraudulent importer will demand, and cannot attempt to rival the Foreign Manufacturer with any expectation of success.

"5th.—That the demand of Foreign Manufacturers has consequently and incalculably increased. That not only do the old establishments in France, Switzerland and Geneva exist, but, our ablest artificers in jewelled work having been driven from England by necessity, and seduced to those countries by hopeful advantage, they prosper and improve; but also new establishments are formed in America, in Sweden, in Denmark, at Berlin, Nuremburg, and Neufchatel, which will annihilate even our domestic trade, as they imitate completely British Manufactures, and as thousand of Watches are annually smuggled, not only formed after the English pattern but with the names of English Manufacturers, and the Hall Marks of the Goldsmiths' Company forged thereon, and

"6th.—That not only are these Countries impairing this Manufacture, but availing themselves of the ingenuity of the Watchmakers (whose emigration they have encouraged and whom they liberally support) they construct machinery for Cotton Manufactories (many of which have been recently established in America) and thus will exclude this Country from the most profitable commerce which it yet retains.

"Second as to Exportation,—

"As great quantities are annually smuggled into the Country, great quantities are also annually smuggled out of the Country with great, although not equal disadvantage to the nation and the Manufactories. Facility is thereby afforded to the evasion of the 9th and 10th Will. 3rd, c. 28. Stolen and imperfect Watches are thereby distributed, and upright Manufacturers and Merchants who pay the export duties amounting to about £4 p cent. besides freight and other charges which Smugglers also elude, are unable to compete in foreign markets with the smuggler who has evaded those duties and charges, and who sells articles attractive in appearance but destitute of real worth.

"To the second Cause of the fearful evils which exist we next proceed and we remark,—

"1st.—That from the principles to which we have reference and the long and practical knowledge essential to the fabrication of a perfect or useful Watch, such fabrication must be attended with considerable labor and expence, but that imperfect Watches constructed by inferior workmen for persons destitute of experimental information may be sold for lower prices, but whilst such fraudulent Articles delude and injure the consumer, these frauds and the inadequate compensation for labor paid by the Vendors of those fraudulent Articles must ultimately destroy equally the Workman and the Employer and annihilate a Manufactory of great actual and relative advantage.

"2nd.—That Pawnbrokers &c. who are prohibited by statute from receiving unfinished Watches as pledges purchase those Watches of dishonest workmen and vend them in a state apparently complete, but really so imperfect as to deprive the article of value, and to be destructive of that public confidence on which the permanence of the Trade must depend.

"3rd.—That to conceal such inferiority of Workmanship and to improve such opportunities for imposition various artifices have been adopted as,—

"1st.—Clocks and Watches are made without the inscription of any maker's name.

"2nd.—They are made with moveable plates whereby other names can be capriciously and instantly substituted, and

"3rd.—They are made with forged and false names, whereby purchasers are scandalously deluded, and an injury is inflicted on the ingenious and able Mechanics whose names are generally adopted, which can never be repaired.

"To trace the existing evils to the causes which we have announced, would superfluously and therefore improperly occupy your time—We therefore proceed rather to suggest the few and intelligible remedies which we request you to invite the Legislature to supply. And first as to the evils resulting from smuggle importation and exportation.

"The only remedies must obviously be the enactment of some measures whereby the payment of the countervailing and export duties may be both enforced.

"As to Importation,—

"We expect by the following provisions to attain

"1st.—That all dealers in foreign Clocks and Watches be required to take out an annual license, that their existence and residence may be known.

"2nd.—That all foreign Watches now in the possession of dealers should be brought in and marked on payment of a trifling charge. That insuperable obstacles may no longer prevent that detection of smuggled Watches which the Manufacturers and the Country must equally desire.

"3rd.—That no foreign Watches be imported but at London.

"4th.—That on all foreign Watches a number and the names of the actual foreign maker, and the place of his residence be engraved.

"5th.—That all such Watches when imported shall be marked so as to be immediately cognisable, and

"6th.—That unmarked Watches may be seized and sold, and penalties be imposed on the possessors similar to those which possessors of other prohibited articles are by various Acts liable to pay.

"To these suggestions we flatter ourselves that no objections can be made, but we will observe that we do not propose that these regulations should have a retrospective operation, but that one year should be allowed for marking all the foreign stock already imported; that the Custom House officers who have been consulted perceive no impracticability in the arrangement; and that in all Cases and various other Articles imported similar restrictions, similar marking, and similar penalties have been long and usefully applied.

"As to Abuses on Exportation, we only propose—

"1st.—That no Watch shall be exported on which the name and residence of the maker shall not be engraved as hereafter suggested, nor without due entry and endorsement on the Cocket at the Custom House.

"2nd.—That no ship master shall receive any of these Articles without liability to their seizure and to his punishment, and to obviate any objection to any ideal harshness in the operation of such regulation we subjoin.

"3rd.—That any person who may incur a penalty by cladestine shipping not being privy thereto shall have a remedy against the owner of the property which may have been so cladestinely deposited with them.

"As to the Second cause of the calamities which we deplore,—

"Justice to our experience, to our opinions, and to our consistancy induces us to avow that we believe the only adequate remedy to the frauds practised on the public and injurious to the Trade must consist in the prohibition of any person from professing to be a Manufacturer of Clocks or Watches, who has not either served an apprenticeship or officiated as a Journeyman for seven years to the Manufactory, or whose practical competence has not been previously ascertained by an examination similar to that Physicians, Surgeons and persons carrying on other professions (not more important) are compelled to undergo, or that every article should be examined and marked in the manner which the Charter of the Company directs, or in the same manner according to the same principles and for similar reasons which have induced the Legislature to submit Plate, Leather and many other articles to similar investigation for the public security. These remedies we therefore urgently request : But as we apprehend that even if the enlightened mind of your Lordship should disdain to be bound by the cobweb theories of Dr. Adam Smith and other modern Speculatists on political Economy (the temerity of which experience and observation cannot but proclaim), yet that your Lordship might not immediately be able to induce other persons to partake your liberation from such prejudices nor to resist the torrents of inaccurate and injurious opinion which flow with fearful rapidity, we will suggest some palliative improvements to which we presume the most enthusiastic friends to the freedom of trade cannot even momentarily object. On this point we indeed only require that the intention of the Legislature in 9th and 10th William 3rd, c. 28, and the Act relating to Pawnbrokers should be rendered operative, and that the evasion of those Statutes should no longer exist. And we therefore suggest,—

"1st.—That all Clock and Watchmakers be required to take out an annual License such as is required from all Manufacturers of Plate, and that they certify every removal in the same manner which many laws require Manufacturers of other articles to adopt.

"2nd.—That the name and evidence of the actual maker of every Clock and Watch shall be engraven on a permanent part of the Watch.

"3rd.—That no subsequent substitution of any other name than that of the real maker shall be allowed, and that such provisions shall by adequate penalties be enforced.

"4th.—That forgeries of the names and residences of other persons shall be punishable as felonies at the discretion of a judge—but not with a punishment exceeding Transportation for seven years, and

"5th.—That the existing law as to the receiving by Pawnbrokers of unfinished Watches shall be extended so as to prevent them from manufacturing Watches, whereby unfinished work fraudently obtained can be consumed, and also for taking into pledge any Watches which have not the name of the maker complete and engraven thereon, and of these provisions which innumerable analogies support and to which we cannot anticipate any objections which can require a reply, we should only add those general clauses which similar acts usually contain.

"Obedient to your wishes we have thus imperfectly explained the evils which we deplore, the causes by which they have been promoted, and the remedies we venture to suggest. We are conscious that those explanations cannot attain the effect which statements more detailed and more abundant in illustration might produce. Our reluctance to intrude on you has however restrained that desire for more expanded communications which we feel.— For we assure your Lordship that on this subject we are most anxious and sincere, representing thousands of distressed and suffering Mechanics we commisserate their affliction, and loving our country we are unwilling that a manufactory which has aided her triumphs and augmented her resources should be eradicated or transplanted to other and to hostile shores, such results however must occur unless some Parliamentary relief be immediately afforded. Knowing this fact and almost reduced to despair by official delays and obstacles which (since the death of Mr. Pitt) our suggestions have experienced, we have been revived by the liberal and stateman-like attention which your Lordship has condescended to display. We now cherish a hope that your compassion for thousands of ingenious and indefatigable men destitute of occupation—your respect for your illustrious predecessors who did not disdain to attend to our applications and to afford us redress—your anxiety to prevent our enemies from depriving us of a trade equally honourable and productive—and your solicitude to preserve to our native country this important manufacture, will induce you to grant to us your further and candid attention and your speedy and effectual support.

"We will only take the liberty to add that we shall be most happy to afford to your Lordship any further personal explanations which you may require—and that as the remedies suggested can only be supplied by Parliament and ought not beyond the present session to be deferred, we will submit to your Lordship a draft of a Bill for effecting those objects which we shall earnestly entreat the Administration to introduce as soon as your Lordship has had the goodness to inform us whether our suggestions are honored with that approbation which we feel honestly confident that you will cheerfully confer.

"We have the honor to be My Lord,
"Your Lordship's most obedient, devoted, humble Servants,
"Signed by Paul Philip Barraud, pro Master.
Isaac Rogers }
John Thwaites } Wardens."
John Roger Arnold }

In May, 1814, in consequence of the distressed condition of the Workmen and the depressed state of the Trade, the Court presented the following Petition to the House of Commons :—

"*The Humble Petition of the Master, Wardens, and Court of Assistants of the Art or Mystery of Clockmaking, of the City of London:*

"SHEWETH,

"That the Art of making Clocks and Watches was long since established, and has been carried on in this country with great private and public advantage, and has attained unequalled excellence.

"That till within a few years past, more than One Hundred Thousand Clocks and Watches have been annually made; whereby the sum of at least £500,000 has been produced by British labour, on materials principally of British produce; and that many thousand artizans were thereby usefully employed.

"That the national advantages derived from the perfection to which the Art of Clock and Watchmaking has been carried in this country, are not limited to the value of its produce, but extend to every branch of manufacture in which machinery is used.

"That, from the operation of various causes, the value of the Clock and Watch Manufactory, as a source of national advantage, has of late years been greatly deteriorated, and continues rapidly declining: the Manufacturers, deprived of adequate employment, are obliged to seek other means of subsistence; and the workmen, in all its branches, are in great numbers reduced to distress, or are dependent on parochial relief for support; and many of the superior workmen, destitute of suitable encouragement at home, have been seduced to foreign countries, carrying with them their knowledge and ability to construct and employ the most valuable and useful machinery, whereby the principal Manufactures of Great Britain will be transplanted, and established in foreign countries, to the exclusion of the British Manufactures.

"That the former prosperity of a Manufacture, intrinsically and relatively important, was in a great measure attained by the enforcement of the restrictions imposed by Act of Parliament on the importation of Foreign Clock and Watch-work, as well in an incomplete as in a complete state.

"That in the year 1787, a Duty of 27½ per centum was imposed on all Foreign Clocks and Watches imported into this country; which Duty has subsequently, from time to time, been increased and now amounts to 75 per centum.

"That, in consequence of the want of provisions adequate to the collection of such Import Duties, the illicit introduction into this country of Foreign Clock and Watch-work has obtained to an extent ruinously injurious to the British Manufactory; and, the advantage derived by the Smuggler having increased in proportion to the increase of the Duties, the illicit trade is now so regularly systematized that the Importers will undertake the safe conduct and delivery of Foreign Clock and Watch-work (without payment of Duty) in this country, for 10 per cent. on its value; thus affording the illicit trader a premium of 65 per cent., which enables him to undersell the British Manufacturer, and to the great injury of the Public Revenue.

"That this facility with which Foreign Clock and Watch-work is illicitly imported into this country, is one of the principal causes of the declining state of the British Manufactory.

"That during the long continuance of the War, the exportation of British Clock and Watch-work has very much diminished, while the illicit importation of Foreign Clock and Watch-work has increased to an unprecedented degree during the same period; and, unless some new remedy be opposed to the evil, there is reason to apprehend that whenever a general Peace shall be made, the condition of the British Manufactory of Clocks and Watches will become still more calamitous from the increased facilities with which Foreign Clock and Watch-work will then be illicitly introduced into this country, as well for home consumption as for the export trade.

"That Foreign Clocks and Watches are illicitly imported for sale in all parts of the Kingdom; and that in order to obviate any impediments which national preference, joined to the acknowledged superiority of English work, might oppose to the sale of Foreign Watches, they are illicitly imported in an incomplete state; and being made to resemble, in their exterior appearance, English Watches, are sold as English, to the great injury of the public, and the ruin of your Petitioners.

"That no permanent nor effectual relief to the distress of your Petitioners can be obtained, unless the wisdom of Parliament should interfere, and remove or mitigate those evils, the existence and consequence of which your Petitioners most humbly represent, and most sincerely deplore, and are prepared to prove to your Honorable House.

> "Your Petitioners therefore humbly pray, that your Honorable House will investigate the extent and the causes of the evils of which they complain, and will afford to your Petitioners such relief as to your Honorable House may seem meet."

"In January, 1816, a Report was presented to the Court from a Committee appointed to acquire information respecting the illicit introduction of Foreign Watches and Clocks and devising means for preventing the same, in which it is stated, as the result of an interview had in the previous December with the Right Hon. Nicholas Vansittart, Chancellor of the Exchequer, that he had desired a memorandum might be sent to him of the means the Company proposed for remedying the evils complained of; in consequence whereof they had forwarded to him the following Statement:—

"1st, No Foreign Clocks or Watches to be imported at any other Ports than those of London, Bristol, or Liverpool.

"2nd, No Foreign Watches to be imported in parcels of less than Fifty each, nor Foreign Clocks in packages of less than Twelve each.

"3rd, No Clocks or Watches to be imported in an incomplete state, nor without their Cases, nor out of their Cases, nor Clock or Watch Cases to be imported without their Movements fixed in them.

"4th, All Foreign Watches or Clocks having any name or place of abode, or freedom, purporting to be the name or place of abode, or freedom of any British Watchmaker, engraven or painted on any part thereof, to be strictly prohibited.

"5th, All Foreign Clocks and Watches to have a mark permanently imprinted on some part of the Movement, or Cases, by the Officers of the Customs, when the Duties are paid.

"6th, All Dealers in Foreign Clocks and Watches, to take out an Annual Licence so to do, not less in amount than the Plate Licence now necessary to be taken out by English Watchmakers, and to write over their doors, ' Dealer in Foreign Clocks and Watches.'

"7th, From and after the   day of   next (twelve months after the passing of this Act), all Foreign Clocks and Watches, which are unmarked, will be liable to seizure, unless the Proprietors (such Proprietors not being Dealers) make Affidavit that they were possessed of them previously to the passing of this Act.

"8th, All Foreign Clocks and Watches seized under the provisions of this Act, to be sold for exportation only."

On the 10th of June, 1822, a Deputation from the Trade waited upon the Court, to request its co-operation in opposing so much of a Bill then before Parliament, entitled, "An Act, to make more effectual provision for permitting Goods imported, to be secured in Warehouses, or other places, without payment of Duty on the first entry thereof, 12th of May, 1823," as applied to Clocks and Watches. Upon which the Court determined to petition the House of Commons on the subject; and a Petition against so much of the Bill as related to the warehousing, under certain restrictions, of Clocks, Watches, and Watch-glasses, for home consumption, upon payment of Duty, and for exportation without payment of Duty, was accordingly presented by Mr. Alderman Bridges on the 11th of June, and ordered by the House to be laid upon the Table and printed. The Bill was eventually adjourned for three months.[1]

On the 20th March, 1823, a Committee was appointed by the Court to communicate with the Right Honorable Mr. Wallace, President of the Board of Trade, on the subject of the Warehousing Bill, which had been again brought before Parliament; when it was resolved that, as Mr. Wallace was determined not to omit Clocks and Watches, and Watch-glasses, in his proposed Warehousing Bill, it would be desirable to obtain the introduction of certain clauses, to render

[1] Journal of the House of Commons, 1822, p. 334.

the measure as little mischievous as possible ; and the following Memorandum was thereupon prepared, and forwarded to Mr. Wallace :—

"That all Clocks and Watches admitted to entry, should have a distinguishing mark impressed upon them, before going out of the King's Warehouse.

" That no Watch should be admitted to entry with marks on the cases similar, approximating, or purporting to be the marks of the Goldsmiths' Company.

" That no Clocks or Watches be admitted to entry with ' London ' engraved on them, or engraved in a way to purport or give colour to their being English.

" That no Clocks or Watches be admitted to entry, unless they have engraved on them a name and place, purporting to be the name and place of abode of the person or persons who made them.

" The object the Company of Clockmakers has in view, is principally that Foreign Clocks and Watches shall not come out of the King's Warehouse to be sold as English Manufacture.

" The Company has only farther to observe, that by a late regulation of the French Government, all Foreign Watches brought into France are subject to a distinguishing mark, which is impressed upon them by the Government officers, without injury to the work."

On the 7th of April, 1823, the Committee reported that Mr. Wallace had stated, that one of the propositions, by far the most material of the four contained in the Memorandum, namely, that of marking the Foreign Clocks and Watches, was inadmissible, but that the other three propositions would be adopted ; and on the 2nd of June, 1823, the Clerk produced a printed Copy of the new Warehousing Act, passed the 12th of May, and read the following Clause, introduced at the request of the Company :—

"And be it further enacted, That no Watch of Foreign Manufacture shall be imported and warehoused under the provisions of this Act, upon the Case or Cases of which any mark or stamp shall be impressed, which shall be similar to, or shall purport to be, or shall be intended to represent, any mark or stamp of the Goldsmiths' Company of London, or other legal British assay marks or stamps ; and that no Clock or Watch of Foreign Manufacture shall be so imported and warehoused, upon the face, or upon any part of which, the word ' London,' or the name of any other town or place of the United Kingdom, shall be engraven or painted, or shall in any way appear so as to purport or give colour that such Clock or Watch is of the Manufacture of the United Kingdom ; and that no Clock or Watch of Foreign Manufacture shall be so imported and warehoused, unless a distinguishing number, and the name or names of some person and place, shall be engraven, and shall appear visible on the frame or other part of such Clock or Watch, independent of the face, purporting to be the name and place of abode of the person or persons by whom such Clock or Watch was made ; and that no Clock or Watch of Foreign Manufacture, shall be imported or warehoused under this Act in any incomplete state, that is to say, not having the Movement, with all its concomitant parts, properly fixed and secured in its Case, on pain of the forfeiture of such Watch or Clock."

On the 8th September, 1823, the attention of the Court was directed by the Officers of the Custom House to a case of Foreign Watches imported and warehoused under the Act, for home consumption or for exportation, free of duty, which bore forged names of well-known foreign as well as English makers, amongst the latter being that of Eardley Norton, of Red Lion Street. An examination of them by Members of the Company proved that they were forgeries, and bore counterfeit marks of Goldsmiths' Hall. The Court thereupon determined to memorialise the Treasury on the subject, with a view to prevent their being taken out from the warehouses until destroyed as watches, and to direct the attention of the Goldsmiths' Company to the forgeries of their marks. They likewise resolved to caution the public by advertisements in the newspapers against purchasing such Watches as of English manufacture.

A further similar importation being reported during the same month of September, the Court again memorialised the Treasury, and intimated that they had received information that a large number of such Watches were ready to be sent to this country if permitted to pass, and urged that those already received should not be released by the Customs, but so disposed of as to prevent the practice in future, protect the English purchaser, and support the home manufacturer.

In the month of November following they received an intimation from the Treasury that proceedings would be taken for the condemnation of the articles in question, according to Law, and that the Customs Officers had been instructed to prevent their being warehoused in future.

In March, 1824, the Court determined to petition the Treasury for an amendment of the Warehousing Act so far as related to Clocks and Watches, the Act not distinctly setting forth the manner in which they were to be disposed of when seized as forgeries, and to direct their attention to the fact that no obstacle existed to such importations, provided they were entered for home use and the duty immediately paid, nor to the importation of unfinished and incomplete goods, which had afterwards an outward appearance put upon them here, and were then sold as entirely of English manufacture. The Petition adopted prayed for an alteration of the Law to meet these objections, and to provide for the destruction of such articles and the conversion of the gold and silver cases into bullion; for the infliction of a penalty for the importation of such fraudulent goods, and for placing Foreign Watchcases, bearing forged marks of Goldsmiths' Hall, under the same regulations as similar frauds against the Act for regulating the manufacture and duties on wrought gold and silver.

In the following month a Deputation of the Court had interviews with the Government upon the subject. Whilst the Treasury were willing to accede to the wishes of the Company, the Chancellor of the Exchequer objected to the breaking of Watches, but thought it highly desirable some distinguishing mark or stamp should be impressed upon them.

In the month of July, 1824, it was reported to the Court that a further seizure of Foreign Watches had been made, which were about to be sold by the Customs Commissioners, and that the forged names on them had, as far as practicable, been obliterated, and the marks punched out of the cases.

It will thus be seen that, although not quite in the manner suggested by the Company, the objects they had in view—viz., the protection of the English Trade—were in a great measure secured, the defacement of the watches having rendered them almost valueless.

This satisfactory result, however, had hardly accrued when, in the following year, 1825, an Act, 6th George IV, cap. cvii, was passed, intituled, "An Act for the General Regulation of the Customs," by which the Clause in the Warehousing Act before mentioned, which had been inserted at the express instance of this Company, was, in fact, repealed, and the new Act, whilst prohibiting the warehousing of forged Foreign Clocks and Watches, did not prevent their being entered for home consumption without being warehoused, or if warehoused, for home consumption only.

This unfortunate circumstance compelled the Company to recommence their agitation, and the following Memorial to the Board of Trade, agreed upon at a Court held on the 6th November, 1826, fully sets out their previous proceedings and the objects for which they again sought the intervention of the Government :—

"SHEWETH,
"That in an Act passed in the 4th year of his present Majesty, cap. 24, entitled, 'An Act, to make more effectual provision for permitting Goods to be imported, to be secured in Warehouses, or other places, without payment of Duty on the first entry thereof,' 12th May, 1823, the following (LXXXI) Clause is introduced. [Here follows the Clause, for which *vide* page 286.]

"This Clause was introduced into the Act, specially to prevent Foreign Clocks and Watches, made in imitation of British, and with British Makers' names and places of abode or freedom thereon, from being warehoused, and afterwards sold, either for home consumption or exportation, as of British Manufacture.

"In or about September 1823, a large parcel of Gold, Silver, and Metal Watches, not less in number than 846, were imported from Hambro', 450 in the ship 'Thetis,' Reed, Master, and 396 in the 'London,' Rumbert, Master, and were seized for not conforming to the above-recited Act.

"This being the first seizure under the Act, the Right Honorable the Lords of the Treasury were pleased to order all the Watches that had the names of British Makers or places thereon, or on the Cases of which were impressed imitative marks of the Goldsmiths' Hall (several of the Cases that purported to be Silver, turned out, on examination by the Officers of Goldsmiths' Hall, to be little better than base metal), to be destroyed, and the remainder restored to the owners, on their paying certain expences, and giving bond to send the Watches back by the same ships to Hambro'. No farther attempts, as far as is known to your Memorialists, have been made to warehouse Clocks and Watches contrary to the provisions of the Act.

"In the 6th year of Geo. IV. an Act was passed, cap. 107, entitled, 'An Act for the general Regulation of the Customs,' (5th July, 1825). In the latter part of Clause LIII. of this Act, under the head of 'Exceptions to be Warehoused,' are the following words : 'Clocks or Watches impressed with any mark or stamp, appearing to be, or to represent any legal British assay mark or stamp, or purporting by any mark or appearance, to be of the Manufacture of the United Kingdom, or not having the name and place of abode of some Foreign Maker abroad, visible on the frame, and also on the face, or not being in a complete state, with all the parts properly fixed in the Case ;' the intention of which is evidently the same as the Clause before recited in the Warehousing Act, but not being sufficiently clear and explicit, the intention of the Legislature is consequently more easily evaded.

"But the great omission in the Act 6 Geo. IV. cap. 107, before recited, and which it is the express object of your Memorialists to represent, is, that the Clause above recited is intended to prohibit the warehousing of Foreign Clock and Watches, purporting to be of British Manufacture, &c. &c. the same as is done by the Clause (LXXXI.) in the Warehousing Act, cap. 24. Yet the Act does not contain any provision whatever, to restrain the importing of such Clocks and Watches, upon their being immediately entered for home consumption, without being warehoused.

"Your Memorialists request to state, that in consequence of this omission, a parcel of Foreign Gold and Silver Watches, engraved 'Charles Stiffenone, Regent-street, London,' were imported on or about the 10th July, 1826, and entered at the Custom-house for payment of Duty, but which were stopped, under the impression that the restrictions in the Warehousing Act, applicable to Foreign Watches and Clocks brought into this country, bearing the names of British Makers or places, &c. &c. were equally enforced by the Importation Act; but on reference to the latter Act, this was found not to be the case; consequently, the Watches were necessitated to be restored to the owner, on the payment of Duty: Clocks have also been imported in a similar manner.

"Your Memorialists beg to represent, that the prosperity, they may say the existence, of the Manufacture of Clocks and Watches in this country, solely depends on the superior character of the British articles to those manufactured in any other part of the world. The estimation in which English Watches and Clocks are held, is proved by the well-known fact, that an immense number are made on the Continent with British names and 'London' on them, and the Cases impressed with marks purporting to be those of the Goldsmiths' Hall, London, and distributed as British to every part of the globe, to the great prejudice and loss of the British Manufacturer.

"This is a misfortune that cannot be prevented; but the immediate effects resulting from the facility now afforded to bring Clocks and Watches into this country, bearing British Makers' names, and places where made, afterwards to re-export or sell them in the home-market as British, will be, first, materially to diminish the Export Trade, already much reduced; and secondly, to greatly injure the Home Trade, which is the legitimate and only certain market left to the British Manufacturer; subsequently, from the bad performance of the articles sold as of British Manufacture, the reputation of the British Manufacturer will be destroyed, and the Export Trade, which depends solely on the superior character of the British Clocks and Watches over those of every other country, will eventually be entirely lost. The Home Trade will also suffer a progressive diminution, until, as an object of Commerce, it entirely ceases.

"The high price of labour in this country (resulting from causes not necessary to be enumerated), compared with the Continent, particularly Switzerland, a country exempt from taxation, where the greater part of the Foreign Watches are made, operates in a peculiar manner on a Manufacture, of which the value of the raw material forms so very small a part of the total value, as is the case in Clocks and Watches, particularly the latter; the total value of the raw material in a Gold Watch of the value of £30, deducting £8 : 15 for the Gold, is not Five Shillings; consequently, it is impossible for the British Manufacturer to enter the lists with the Foreigner on the score of price; the success of the former depends entirely on the superiority of the article he manufactures.

"The evils resulting from these practices are not confined to the Manufacturer alone : the Public are grossly imposed upon and defrauded by these Anglo-Foreign Clocks and Watches, which almost without exception are of a very inferior quality; for it is very difficult, in the present state of the Art, for an individual not of the profession, or at any rate, not professing a knowledge of mechanics, to distinguish from the external appearance only, a Foreign from a British Watch or Clock

"Your Memorialists therefore pray, that as soon as can consistently be done, the Act 6 Geo. IV, Cap. 107, Clause LIII, may be so amended, in relation to Watches and Clocks imported, to pay the Duty and also to be warehoused, that they shall in either case be subject to the same regulations and restrictions as are contained in the 81st Clause of the Warehousing Act; which Clause was inserted at the solicitation of your Memorialists, for the two-fold purpose of protecting the Public at large from fraud and deception, and of upholding and supporting the British Manufacturer"

A second Memorial to the Board of Trade was adopted at the Court held on the 8th January, 1827, in which, after recapitulating the facts as stated in their former one, they continue as follows :—

"As the Law now stands, Clocks and Watches bearing the names of British Makers and of British towns and places, with the Cases of the Watches impressed with marks resembling those impressed on British Gold and Silver Watch Cases, can be imported without let or hindrance, either on payment of Duty, or to be warehoused, provided only that in the latter case they are not warehoused for exportation; and the British Manufacturer has to compete with a Manufacture carried on in countries mostly exempt from taxes, rates and tithes (this is particularly the case with regard to the Watches made in Switzerland, where by far the greater number are made), the very existence of this Trade depending solely on the superior character of the article he manufactures.

"Your Memorialists therefore feel it incumbent on them to renew the prayer of their former Memorial, and to request, that as soon as can be properly done, the Act 6 Geo. IV. Cap. 107, Clause LIII. may be amended to this effect: That no Watch of Foreign Manufacture shall be imported, upon the Case or Cases of which, any mark or stamp shall be impressed, which shall be similar to, or shall purport to be, or shall be intended to represent, any mark or stamp of the Goldsmiths' Company of London, or other legal British assay marks or stamps; and that no Clock or Watch of Foreign Manufacture shall be so imported, upon the face, or upon any part of which, the word 'London,' or the name of any other town or place, or person, of the United Kingdom, shall be engraven or painted, or shall in any way appear, so as to purport or give colour that such Clock or Watch is of the Manufacture of the United Kingdom; and that no Clock or Watch of Foreign Manufacture shall be imported, unless a distinguishing number, and the name or names of some person and place shall be engraven, and appear visible on the frame, and also on the face, purporting to be the name and place of abode of the person or persons by whom such Clock or Watch was made; and that no Watch or Clock of Foreign Manufacture shall be imported in any incomplete state, that is to say, not having the Movement, with all its concomitant parts, properly fixed and secured in the Case, and finished in a state to go and shew the time, on pain of the forfeiture of such Clock or Watch.

"Your Memorialists are aware, that it has been urged as an objection to their desire for protection for the Public and themselves, that if Clocks and Watches are prohibited from being legally imported (but subject to certain restrictions), that they will be clandestinely brought into this country; to which in reply they observe, that in its present state, the Law not prohibiting such fraudulent practices in the importation of Foreign Clocks and Watches, it may be said to countenance the evils complained of, and to encourage practices abroad which are realized here, although they could not be originated in these realms. It certainly is an anomaly, that Clocks and Watches can be imported into, and openly sold in this country, that could not be legally manufactured in the country."

In May, 1828, they again memorialized the Board of Trade, and expressed their disappointment at the great length of time which had elapsed without their receiving any answer, and called the attention of the Board to the following facts :—

"In or about September 1827, a parcel of Watches in Silver Cases, with the name 'Eardley Norton, London,' engraven upon them in the English fashion, and the Cases impressed with marks resembling those of the Goldsmiths' Hall of this City of London, were entered at the Custom-house for payment of Duty, and seized, not because they were engraven and marked as above described, but because they were entered for Duty at the supposed undervalue of Five Shillings each : at the following regular Custom-house sale, Mr. Owen, of Wallingford, a general dealer, purchased 23 of these Watches, all engraven and marked as above described, for about Nine Shillings each.

"It is scarcely necessary to add, that these 23 watches, which were of the very worst quality, were purchased to be resold, and will supply the place of so many English Watches. The individuals who may eventually purchase these Watches as English, will be most grossly deceived, and the reputation of the English Artists suffer in consequence.

"In conclusion, your Memorialists beg leave to state the following fact, connected with these Anglo-Foreign Watches, particularly deserving the notice of His Majesty's Government. Had the above mentioned Watches been manufactured in Great Britain, the parties making and selling them, would have been amenable to the Civil Law for using the name of another Maker, and to the Criminal Law, for applying false marks to the Cases; from whence it follows that Foreigners can do that with impunity, for their own advantage, and to the great prejudice of His Majesty's subjects, which would subject the latter, were they to do the same, to severe pains and penalties."

In July of the same year, the Court directed a Memorial to be prepared to the Treasury, but at the next Meeting it was reported that an Act had been passed which had rendered its presentation unnecessary. The Act referred to being the Act 9th, George IV, cap. lxxvi, intituled : "An Act to amend the laws relating to the Customs," clause 4, of which enacts as follows :—

IV. "'And whereas it is expedient to prohibit the importation of Clocks and Watches having false marks or names thereon; be it therefore enacted,

"That it shall not be lawful to import any Clock, nor any Watch, impressed with any mark or stamp, appearing to be or to represent any legal British assay mark or stamp, or puporting by any mark or appearance to be of the manufacture of the United Kingdom, or not having the name and place of abode of some Foreign Maker abroad, visible on the frame, and also on the face, or not being in a complete state, with all the parts properly fixed in the Case ; and that such prohibition shall be complied with and enforced, in like manner as if the same were set forth in a certain Table, denominated, 'A Table of Prohibitions and Restrictions Inwards,' contained in the said Act for the general Regulation of the Customs.'"

The Court, at a subsequent Meeting, held on the 25th November, 1828, caused copies of the above Clause to be officially communicated to the Swiss and French Consuls General, with a view to its provisions being made known in their respective countries.

Though, as has been shewn, the law was at length so amended as to meet the views of the Trade, it appears that the same illicit practices were continued, and Watches, etc., continued to be imported bearing the forged names, etc., of the same English makers as formerly, and within two years after the passing of the Act, viz., in February, 1830, the Court again memorialized the Treasury in the following terms :—

"*The Memorial of the Master, Wardens, and Court of Assistants of the Company of Clockmakers of the City of London :*

"SHEWETH,

"That in or about the month of December last, three dozen of Foreign Watches, in Silver Cases, supposed to be the property of a Russian Jew, were seized, under the provisions of the Act 6 Geo. IV. cap. 107, sec. 53, in consequence of their being engraved with an English name and place thereon, viz. 'Eardley Norton, London,' in violation of the said Act, but without any marks or impressions on the Cases, purporting to be those of the Goldsmiths' Hall ; as all English Watches, Silver as well as Gold, must have the Cases assayed and marked at Goldsmiths' Hall, before the Watches can be sold, otherwise the party selling the same, are liable to a heavy penalty, and the articles destroyed.

"Your Memorialists beg very respectfully to submit to your Lordships, that if these Watches are permitted to be sold at the Custom-house, as is customary with seized goods, they will eventually be resold in detail as English Watches, to the prejudice of the English Manufacture, which, from causes which it is unnecessary to refer to on the present occasion, is in a most depressed state, and a great number of industrious workmen are out of employment, and consequently in great distress—themselves and families wanting the necessaries of life.

"Moreover, should these Watches be subsequently resold, as of English Manufacture, after having been sold at the Custom-house sale, such resale will, upon the face of the transaction, be illegal, in consequence of the Cases not bearing the marks of the Goldsmiths' Hall, which, being of Foreign Manufacture, they cannot have; it becomes therefore very probable, that to render the Watches more saleable, false or forged marks will be applied to the Cases; thus adding a second fraud to the first.

"It is further to be observed, that these Watches are of very inferior quality, and if exported, would certainly be sold for English, to the great prejudice of the character of the English work.

"Your Memorialists therefore pray, that your Lordships will order these Watches not to be so sold, but that the Cases may be dealt with as with Plate seized of Foreign Manufacture, and the Movements to be destroyed."

To this an answer was received from the Treasury, intimating that instructions had been given to the Commissioners of Customs for the destruction of the Watch Movements in question, and the rendering the Cases unfit for use as well, and for their disposal as Plate seized, of Foreign Manufacture.

In January, 1832, the distress existing in the Trade induced the Court again to take up the question, and they agreed to another Memorial to the Treasury, and a letter to Lord Althorp, then Chancellor of the Exchequer, in support of it. The Memorial itself contains a succinct statement of the case of the English makers, the disadvantages under which they had so long laboured, and the various alterations made in the law with a view to alleviate these disadvantages, and protect the King's subjects from undue and unfair foreign competition; and is as follows :—

"*The Memorial of the Master, Wardens, and Court of Assistants of the Company of Clockmakers of the City of London:*

"SHEWETH,
"That on or about the period of the Right Honourable William Pitt's Commercial Treaty with France, an *ad valorem* Duty of 75 per cent. was imposed upon all Foreign Clocks and Watches imported into this country, which Duty was commonly known by the very appropriate appellation of 'a Countervailing Duty.' That so long ago as previous to the year 1787, the Manufacture of Clocks and Watches in this country was found to be materially affected by the illicit importation of Foreign Clocks and Watches; and in consequence, a Representation was addressed to the Lords of Trade on the 19th of February, 1787; and the subject of the Representation being found to be one that immediately affected the Revenue, it was a few days after laid before the Lords of the Treasury.

"That the War with France, which commenced in 1793, and continued until the short Peace of Amiens in 1802, and subsequently until 1815, prevented in a great measure the increase of the evil; and it does not appear that any further communications took place between His Majesty's Government and the Company, on the subject of Foreign Clocks and Watches (with one exception in 1789), until 1816; after which period they became much more frequent. But since the general Peace in 1815, the evil has been progressively increasing, until it has arrived at so alarming a height, as to threaten the speedy and entire annihilation of the Manufacture of Clocks and Watches in this country.

"That an Act was passed, 6 Geo. IV., cap. 105, entitled, 'An Act to repeal the several Laws relating to 'the Customs,' (5th July, 1825), whereby all former Acts were repealed; and that an Act was passed, cap. 107, entitled, 'An Act for the general Regulation of 'the Customs,' (5th July, 1825), by which a Duty of only 25 per cent. *ad valorem*, was imposed upon all Foreign Clocks and Watches imported into these realms. But from the absence of some Legislative Enactments, whereby the fact of the article having paid the Duty, can be satisfactorily ascertained, the provisions of the Act, particularly as applied to Watches, are become a dead letter, and the intention of the Legislature is entirely frustrated.

"Your Memorialists have been informed from good authority (the truth of which information may be easily ascertained by an application to the Honorable Board of Customs), that scarcely an entry of Watches for payment of Duty has been made at the Custom-house within the last two years, during which time the number of Watches illicitly imported, and exposed for sale in the public shops and private establishments, has increased twenty-fold, without the smallest benefit to the Revenue. A certain number of Clocks, though far from the total quantity brought into the country, are entered for payment of Duty; but those are generally very much undervalued.

"The Foreign Manufacturers have their respective Agents in London, to whom they consign their goods; and there are certain individuals, a species of nondescript Smugglers, who carry on a very lucrative business, without, as in the case of the operating Smuggler, any personal risk, by insuring the safe delivery of the articles, for a very small per centage upon their value. In like manner, private individuals procuring, or having Watches made abroad for their own use, have the option of having their Watches delivered to them free of Duty by the London Agent of the Foreign Maker, and are not required to pay for them until they are received in London. By these arrangements, the Foreign Manufacturer possesses great facilities for importing his Clocks and Watches, particularly the latter, into the country; and the persons dealing in them are enabled to procure them to the best advantage, and without risk of loss: all this without in the smallest degree benefiting the Revenue, but to the utter ruin of the British Manufacturer.

"Your Memorialists have lately been informed, and they believe the information to be correct, that in consequence of the decrease in the number of English who have visited Paris since July 1829, and consequently of the number of Swiss Watches sold there, that the Swiss Manufacturers have it in contemplation, to remove their principal establishments from Paris to London; which, for the reasons above stated, they can do to great advantage to themselves, and proportionate injury to the English Manufacturer.

"That the home market is almost the only market remaining to the English Clock and Watch Manufacturer; for in consequence of the superior estimation in which English Clocks and Watches have for a great length of time been held, and the consequent demand for them in most parts of the world, the Foreign Manufacturers have been induced to make Watches as nearly as possible to resemble English, and engraved with English names, and 'London,' and with forged marks of the Goldsmiths' Hall of London impressed upon the Cases, for the purpose of being exported to the foreign markets commonly supplied by the British Manufacturer; who, from the comparative low prices at which they (the Foreign Manufacturers) can afford to sell them, compared with the unavoidable high price of the English Watches, the latter are completely driven out of the market, to the great prejudice of the English Manufacturer; and Clocks and Watches will necessarily cease to be an article of export trade, except to a very limited extent. As a proof of the superior quality of the English Manufacture, your Memorialists beg particularly to call your attention to this circumstance,—that they are not aware that a single instance has been adduced, of English Clocks or Watches having been made to imitate Foreign, with Foreign names of makers and places upon them. The disadvantages the English Manufacturer labours under, as above-mentioned, were much increased in the year 1822, by the passing of the Warehousing Act; which, although it prohibited the warehousing of any Clocks and Watches having English names or 'London' engraved on them, or marks on the Cases in imitation of those of the Goldsmiths' Hall, still enabled the Foreign Manufacturer to keep his goods, free of expence, for a considerable period in the King's Warehouse, ready to be exported to the first market that offered, at a very much lower price than similar goods made here could be afforded. It is true, this particular Act was repealed by the Act 6 Geo. IV. cap. 105 (5th July, 1825), but its provisions are contained in an Act 'for regulating the Customs,' passed the same year, cap. 107; and the Foreign Manufacturer still enjoys the advantage of warehousing his goods at a very trifling expence, and of deferring the period for payment of the Duty, to suit his own convenience.

"That with very few exceptions, the Watches brought into these realms, and commonly called French Watches, are not made in France; but are in fact made, part at Geneva, but by far the greater number at Neufchatel, in Switzerland, in a country in which the price of the necessaries of life is not influenced by Corn-laws; and where there are neither Taxes, Poor's-rates, or Tithes, or scarcely impositions of any sort or kind whatever; and where the expence of living, and consequently the value of labour, is infinitely less than in a country like England, by far the highest taxed of any in Europe; and where, moreover, the high price of labour is maintained by Corn-laws, the effect of which is to enhance the cost of the first necessaries of life. From these causes, the relative situation of the English and Foreign Manufacturer is so very different, and the advantage so decidedly in favour of the latter, that were the Duty of 25 per cent. imposed upon all Foreign Watches brought into this country levied, the same would afford a very inadequate protection to the home Manufacturer. Probably no amount of Duty short of 75 per cent., as first imposed by Mr. Pitt, upon all Foreign Clocks and Watches imported, would be equivalent to the relative situation in which the British and Foreign Manufacturers are placed.

"That the cost of manufacturing Clocks and Watches, but more particularly the latter, depends entirely upon the price of labour; because, exclusive of the Gold or Silver of which the Watch Cases are made, the value of the raw materials of which the Watch Movement is composed, compared with the article when finished, is exceedingly small. The cost of manufacturing a Watch may be divided as follows: 1st, The value of the labour employed, forming by far the greater part of the total value: 2nd, The value of the material, Gold or Silver, of which the Case is made: 3rd, The value of the raw material of which the Movement is made; which last is by very much the smallest part. The average value of the raw material employed in making a Watch, may be estimated at from Two to Four Shillings each Watch Movement.

"What is above described under the denomination of raw material, is not strictly so; but has been brought into a certain preparatory state by the help of machinery, particularly the steel wire of which the pinions and pendulum-springs are made.

"That the raw materials, as above described, and generally all the steel employed in the manufacture of Watches, is exported from this country to Switzerland. Until the year 1825, the exportation of any unfinished part or parts of Watches was strictly prohibited by a former Act. In the present state of the Law, the Foreign Manufacturer draws his raw material, wrought into a preparatory state as above described, from this country; and is thereby enabled to furnish better articles, and at a cheaper rate than he could otherwise do. To satisfy themselves of the truth of the above statement, your Memorialists employed a person to apply at Locle, in the Canton of Neufchatel, the principal seat of the Watch Manufactory in Switzerland, to purchase the above-named Articles (steel pinion wire, pendulum spring wire, and steel prepared for various purposes), where he was unhesitatingly told, they were all brought from England, and that if he required any quantity, his better plan would be to employ an agent to procure them direct from London.

"That the assertions made by some writers upon Political Economy, and of sundry articles in some of the Encyclopediæ, that machinery had been brought to such perfection, that little now was required in the manufacturing of Clocks and Watches, but what could easily be accomplished by the use of machinery, are entirely false. The contrary is the case; for there is no manufacture so dependent upon manual labour and dexterity, or for which so little can be done by the aid of machinery; except indeed as described under the head of raw material. But this, in the present state of the Law, is as much to the benefit of the Foreign as to the English Manufacturer. In the entire catalogue of articles manufactured in this country, there is probably not one in which manual labour forms so large a proportion of the cost of production, as in Clocks and Watches, but more particularly the latter; and consequently so valuable in a thickly-peopled country like England; and more especially at a time when it is the fashion, with a certain class of Political Economists, to attribute a considerable portion of the distresses under which the lower classes are at present labouring, to an excess of population.

"That although the superiority of the English Watches, as to quality and performance, is not disputed, still it has been asserted, and too generally credited, that English Watches cannot be made so flat and so neat as Foreign Watches. This is not the fact: Watches are, and can be made in London, as small, as flat, as neat, and as beautiful to the eye, as any made on the Continent; but they cannot be made at the same cost, and consequently cannot be sold at the same price; but the attempt on the part of the British Manufacturer to compete with the Foreign artizan in the price of Clocks and Watches, has a natural tendency to deteriorate the quality of the article and must eventually lose to the British Clock and Watchmaker the superior character he has hitherto maintained in his branch of manufacture.

"That the Art of Clock and Watchmaking employs a great number of persons in various parts of the United Kingdom, particularly in London, Liverpool, Coventry, and Prescot in Lancashire; not only in the immediate manufacture of Clocks and Watches, but also of various tools employed in that manufacture.

"That for some time past, the situation of those individuals, from the want of employment, has been progressively getting worse; and that the period is fast approaching, when, in the full enjoyment of the faculties Nature has given them to obtain a decent livelihood, and provide for themselves and their families, as their fathers had done before them, they will, for the want of employment, be reduced to a state of absolute pauperism, and become dependent upon the Poor's-rate for support: thereby increasing the total mass of pauperism, and the already overgrown amount of the Poor's-rates, and all the moral evils resulting from such an artificial state of society.

"That for some time past, the earnings of the working classes, in consequence of the extent to which the illicit introduction of Foreign Clocks and Watches into this country has prevailed, have been gradually decreasing, and have now reached the minimum at which those who are fortunate enough to obtain employment, can earn a bare maintenance. That the only persons who really benefit by this state of things, are, 1st, The Foreign Manufacturer; and, 2nd, The home wholesale Smuggler, who carries on a most profitable agency, with very little pecuniary risk, and without any personal risk whatever.

"That the return of the number of Watch Cases assayed and marked at the Goldsmiths' Hall, forms no just criterion of the number of Watches made in this country. For some time past, but more particularly since the general Peace in 1815, a practice has been carried on by certain Foreigners to a considerable extent, of illicitly importing Foreign Watches in a nearly or quite finished state, particularly Repeaters, but without Cases, which are put into Cases made here, and invariably sold as English Watches, and at as near the price of English Watches as the parties practising these frauds can obtain. Great numbers of these Watches are also exported, and sold as of English manufacture; but being of very inferior quality, are doubly injurious to the British Manufacturer, as they not only deprive him of his legitimate share of trade, but, by their bad performance, bring unmerited discredit upon the British Manufacture. This practice has increased to so great an extent, that your Memorialists have repeatedly cautioned the Public against it by Advertisement in the Daily Papers.

"That the Art of Clock and Watchmaking, which has universally been allowed to hold the first class in the mechanical arts, has been carried to the highest degree of excellence in this country. England produced the first Marine Chronometers deserving that appellation. English Clocks and Watches are valued and sought after in every quarter of the globe where civilization has made any progress; and wherever the Foreign article has usurped the place of the English, it has been under the mask of English names, and disguised to resemble English Manufactures.

"That the claims of the individuals practising the Art of Clock and Watchmaking to the protection of the Legislature, have been fully allowed, upon every occasion, when a Deputation from the Court of Assistants of this Company has had business to transact with any of the Members of His Majesty's Government; and moreover, that Legislative Enactments have been made at the special solicitation of the Court of Assistants, of which it will be sufficient to notice two, viz. the Clause (LXXXI.) in the Warehousing Bill, (12th May, 1823), and the Clause (IV.) in the 'Act to Amend the Laws relating to the Customs,' (25th July 1828); but your Memorialists regret to add, that in consequence of the present state of the Trade, and the little prospect that exists of its improvement, that several workmen of the superior class, men of considerable talent as workmen, and possessing some property; precisely those who, on every account, it is desirable should not leave the country, are about to emigrate to America. The inferior class of workmen, and consequently those the least useful, have not the means of emigrating; and their entire ignorance of all agricultural pursuits, precludes their being engaged by individuals forming establishments in the British Colonies; and the prospect that awaits them, from the want of employment in their legitimate calling, is to end a life of wretchedness and misery in a workhouse.

"Your Memorialists therefore very respectfully beg to submit to your Lordships,—That from the best consideration they can give the subject it appears to your Memorialists, that the only prospect that remains for restoring the Manufacture of Clocks and Watches to its former state of prosperity, and preserving it to the country, may be stated under the following heads :

" 1st, That the Duty upon Foreign Clocks and Watches imported, be made to assimilate to the relative situation of the working classes in this country, and in France and Switzerland.

" 2nd, That the collection of the Duty be rigidly enforced; for which purpose, all Foreign Clocks and Watches to be marked when the Duty is paid: the mark to be the proof of the Duty having been paid. That the said marking be done at the Custom-house, and by an Officer appointed by the Commissioners of His Majesty's Customs. The marking Foreign Goods imported, upon payment of Duty, is not new in principle; and to adopt it in the case of Clocks and Watches, has been pressed upon His Majesty's Government since the year 1787.—If the principle of marking is conceded, there will be no difficulty in regulating the detail, and it can be effected without any prejudice whatever to the article marked.

" 3rd, That no Clocks or Watches unfinished, or in an incomplete state, or without Cases; or parts of Clocks or Watches finished or unfinished, or without name of maker, and place where made, be allowed to be imported.

"4th, That no incomplete Clocks or Watches, or parts of Clocks or Watches, or raw material prepared for the manufacture of Clocks or Watches (such as steel pinion wire, or pendulum spring wire), be allowed to be exported.

"5th, That efficient Legislative Enactments be adopted, to cut short the proceedings of the home wholesale Smuggler, who furnishes the capital employed in the illicit trade, in a similar manner to what was adopted to put a stop to the investment of British capital in the Slave Trade."

The reply of the Treasury to this Memorial was laid before the Court on the 5th March, 1832, in the following terms:—

"GENTLEMEN,

"I am commanded by the Lords Commissioners of His Majesty's Treasury to acquaint you, that on the fullest consideration of your Memorial, in which you request that you may be relieved from the injury sustained by the Trade from the illicit importation of Foreign Clocks and Watches; and after having taken the opinion of the Board of Trade thereon, *it does not appear to my Lords, that any attempt to relieve you from Foreign competition, by rigid Custom-house regulations, would have a beneficial effect in protecting your Trade.*

"I am, Gentlemen,
"Your obedient Servant,
(Signed) "SPRING RICE.

"*Treasury Chambers,
2nd March, 1832.*"

On the 6th of May, 1833, the Court determined again to appeal to the Treasury, more especially since the Trade had in the interim become still further depressed.

The Memorial adopted by them and the correspondence which thereupon ensued with the Treasury, are set out at length, as follows:—

"*To the Right Honourable the Lords Commissioners of His Majesty's Treasury:*

"*The Memorial of the Master, Wardens, and Court of Assistants, of the Company of Clockmakers of the City of London,*

"SHEWETH,

"That upwards of Twelve Months have now elapsed since your Memorialists last addressed your Lordships, during which period the state of the Clock and Watch Manufacture in this Country has, from various causes, been progressively more and more depressed. The principal cause of this depression is indisputably the immense number of Foreign Clocks and Watches brought into the Country.

"By an Act passed in the 6th year of George IV., cap. 107, entitled 'An Act for the Regulation of the Customs,' (5th July, 1825), the Duty to be paid on the importation of Foreign Clocks and Watches was reduced to and definitely fixed at 25 per cent. *ad valorem*, which is a reduction of 50 per cent. from the protecting Duty established at the period of the late Mr. Pitt's Commercial Treaty with France.

"This reduced Duty of 25 per cent. Lord Wallace (then President of the Board of Trade), stated to a Deputation from your Memorialists he considered preferable to a higher Duty, because it afforded less inducement for Smuggling, adding that it was the determination of His Majesty's Government to take the necessary steps for enforcing the payment of the reduced Duty. Your Memorialists without entering at present into the question of the good policy of thus reducing the protecting Duty, beg to submit respectfully but firmly to your Lordships that they have a right to expect that the enforcement of the reduced Duty should be carefully and strictly attended to. They regret that this has not been the case. From the period of the reduction of the Duty to the present time the evil of the contraband importation has been daily increasing, but from the facilities afforded by the small bulk of the article, the Smuggling of Watches has very far exceeded that of Clocks. A number of Foreign Clocks have certainly been entered for the payment of Duty, but even in this case the Home Manufacture has not due protection; since from the circumstance of their being under-valued, they have paid much less duty than they should have done. Moreover, your Memorialists have reason to believe that a great many Clocks have been clandestinely imported. With regard to Watches, the number which has been entered and has paid duty bears a very small proportion to those which have been illegally imported. Your Memorialists are aware that from the nature of the circumstances upon which they address your Lordships, they cannot produce strict demonstration of the facts of which they complain, and the difficulty in this respect is increased by the defective manner in which the Custom House Registry of Watches imported is kept. In that Registry, as your Memorialists understand, no account is taken of the number of the Watches imported, or whether they are Gold or Silver, nothing is stated but their gross value. It is very desirable that this defective registration should be remedied. The fact, however, of the enormous amount of the contraband trade in the articles of your Memorialists' Manufacture, which they complain of will, they think, be as plainly apparent to your Lordships as it unfortunately is to themselves, from the following circumstance : The total value of the Clocks and Watches, for which duty was paid at the Port of London for the four years ending with 1832, was as follows :—Clocks valued at £99,600 11s. 1d., Watches only valued at £2937 17s. 0d., but, as has been before noticed, these articles being generally entered for payment of duty at very far below their real value, particularly when imported for sale, the above sum of £99,600 11s. 1d. was probably not much more than half their value, and it may fairly be inferred that the total value of the Clocks, only, imported was not less than £200,000. With respect to Watches the disproportion of the value entered at the Custom House to the number everywhere publicly offered for sale, is so palpable that there can be no doubt of the immense contraband trade that must be carried on. Taking the value of Foreign Gold Watches at an average of £7 each, it would appear that in the four years above mentioned, and supposing all the Watches imported to have been Gold Watches, no more than 420 Foreign Gold Watches were imported ! It is notorious to every man in the trade that ten times that number might be counted in the shop windows any morning in a walk from Whitechapel to Hyde Park, besides the immense number that are not open to public view. There cannot be a doubt therefore that the *revenue is enormously defrauded,* and the protection intended to be afforded to the Home Manufacturer wholly lost. Independently of the Watches publicly exposed for sale, Foreign

Watches (the same remark applies to Foreign Clocks) are now commonly sold as an article of commerce by Jewellers, Haberdashers, Milliners, Dressmakers, Perfumers, French Toy-shops, &c.; and are even hawked about the streets. Probably at no period was so large a number of Foreign Gold Watches brought into the country as within the last four years, and your Lordships' Memorialists are of opinion that they do not estimate the value of these Watches at all too highly at the sum of £700,000. Your Memorialists are fully aware of the difficulty of forming a correct estimate upon a question of this sort, with the very slender official data that can, in the present defective manner of making the entries, be obtained. But your Memorialists, with the sources of information which their intercourse in the trade supplies, are satisfied they are much under the mark when they estimate the number of Gold Watches brought into this country by various channels during the last four years to average not less than 25,000 each year, giving a total of 100,000 Gold Watches. Now taking £7 as the average value of each Watch, the total amount will be £700,000. The number and value of the Silver Watches imported is much less in proportion than that of Gold Watches; they may fairly be estimated at 10,000 Watches each year, at an average value of 15s. each, which gives a total of 40,000 Watches, value £30,000, making the total value of Gold and Silver Watches £730,000. The value of the Clocks has been previously estimated at £200,000, making the total value of the Clocks and Watches brought into the country the last four years £930,000, upon which sum, had the Duty been enforced, it would have amounted to £232,500, whereas the Duty paid has been only £25,634 12s. 0¼d., *being very nearly £200,000 less than it would have been had the Duty been properly collected.*

"Your Memorialists very respectfully submit to your Lordships that if it is fitting a Duty should be imposed upon Foreign Clocks and Watches, it is equally so to enforce the payment. That to nominally protect a Home Manufacture by imposing an import duty upon a similar Foreign Manufacture, and at the same time to omit to adopt such measures as can alone ensure the collection of the Duty, *and thus virtually to sacrifice both the Revenue and the Home Manufacturer for the benefit of the Foreign Manufacturer who does not contribute one shilling towards the expense of the State or the support of the poor, is to practise a cruel mockery upon the heavily taxed and rated British Manufacturer.* Further, that the Foreign Watches of the illicit importation of which into these realms your Memorialists have so much cause to complain, are made principally in Switzerland, a country exempt from Taxes, Rates and Tithes, and without Corn Laws to force up the value of labour. Moreover, your Memorialists are not aware that any articles of British Manufacture are exported to Switzerland.

"The Foreign Dealers openly boast of the facility with which they smuggle their Watches into this country, the few they enter for payment of Duty serving as a cover for the others; and they do not scruple to avow that so long as the Legislature abstains from adopting some measure to identify the Clocks and Watches that have paid the Duty, and thus distinguish them from those that have not, that nothing as the law at present stands can or shall prevent their importing as many as they please without payment of Duty.

"Your Lordships' Memorialists have been induced to trouble your Lordships at this time, in consequence of having noticed in the Reports of the Proceedings in the House of Commons as given in the daily papers, that the various Acts for the regulation of the Customs were about to be revised and consolidated, in the hope that your Lordships would be induced to embrace the present opportunity to bestow some consideration on a subject involving the interests, nay, the very existence, of a great number of industrious and deserving mechanics and their families. For your Memorialists regret to add that the distresses under which the English artizan has for a long time laboured have not diminished, but are, on the contrary, considerably aggravated, principally by the cause above mentioned.

"No consideration but an imperative sense of the duty your Lordships' Memorialists owe the trade at large, of which they are the legally-constituted guardians, added to the interest they take in the happiness and well-being of the working classes, would have induced them to trouble your Lordships at the present conjuncture, but, having so done, they think it right to state unreservedly to your Lordships that unless some efficient relief is afforded to the British Manufacturer, which cannot be done unless the payment of the duty as by law established is enforced, he must, from inability to meet the Foreign manufacturer in the home market—almost the only market now left to him— cease to manufacture, and thus throw out of employment a great number of workmen, thereby increasing the distress and misery which, for want of employment, now prevails among the lower classes, and is one principal cause of the existing discontent. Your Lordships' Memorialists beg leave here also to observe that the greater cheapness of Foreign Watches is no compensation whatsoever to the classes who are thrown out of employment by their illicit importation. It is not the industrious or the lower classes who use Foreign Clocks and Watches.

"In conclusion, your Lordships' Memorialists think it right to state to your Lordships that, although they do not consider the duty of 25 per cent. *ad valorem* to be a sufficient protecting duty for the English Manufacturer, burthened as he is with taxes and poor's rates—particularly in the article of Watches, which are manufactured in an untaxed country—yet aware of the feeling that so generally prevails in the present day against high protecting Import duties, they abstain from urging any increase of the amount of duty, and only pray that they may possess in fact the protection which, according to the existing law, they ought to have.

"Your Lordships' Memorialists will now briefly state to your Lordships, under the two heads of Imports and Exports, points to which they particularly wish to call your Lordships' attention.

"IMPORTS.

"That the collection of the Duty upon all Foreign Clocks and Watches brought into these realms be enforced with the same exactness as is done in the case of various other articles, and in such a manner that those that have paid the Duty can be readily distinguished from those that have not.

"That no Clocks or Watches be admitted to entry with 'London,' or the name of any other place in the United Kingdom, engraved on them, or engraved or painted in any way to give colour to their being English.

"That no Clocks or Watches be admitted to entry unless they have engraved on them a name and place purporting to be the name and place of abode of the person who made them.

"That no Clocks or Watches be admitted to entry in an incomplete state, that is to say, without having the movement and all its concomitant parts properly fixed and secured in its case.

"That no Watch shall be admitted to entry with marks on the case similar or approximating to or purporting to be marks of the Goldsmiths' Company of the City of London.

"EXPORTS.

"That no incomplete Clocks or Watches, or parts of Clocks or Watches, or material prepared for the manufacture of Clocks or Watches (such as pendulum spring wire, and steel pinion wire) be allowed to be exported, as it is well known that the Foreign Manufacturer derives his supply of these articles (which are in fact the most useful parts of the material of Watches) from this country.

"That all Clocks and Watches exported shall bear the name and place of abode of the person by whom they are made engraved upon them; and Clocks and Watches without names not to be allowed to be exported.

"*Office of Committee of Privy Council for Trade,*
"*Whitehall, 24th May, 1833.*

"SIR,

"The Lords of the Committee of Privy Council for Trade have received an application on behalf of the Watch Case Makers of Liverpool, stating that the works of Watches made in England are exported without cases, and that they are afterwards put into cases of Foreign Manufacture on which imitations of the marks of British Makers and of the Assay Offices of this Country are impressed, the metal being far below the English standard, and that the Watches, when so completed, are sold as entirely of British manufacture, to the injury and disrepute of the British makers; and it is further stated that by the Act of the 9 and 10, Will. III. chap. xxviii., the exportation of any case or dial plate for a Clock or Watch is prohibited, without the movement being put therein and made up for use, which Act was intended to protect the Watchmakers in this country; and the Watch Case Makers pray that similar protection may be afforded to their trade by a legislative enactment prohibiting the exportation of Watches, except in Gold and Silver Cases.

"Before the Lords of this Committee proceed to take this matter into consideration, they would be glad to receive any remarks which the Members of the Company of Clockmakers in London may have to offer on the subject, and I have therefore been directed to communicate their Lordships' wish to you accordingly.

"I am Sir,
"*Mr. G. Atkins,*   "Your obedient Servant,
  "*Cowper's Court, Cornhill.*   (Signed)   "THOMAS LACK.

"Cowper's Court,
"May 28th, 1833.
"SIR,

"I am directed by the Master and Wardens of the Company of Clockmakers of the City of London, to acknowledge the receipt of your letter of the 24th instant.

"I am further directed to say that it is their decided opinion, as expressed on former occasions, that the exportation of Clocks and Watches without their cases, or in any respect in an unfinished state, as well as parts of Clocks and Watches, is highly prejudicial to the best interests of the British Manufacturer. In the first place a number of workmen are thereby deprived of the means of gaining a livelihood, and in the second it opens a wide door to every species of fraud, as alluded to in your letter.

"You will find this opinion expressly stated in two Memorials from the Company of Clockmakers of the City of London, addressed to the Lords of His Majesty's Treasury, dated February 8th, 1832, and the 8th instant. And in a Letter from Mr. Spring Rice, dated 2nd March, 1832, it is mentioned that the Memorial of the 8th February has been referred to the Board for Trade.

"I am directed to add that, if you have not easy access to these Memorials, copies of the same will with much pleasure be furnished, as well as any information the Court can give that you may require.

"I am, Sir,
"Your obedient Servant,
(Signed) "GEORGE ATKINS,
"Clerk to the Company.

"Thos. Lack, Esq.
"Offices of the Commissioners of Privy
Council for Trade, Whitehall."

"Custom House,
"4th June, 1833.
"SIR,

"The Lords Commissioners of His Majesty's Treasury having transmitted to the Board of Customs a Copy of a Memorial from the Master and Wardens of the Company of Clockmakers, containing suggestions in order to prevent the illegal importation of Watches and Clocks, or their admission at under valuation, I have it in command to acquaint you that the Board of Customs are ready to consider any further regulations which the Company of Clockmakers may have to propose, with a view of attaining the object of their application.

"I am, Sir,
"Your most obedient Servant,
(Signed) "J. KER.

"Mr. G. Atkins.

"Office of Committee of Privy Council for Trade,
"Whitehall, 5th June, 1833.
"SIR,

"I am directed by the Lords of the Committee of Privy Council for Trade to acquaint you that your letter of the 28th ultimo, on the subject of the exportation of Clocks and Watches in an unfinished state, has been duly received, and will be considered by their Lordships.

"I am, Sir,
"Your obedient Servant,
"*Mr. G. Atkins.* (Signed) "THOMAS LACK.

" Treasury Chambers,
" 10151¼ " 7th June, 1833.

"GENTLEMEN,
"Having laid before the Lords Commissioners of His Majesty's Treasury your Memorial on the subject of the Duties on Foreign Clocks and Watches, I have it in command to acquaint you that my Lords have given directions to the Board of Customs, to ensure the utmost vigilance on the part of their officers to guard against the illegal importation of Watches, as well as to ensure the payment of the full duties on Watches when imported. I am at the same time to add that if it be true, as now stated, that Watches are smuggled in, the increase of duty would only increase the temptations to such clandestine traffic, and that the affixing the name of a foreign maker and a mark importing the payment of duty, could not give much additional security, unless means were adopted of searching and inspecting Watches worn by individuals, and of seizing Watches if not so marked. This power of search and seizure, it is obvious, never could be granted; independently of which the facility of counterfeiting the proposed marks would in itself be a bar to a compliance with this suggestion.

"I am, Gentlemen,
"*To the Company of Clockmakers,* "Your obedient Servant,
"*Mr. G. Atkins.* (Signed) "SPRING RICE.

" *Cowper's Court, Cornhill,*
" *June 11th, 1833.*
"SIR,
"I am directed by the Master and Wardens of the Company of Clockmakers of the City of London to acknowledge the receipt of your Letter of the 5th instant.

"I am further directed to say that the object the Company have in view in the Memorial, dated May 7th, to the Lords of the Treasury on the subject of Foreign Clocks and Watches not being the alteration of the existing law, but merely the *bonâ fide* and vigilant carrying the same into effect, they have in point of fact, no suggestions to make to your Board further than those contained in their Memorial, of which it appears by your Letter the Board of Customs have been furnished with a copy by the Lords of the Treasury.

"I am, Sir,
" Your most obedient humble Servant,
"*To J. Ker, Esq.,* (Signed) "GEORGE ATKINS,
" *Custom House, London.* "Clerk to the Company.

"My LORDS,

"6, Cowper's Court, Cornhill,
"June 13th, 1833.

"I am directed by the Master and Wardens of the Company of Clockmakers of the City of London, to address your Lordships in reply to a Letter I have received from Mr. Spring Rice, dated th 7th instant (and marked 10151⅞), in answer to a Memorial addressed to your Lordships dated the 7th May last, by the Master, Wardens, and Court of Assistants of the Company.

"I am directed in the first place to observe that Mr. Spring Rice's Letter appears to have been written under the impression that, in their Memorial before mentioned, the Court had applied to have the amount of duty on Foreign Clocks and Watches imported increased. If your Lordships will have the goodness to refer to the Memorial you will find that it is especially mentioned that an increase of duty is not asked for. The words in the Memorial are : 'yet, aware of the feeling that so generally prevails in the present day against high protecting Import Duties, they abstain from urging any increase of duty, and only pray that they may possess in fact the protection which, according to the existing law, they ought to have.'

"I am directed, in the second place, to observe that Mr. Spring Rice, in his Letter, objects, *in toto*, to the proposed plan of marking Foreign Clocks and Watches imported, as affording no valid security, unless accompanied by the right of search and seizure, which, he says, never could be granted. In answer to this objection, I am directed to call your Lordships' attention to a case very much in point, namely : that the very considerable revenue derived from the duty upon wrought gold and silver in this country is entirely secured by the marks imposed upon the articles manufactured, which marks are imposed when the duty is paid ; and that all articles of gold and silver plate are obliged to be sent to certain offices, where they are marked and the duty paid before they can be offered for sale. Any breach of the law in this respect subjects the parties offending to very severe and heavy penalties, and there are but very few instances known of its being evaded. In reference to the second part of the objection—the right of search and seizure—it certainly does appear singular that British born subjects, dealers in wine, spirits, tobacco, &c., &c., should be subject to inconvenience from which Foreigners, dealers in Foreign Watches and Clocks, are exempt; and also *that so much vigilance to protect the revenue should be exercised with regard to some persons, and so much laxity be permitted with respect to others.*

"This right of search and seizure is not a new suggestion, and at one time (before the year 1823) was frequently acted upon by the Custom House Officers in reference to Clocks and Watches.

"The securing to the *Revenue the Duty upon Foreign Clocks and Watches* by the operation of marking, to which so much objection is urged, would not be a difficult operation, and though at first it might be attended with some trouble would very soon work well *for the benefit of the Revenue* and for the protection of the British Manufacturer. The Swiss Watches sold at Paris are marked with reference to the quality of the gold of which the cases are made, and what is feasible in Paris is equally so in London. The importance of this measure for the *benefit of the Revenue* and the protection of the English Manufacturer has been insisted upon in several communications that have taken place with the Lords of the Treasury, but as your Lordships may find it difficult to refer to the original documents, I am directed by the Master and Wardens to forward you the accompanying copy of 'A statement of the various proceedings and transactions that have taken place between the Court of Assistants of the Clockmakers' Company of the City of London and His Majesty's Government, in relation to the importation of Foreign Clocks and Watches into these realms. Ordered by the Court to be printed for the use of the Members of the Court the 6th February, 1832.' I am further directed more particularly to refer your Lordships to page 15, in which will be found the heads of a plan, which, if embodied in an Act of Parliament, would no doubt operate for the *benefit of the Revenue*, while it would give the home manufacturer the protection of which he so much stands in need, and to which he is so justly entitled.

"Should the measures proposed in the Memorial be found upon trial insufficient to protect the interest of English manufacturers, the Master and Wardens then propose to submit to your Lordships the propriety of subjecting Foreign Clocks and Watches, and those who deal in them, to the operation of the Excise Laws. If that were done there can be no doubt that the grievance so justly complained of would be in a great measure, if not entirely, abated. There is nothing unreasonable in this proposition, as it does not appear why Foreign Clocks and Watches should not be under the supervision of the Excise, as well as other articles. *The English Watchmakers have always been obliged to take out a licence annually at the Excise Office, without which they cannot sell Gold or Silver Watches.*

"In conclusion, I am directed to state to your Lordships that there is one fact connected with the importation of Foreign Clocks and Watches that should not be lost sight of, namely, that these articles are imported almost entirely for the use of *the upper classes of Society ;* that it is their pecuniary interests chiefly that will be affected by any measures that may be adopted to enforce the payment of the Duty, and that so long as the present state of things is suffered to continue *both the revenue and the interests of the British Manufacturer and of the working classes are sacrificed for the pecuniary advantage of the higher classes.*

" *That the revenue is completely sacrificed is sufficiently proved by the statement in the Memorial, dated the 7th of May last, presented to your Lordships, of the value of the Watches entered for payment of Duty at the port of London in the four years ending 31st December,* 1832.

"To this state of things the Court has reason to believe the working classes are feelingly alive, and their complaint, that while they are heavily taxed, they are at the same time deprived of the means of earning wherewithal to pay these taxes, is, in the case of the workmen employed in the manufacture of Clocks and Watches, but too well founded.

" I have the honour to be,
" My Lords,
" Your Lordships' most obedient humble Servant,

" *To the Right Honourable the Lords*   (Signed)   " GEORGE ATKINS,
   Commissioners of His Majesty's Treasury.   ' Clerk to the Company.

"Custom House,
"21st June, 1833.
"SIR,

"Having laid before the Board of Customs your Letter of the 11th instant, stating, in reply to my letter of enquiry, dated the 5th preceding, that the Master and Wardens of the Company of Clockmakers have no suggestions to offer with a view of more effectually preventing the illegal importation of Foreign Watches and Clocks further than those contained in their Memorial to the Lords of the Treasury, of the 7th ultimo, their object not being the alteration, but the enforcement of the existing Law, I have it in command to acquaint you, for the information of the Master and Wardens of the Company, that the Board have issued a General Order to their Officers in London and at the several out-ports, enjoining them to the most vigilant attention, in order to prevent the illegal importation of Watches and Clocks, or their admission at an improper valuation.

"I am, Sir,
"*George Atkins, Esq.,*   "Your most obedient Servant,
   Cowper's Court, Cornhill.   (Signed)   "J. KER.

"*Cowper's Court, Cornhill,*
"29th June, 1833.
"SIR,

"I am directed by the Master and Wardens of the Company of Clockmakers of the City of London, to acknowledge the receipt of your Letter of the 21st inst.

"I am further directed to forward through you to the Honourable Commissioners of His Majesty's Customs, a copy of 'A statement of the various proceedings and transactions that have taken place between the Court of Assistants of the Clockmakers Company of the City of London, and His Majesty's Government, in relation to the importation of Foreign Clocks and Watches into these realms;' to which proceedings it will be necessary to refer in the course of this Letter.

"The statement in your Letter that the object the Master and Wardens have in view is not the alteration, but the enforcement of the existing law, is perfectly correct. But the Master and Wardens beg to submit that for this purpose much more is requisite on the part of the Honorable Commissioners of the Customs than merely exercising vigilance at the Custom Houses of London and the out-ports. From the small bulk of the article many Watches (if not Clocks) will, in spite of the exertions of the Custom House Officers, be clandestinely brought into the country, and it becomes necessary, as well for the future *security of the Revenue as the protection of the British manufacturer,* that the Clocks and Watches that have in the first instance escaped the vigilance of the officers, should be caught while in the hands of the wholesale dealers (who bear the same relation to their operative contrabandists as the receivers of stolen property bear to the thieves). For this purpose the Officers of His Majesty's Customs might, as was formerly done, exercise the right of search for and seizure of Foreign Clocks and Watches in the hands of dealers and importers, leaving on them the *onus* of shewing that they have paid the duty. This has been repeatedly done, and at no distant period, and recourse might again be had to similar measures.

"That a vast number of Watches have been clandestinely brought into this country, is a fact proved to a demonstration, by the great number exposed publicly for sale, (a great many of which are without names, which circumstance sufficiently proves that they have not passed the Custom-house; since all Watches entered for Duty must have the maker's name and place of abode engraved on them); and the exceedingly small amount of the value (under 3000*l.*) of those entered for the payment of Duty at the Port of London, in the four years ending at Christmas 1832. It is the opinion of persons well qualified to form a just opinion on the subject, that if the whole of those Watches had paid the Duty, they would have been valued at a sum little short of 500,000*l.*, or perhaps even more; the Duty upon which would have amounted to 125,000*l.*—to which amount, at the least, the Revenue has been defrauded, in consequence of the very imperfect manner in which the Duty has been levied.

"It appears to the Master and Wardens of the Clockmakers' Company, that the most effectual, and the least expensive, and in all respects the best method, of securing the payment of the Duty, would be to mark all Clocks and Watches when the Duty is paid: the adoption of this method, by shewing which have, and which have not, paid the Duty, would prove highly advantageous to the Revenue; and it has been repeatedly urged upon His Majesty's Government, but, unfortunately for the Revenue and the British Manufacturer, without success.

"In conclusion, I am directed to say, that the Master and Wardens of the Company of Clockmakers of the City of London, trust the Honourable Commissioners of His Majesty's Customs will adopt such measures as will virtually, not nominally, enforce the existing Law; and that it will no longer remain, to all intents and purposes, a dead letter; which, from some cause or other, has been much too long the case.

"I am, Sir,
"Your most obedient humble Servant,

"*J. Ker, Esq.,* (Signed) "GEORGE ATKINS,
"*Custom House, London.* "Clerk to the Company.

"*Custom-house,*
"*11th July, 1833.*

"SIR,

"Having laid before the Board of Customs your Letter of the 29th ultimo, transmitting, with reference to the communication made to you by Mr. Ker's Letter of the 21st preceding, some further observations on the subject of the illegal importation of Watches and Clocks, together with a Statement of the Proceedings between the Court of Assistants of the Clockmakers' Company and His Majesty's Government, relative thereto;—I have it in command to acquaint you, for the information of the Master and Wardens of the Company of Clockmakers, that the Board of Customs are not prepared to recommend any further measures for adoption in respect to the importation of Clocks and Watches.

"I am, Sir,
"Your obedient Servant,
(Signed) "C. A. SCOVELL,
"*George Atkins, Esq.* "Sec^y.

"Treasury Chambers,
"20th July, 1833.
"11506¹⁶/₇.
"GENTLEMEN,

"The Lords Commissioners of His Majesty's Treasury having had under their consideration your further Memorial of the 13th ultimo, on the subject of the injury done to your Trade by the unlimited importation of Foreign Clocks and Watches; I have it in command to acquaint you, that my Lords have given every attention to this subject which its importance deserves, and that they have directed the utmost care to be given by the Customs department to guard against the fraudulent introduction of Foreign Watches without payment of Duty; but that they apprehend any increase of protection, in the way of augmented Duty, could only add to the inducement to smuggling; and that they are not aware of any other course that could be resorted to with beneficial results. To bring an entire branch of trade under the supervision of the Excise, appears to my Lords a very objectionable mode of proceeding, and not likely, with respect to the sale of Watches and Clocks, to attain the object sought for.

"I am, Gentlemen,
"Your obedient Servant,

"The Clockmakers' Company, (Signed) "SPRING RICE.
"6, Cowper's Court, Cornhill.

"Cowper's Court, Cornhill,
"July 26, 1833.
"SIR,

"I am directed by the Master and Wardens of the Company of Clockmakers of the City of London, to acknowledge the receipt of your Letter of the 20th inst., 11506¹⁶/₇, addressed to the 'Clockmakers' Company.'

"In the first place, I am instructed to express to you the great satisfaction it has afforded the Master and Wardens of the Company, which they are sure will be equally felt by all the members of their body, to learn that the Lords of His Majesty's Treasury have taken into consideration the peculiar situation of the British Clock and Watchmaker, and in consequence, given the directions you describe, with regard to enforcing the collection of the Duty upon Foreign Clocks and Watches imported into this country. For this they are exceedingly obliged to their Lordships, and beg to return them their best thanks.

"At the same time I am directed to request the favour of you to state to their Lordships, that it is the decided opinion of the Master and Wardens, founded upon long experience, that something more is still requisite to be done for the *security of the Revenue and the protection of the British Manufacturer*. From the small bulk of the article, Watches (if not Clocks) will, in spite of the exertions of the Custom-house Officers, be clandestinely brought into the country in great numbers; and it becomes absolutely necessary, to effectually put a stop to this contraband traffic, for the Custom-house Officers to exercise the right of seizure of such as have not paid the Duty, while in the hands of the dealer. Many of the parties who receive these Watches, do so as a matter of regular trade, and stand in precisely the same situation to the smuggler that the receiver of stolen goods does to the thief.

"This right of search has been repeatedly exercised, and at no distant period; and unless this is again done,—as the Watches, when once in the country, will be considered to be perfectly safe,—means will soon be discovered of clandestinely importing them; and the good intentions of their Lordships will thereby be completely frustrated.

"So vigilant were the Officers at one time, that it is a well-known fact, that the foreigners, who were then the wholesale dealers in Foreign Watches, rarely kept their Watches three nights consecutively at the same place; and scarcely ever at their own place of residence.

"This mode of proceeding may, at first sight, appear harsh and severe, but it must be borne in mind that the smuggler, and the person by whom he is employed, voluntarily expose themselves to this inconvenience. *Equally severe measures are daily had recourse to for the protection of the Revenue; in proof of which fact, it will be sufficient to notice the recent proceedings in connection with the collection of the Post Office Revenue.*

"That a vast number of Watches have been clandestinely brought into this country, is a fact proved by the immense number publicly exposed for sale, to say nothing of those not so publicly exposed, *and the exceedingly small amount of the value* (2937*l.* 17*s.*) *of those entered for payment of Duty at the Port of London, in the four years ending Christmas* 1832, *upon which the amount of Duty paid was only* 734*l.* 9*s.* 3*d.* The total value of the Watches brought into the country during those four years, is certainly considerably under-rated at the sum of 500,000*l.*; upon which the Duty would have been 125,000*l.*; *making a positive loss to the Revenue of* 124,265*l.* 10*s.* 9*d.—an example of loss of Revenue, from want of attention to the collecting it, probably without example in modern times.*

"I am directed to again call your attention to the fact, that the *English Watchmaker has from time immemorial, been obliged to take out an Annual Licence at the Excise*, where he is duly registered, to enable him to sell Gold or Silver Watches. Now, it is the opinion of the Master and Wardens, that if all persons who deal in Foreign Clocks and Watches were compelled by Law to take out an Annual Licence, as is the case with persons dealing in a great variety of articles, viz. Lace, Plate, Watches, Horses, Tea, Coffee, Tobacco, Wine, Spirits, &c., &c., &c.; and in a similar manner to write up over their door, '*Licensed Dealer in Foreign Clocks and Watches*,' that such a measure would, next to marking the Clocks and Watches when the Duty is paid, from the publicity that would be given to the parties dealing in these articles, afford the best security that can be adopted for the due collection of the Revenue, and the protection of the British Watch and Clockmaker. Moreover, it would benefit the Revenue, by the amount of the Licences taken out, without any expense in the collection. The Master and Wardens earnestly entreat of you to request the favour of the Lords of the Treasury to take this proposal of theirs into consideration at their earliest convenience: there cannot for an instant be a doubt of the facility with which it would be carried into execution; it is divested of all feature of harshness or oppression, and is requiring no more of the dealer in Foreign Clocks and Watches than is required of the dealers in a great variety of other articles, as well luxuries as necessaries of life. Some individuals, Auctioneers for example, are obliged to take out a Licence as Auctioneers, and separate Licences to enable them to sell by auction Plate, Wine, Spirits, &c.

"In conclusion, I am again directed by the Master and Wardens to call your attention to a misconception which (judging from the latter part of your Letter of the 20th instant) the Lords of the Treasury and yourself still appear to labour under. You there express yourself as though their Lordships supposed the Master and Wardens had asked for an increase of the amount of the Duty levied on Foreign Clocks and Watches: now the precise contrary is the case. If you will have the goodness to refer to the conclusion of the Company's Memorial to the Lords of the Treasury, dated the 7th May last; and to the beginning of a Letter addressed to their Lordships, dated the 13th June last; you will find the opposite sentiment expressly stated. The words in both are—'*Yet, aware of the feeling that so generally prevails in the present day against high protecting Import Duties, they abstain from urging any increase of Duty; and only pray that they may possess, in fact, the protection which, according to the existing Law they ought to have.*' To setting this mistake right the Master and Wardens attach considerable importance.

"I am Sir,
"Your most humble Servant,
(Signed) "GEORGE ATKINS,
"*To the Right Hon. Spring Rice,*   " Clerk to the Company.
Secretary to the Treasury,
&c. &c. &c.

" *Treasury Chambers,*
" *19th October, 1833.*
"GENTLEMEN,
" I am directed by the Lords Commissioners of His Majesty's Treasury to transmit herewith for your information the copy of a report of the Commissioners of Customs on the subject of the illegal importation of foreign Clocks and Watches, and I am to acquaint you that my Lords are willing to receive any further communication from you, and to take any steps which, on full consideration, may appear desirable for the purpose of preventing or of repressing any illicit importation of Foreign Watches.

" I am, Gentlemen,
" Your obedient Servant,
" *The Clockmakers' Company,*   (Signed)   "J. STEWART.
" *Cowper's Court, Cornhill.*

(COPY ENCLOSED IN THE FOREGOING.)

" May it please your Lordships.—Mr. Spring Rice having, in his letter of the 13th September signified, that in consequence of a further application from the Watch and Clockmakers' Company, complaining of the injury done to their Trade for want of proper vigilance on the part of the Revenue officers, he (Mr. Spring Rice) was directed to desire that we would report to your Lordships whether we have reason to apprehend that any illegal importation of Watches and Clocks takes place, and in the event of such question being answered in the affirmative, that we would suggest whether any and what regulations, legislative or departmental, are necessary for checking such contraband traffic.

"In obedience to your Lordships' commands, we report :—

"That as regards Foreign made Watches, adverting to the portableness of the article, the facility with which they may be concealed, and the rate of duty payable thereon ; viz. 25 per cent., we are not prepared to deny the possibility of it being an article of traffic with the smuggler ; but we have no reason to believe that it is carried on to any great extent as a system of smuggling.

"The laws and regulations, however, which are in force for the prevention of smuggling, are equally applicable to Clocks and Watches as to any other goods liable to duty on importation into the United Kingdom ; and as regards the articles in question, we are not aware of any regulation, legislative or departmental, the adoption of which would efficiently check the illicit traffic therein.

"With regard to the complaint of the Memorialists, that injury is done to their trade for the want of proper vigilance on the part of the Revenue officers, we have to observe, that in consequence of a former representation from these parties to the same effect (copy of which your Lordships were pleased to transmit to us in Mr. Spring Rice's letter of the 18th May last), we called upon them to propose such further regulations as might appear to them advisable, with a view to detect or prevent the improper introduction of Foreign Clocks and Watches ; and in reply, they stated that their object was not an alteration of the law, but merely the vigilant carrying the same into effect, and as they had asserted that the officers of the revenue had permitted the importers of Foreign Clocks and Watches to enter those articles for the duty at a less amount than their real value, we issued a circular notice, dated 13th June, enjoining the officers at this port, and at all the outports, to the most vigilant attention, with a view to prevent the admission of Clocks and Watches at an improper valuation.

"We beg to add, that in the case of recent importation of Gold Watches which were entered for duty as being of the value of £90, the officers consulted some of the Members of the Committee of Watchmakers as to the correctness of the entry, and after having inspected the articles, they declared them to have been undervalued at least £50. per cent., whereas, on their being sold, under the provisions of the Regulation Act, the articles only realized eight per cent. more than the Crown paid for them, a result tending to prove that the opinion of the Committee was not altogether to be relied on.

(Signed)
"*Custom House,*
September 13, 1833.

"*Cowper's Court, Cornhill,*
January 10, 1834.

"SIR,

"I am directed by the Master and Wardens of the Company of Clockmakers of the City of London to acknowledge the receipt of a letter from Mr. J. Stewart, dated Treasury Chambers, 19th October, 1833, 1794. 2 . 1$\frac{4}{0}$, addressed to the Clockmakers' Company, Cowper's Court, Cornhill, and enclosing a copy of a letter, and report from the Honourable Commissioners of Customs to the Lords of the Treasury, dated 13th September, 1833.

"I am further directed to request the favour of you to thank their Lordships for this mark of their attention, as well as for the assurance contained in Mr. Stewart's letter of their Lordships' willingness to attend to any further suggestions the Master and Wardens may think proper to offer; and to adopt such measures as may on further consideration appear desirable for repressing the importation of Foreign Watches and Clocks, particularly the former.

"The Master and Wardens beg in the first place to offer some remarks on the letter and report of the Honourable Commissioners of Customs, and then, availing themselves of their Lordships' permission, they will state what they conceive will most conduce to the security of the revenue and the benefit of the Trade at large.

"To begin with the letter from the Honourable Commissioners of Customs to the Lords of the Treasury, which accompanies their report. The Commissioners there observe that the Company of Clockmakers, in a recent communication to the Treasury, complain of want of vigilance on the part of the Custom House Officers. The Master and Wardens of the Company certainly do complain of smuggling to an enormous and most injurious extent; from which they cannot avoid inferring the extreme negligence of the officers, and with very great reason. For, be it observed, that by a clause in the Act, entitled 'An Act to amend the Laws relating to the Customs' (25th July, 1828), passed five years ago, it is provided that all Clocks and Watches imported shall bear on two places, that is to say, on the works and on the dial, a name of a person and town, purporting to be the name and place of abode of the person who made them. This clause was added to the Bill at the express solicitation of the Company of Clockmakers; and that no excuse might be afforded for evading this clause by the Foreign Manufacturer, or for pleading ignorance of its existence, the Clerk of the Company (see pages 51, 52, and 53 of a printed statement of proceedings between the Company of Clockmakers and his Majesty's Government, London, 1832, of which a copy was sent to the Treasury, 13th of June, 1833), was directed to write to the French and Swiss Consuls, informing them of the circumstance, and enclosing a copy of the clause, not only in English, but translated into French The receipt of these letters and their enclosures was acknowledged by the two Consuls, accompanied by a promise to communicate their contents to their respective Governments. After this the plea of ignorance of the law cannot be offered, indeed it is one which is never allowed as an excuse when the revenue is concerned. Now, what is the fact? Warehouses, and even shop windows innumerable, not merely in the Metropolis, but in all the principal Cities and Towns in the Empire, but more particularly the watering places, such as Brighton, are full of Foreign Watches, publicly exposed for sale, which, in the face of the Act of Parliament, passed on purpose to meet the case, do not carry upon them a single name, much less a name of maker, and of place where made in two places, namely, on the dial and on the works, which, in conformity of the Act, they ought to bear. It follows as a matter of course, and to this fact your attention is particularly requested, that the whole of these Watches without names have been clandestinely brought into the country, because, in the state described, they are strictly prohibited, and could not be entered for payment of duty; and as a necessary consequence, that the revenue has been defrauded of the amount of duty they ought to have paid. So much in proof of the truth and justice of the complaint of the want of vigilance on the part of the officers. Some few solitary examples of the contrary have occurred, but they are extremely rare, and only show what might be done if proper vigilance were exercised.

"A seizure was recently made at a private house of 24 Gold Watches without names, and on the 15th November last 14 Gold Watches were seized in the Port of London, on board the William Jolliffe, from Hambro', Downie Master, addressed to H. Warburg, 17, Leman Street, Goodman's Fields, which were packed in a tin box, and attempted to be passed as a sample of clover seed. This last seizure was made in consequence of the suspicions of the Master of the vessel being raised by the weight of the box, and not through the vigilance of the officer on board.

"Though it were admitted, that from the portable nature of the article it is extremely difficult to prevent the illicit importation of Foreign Watches; still the immense quantity exposed for sale should lead to very strict measures for the prevention of a fraud so injurious to the revenue and ruinous to the British Watchmakers' Trade; and, if even these measures did not prove successful, still the illicitly imported Watches might legally be seized wherever they are secretly deposited or openly exposed for sale.

"I am now directed to offer the following observations upon the report :—

"In the first paragraph of their Report the Commissioners say, in reference to the illicit importation of Foreign Watches, 'We have no reason to believe it is carried on to any great extent as a system of smuggling.' Surely the Commissioners must totally have lost sight of the return, which it is most natural to suppose was furnished by themselves, laid upon the table of the House of Commons on the motion of Mr. Ewart, and ordered to be printed 5th July, 1833, which not only fully contradicts the above statement, but officially proves that the direct reverse is the case. It appears by this printed return, that the total value of the Foreign Watches imported in the last four years, ending with 1832, was £10,428. 12s.; and of the same exported, £9,714.; the value of the Watches remaining in the country being only £714. 12s. The absurdity of supposing such a conclusion to be even an approximation to the truth is so palpably evident, that it would be only a waste of time to contradict it further than by stating the fact that Foreign Watches to a greater amount in value may every day be seen exposed for sale in several individual shops in the Metropolis.

"In the second paragraph they say, 'The laws and regulations, however, which are in force for the prevention of smuggling, are equally applicable to clocks and watches, as to any other goods liable to duty on importation; and that they are not aware of any regulations, legislative or departmental, the adoption of which would effectually check the illicit traffic therein.' The first part of this statement is no doubt correct; but it does not follow that such regulations as are fitting to prevent the smuggling of bulky goods, are the best that can be adopted for small articles like watches; and the second part is evidently erroneous, inasmuch as a system of regulations has been distinctly pointed out to the Lords of the Treasury, and by their Lordships transmitted to the Board of Customs, (see letter signed J. Ker, dated Custom-house, 4th June, 1833), by the Company of Clockmakers, by the adoption of which, the evil complained of, though it would probably not be entirely done away with, yet would be very considerably diminished.

"Your attention is now requested to the next paragraph of the Report, in which the Commissioners state that they had 'called upon them (the Company) to propose such further regulations as might appear to them advisable, with a view to detect or prevent the improper introduction of foreign Clocks or Watches, and in reply they stated, that their object was not an alteration of the law, but merely the vigilant carrying the same into effect.' What is here stated is true to a certain extent ; but the Company had at that time, in fact, suggested regulations for enforcing the payment of duties on foreign Clocks and Watches, and for detecting such as were clandestinely introduced into this country, without requiring a legislative enactment new in principle, as before mentioned.

"In reference to the last paragraph of the Commissioners' Report, it is only necessary to observe, that the sales at which the Watches therein referred to were sold, are practically under the influence of the Jews, and that the Watches producing no more than they did, at sales conducted as these sales are, is no proof whatever that they were not worth more than they realised, which, however, it is admitted was more than the value at which they were attempted to be entered.

"Thus far it appeared proper to the Master and Wardens to notice the erroneous statements contained in the Letter and Report from the Honourable Commissioners of Customs to the Lords of the Treasury.

"There is another circumstance which I am directed very briefly to notice, as the Company do not allude to it but with great reluctance : it is the great quantity of smuggling understood to be carried on through the medium of the Foreign Office, by means of the immense bag brought over twice a week by the Messenger who is the bearer of the bag with the Government Despatches and Papers ; and also through the means of the Messenger of the French Embassy. A recent investigation has shewn, that even the French official seals have been surreptitiously made use of to forward such disgraceful proceedings.

"I am now directed by the Master and Wardens to observe, that when they addressed you on the 26th of July last, they were ignorant of the return moved for by Mr. Ewart, and ordered by the House of Commons to be printed the 5th of July, 1833. This return affords the most ample proof of the substantive correctness of the statements contained in the various Memorials and Letters addressed by them to the Lords of the Treasury, the Commissioners of Customs, and yourself.

"To insist further on the great number and great amount of value of the Watches clandestinely brought into the country, and the enormous amount of the loss that in consequence is sustained by the Revenue, and by the British manufacturer is quite unnecessary, and I am only directed to add, that the evil is daily and hourly increasing.

"All that has been advanced on the subject in the long-protracted and unfortunately hitherto fruitless correspondence that has taken place between the Company of Clockmakers and his Majesty's Government, is fully borne out by the Parliamentary document so repeatedly referred to; and this account, moved for by Mr. Ewart, may be considered, so far as regards the Manufacture of Clocks and Watches in these realms, as one of the most important documents ever laid on the table of the House of Commons.

"In answer to the second part of Mr. Stewart's letter, in which that gentleman states that the Lords of the Treasury 'are willing to receive any further communication from the Company, and to take such steps as, on full consideration, may appear desirable for the purpose of preventing, or of repressing any illicit importation of Foreign Watches,' I am directed to state, that it is the opinion of the Master and Wardens that great good would result from a simultaneous seizure in all parts of the kingdom of all Foreign Clocks and watches not bearing names of Maker and Place where made (in strict conformity with the Act of Parliament before referred to) in the possession of all wholesale and retail traders and dealers of whatever description they may be, whether foreigners or natives, and whether calling themselves Watchmakers, Jewellers, Warehousemen, General Dealers, Milliners, or by any other denomination. Such a proceeding, which in itself is strictly legal, and perfectly in accordance with the usual practice for the protection of the Revenue, followed by the adoption of the plan so repeatedly pressed, but hitherto in vain, by the Company upon the notice of the Lords of the Treasury, of causing all Clocks and Watches imported to be marked when the Duty is paid, such mark to be the proof of the duty having been paid; joined to compelling all persons dealing in those articles to take out an annual licence, as is the case with dealers in a variety of manufactured goods, and raw produce, would tend more to the benefit of the Revenue and the British Manufacturer, than any other measures that could be adopted. The watches seized would be sold for exportation, and the Home Market would thereby be relieved from a great quantity of Foreign Clocks and Watches now on sale; moreover the Foreign Manufacturer and his agent would be taught that the law was no longer to be infringed with impunity, and that the demi-official countenance they for so many years fancied they enjoyed, was at an end. It is respectfully and earnestly desired that the Lords of the Treasury would come to a determination as to the course to be pursued in this matter. The question is reduced to a very narrow compass: is the law of the land to be set at naught—the Revenue to be sacrificed, and the British Manufacturer to be seriously injured for the profit of the Foreign Manufacturer and the smuggler, and the pecuniary advantage of that class of British society, which, of all others, can best afford to pay for the article of home manufacture? This is what the question is reduced to—it is idle any longer to attempt to disguise the fact; and although nothing can be further from the intention of the Clockmakers' Company, than to assume a tone of unbecoming haste or positiveness; yet they feel that in order to do their duty to themselves, and to save their Lordships any further doubt as to the real facts of the case, they should state plainly, that unless it be the desire of the Government to sacrifice both the Revenue and the interest of the Home to the Foreign Manufacturer, immediate means should be taken to put an end to the illicit traffic complained of.

" I am, Sir,
" Your most obedient humble Servant,

(Signed) " GEORGE ATKINS,
" *Clerk to the Company.*

"*To the Right Hon. Spring Rice,*
" *Secretary to the Treasury, &c., &c., &c.*

"Treasury Chambers,
"May 7, 1834.
"Gentlemen,

"I have laid before the Lords Commissioners of His Majesty's Treasury your further Memorial on the subject of the illegal importation of Foreign Clocks and Watches.

"In reply I am directed by their Lordships to inform you, that they do not consider that either of the suggestions submitted by you would be attended with any beneficial results, even if it were possible to carry them into practice; and it does not appear to my Lords that any further measures can be adopted for the prevention of smuggling in Clocks and Watches.

"I am, Gentlemen,
"Your obedient Servant,

"*Mr. G. Atkins and Others,* (Signed) "J. STEWART.
"*Watch and Clockmakers, Cowper's-court, Cornhill.*

"(COPY, No. 4.)

"*Seventh Article of the Ordonnance of the King of the French,*
"*published in Paris on the 4th inst.*

"HORLOGERIE.—Montres d'or 6 per 100 de la valeur: montres d'argent 19 per 100 de la valeur. Mouvements de toutes sortes, sans boitiers, 10 per 100 de la valeur.

"L'importation en sera permise par les seuls bureaux ouverts au transit de marchandises prohibées. Les montres ainsi introduites seront dirigées par acquit a caution, et sous le plomb des douanes, sur l'un des cinq bureaux de garantie de Paris, Lyon, Besançon, Montbeliard, et Lons-le-Saulnier, pour y etre *essayées* et *marquées* et y acquitter le droit de garantie.

"TRANSLATION OF THE ABOVE.

"WATCH-WORK.—Gold Watches to pay six per cent. *ad valorem* duty, Silver Watches ten per cent., movements of every description, not in cases, ten per cent.

"Importation will only be permitted through the bureaux for prohibited goods. Watches thus introduced shall be forwarded, under bond, and under the seal of the Customs, to one of the five examining establishments at Paris, Lyons, Besançon, Montbeliard, or Lons-le-Saulnier, there to be examined and marked, and the duty paid."

On the 6th of February, 1837, the Court of Assistants again approached the Board of Trade with a complaint as to the still increasing illicit importation of Foreign Clocks and Watches which, whilst continuing to cause great injury to the Revenue, was also destroying the English Manufacture.

Their Memorial recapitulates the practical remedies for this state of things which they had so frequently urged on former occasions, unfortunately to no purpose, viz. :—

1st.—Marking the Watches as in France.
2nd.—Rendering all unmarked Watches exposed for sale liable to seizure.
3rd.—Obliging the Dealers in them to take out an Annual Licence, as Dealers in a variety of other imported articles were obliged to do.

The Memorial then proceeds to suggest two other remedial measures, for both of which it is urged abundant precedents exist, viz. :—

1st.—A new enactment for regulating the conditions under which Foreign Clocks and Watches should be allowed to be imported.
2nd.—To place the Customs Officers on the same footing with regard to the seizure of Watches and Clocks as they were with regard to the seizure of Silks, viz., to give them the benefit of the seizures to the full extent of their value instead of one half only as was then the case.

And in support of the suggestions, advances the following arguments :—

"From the very loose wording of so much of the last Act (viz. 3rd and 4th William 4, Cap. 52, Sec. 58), for regulating the duties on imports and exports as relates to the importation of Clocks and Watches, those Articles are now allowed to be entered for the payment of duty with the name of the maker and the place where made merely painted on them, a former Act (4th George 4, Cap. 24, Sec. 81) required them to be engraved; the consequence resulting from Clocks and Watches being imported with the names, &c., only painted on them is that these names are subsequently taken out and English names and places substituted, and they are then sold as articles of English manufacture.

"An individual of the name of Vieyres, residing at No. 40 Pall Mall, has sold a number of Foreign Watches with his name and address in full upon them, the cases of which were also Foreign. The same fraud is also practised in Clocks, the name, real or fictitious of the maker and his place of abode being painted on the back of the clock and the dial, and having passed the Custom House are then taken off without difficulty or injury to the work by Alcohol, and any other name that may be required substituted in their place. Mr. Thomas Cox Savory, of 47 Cornhill, in his innumerable daily advertizements advertizes Clocks, and among others Clocks to strike the hour and half hour, at Five Guineas each.

"From the wording of the advertizement any person not alive to the imposition would suppose that these Clocks were made by Mr. Thomas Cox Savory, and consequently that they were English. The fact is otherwise, they have it is true his name and 'London' on them, but every part is foreign.

"Very recently the late Master and one of the Members of the Court of Assistants, at the request of some of the Officers of H. M. Customs, inspected sundry Clocks and Watches at the Custom House that had been detained for further examination in consequence of the names being only painted on them. The Clocks were precisely similar to those sold by Mr. Thomas Cox Savory with foreign names painted on the back plates and dials. In the presence of the Officers of the Customs the names were removed from one of the Clocks by the application of Spirits of Wine without injury to any part of the work. The names on the Watches were affixed to little metal slips dovetailed into the work which could easily be removed, and other slips bearing different names substituted in their stead.

"The whole matter was got up with a fraudulent intent to deceive the unwary and ignorant, for the Balances of some of the Watches shown to the Master and Assistants were made to resemble Chronometer Balances, but in point of fact were not such, and could not be converted into Chronometer Balances at all. These Watches were large, of the shape and appearance of English Watches, and evidently brought into this Country to be re-exported, and it is more than probable they were re-exported with an English name and 'London' upon them.

"A great number of other persons might be named who notoriously sell foreign Clocks and Watches with their own names and 'London' engraved upon them, but it was thought sufficient to name only two, and the ungracious task of particularizing persons by name would not even now be resorted to, but for the purpose of meeting by anticipation a direct denial of the facts.

"In reference to the condition in which foreign Clocks and Watches should be allowed to be entered for payment of duties, the Master, Wardens, and Court of Assistants beg to propose to your Lordships that the following Clause (being very similar to 4 Geo. IV., Cap. 24, Sec. 81) should be forthwith substituted for the one now in force. 'And be it further enacted, That no Watch of Foreign Manufacture shall be imported or warehoused under the provisions of this Act, upon the Case or Cases of which any mark or stamp shall be impressed, which shall be similar to, or shall purport to be, or shall be intended to represent any mark or stamp of the Goldsmiths' Company of London, or any other legal British assay marks or stamps, and that no Clock or Watch of Foreign Manufacture shall be so imported or Warehoused, upon the Face or upon any part of which the word 'London,' or the name of any other Town or place of the United Kingdom shall be engraven or painted, or shall in any way appear so as to purport or give colour that such Clock or Watch is of the manufacture of the United Kingdom, and that no Clock or Watch of Foreign Manufacture shall be so imported or warehoused unless a distinguishing number and the name or names of some person and place shall be permanently and visibly engraved, and shall appear distinctly upon the frame or plate of such Clock or Watch, purporting to be the name or names and place of abode of the person or persons by whom such Clock or Watch was made; and also upon the face or Dial of such Clock or Watch, but, if made of Enamel or Glass, the name and place shall be thereon visibly painted, and the painting burnt in, and that no Clock or Watch of Foreign Manufacture shall be imported or warehoused under this Act in an incomplete state, that is to say, not having the movement, with all its component parts, finished and properly fixed and secured in its case, on pain of forfeiture of such Clock or Watch.'"

"I now proceed to the second regulation to which the Master, Wardens, and Court of Assistants wish to call your Lordships' attention, viz., to place the Officers of the Customs on the same footing in reference to seizures made of Clocks and Watches, as they are with regard to seizures of Silks. In the case of Silks the Officers have the full benefit of the proceeds of the seized property. In the case of Clocks and Watches they have only the ordinary portion of the produce of the seizure. This boon was conceded to the British Silk Manufacturer some time since, and has been attended with the greatest advantage to them and to the Revenue :—Clocks and Watches, but more particularly Watches are articles that are very easily smuggled and much vigilance is requisite to detect the operations of the Smugglers, moreover they are Articles that are easily damaged and produce but little when sold at the different Custom house sales. These circumstances render it more necessary that the inducement to exertion on the part of the Officers should be made as great as possible."

"There is no branch of Manufacture that requires legislative support more than that of Clocks and Watches, particularly the latter; the foreign Watches are made almost without exception in Switzerland, and the difference in the cost of production between that Country and England is so great that it is impossible for the English Manufacturer to enter into competition with the Swiss Manufacturer, for even in France where the value of labour is less than in England, the Watch Manufacturer has been ruined by the cheaper Swiss Watches. This is a fact that has been long known to the Master, Wardens, and Court of Assistants of the Company of Clockmakers, but which has never been so publicly stated as it is in Dr. Browning's Report on the Commerce and Manufactures of Switzerland, presented to both Houses of Parliament in the last Session by command of His Majesty, wherein it is mentioned at Page 34 that (recently) 'not ten Watches are made in Paris in one year.' Surely it is necessary to preserve the British Manufacturer from a similar fate."

On the 6th of March following, an answer was read from the Board of Trade, dated 23rd February, intimating that they could not undertake to recommend to Parliament the enactment of any more restrictive or severe law than was then in force.

On the 22nd November, 1841, the Court agreed to a Memorial to the Lords of the Treasury, in which reference is made to the history of their numerous previous communications with the Government already set out in these pages. All that is material in this document is contained in the following Extracts therefrom, viz. :—

"The Master, Wardens, and Court of Assistants had considered the matter set entirely at rest, by Mr. J. Stewart's Letter of the 7th of May, 1834, and that all further application to Her Majesty's Government on the subject would be perfectly useless; they have however been induced to alter that opinion, in consequence of the Appointment of a Commission to enquire into abuses in the collection of the 'Revenue,' and of certain Proceedings that took place in reference to a seizure of Foreign Watches, to a very considerable amount (the property of M. Moulinie, of Geneva), that took place last spring, and which, after a motion for a new trial in the Court of Exchequer, has very recently ended in the condemnation of the Goods seized. Another circumstance has also caused the Master, Wardens, and Court to adopt the present course of proceedings. It would seem by an Official Letter, addressed to one of the Members of the Court, who had been subpœnaed to give evidence on the part of the Crown, on the trial above alluded to, by the Solicitor to the Customs, of which a copy accompanies this Memorial, that in the present state of the law no seizure can be made of Foreign Clocks and Watches, though they should, from the circumstance of their not carrying the name of a maker, as directed by the Act of Parliament, be known not to have paid the Duty, unless seized *in transitu;* or, as in the case of Moulinie, seized in the possession of the original Importer or Smuggler.

"One of the objects of the present Memorial is to call the attention of the Lords of the Treasury to the above fact of the defect in the legal enactments, for the protection of the Revenue and the Trade, trusting that, at the first convenient opportunity, the Law will be amended so as to render it as effective as the importance of the subject deserves. The subject brought before the consideration of their Lordships, is divided into two heads—1st. The Collection of the Revenue; and, 2nd. The Protection of the Home Manufacture. Both these considerations have been so repeatedly urged upon the notice of Her Majesty's Government, that the Master, Wardens, and Court have considered that the best mode of attaining the desired object would be to forward to their Lordships a printed Copy of all the proceedings that have taken place between Her Majesty's Government and the Company, from the 27th of February, 1787, to the present time, embracing a period of upwards of half a century; and to refer to such parts of the same as appear to be most important in reference to the present state of things.

"It appears that the Duty upon Foreign Clocks and Watches has varied from 75 to 25, the present duty, per cent. *ad valorem*. Such a Duty, if effectually collected, would have proved very productive to the Revenue : the contrary is well known to be the case. Indeed the fact is put beyond a doubt, by the return of the amount of Duty paid upon Watches imported during the four years ending with 1832, as shewn by an Official Return, made by order of the House of Commons, upon the motion of Mr. Ewart, and ordered to be printed the 5th of July, 1833; and there is every reason to believe that the duty has not been more productive since.

"The following is a copy of the Return :—

	1829.			1830.			1831.			1832.		
	£.	s.	d.	£.	s.	d.	£.	s.	d.	£.	s.	d.
Value of Foreign Watches entered	3043	5	0	2399	1	0	2688	2	0	2295	4	0
Value of Foreign Watches exported on which Drawback was paid	2838	15	0	2278	0	0	2509	0	0	2088	5	0
	204	10	0	121	1	0	179	2	0	209	19	0

Shewing a total balance of the value of the Watches imported for home consumption of 714*l*. 12*s*., upon which a Duty of 178*l*. 13*s*. was paid, giving an average of 44*l*. 13*s*. 3*d*. for the amount of Duty paid in each of the four years.

"The following may be quoted, as one of a great many facts that might be offered in proof of the correctness of the assertion that very few of the Watches brought into the country pay Duty. There were recently exposed for sale in one shop window in the Strand, 24 dozen or 288 Gold Foreign Watches, and as many Silver. Taking the average value of the Gold at 7*l*. each, and of the Silver at 2*l*. 10*s*. each, as the import value, which is considerably less than their real value, the total amount will be 2736*l*., on which the amount of Duty that ought to have been paid is 684*l*., being only 30*l*. 12*s*. less than the total amount of Duty paid in the four years, 1829, 1830, 1831, and 1832.

"The great increase in the illicit Importation of Watches has been since the Peace in 1815. The value of the Watches brought into these realms, by dealers and private individuals, since that period does not average at the lowest computation, less than 200,000*l*. annually, upon which the amount of Duty, at 25 per cent. would have been 50,000*l*. annually. Twenty-six years have elapsed since the Peace, consequently, supposing the above calculation to be correct, which, from the data on which it is founded, there is good reason to believe it is, the total amount of Duty received would have been the very large sum of 1,300,000*l*. This calculation agrees very nearly with a similar one made in the year 1833. In a Memorial addressed to the Lords of the Treasury, dated the 7th of May, of that year, the value of the Watches imported, in the four years ending 1832, was estimated at 730,000*l*., averaging 182,500*l*. each year. It may be said, in reply to this statement, that if the Duty had been rigidly enforced, the number of Watches imported would have been less. Suppose, for argument's sake, Watches to the amount of only half the value; namely, 100,000*l*. a year to have been imported; in that case the amount of Duty received would have been 25,000*l*. a year, or 650,000*l*. in the 26 years since 1815. Whereas the total amount of the Duty received in 26 years, taking for data the average of the Duty paid in the years 1829, 1830, 1831, and 1832, which is 44*l*. 13*s*. 3*d*. a year, as shewn by the Return printed in the order of the House of Commons before-mentioned, will be only 1164*l*. 4*s*. 6*d*. shewing a loss to the Revenue of 648,838*l*. 15*s*. 6*d*. If the correctness of this statement is doubted, the exact amount of the Duty paid on Watches imported since the Peace can, it is presumed, very easily be ascertained by reference to the Board of Customs, which will shew whether or not the average amount of Duty paid has increased since 1832.

"The great loss sustained by the Revenue had been fully brought under the notice of His late Majesty's Government, on several occasions.

"The second consideration to which the Master, Wardens, and Court of Assistants are anxious to call your Lordships' attention, is the situation of the Home Manufacture. So much has been said in the former communications from the Court to Her Majesty's Government on this subject, that the Master, Wardens, and Court abstain from doing more than to refer your Lordships to the same.

"The suffering Foreign Watches to be bonded for exportation without payment of Duty, has proved extremely injurious to the British Manufacture. This most perfectly non-reciprocal measure was introduced in 1822 by the Right Hon. Mr. Wallace; a measure that in the case of bulky goods might be useful as the means of employing British Shipping, but in the case of such small articles as Watches utterly useless, but to promote the interests of the Foreign Manufacturer to the prejudice of the English Manufacturer. In order to obviate, as far as was practicable, the evil consequences that it was foreseen would result from this, so far as the Watch Manufacture was concerned, most mischievous measure, it was proposed to Mr. Wallace to introduce certain Conditions or Regulations, four in number, into the Warehousing Bill before Parliament, for the protection of the British Manufacture, a Copy of which was sent to that gentleman. By much the most important of the four, of which notice will be taken hereafter, was declared by Mr. Wallace to be inadmissible; the others were adopted. The original Warehousing Bill, your Lordships' Memorialists believe, was subsequently repealed, and embodied in the General Customs Bill since passed. Owing to the ambiguous mode in which the Clause in the Act is worded, it has not afforded the protection required; and the permission granted by the Legislature to Bond Watches for exportation without payment of Duty, has proved most ruinous to the British Manufacturer, and opened a wide door to frauds and deceptions of various kinds.

"The Master, Wardens, and Court of Assistants, will now as briefly as possible allude to the measures which have been repeatedly urged upon the notice of Her Majesty's Government; and which, had they been adopted, they think they may confidently venture to assert would have secured the due collection of the Revenue, and the protection of the British Manufacture. The principal of these, and the only one that will at present be urged at any length, is marking the Watches when the Duty is paid. The immense advantage that would attend this measure is this; that, as in the case of Gold and Silver Plate, so long as the article is in existence it carries on itself the proof of having paid the Duty. This plan of marking was proposed to the Lords of the Committee of Trade so long since as February 22nd, 1787. In a Memorial of that date, addressed to the latter, such a measure is very expressly recommended. In this Memorial the Company claims the right of marking the Watches by virtue of their Charter. But that in no way affects the general merits of the case, and the claim has not been pressed since. The same measure was again urged upon the Right Honourable Nicholas Vansittart, Chancellor of the Exchequer, in a Memorandum forwarded to him December 21st, 1815, as follows. '5th. All Foreign Clocks and Watches to have a mark permanently imprinted on some part of the movement or cases, by the Officers of the Customs, when the Duty is paid.' Again, in 1823, at the period of the passing of the Warehousing Bill, in which the permission to Bond Watches was included, a Committee was appointed to communicate with the Right Honourable Mr. Wallace on the subject, when it was resolved, as Mr. Wallace was determined not to omit Clocks and Watches in his proposed Warehousing Bill, to endeavour to obtain certain Clauses to render the Measure as little mischievous as possible; and a Memorandum was sent him, of which the following was the first Clause, 'That all Foreign Clocks and Watches admitted to entry, should have a distinguishing mark impressed upon them before going out of the King's Warehouse.' This proposition, without stating any reason for omitting to adopt it, Mr. Wallace declared was inadmissible. The marking was again pressed upon the notice of the Lords of the Treasury, in a Memorial addressed to their Lordships, dated February 8th, 1832, as follows, '2nd. That the Collection of the Duty be rigidly enforced; for which purpose all Foreign Clocks and Watches to be marked when the Duty is paid: the mark to be the proof of the Duty having been paid. That the said marking be done at the Custom House, by an Officer appointed by the Commissioners of His Majesty's Customs.'

"The marking was again brought to their Lordships' notice, by implication, in a Memorial addressed to the Lords of the Treasury, dated 7th May, 1833, as follows. ' 1st. That the Collection of the Duty upon all Foreign Clocks and Watches brought into these Realms, be enforced with the same exactness as is done in the case of various other articles; and in such a manner that those that have paid the Duty can be easily distinguished from those that have not.'

"No reason was ever directly given why the marking the Clocks and Watches was objectionable, or should not be adopted. Mr. Wallace contented himself with saying the proposition was inadmissible, without assigning any reason whatever. In a Letter from the Right Honourable Spring Rice, dated Treasury Chambers, 7th June, 1833, addressed to the Clerk of the Company, in reference to the proposed marking, that Gentleman makes the following remark,—'The facility of counterfeiting the proposed marks would be a bar to a compliance with this suggestion.' The short Answer to this objection is, that a considerable revenue is derived from a duty imposed upon all manufactured Gold and Silver Plate, which is entirely realized and collected by marking the plate ; and that the marks and stamps impressed on the plate have very rarely been attempted to be counterfeited. The Master, Wardens, and Court are, however, aware that it has been privately stated that such delicate articles as Watches could not be marked without, to a certain degree, damaging the same. That this is quite a fallacy is proved by the fact, that all the Foreign Watches imported into France have, for some time past, been marked on the case of the Watch, without injury or detriment to the Watch in any respect. The Master, Wardens, and Court abstain from entering into any detail how the marking is effected, contenting themselves with confidently asserting that whatever results can be produced by mechanical skill and dexterity in France, the same can most certainly be done in England. The marking Foreign Watches was, your Memorialists believe, commenced in France some time in 1833 or 1834, and has been found to work extremely well. It is worthy of notice, that in France the Government mark on the Foreign Watches imported certifies not only that the import duty has been paid on the Watch, but also that the gold of which the case is made, is of the quality of 18 carats. For this purpose each case is assayed, which is a nice and difficult operation, much more so than mere marking, but still it is done, and most rigidly ; but without the least injury to the Watch or its Case.

"All that the Master, Wardens, and Court ask of your Lordships is, that the mark should be the voucher of the import duty having been paid, without reference to the quality of the gold of which the case is made. The subject of marking the Watches, as practised in France, has recently been entered into very much in detail, in a Correspondence between Mr. Ross, Surveyor-General of the Customs, and the Member of the Court before alluded to, in which the mode of assaying and marking the Watches, and levying the duty, as practised in France, is fully explained. It is presumed your Lordships can, as a matter of course, have access to this Correspondence ; but if your Lordships prefer it, the papers being in the possession of the Clerk of the Company, a copy of the same shall be furnished.

"Several minor regulations might be offered to the consideration of your Lordships, that would greatly tend to ensure the due collection of the Revenue, and at the same time protect the Home Manufacture. One of these would be to require all dealers in Foreign Watches to take out an annual licence, (English Watchmakers are obliged to take out a licence in the shape of a Plate licence, at the annual cost of 2*l*. 6*s*. at the least,) but the Master, Wardens, and Court decline noticing them further at present. The result of the experience of upwards of 50 years, sufficiently proves the total uselessness of all Custom-House regulations unaccompanied by marking, and for this reason they will not propose any further measure, until made acquainted with your Lordships' determination, on the subject of marking all Clocks and Watches imported.

" Should your Lordships, on mature consideration, determine to adopt a measure that has been found to answer the desired purpose in France, they will request the favour of an interview for two or three Members of the Court with the Right Honourable the Chancellor of the Exchequer. Should your Lordships, on the other hand, decline to adopt the measure, the Master, Wardens, and Court, will not trouble you further on the subject, persuaded that so doing would be only needlessly to occupy your Lordships' most valuable time, to produce no beneficial result.

" The Master, Wardens, and Court, will now mention a circumstance connected with the illicit importation of Foreign Watches, that they consider deserving of your Lordships' notice. In a Memorial addressed to the Lords of the Treasury, dated February 1832, it is stated, that the Foreign Manufacturers had it in contemplation to remove their principal establishments from Paris to London. This has come to pass, and London is now the head quarters of all the principal Foreign Watch Manufacturers : and there is no description of Foreign Watch that, if wanted, cannot be immediately procured in this City. A further inducement with the Foreign Watch Manufacturer to prefer London to Paris is to be found in the following circumstance—That the Cases of all Gold Watches imported into France, must, as before-mentioned, be made of Gold of the value of 18 carats, otherwise they are liable to be seized, and the parties in whose possession they are found severely punished. Such is not the case with the Foreign Importer here. But the English Watchmakers are by law compelled to make the cases of their Gold Watches of 18 carat Gold. The Act of Parliament not applying to Foreign Watches, the cases of a great many of the Gold Watches brought into these realms are made of Gold of 16 carats only ; and your Memorialists are credibly informed that it is in contemplation to send over Watches in cases of the quality of only 14 carats. The making the Watches in cases of such inferior Gold is a great pecuniary advantage, though not very creditable, in a moral point of view, to the Foreign Manufacturer, for the whole of these Watches are sold as though the cases were of 18 carat Gold. This is a fraud that could not be practised in France.

" With regard to the Foreign Clocks, the Master, Wardens, and Court, are of opinion, the article being more bulky, and comparatively of much less value than Watches, that the duty is more generally collected than it is upon Watches, with the exception of Clocks of a particular description called Balance or Carriage Clocks, of which great numbers are smuggled into the country, particularly at the different watering places on the coast ; but that, nevertheless, from the very loose manner in which the Customs Act is worded, many frauds are practised which might easily be prevented. For example, the name of the maker and place where made, required by the Act to be shewn on the dial, in the place of being indented by stamping, or cut into the dial by engraving, in the case of metal dials, or burnt in in the case of enamel dials, as is customary in English Clocks, is merely painted, and can be removed by the application of alcohol, without difficulty, or injury to the appearance of the dial. This experiment has been made with complete success in the King's Warehouse at the Custom House. In the case of a great many of these Clocks, before they are exposed for sale, the painted name is removed, and an English name and 'London' substituted in its place; they are then sold as English Clocks. As these articles are almost always of very inferior quality, this fraud is extremely prejudicial to the character of the British Manufacture as well as to the interests of the Manufacturer.

> In conclusion, the Master, Wardens, and Court of Assistants of the Company of Clock Makers of the City of London, very respectfully beg the favour of your Lordships, to take the subject of the present depressed state of the Manufacture of Clocks and Watches in this Country into your most serious consideration, in reference to the injury the trade sustains by the illicit importation of Foreign Clocks and Watches."

To this Memorial an answer was received in a Letter from the Treasury, dated the 29th January, 1842, to the effect that, after consultation with the Board of Trade, the Treasury, whilst regretting the existing evils under which the Trade was stated to labour, were of opinion that they would not be removed by the stamping of Foreign Watches, which would, moreover, be attended with serious inconvenience. They further intimated that Vendors of Foreign or Home-made Gold or Silver Watches were equally liable to the usual plate licence duty; that prosecutions had been equally instituted against both classes, and that there was no reason to think that the duty was not as regularly paid by one as by the other.

This reply provoked a rejoinder from the Company in the shape of a fresh Memorial, in which they reminded the Treasury that whilst the Revenue lost to the extent of from £20,000 to £25,000 per annum :—

> "The only persons who benefit from the present state of things are the Swiss Manufacturers and the Smugglers, for it is well to bear in mind that every (so called) French Watch smuggled into this country is made in Switzerland, the only country in Europe the inhabitants of which pay neither rates nor taxes, and with whom it is, therefore, impossible for the English Manufacturer to compete. It is further to be observed, and this is very important, that not anything new is asked of their Lordships, the prayer of the Company's Memorial of the 9th December last being merely that the existing Law should be put in force, and not suffered to become a dead letter for the benefit of Foreigners and Contrabandists.

> " Having thus shown the importance of the subjects the Master, Wardens, and Court of Assistants have with much reluctance resolved again to address

your Lordships, being persuaded that the 'serious inconvenience,' which you stated in your answer of the 29th January would result from 'stamping Foreign Watches,' must be the result of some misconception as to the difficulties attendant upon the marking, or mis-information derived from parties who have a personal interest in perpetuating a state of things equally ruinous to the revenue and to the individuals engaged in the manufacture of Clocks and Watches in this Country.

"As the best and most convincing proof that can be offered to your Lordships, that the Cases of the Swiss Watches are marked in France without injuring them, the Master, Wardens, and Court of Assistants have forwarded to your Lordships the Gold Case of a Swiss Watch, particularly light and delicate, weighing only 9 dwts., which has been marked in France on the front of the pendant; the mark, which is extremely distinct and visible, notwithstanding the Watch has been made and in use many years, is a voucher that the Gold is of the quality of 18 carats, and that the Watch has paid the import duty into France; that the case has not sustained any injury from the marking is perfectly clear. This case is of no value but as bullion, and is quite at your Lordships' service as long as you choose to keep it. It may be asserted as an objection to stamping, that the marks may be counterfeited, but so may the marks impressed on the Gold and Silver plate at Goldsmiths' Hall when the duty is paid, as a proof that it has been paid; yet this is the only security for the collection of that branch of the Revenue, as instances are very rare of the marks having been attempted to be forged.

"The Master, Wardens, and Court, from motives of delicacy, abstain from offering any opinion how the marking should be effected. Their Lordships will find no difficulty in obtaining information on this subject, and they will venture to name one individual, Mr. Holtzapffel, the well-known maker of machines of every description, who from his knowledge of the subject is peculiarly qualified to afford their Lordships the best information. In the present state of the relations between this country and France, there would probably be no difficulty in obtaining permission for an individual sent by the Government to see how the stamping is effected in that country. This would remove all practical objections, because no individual, however interested in perpetuating the present state of things, will venture to assert that Watches cannot be equally well marked in England as in France. The Master, Wardens, and Court are sorry to observe that your Lordships have not taken any notice of that part of their Memorial which related to certain abuses in reference to the importation of Foreign Clocks.

"The Master, Wardens, and Court regret that they did not express their meaning more distinctly in their Memorial of the 9th December on the subject of Licences. What they stated was not in reference to the Plate Licence as applied to Foreign Watches; their intention was to suggest that a separate licence should be taken by all persons dealing in Foreign Clocks and Watches for permission so to do, without reference to any other licence. A licence of £2 a year would produce a revenue of not less than £10,000.

"There are abundant authorities for such proceeding. The case of an Auctioneer is particularly in point. An Auctioneer in an extensive line of business, independent of an annual licence of £5 5s., is obliged to take out additional licences to the amount altogether of £35 4s. For the details of these licences your Lordships are referred to a letter to, and answer from, a Firm of the first respectability, copies of which accompany this Memorial.

"In conclusion, the Master, Wardens, and Court of Assistants of the Company of Clockmakers of the City of London would feel very much obliged if the Right Hon. the Chancellor of the Exchequer, and the Vice-President of the Board of Trade, would have the goodness to grant an interview to two or three members of the Court, as they cannot help being convinced that such a proceeding would, by mutual explanation, remove the difficulties that at present exist, to the adopting the same mode of distinguishing the Clocks and Watches that have paid the import duty from those that have not, as is practised in France."

This last Memorial only received the courtesy of an acknowledgment at the hands of the Government, and the return of the Gold Watch Case with which it was accompanied.

In July, 1843, a Bill was before Parliament, entitled "A Bill to amend the laws relating to the Customs," which, by Clause 10, proposed to repeal the restrictions and prohibitions which had been made in accordance with the Act, 3rd and 4th William IV, cap. lii, sec. 58, relating to the importation of Foreign Watches and Clocks; and the Company agreed to a Petition to Parliament against such Clause, which they asserted would be absolutely fatal to the English manufacturer. They, moreover, on the 2nd August, presented a Memorial to the Treasury on the subject, and urged them to withdraw the Clause from the Bill, which, they alleged, if passed, would enable unprincipled individuals to import articles in parts at different periods, and in different places, incomplete and consequently of little value, the amount of duty being proportionately small; a trick of a similar character having been played with gloves, by importing separately parcels of right and left-hand gloves. They contended that the Clause would utterly destroy the very small amount of protection afforded to the British manufacturer who had suffered by the then recent reduction of duty on Foreign Watches, which reduction the President of the Board of Trade had admitted in the House of Commons had proved a failure so far as preventing smuggling was concerned.

The Memorial concludes as follows:—

"It may not be amiss to notice that all English Clocks and Watches, entered for exportation, must carry the name and place of abode of the Maker on the frame and on the dial. In point of fact the Law is more indulgent to the Foreign than to the English Manufacturer. The justice of such a proceeding it is difficult to understand.

"The Master, Wardens, and Court of Assistants consider they have good reason to complain of the little courtesy with which they have been treated by your Lordships. The first intimation that a measure of such great interest to the Trade was in progress came from the Member for Finsbury. During the long period the Right Hon. William Pitt was in office, a communication was regularly made to the Master, Wardens, and Court of Assistants, generally through the medium of the Secretary to the Treasury, whenever he had it in contemplation to make any alteration in the Laws relating to Clocks and Watches. During this period some very important measures were brought before Parliament, among others the Tax on Wearers of Watches, and the alteration of the Standard of the Gold of which the Watch Cases were made.

"In conclusion, the Master, Wardens, and Court of Assistants of the Company of Clockmakers of the City of London, very respectfully beg the favour of your Lordships to take this subject into your most serious consideration, not doubting but you will see the necessity that exists for continuing the Law as it now stands, and that you will direct Clause No. 10 to be withdrawn from the Bill, now in progress through Parliament, to amend the Laws relating to the Customs."

On consideration of this Bill by the House of Commons in Committee, on the 5th August, Clause 10, to which the Company had thus objected, was thrown out.

In January, 1849, the attention of the Court was directed to the fact, that a number of Foreign Watches in Metal Cases in imitation of Gold, had been advertized for sale as "Gold Watches" in the Catalogue of the Custom House Sale of the preceding Quarter, but had been subsequently withdrawn, and that they had been again catalogued in the then forthcoming Quarterly Sale as "Watches" only, but with the prices on which the advances were to be made as high as Gold Watches.

It was thereupon determined to issue an Advertisement in the Daily Newspapers, cautioning the public with regard to them, seeing that they might be purchased by interested persons, who might avail themselves of the circumstance of their very great resemblance to Gold Watches, to sell them as such, and thereby defraud the public.

On the 2nd February, in the same year, the Court agreed to the following Memorial, by way of protest, to the Lords of the Treasury :—

"*To the Right Honourable the Lords Commissioners of Her Majesty's Treasury :*
"*The Memorial of the Master, Wardens, and Court of Assistants, of the Company of Clockmakers of the City of London,*

"SHEWETH,
"That there were in the spring of 1848 imported into the Port of London, and entered at the Custom House for Duty, but without the

customary distinction of Gold, Silver, and Metal, a parcel of Watches, in number about 330, which were made at Lausanne, in the Canton de Vaud, for the express purpose of defrauding the Revenue of this Country. They are supposed to have been entered by a person calling himself Piccard, as Agent for the Maker, an individual of the name Bonnet, notorious for the manufacture of Gold Cases of only 6 and 8 carat Gold, but mark'd purporting to be 18 carat Gold. The Watches were made to resemble Gold Watches, but entered merely as Watches, that in the event of their being discovered to be not Gold, but Metal, they might not be liable to seizure. They were valued at an extremely low price, supposing them to be Gold, which they purported in appearance to be, but at very much above their value as Metal Watches which they really are. The Watches were seized for being under-valued under the supposition that they were Gold, and paid for with an addition of 10 per cent. *ad valorem*, and the parties concerned openly boasted in Switzerland of the trick they had played the Custom House in London. The Watches were brought forward at the November customary sale, and catalogued as 'Gold Watches.' While on public view it was first discovered that the Watches were not Gold, but Metal, and in consequence they were withdrawn. At the last sale (January 27th) they were again brought forward, but this time they were merely designated in the Catalogue as 'Watches.' Now this same Catalogue contains no fewer than 769 Watches, and, these excepted, the whole are accompanied by the proper and customary description, of whether of Gold or Silver, with the prices at which they were put up and the advances to be made were quite as high as those of many of the Gold Watches. The Watches should have been described as what they are, 'Metal Watches,' and a proportionate price put upon them. The omission of the word 'Metal' was repeated too often to be a mistake of the Printers, and no other construction can be put upon the omission but this, that it was for the same purpose it had been previously made by the Importer, which supposition is confirmed by the prices put upon the Watches in the Catalogue.

"It is perfectly true that a gross fraud was practised by the foreigner, and that the Revenue was defrauded to a considerable amount, but it will ever be a subject of regret that an attempt should have been made to recover the loss at the expense of the public, by a similar mode of proceeding to that by which the loss was occasioned.

"Your Memorialists beg to submit to your Lordships that more caution should be used when Watches are entered for Duty, to ascertain whether they are *bonâ fide* Gold, Silver, or Metal. This description embraces all the Watches made; and that the same should be duly noticed in the Catalogue of sale. There are one or two instances on record of Watches made in Steel and Platinum cases, but the number is so few that it is not necessary to notice them. In the year 1848 no fewer than 2,618 Watches and 770 Clocks were sold at the Custom House sales. Now the selling these Watches in lots of two each, and the Clocks singly, offers a convenience to private purchasers which was not contemplated by the Legislature, and is very prejudicial to the English Manufacturer and Shopkeeper, who is compelled to take out an Annual Licence to carry on his trade. Formerly, to obviate this inconvenience, the Watches were sold in lots of ten and twelve each, and the Clocks in a similar manner. As the sales are at present conducted the Great Warehouse at the Custom House is converted into a Government Bazaar in which there are quarterly sales of Clocks and Watches, and the Commissioners of Customs into ordinary retail dealers. These two last, which are very serious inconveniences under which the Trade labours, are possibly of such a nature as can only be remedied by an Act of Parliament."

On the 5th of the same month, they adopted the following Petition to the House of Commons, which was presented on the 9th, and ordered to lie on the Table.

" *The Humble Petition of the Master, Wardens, and Court of Assistants of the Art or Mystery of Clockmaking of the City of London,*

" SHEWETH—

" That some time in 1848, 326 Watches, merely designated as Watches, but omitting the ordinary description of Gold, Silver, or Metal, were entered for payment of Duty at the Custom House, London, and seized for being under-valued, and as is customary in these cases paid for with 10 per cent. *ad valorem*, in addition. At the periodical Quarterly Sale at the Custom House in November last, these Watches were offered for sale as 'Gold Watches,' and catalogued as such, but upon a close examination were found to be Metal, and in consequence withdrawn, it being then discovered that a fraud had been practised upon the Customs. At the Quarterly Sale, January 27th, however, these Watches were again brought forward, and entered in the Catalogue as Watches, but without the distinguishing appellation of Gold, Silver, or Metal, though at quite as high a price and subject to the same advances each bidding as Gold Watches, thereby leaving the public to infer that they were in reality what they appeared to be, namely, Gold Watches.

" The remaining Watches in the sale, 443 in number, were distinctly catalogued as Gold and Silver Watches; in like manner the former ought to have been distinguished as Metal Watches. Their true character being detected at the sale, no biddings were made, and they still remain in the Queen's Warehouse.

" That with very few exceptions the whole of these Watches were lotted in pairs, and the Clocks singly, the Commissioners thereby departing from a rule generally observed with other merchandise of selling goods in bulk (the correctness of this assertion is shown by the printed catalogue), or, as regards Watches, in parcels of not less than 10 or 12, as was formerly the practice. The Clock and Watchmakers, therefore, complain of being made an exception to a general rule, and one which operates to their serious injury.

" That in the year 1848, no fewer than 2,730 Watches and 789 Clocks, lotted as before described, were sold at the Custom-House sales, thereby converting the great warehouse into a bazaar, and the Commissioners of Customs into ordinary retail dealers in Clocks and Watches.

" That the Chronometer is, next to the Compass, the most important instrument used in Navigation, and that, deprived of Chronometers, the War Navy of this Country would on Foreign service be very soon reduced to the same state Lord Anson describes the Squadron under his command to have been after doubling Cape Horn in the memorable expedition to attack the Spanish Settlements in the West Coast of South America.

"The workmen employed upon Chronometers may be designated as the *élite* of the workmen, selected out of the great mass, and unless the manufacture of Clocks and Watches is duly protected and the makers placed upon the footing of the most favored manufacturers, the nursery for workmen will be destroyed and ultimately the War Navy become dependent upon foreigners for Chronometers. It is especially deserving of notice, that the Chronometers that have performed the best, have hitherto invariably been made in England.

"Your Petitioners therefore humbly pray that your Honorable House will investigate the extent and the causes of the evils of which they complain, and will afford to your Petitioners such relief as to your Honorable House may seem meet."

An answer, dated the 31st March following, was received from the Treasury to the Memorial to that body, to the effect that they saw no reason to depart from the existing Regulations.

On 30th January, 1852, it was agreed to present a Petition to the House of Commons, and a Memorial to the Lords of the Treasury, directing their attention to the great injury likely to be done to the Trade by reason of the Treasury Minute to the Customs, on the subject of the *importation* or *exportation* of Foreign Watches having counterfeit British names and places of abode thereon, which Petition and Memorial are as follow :—

"*To the Honorable the Commons of Great Britain and Ireland in Parliament assembled,*

"*The Humble Petition of the Master, Wardens, and Fellowship of the Art and Mystery of Clockmaking of the City of London,*

"SHEWETH,

"'That in the 4th year of the reign of George 4, an Act was passed entitled an 'Act to make more effectual provision for permitting goods imported to be secured in Warehouses or other places without payment of duty on the first entry thereof, in which a clause was introduced specially to prevent Foreign Clocks and Watches made in imitation of British, and with British names and places of abode, from being warehoused and afterwards exported, and also by the 68th section of the 8 and 9 Victoria, Cap. 86, they are still further prohibited from being admitted into this Country *in transitu* agreeable to the above-named Act.

"Your Petitioners have seen with much concern that, notwithstanding the above Acts, condemning all Watches imported into this Country with counterfeit British names and places of abode, the following letter has been addressed from the Lords of the Treasury to the Commissioners of Customs, whereby all Clocks and Watches *in transitu*, with counterfeit British names and places of abode, are placed upon the same footing as Watches imported without a name, and allowed to be exported, viz. :—

"GENTLEMEN,

"I have laid before the Lords Commissioners of Her Majesty's Treasury your Reports on the subject of the admission of goods into this country *in transitu*, which are included in the List of Articles prohibited by the 63rd Section of the 8 & 9 Victoria, cap. 86, from being admitted into this country for home use, and I am directed by their Lordships to transmit to you a copy of a Report which they have received on this subject from the Lords of the Committee of Privy Council for Trade. Upon a careful consideration of all the circumstances of the case my Lords are of opinion that some alteration may be made in the regulations which at present govern your Officers when cases of this description arise. My Lords perceive that it has hitherto been the practice to allow the exportation of Foreign Watches brought to this country although not marked with the Foreign Maker's name, &c., as required by the above-named Act, but that Foreign Watches having a British Maker's name attached to them have been seized when discovered and condemned as prohibited to be imported. It is their Lordships wish that the regulation which has been applied to Watches without the Foreign Maker's name should be henceforth extended to Watches on which an English Maker's name is counterfeited, it being understood that the search by your Officers of Foreign Goods in Port, intended for tranship-ment, is to be confined to the prevention of the introduction of contraband goods into this country, and that the regulation in question is not to be extended to Watches in Warehouse.

"I am, Gentlemen,
"Your obedient Servant,
"The Commissioners of Customs.   (Signed)   "G. CORNEWALL LEWIS.

"Your Petitioners submit that the facility thus afforded to dishonest foreigners, to impose upon the purchasers of Watches, imported as above described, is immoral in principle and destructive to the character of the British manufacturer, for it must be recollected that the English name is assumed for the purpose of insuring a higher price for these Watches than could otherwise be obtained, the preference given to them in the market being the result of their acknowledged superiority over the Foreign. This deception is still further assisted by the facility the warehousing affords for exporting them in British ships.

"Your Petitioners in calling the attention of your Honourable House to this important subject, desire to impress upon your Honourable House their firm conviction that the strongest necessity exists for condemning all Watches and Clocks imported into this country with counterfeit British names and places of abode, in accordance with the above recited Acts, whether intended for home consumption or to be bonded for exportation, as the only means of securing both the English maker and Foreign purchaser from the most gross and fraudulent imposition.

"Your Petitioners therefore humbly pray that your Honourable House will take into consideration the serious evils arising to the Watch Trade of this country from the proposed adoption of the Treasury-minute above referred to, which will, if acted upon, speedily be converted into a measure for the encouragement of every species of fraud and deception.

"And your Petitioners will ever pray, &c.

"*To the Right Honorable the Lords Commissioners of Her Majesty's Treasury.*

"*The Memorial of the Master, Wardens, and Court of Assistants of the Company of Clockmakers of the City of London,*

"SHEWETH—

"That your Memorialists have seen with much concern the following communication from your Lordships to the Commissioners of Customs on the subject of Foreign Watches and Clocks *in transitu* for Foreign Counties, viz.

[*Vide Letter in the preceding Petition to the House of Commons.*]

"Your Memorialists submit that the encouragement thus afforded to dishonest Foreigners to impose upon the purchasers of Watches exported as above described, whose object will be to export them in British Ships as a proof that they are of English Manufacture, is immoral in principle and destructive to the character of the British Manufacturer. It affords a facility for practising a gross fraud upon the Foreign Purchaser, who is led to suppose he is procuring an English Watch, while in fact he is obtaining a Foreign one, the inferior quality of which is very destructive to the character of the British Maker, for it must be recollected that the English name is assumed for the sole purpose of ensuring a higher price than could be otherwise obtained for the article, the preference given in the Market to the English Watch being the result of its acknowledged superiority over the Foreign.

"Your Memorialists beg to call your Lordships' attention to the following clause in an Act passed in the 4th year of George 4, Cap. 24, entitled 'An Act to make more effectual provision for permitting goods imported to be secured in Warehouses or other places without payment of duty on the first entry thereof,' which Clause was introduced into the Act specially to prevent Foreign Clocks and Watches made in imitation of British, and with British names and places of abode, from being warehoused and afterwards exported, viz.—'And be it further enacted that no Watch of Foreign Manufacture shall be imported and warehoused under the provisions of this Act upon the case or cases of which any mark or stamp shall be impressed, which shall be similar to, or shall purport to be or shall be intended to represent any mark or stamp of the Goldsmiths' Company of London, or other legal British assay marks or stamps, and that no Clock or Watch of Foreign Manufacture shall be so imported and warehoused upon the face or upon any part of which the Word 'London,' or the name of any other Town or Place of the United Kingdom shall be engraven or painted, or shall in any way appear so as to purport or give colour that such Clock or Watch is of the Manufacture of the United Kingdom, and that no Clock or Watch of Foreign Manufacture shall be so imported and warehoused unless a distinguishing number, and the name or names of some persons or place shall be engraven, and shall appear visible on the frame or other part of such Clock or Watch, independent of the face purporting to be the name and place of abode of the person or persons by whom such Clock or Watch was made, and that no Clock or Watch of Foreign Manufacture shall be imported and warehoused under this Act in any incomplete state—that is to say, not having the movement with all its concomitant parts properly fixed and secured in its case on pain of the forfeiture of such Clock or Watch.'

"Your Memorialists in calling your Lordships' attention to this important subject desire to impress upon your Lordships their firm conviction that the strongest necessity exists for condemning all Watches and Clocks imported into this country with counterfeit British names and places of abode, in accordance with the spirit of the above-recited Act, as the only means of securing both the English Maker and Foreign Purchaser from the most gross and fraudulent imposition.

"Your Memorialists therefore pray that your Lordships will take into your most serious consideration the very grevious consequences to the trade of this country that will result from the adoption of the Treasury Minute above referred to, which will, if permitted to be acted upon, speedily be converted into a measure for the encouragement of every species of fraud and deception."

An answer was received from the Treasury, dated the 20th February, 1852, in the following terms :—

"Treasury Chambers,
"*20th February, 1852.*
"GENTLEMEN,
"I am commanded by the Lords Commissioners of Her Majesty's Treasury to acquaint you in reply to your Memorial of the 19th ultimo that the regulations respecting the admission of Foreign Watches and Clocks into this country when *in transitu* for Foreign Countries, were adopted after a careful consideration with a view of affording commercial facilities to the Mercantile interests of the country, and their Lordships are not prepared to revoke or make any alteration in such regulation.
"I have the honor to be,
"GENTLEMEN,
"Your very obedient Servant,
(Signed) "G. CORNEWALL LEWIS.
"The Master, Wardens, &c.,
"Comp^y of Clockmakers."

A Deputation of the Court had an interview with the Chancellor of the Exchequer in the March following, who promised to give the subject his best attention, and requested that a further short Memorial, embodying the sense of the former, might be transmitted to the Treasury. This was accordingly done, and the Memorial was in effect a *duplicate* of the previous one, with an additional paragraph, as under :—

"Your Memorialists have subsequently been informed, and are perfectly satisfied as to the correctness of the information, that a number of Watches had been prepared without names to be ready, in the event of this alteration in the law, to receive such names as it might at the time be more desirable to employ, and that Adams, French and McCabe, London makers, and Roskell and Tobias, Liverpool makers, have principally been used. The entire transaction is too recent to allow any practical results to have occurred, much less to be known, the whole has been managed with an unusual degree of privacy your Memorialists not being aware that such a minute was passed until it appeared in the 'Times' of the 9th of January last. In former times your Memorialists would have been made aware of so important an alteration in the law, through a widely different channel than that of a public print. Of so much importance was this regulation considered at the time the Act passed, A.D. 1828, that immediately notice of the same was given by your Memorialists to the French and Swiss Consuls, the receipt of which was acknowledged by Baron Seguier, the Swiss Consul, under date of the 21st of November, 1828. It will be urged in extenuation of the evil complained of that Watches having English names have for a considerable period been manufactured abroad, to be sold as English, and that this is a practice that cannot be prevented. But from 1828 to the present time these Watches could not be exported in English bottoms or direct from this country. These circumstances were felt by the Foreign manufacturer to prove a considerable obstacle to the sale of his Watches, and one that it was important for him to get removed.

"Your Memorialists therefore pray that Your Lordships will take into your most serious consideration the very grievous consequences to the Trade of this country that will result from the adoption of the Treasury Minute above referred to, which will, if permitted to be acted upon, speedily be converted into a measure for the encouragement of every species of fraud and deception."

To this further Memorial the Treasury eventually caused the following reply to be sent:—

"Treasury Chambers,
"*1st May*, *1852*.
" GENTLEMEN,
"The Lords Commissioners of Her Majesty's Treasury have had under their consideration your further Memorial of the 1st ultimo respecting the admission of Foreign Clocks and Watches in transit for Foreign Countries, in which Memorial you refer to the Act 4, Geo. 4, Cap. 24, which prohibits any Foreign Clocks or Watches bearing counterfeited names of English makers from being imported or warehoused for exportation, and state that 'the strongest necessity exists for condemning all Clocks and Watches imported into this country with counterfeit British names, as the only means of securing both the English maker and the Foreign purchaser from most gross and fraudulent impositions.'

"I am directed by their Lordships to state that the Treasury Order of the 31st December last merely permits such articles, when brought from a Foreign Port in transit to another Port, and without any intention of being landed in this country, to be immediately transhipped for that purpose, and by no means permits them to be imported or warehoused in contravention of the existing law. This order was adopted for the purpose of removing the prohibition, which interfered materially with the carrying trade of the British Ship owner, while it afforded no effectual protection to the English Watch manufacturer, and my Lords cannot but feel, that while it has always been in the power of the Foreign maker to export Watches bearing any mark from one Foreign Port to another, without the British Government having any ground for interference, the mere fact of their now passing in transit through a British Port is not likely to enhance their value in the Foreign market, when the true purport of the recent regulations becomes generally known.

"Under these circumstances my Lords must adhere to the decision already communicated to you, as they do not consider that they would be justified in revoking or altering the regulations in question.

"I have the honor to be,
"Gentlemen,
"Your obedient Servant,
(Signed) "GEO. A. HAMILTON.

"*To the Master, Wardens, and Court of Assistants of the Company of Clockmakers.*"

In October, 1852, at a Special Court, an Assay Officer of the Goldsmiths' Company produced 2 Watches in Gold Cases, the one containing an imitation English Movement, bearing the name of "French, Royal Exchange," and the other being an ordinary Swiss Watch, both the Cases having thereon forged Assay marks of the Goldsmiths' Company.

After serious deliberation the Company decided to submit the facts disclosed to the Treasury and invoke their assistance to put a stop to this pernicious and fraudulent practice, and embodied their views in a Memorial to which they ultimately received the following reply :—

"Treasury Chambers,
"*16th November, 1852.*
"GENTLEMEN,
"The Lords Commissioners of Her Majesty's Treasury have had before them your further Memorial relative to the admission for exportation of Watches, &c., from Foreign Ports, and their Lordships have directed me to state they see no reason for altering the regulations relating to the transhipment of Watches, &c., brought from one foreign Port in transit for another foreign Port, which were communicated to you by their Lordships directions the 1st of May last.

"I am to state further that were the present regulations relaxed the fraud complained of could not be prevented, as the only result would be to transfer the carrying trade in these articles to the Merchants and Ship Owners of other Countries.

"I remain,
"Gentlemen,
"Your obedient Servant,
(Signed) "GEO. A. HAMILTON.

"*To the Worshipful Company of Clockmakers.*"

The unsatisfactory results of their appeals to the Government on behalf of the Trade, evinced in these later Letters from the Treasury, seem to have induced the Court to discontinue their efforts, and for the next 20 years their Records contain no entries of any further similar action being adopted by them.

In the year 1873, however, the subject of Hall-marking Foreign Watch Cases again occupied their deliberations, and the Master having on behalf of the Court addressed himself to the Board of Trade, thereon the Court, on the 13th of October in that year, received and considered the following Letter from the Board of Trade in reply.

"Board of Trade,
"Harbour Department,
"Whitehall Gardens, *July 21st, 1873.*

"GENTLEMEN,

"I am directed by the Board of Trade to acknowledge the receipt of a Memorial, signed by the Master of the Clockmakers' Company, on the subject of the Hall-marking in this Country of the Gold and Silver Cases of Watches of foreign manufacture, and suggesting the introduction of a Bill into Parliament for the better protection of the English trade in Watches.

"In reply, I am to state that the Board of Trade, whilst regretting that the English Watch Makers should suffer loss, as alleged in the Memorial, by the practice of re-exporting and fraudently selling, as English, foreign-made Watches after their Cases have been Hall-marked in this country, would pause before introducing a Bill into Parliament for prohibiting the marking any Watch Cases not of English manufacture.

"It appears to this Board that the English buyers of foreign-made Watches, allowed, under the system of free trade now established, to be imported free of duty, are entitled to the guarantee of the quality of the metal in the Watch case afforded by the Hall-mark, and that there is already a provision of law which sufficiently meets the circumstances of the case at present under discussion, as the 24th Section of the 'Customs Amendment Act, 1867,' (30 and 31 Vic., Cap. 82), expressly requires all Gold and Silver Plate of Foreign Manufacture brought to any Assay Office in the United Kingdom to be impressed with a distinctive mark.

"I am, Gentlemen,
"Your obedient servant,
(Signed)   "ARTHUR W. PEEL."

The Master was thereupon authorized to place himself in communication with the Goldsmiths' Company upon the subject, and subsequently reported, as the result, that by Act of Parliament the Goldsmiths' Company were required to stamp all Foreign Cases, brought to their Hall to be assayed, with the letter F in an Oval, but that the Act was occasionally evaded by some unprincipled Casemakers in this country putting upon them their own marks as of English manufacture.

In January, 1875, the name of an English Casemaker who had adopted this practice, was brought under the notice of the Court, who thereupon directed an intimation to be made to him, that unless he discontinued it proceedings would be taken against him.

An interview was again sought with the Goldsmiths' Company by a Deputation of the Court, and it was found that the Act of Parliament did not empower the marking of Cases with the letter F merely on suspicion, and that in the absence of proof to the contrary it was imperative that they should be marked on presentation at Goldsmiths' Hall as of English manufacture.

As a remedy for this state of things, the Deputation suggested that in all cases where there existed reasonable ground for suspicion, that the goods were of Foreign manufacture, a Statutory declaration should be required before stamping them as English, that they were not merely partially but entirely of English make.

This suggestion was embodied in a Letter to the Goldsmiths' Company, and was by them subsequently submitted to the Board of Trade, from whom a reply was received, of which the following is an Extract :—

"In thanking you for your communication, I am to state that my Lords before expressing their opinion upon the suggestion now made by the Wardens of the Goldsmiths' Company, would be glad to be favoured with the views of the Wardens as to how far such a step would be really efficacious in removing the alleged grievance of the English Watch Manufactures; the assumption is that English-made works are superior to those of foreign manufacturers, and that the foreign makers by getting their cases stamped at Goldsmiths' Hall, induce the English public to believe that their foreign works are of English make. If this really be the case, and if the foreign manufacturer does reap an advantage thereby, what is to prevent him from putting his foreign works into English-made cases?"

To this inquiry the obvious answer was returned by this Company, that the Cases were made much cheaper abroad than they could possibly be manufactured here, and that it was much easier and less expensive to make cases to works than works to cases, indeed, that the cost of doing so in this Country would be to a great extent prohibitory of the practice.

The Board of Trade having taken time to consider the subject, on the 10th September, 1875, transmitted a Letter, in which they stated that after careful consideration they did not think it would be advisable for the Government to undertake to submit to Parliament a Special Bill requiring a Statutory declaration to be made as to the origin of Watch Cases when taken to the Assay Office to be stamped.

These proceedings were the subject of comment in the public press, both in London and some of the other centres of the Trade, and meetings were held at which resolutions were adopted, with a view to obtaining legislative enactments favorable to the course suggested by the Company.

In February, 1878, a Deputation of the Trade from London, Liverpool, and Coventry, had an interview with the President of the Board of Trade (Sir Charles Adderley), to urge the desirability of the appointment by the House of Commons of a Committee of inquiry into the Hall-marking of Gold and Silver. The President advised the introduction of a Bill by private Members, limited to the question of Watch Cases rather than to Hall-marking in general.

On the 26th February, 1879, Sir Henry Jackson accordingly brought a Bill into the House of Commons for the purpose suggested, which was then read a first time, but not further proceeded with.

On the same day the appointment of a Select Committee was agreed to "to enquire into the operation of the Acts relative to the Hall-marking of Gold and Silver Manufactures." On the 5th March the Committee were nominated, who presented their report on the 19th May following.

Upon this report no legislation has up to the present time been based, but it may be desirable to quote such of its recommendations as more particularly refer to the articles manufactured for the Trade with which this Company is especially concerned.

"The chief complaint against the operation of the existing law comes from the manufacturers of Watches and Watch-cases. They have established by evidence that within the last few years a practice has sprung up, and is rapidly increasing, under which foreign-made Watch-cases are sent to this country to be hall-marked with the British hall-mark, and are afterwards fitted with foreign movements, and are then not unfrequently sold and dealt in as British-made Watches; and they assert that this not only injures their own reputation and lowers the credit of British workmanship, but is contrary to the spirit and intention of our legislation. The Assay Offices are unable legally to refuse to hall-mark these foreign Watch-cases when brought for assay by registered dealers, though their officials are practically able to distinguish them from cases of British manufacture.

"Until the practice of hall-marking foreign Watch-cases sprang up, the British hall-marks were taken to indicate British workmanship, and your Committee cannot doubt that foreign Watches in Watch-cases so hall-marked are frequently sold as of British manufacture.

"Your Committee are therefore of opinion that all foreign-made Watch-cases assayed in this country ought to be impressed with an additional distinctive mark (the letter F, by reason of its resemblance to existing marks, is not sufficiently distinctive) indicative of foreign manufacture, and that the law ought to be altered accordingly.

"Your Committee are further of opinion that the Acts now in force require to be amended in regard to the following matters:—

"*(a.)* The assaying authorities should be allowed to return imported articles which are found below standard, instead of breaking them up, as at present.

"*(b.)* A dome made of base metal should not exclude Watch-cases from being hall-marked.

"*(c.)* The assay authorities should have power to mark articles which, though standard, have enamel or other metals or substances added for purpose of ornament only.

"*(d.)* The lower standards of Gold, viz., 15, 12, and 9 carats (equal respectively to $\frac{15}{24}$, $\frac{12}{24}$, and $\frac{9}{24}$ of pure metal), should be discontinued. A composition containing less than two-thirds of pure metal ought not to be called by the name of that metal.

"*(e.)* The whole of the Assay Offices should be placed under the direct supervision of the Mint, so that a uniform standard of quality shall be guaranteed.

"*(f.)* So long as a licence duty is maintained it should be levied at a uniform rate."

The foregoing documents and extracts tend to show that it is in no boasting spirit this Company claim to have always identified themselves with the Trade, in whose interests they were originally incorporated, and with which they have ever maintained and still continue to preserve a close and, as they believe, a beneficial connexion, and to have been ready at all times with their best advice and assistance whenever called upon to use their influence and prestige as a rallying point when unjust or oppressive legislation threatened to well-nigh extinguish this important branch of British Industry, to the maintenance of which, as a maritime nation, so much importance is attached.

CHRONOMETER PRIZES.

The Company have for some time past had under their consideration the question of the best means of promoting improvements and excellence of production in the art of Horology, and on the 8th April, 1878, appointed a Committee to consider the best means of effecting this object, whether by the establishment of prizes for essays, superiority of workmanship, or for the more accurate performance of the Marine Chronometer, or otherwise.

On the 8th of July, 1878, the Committee presented their Report, in which they stated that having regard to the large number of industries, and the great subdivision of labour employed in the manufacture of Chronometers, Watches, and Clocks, they did not recommend that prizes should be offered for any particular branch of their manufacture, but rather that they should be awarded according to the merit attached to the performance of the Time Keeper, shewing the best results as a whole, and with this view suggested that prizes should be awarded to the makers of the two Chronometers performing with the greatest accuracy at the annual trial for Government purchase at the Royal Observatory, Greenwich. The Committee did not advise any expenditure with a view to obtaining essays on the Art of Horology, deeming it desirable to confine the prizes rather to practical that theoretical limits.

The Court having adopted the Report, placed themselves in communication with the Astronomer Royal (Sir G. B. Airy, K.C.B., F.R.S., &c.), and, ultimately, with his concurrence, agreed to a scheme with regulations for giving effect thereto, public notice of which was given to the trade through the usual channels of the press.

The Regulations are as follow :—

"1. THE CLOCKMAKERS' COMPANY, with a view to encourage the highest excellence in the production of the Marine Chronometer, on which Navigation so largely depends, have determined to award annually two Prizes to the makers of the two Chronometers which shall perform with the greatest accuracy, and respectively stand first and second (as tested on the criterion adopted by the Astronomer Royal, and be so certified under his hand) at the annual trials for Government purchase, at the Royal Observatory, Greenwich.

"2. The First Prize will consist of a sum of Ten Guineas, together with the Freedom of the Company, and the Second of a sum of Five Guineas, without the Freedom.

"3. The Company reserve to themselves the right to modify the above Prizes from time to time, as they may deem expedient, or, in the absence of sufficient merit, withhold them altogether.

"4. Any maker or firm depositing a Chronometer at the annual trials, desirous of competing for either of the above prizes, shall have the name of such maker or firm, and a distinguishing number legibly engraved, both on the dial and upper plate of the frame, and shall prove to the satisfaction of the Court of Assistants (if necessary) that he or they, as the case may be, is or are the *bonâ fide* owner or owners thereof, and that the same has been in his or their possession at least six months prior to the trial, and shall produce its rate of going antecedently, if required.

"5. No Chronometer maker or firm shall be eligible to take either of the above Prizes unless the instrument obtaining it becomes the property of the Government by purchase.

"6. If the instrument obtaining the First Prize be the property of a firm, the name of the partner (who must have been such at the time of depositing the instrument and until the results of the trials have been declared) to whom the Freedom is to be awarded shall be submitted to and approved by the Court of Assistants.

"7. If the person entitled to the First Prize be already a Freeman of the Company, the Court of Assistants may, if they think fit, award a Certificate of Merit, or such other addition to the Prize, in lieu of the Freedom, as may seem to them desirable, on due consideration of the special circumstances of the case.

"8. No Chronometer Maker having obtained a First-class Prize, together with the Freedom of the Company, shall be eligible to obtain a similar award, but that circumstance shall not affect his right to compete for the Second-class Prize in subsequent trials; neither shall the holder of the Second-class Prize be debarred from competing for the superior Prize and Freedom in future years.

"9. Any contravention of the Rules settled by the Company or the Astronomer Royal for regulating the competition, will render the award of either Prize null and void.

"10. Any competitor for the foregoing Prizes must be *bonâ fide* engaged in and carrying on the business of either a Chronometer, Clock, or Watch Maker.

"11. Chronometer Makers desirous of competing for the above Prizes must send their names and addresses, and a statement of how many instruments they intend to deposit on trial, with the distinguishing number of each, to the Clerk to the Company, at Guildhall, at least one week before the commencement of the annual trials. Each successful competitor shall make and sign a declaration in the form hereunto annexed, or to that effect.

"CLOCKMAKERS' COMPANY.

" FORM OF DECLARATION.

" *To be made by successful Competitors for Annual Prizes given by the Company.*

"I———of———carrying on the business of a Chronometer, Clock and Watchmaker, do hereby declare that I am the *bonâ fide* owner of the Chronometer bearing my name, and numbered———, standing first* on the List at the conclusion of the last annual trial of Chronometers for Government purchase, as certified under the hand of the Astronomer Royal; that the same has been purchased by the Government, and that *all the conditions regulating the competition* have in every case been fully complied with.

"I, therefore, (subject to the approval of the Court of Assistants) respectfully claim to be entitled to the award of Ten Guineas†, and to be admitted as a Prize Freeman of your Worshipful Company.

"*(Signature)*———
"*(Date)*———"

" * or ' Second.' † or ' Five Guineas,' omitting the subsequent words."

www.ingramcontent.com/pod-product-compliance
Lightning Source LLC
Chambersburg PA
CBHW032018220426
43664CB00006B/290